POWER RANGERS

THE ART OF DAN MORA

Published by

BOOM!

DESIGNER
MARIE KRUPINA

EDITOR
KWANZA OSAJYEFO

EDITOR-IN-CHIEF
ANDY SCHMIDT

BOOM! STUDIOS
WWW.BOOM-STUDIOS.COM

BOOM! Studios, 5250 Lankershim Blvd, Suite 750, North Hollywood, CA 91601.
Printed in China. First Printing.

ISBN: 979-8-89215-875-6, eISBN: 979-8-89215-881-7

Licensed by:

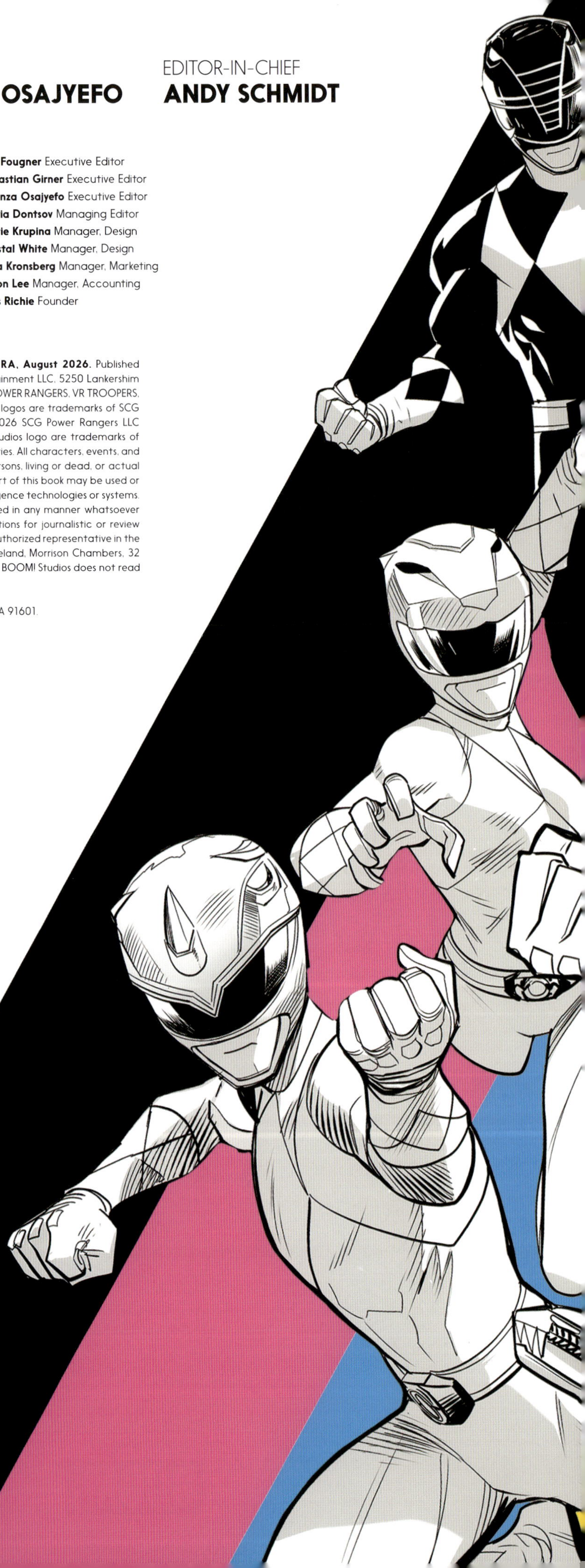

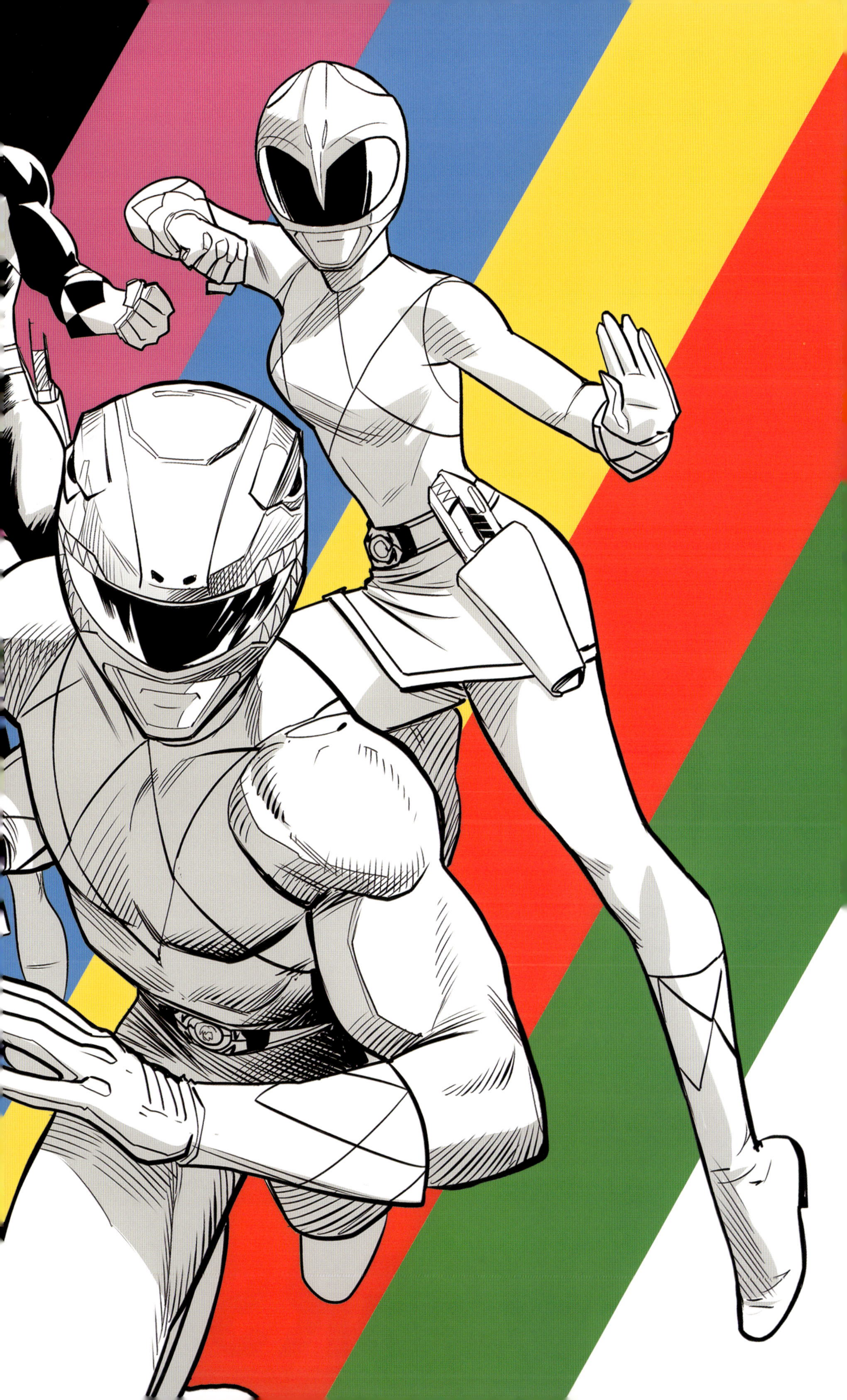

PAGE 6 Power Rangers 100 character designs

PAGE 7 Mutant Rangers - Mighty Morphin Power Rangers / Teenage Mutant Ninja Turtles

PAGE 8 Olivia Hart, daughter of the Green Ranger - Mighty Morphin Power Rangers: The Return

PAGE 9 Adult Kimberly - Mighty Morphin Power Rangers: The Return

PAGE 10 Adult Billy - Mighty Morphin Power Rangers: The Return

PAGE 11 Adult Jason - Mighty Morphin Power Rangers: The Return

PAGE 12 Adult Zack - Mighty Morphin Power Rangers: The Return

PAGE 13 Selena Repulsa: Yellow Ranger daughter of Rita Repulsa and Lord Zedd - Mighty Morphin Power Rangers: The Return

PAGE 14 Billy

PAGE 15 Jason

PAGE 16 Kimberly

PAGE 17 Trini

PAGE 18 Trini + Sabertooth Tiger

PAGE 19 Pterodactyl + Mastodon

PAGE 20 Triceratops + Tyrannosaurus

PAGE 21 Armored Red Ranger

PAGES 22-23 Original designs to celebrate 20 issues of Go Go Power Rangers

PAGES 24-25 Squadron Rangers - early designs

PAGE 26 Power Rangers Prime designs

PAGE 27 Power Rangers White Ranger Power Coin

PAGE 28 Drakkon Rangers

PAGE 29 Powered Up Green Ranger

PAGE 30 Gold Omega Ranger

PAGE 31 The Death Ranger

PAGE 32 Red Omega Death Ranger

PAGE 33 Feral Drakkon Power Suit

PAGE 34 Dark Grid Ranger

PAGE 35 Unknown Ranger

DESIGN LAB:

RANGERS

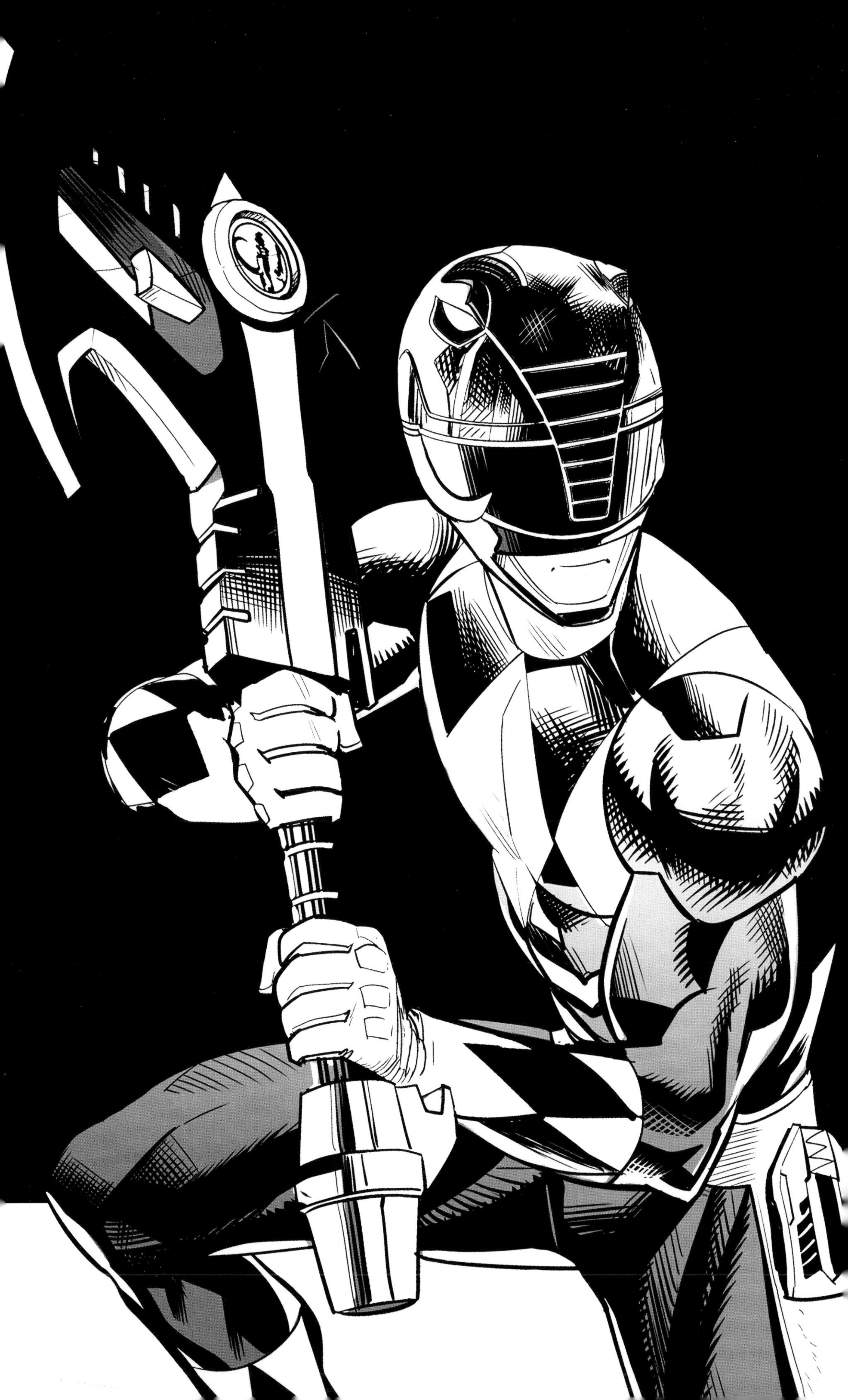

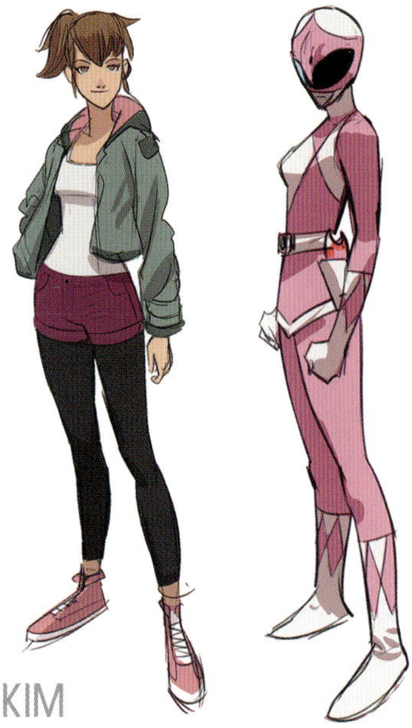

KIM

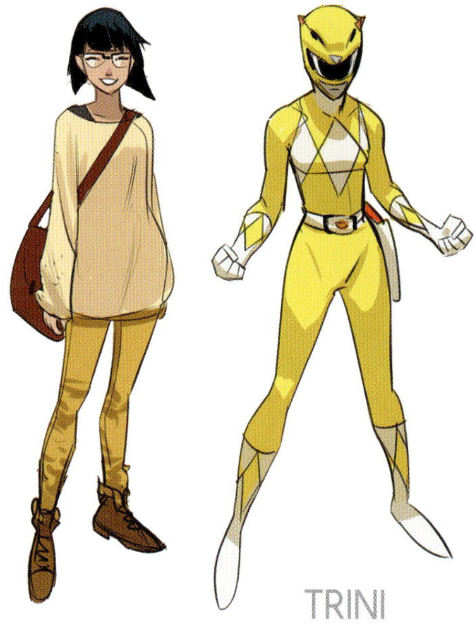

TRINI

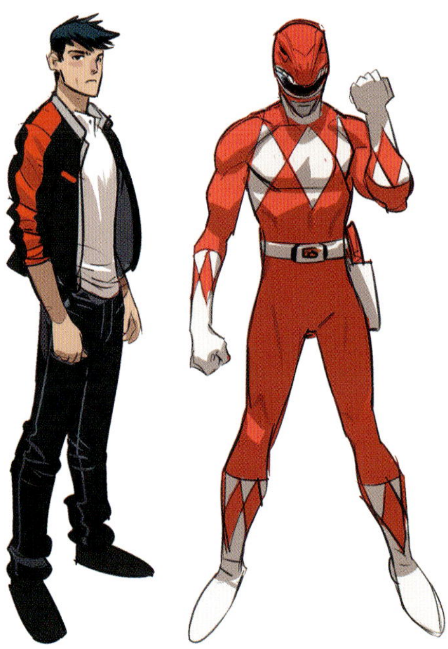

JASON

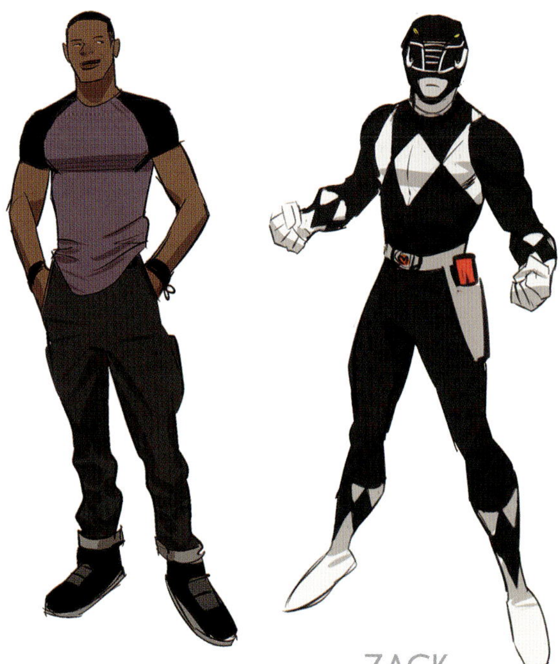

ZACK

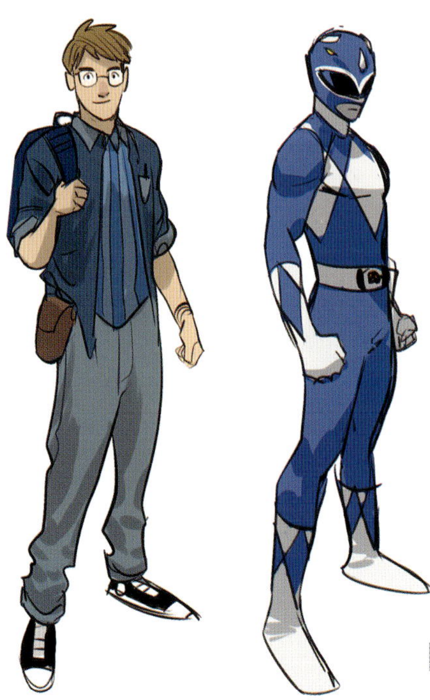

BILLY

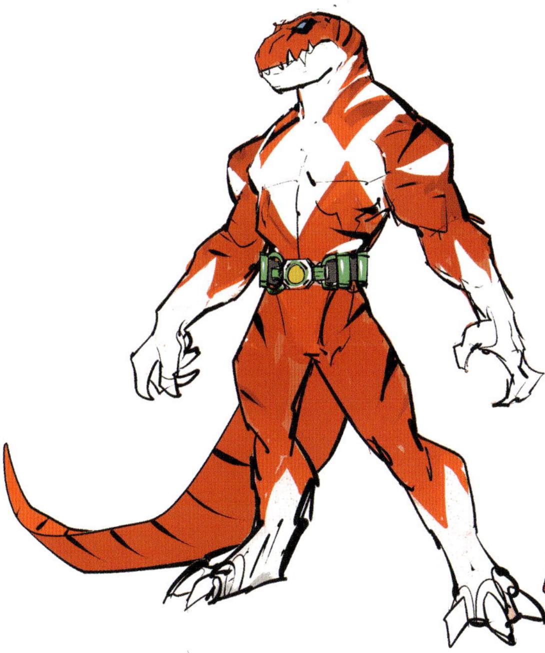
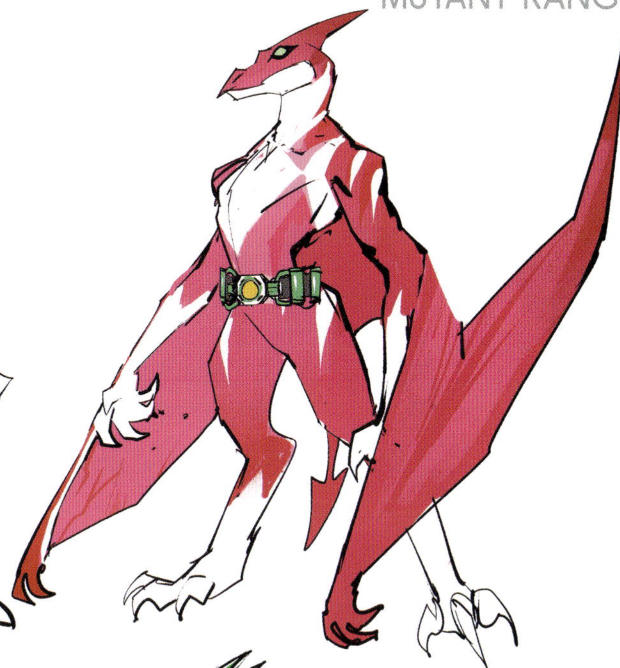
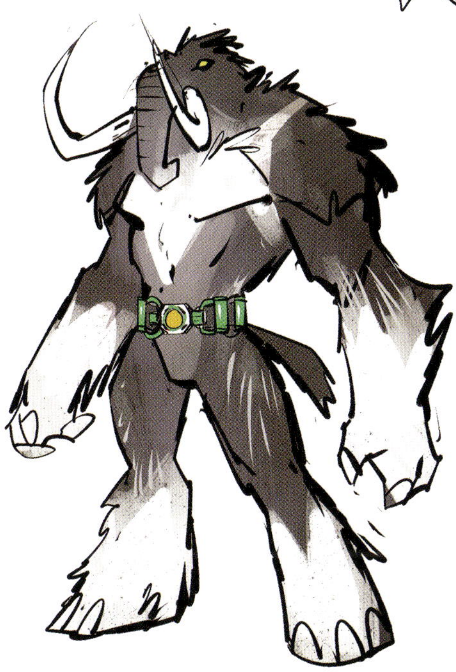
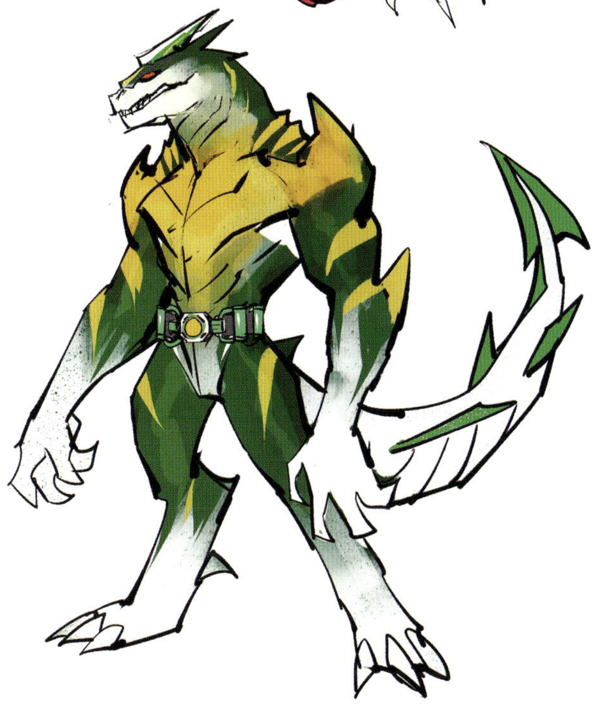
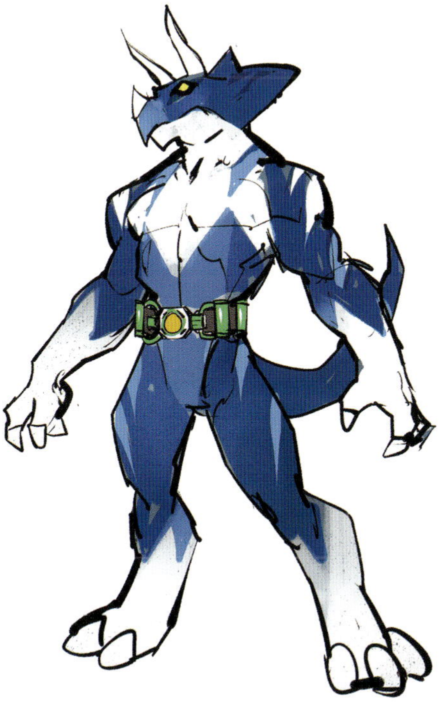
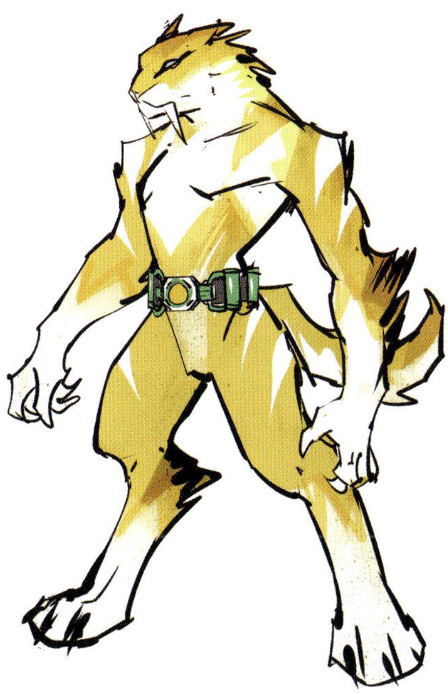
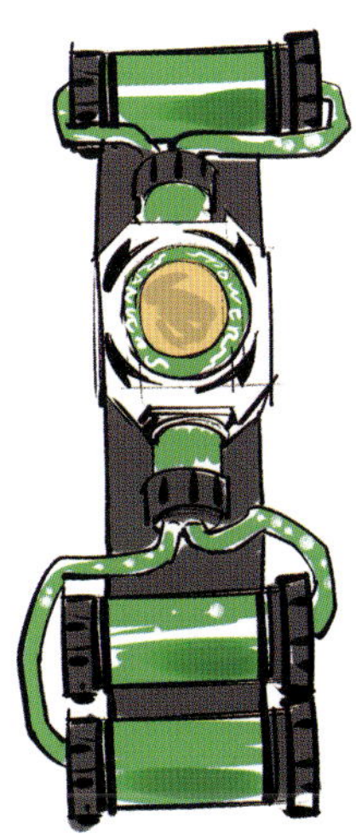

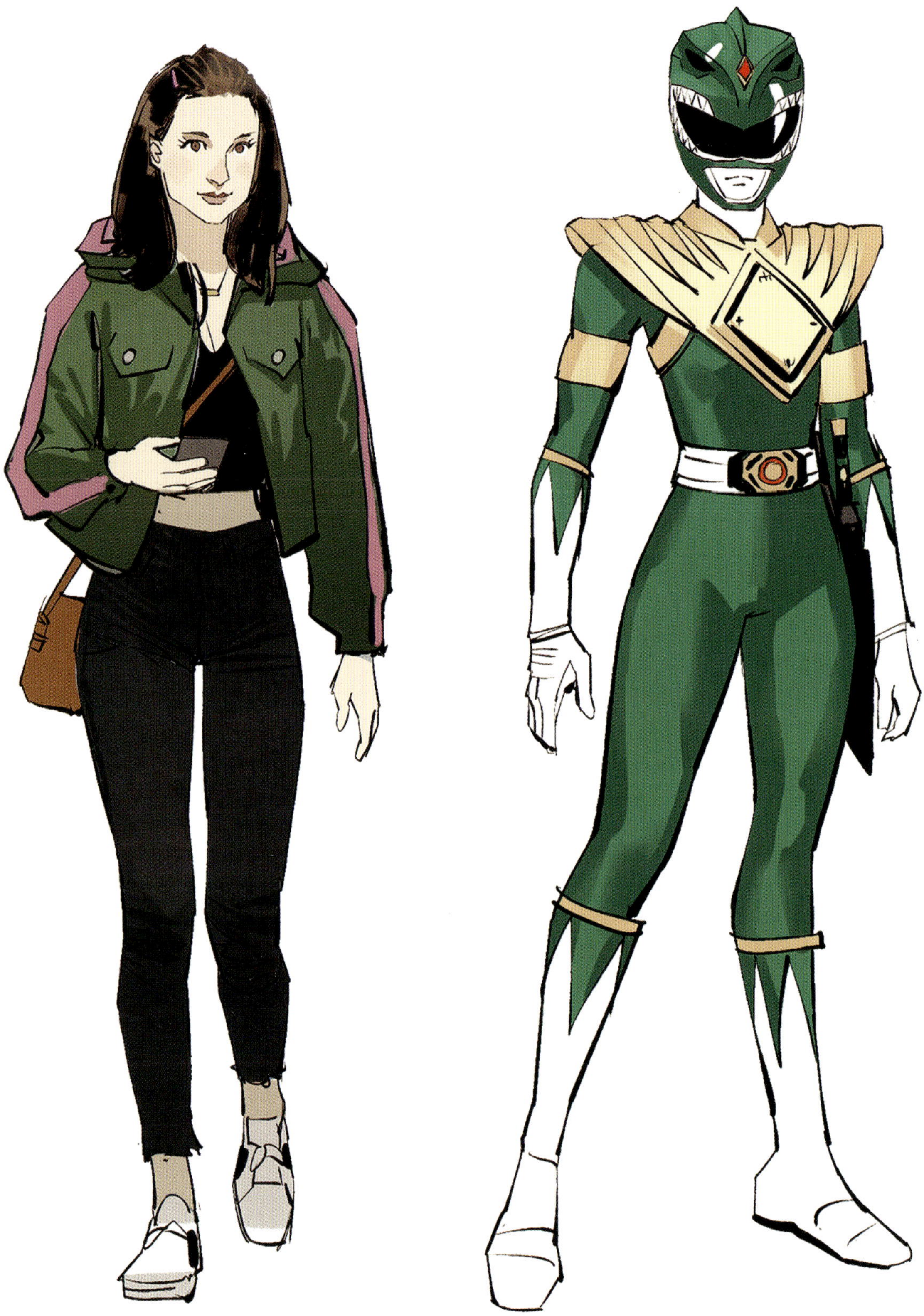

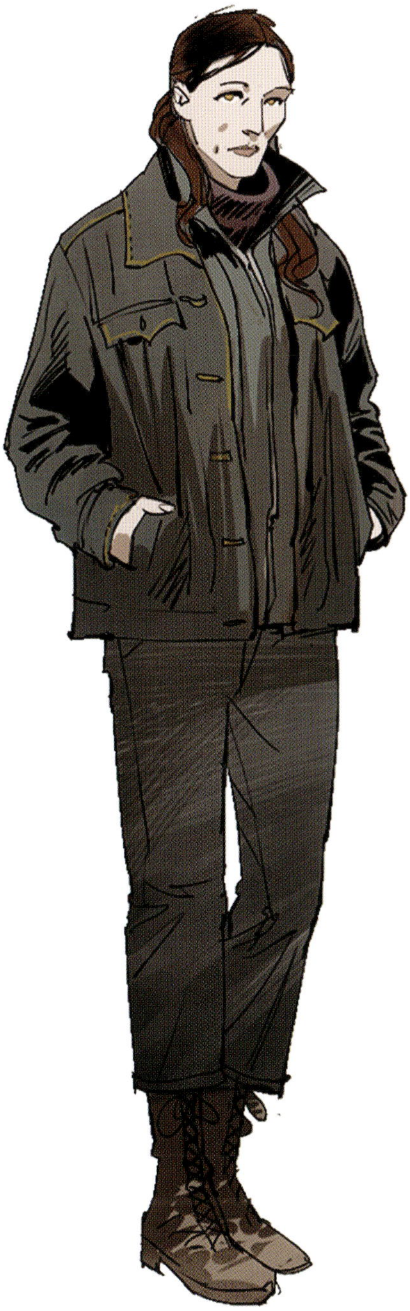

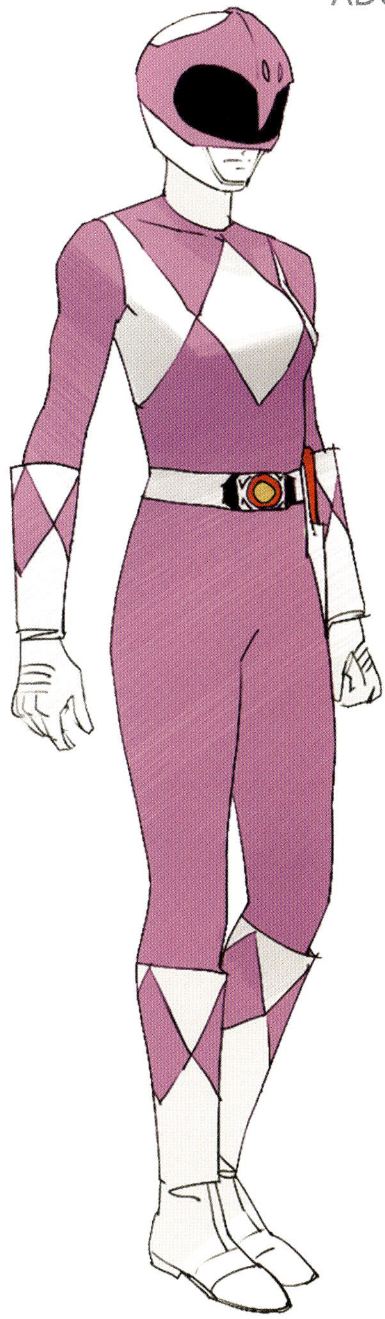

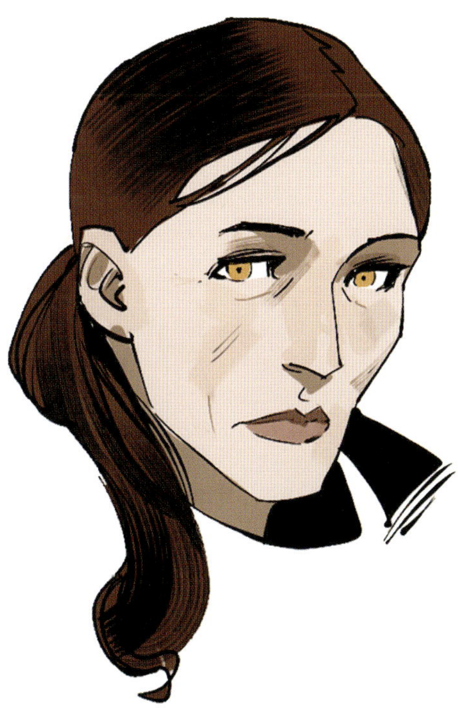

ADULT BILLY

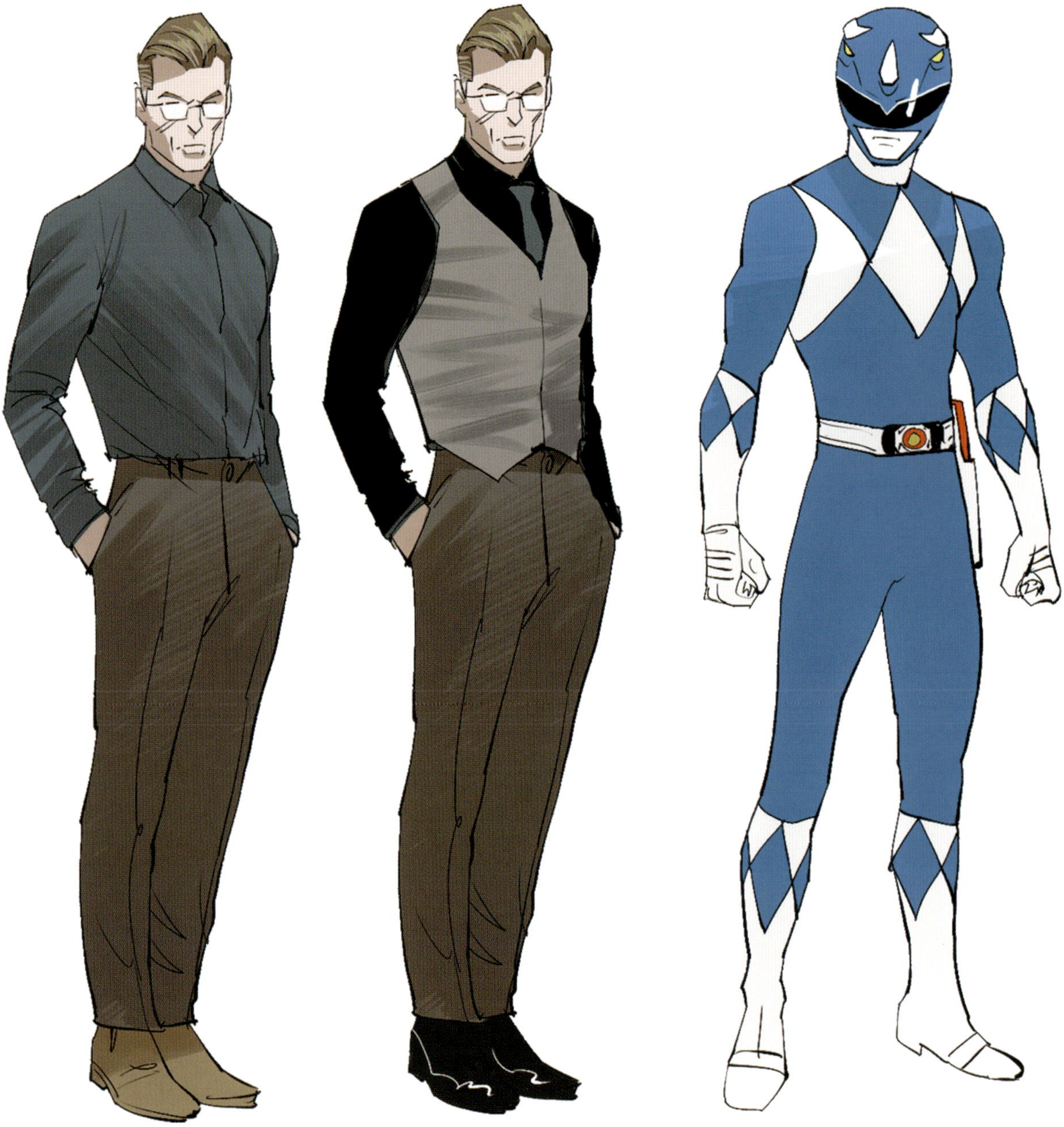

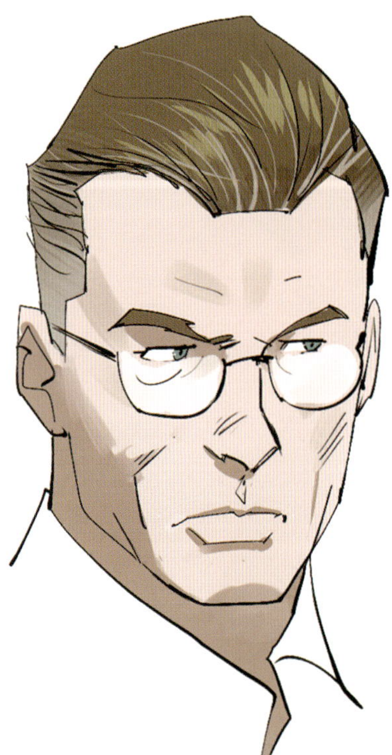

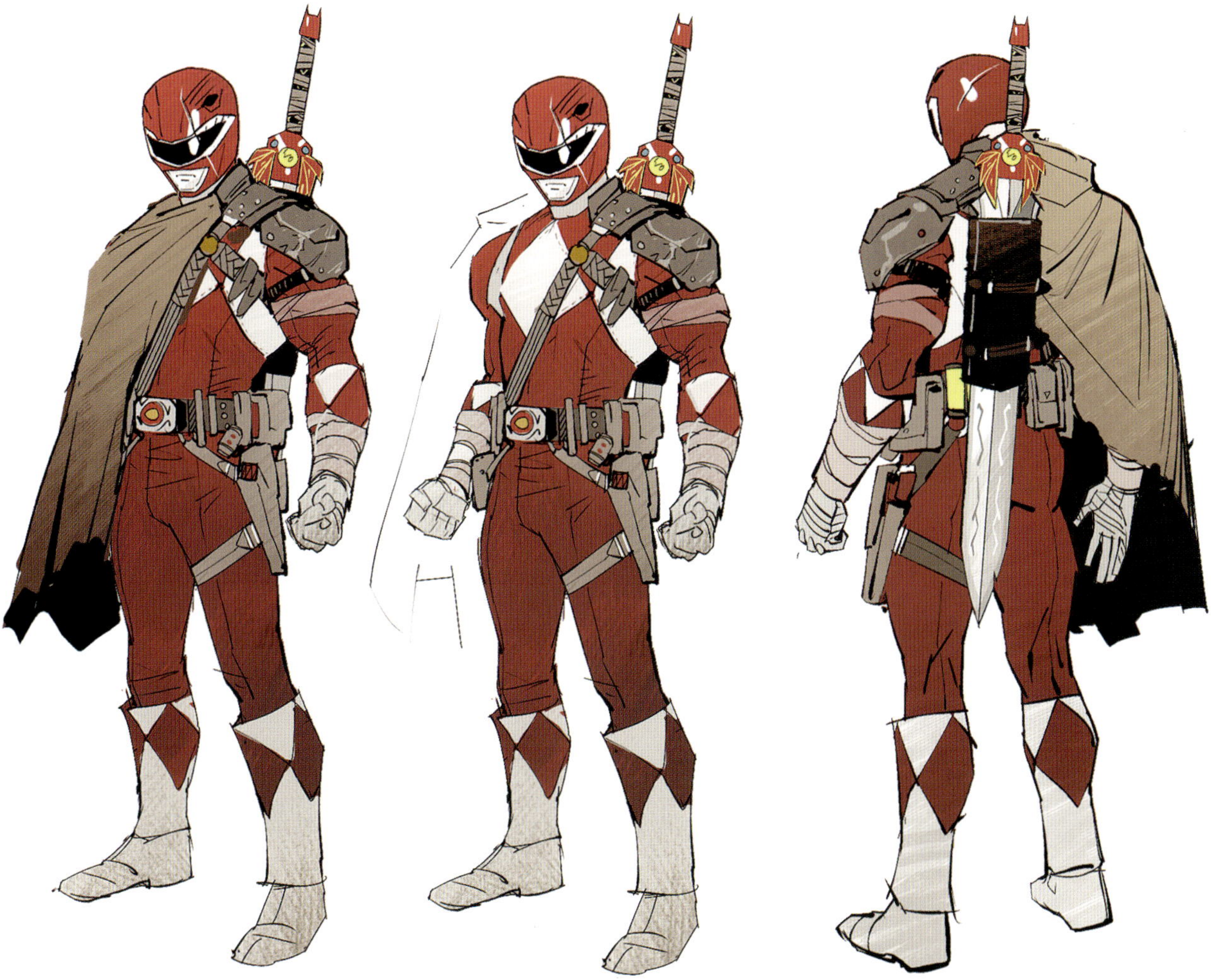

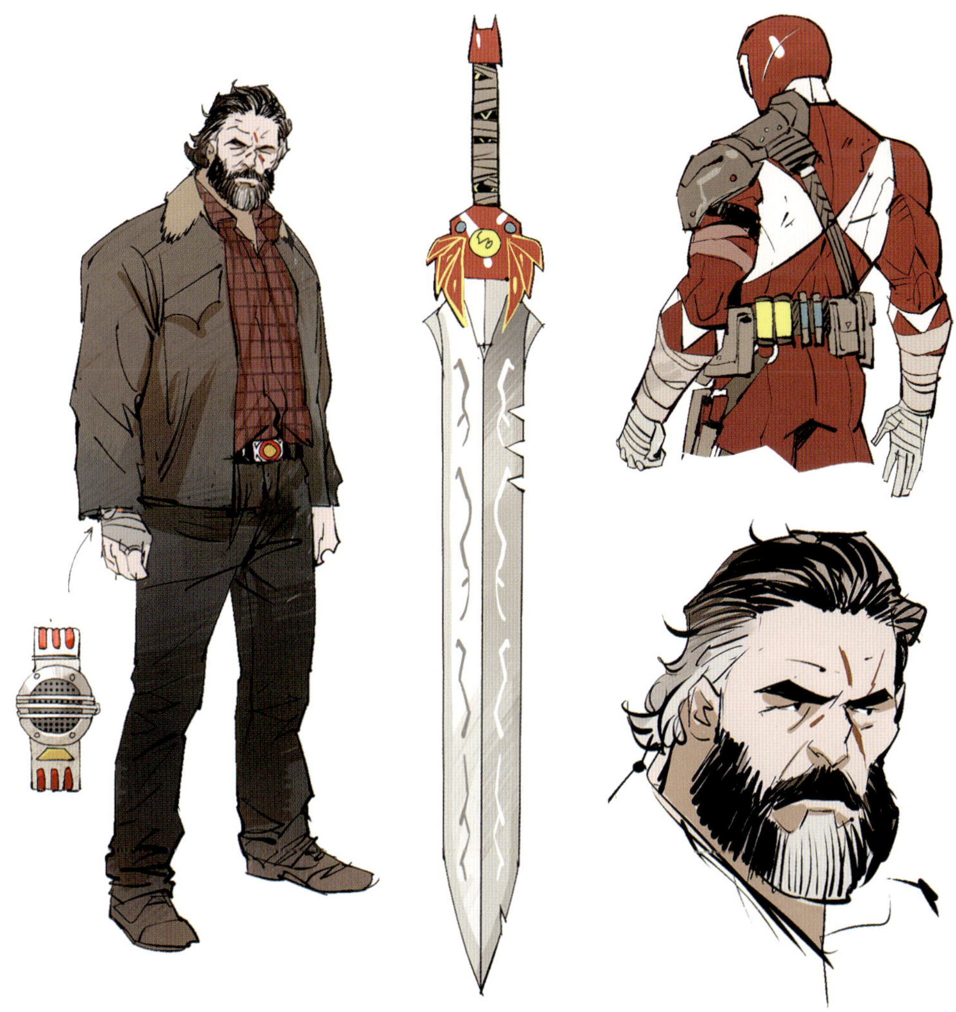

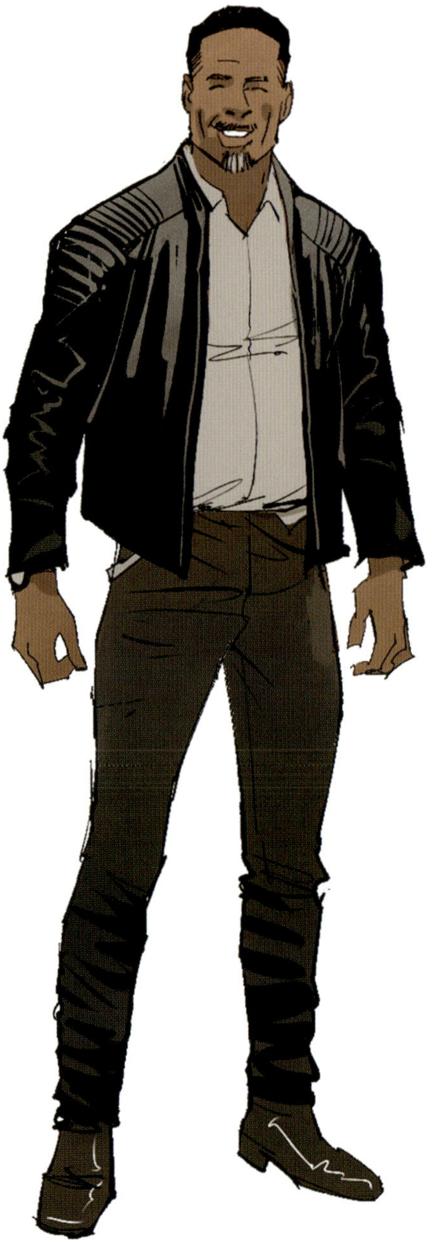

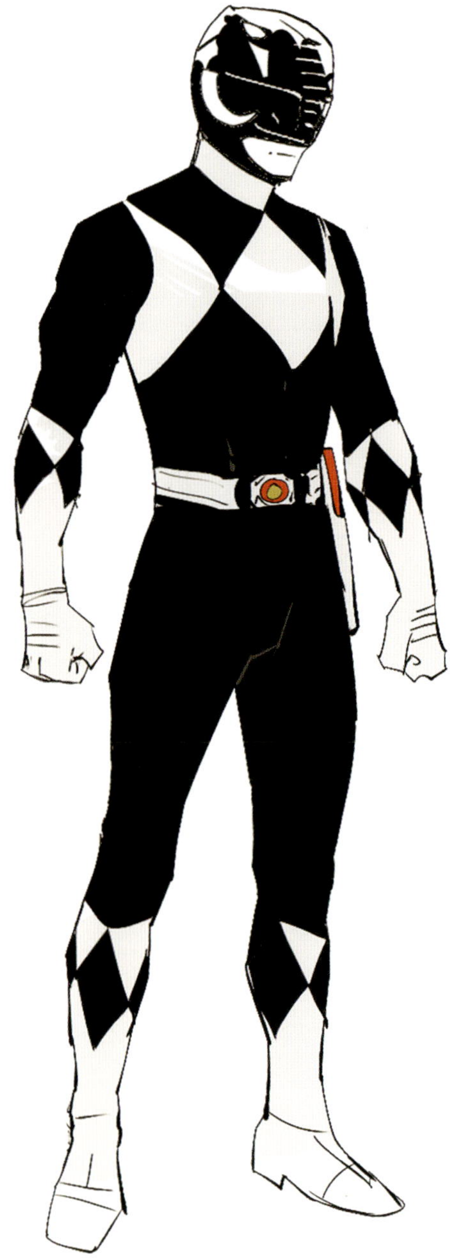

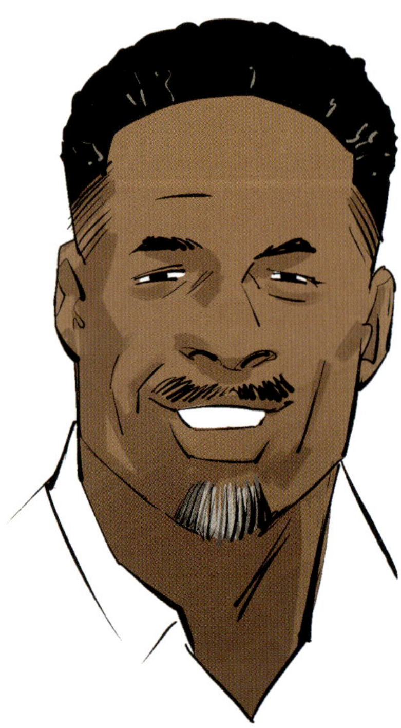

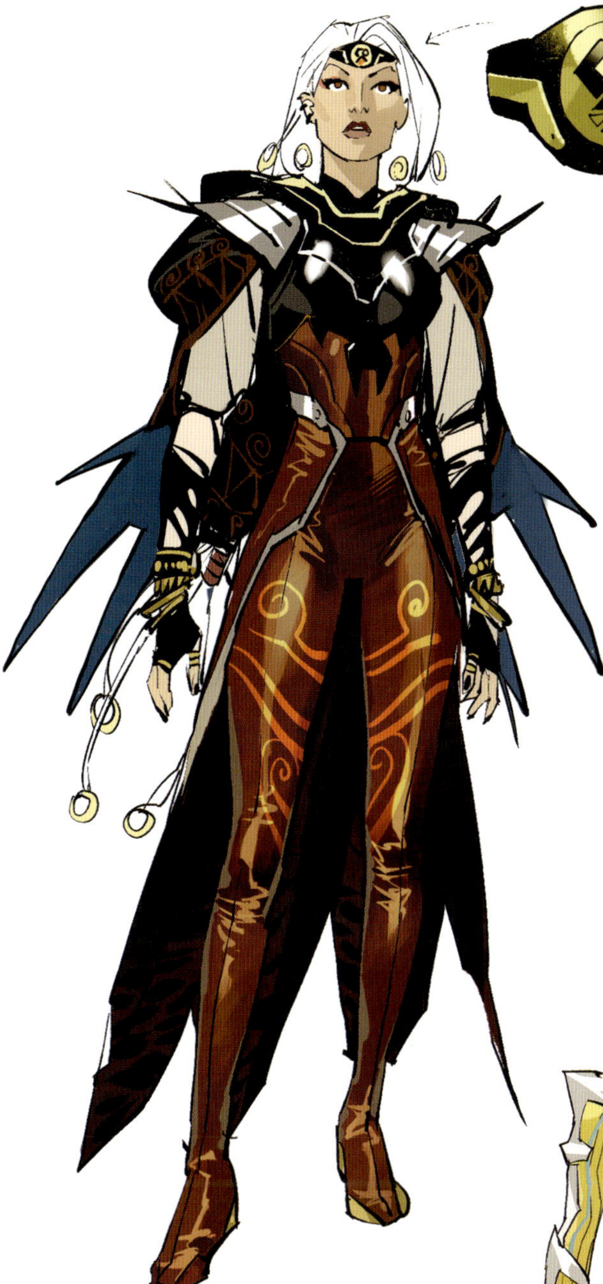

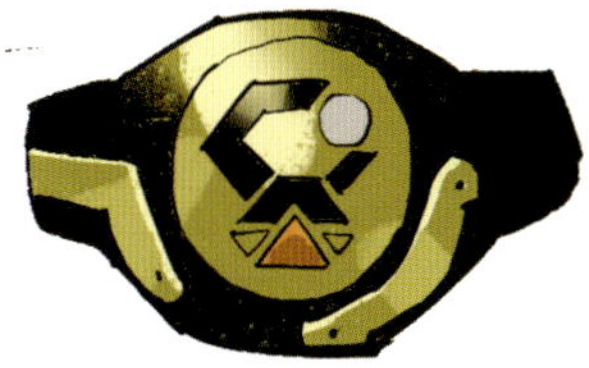

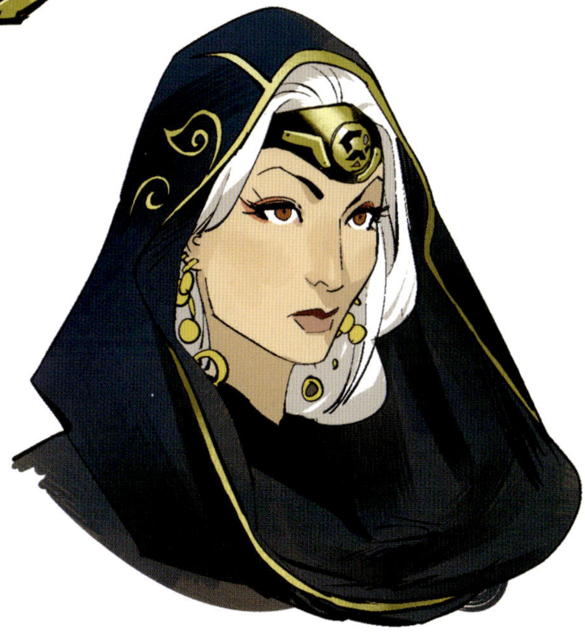

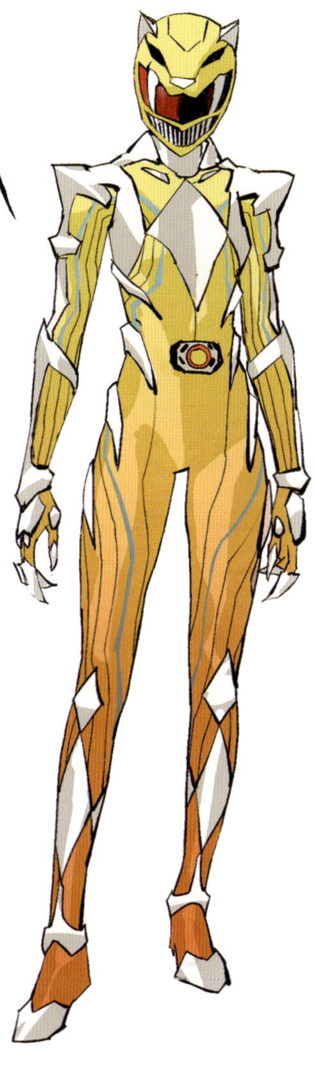

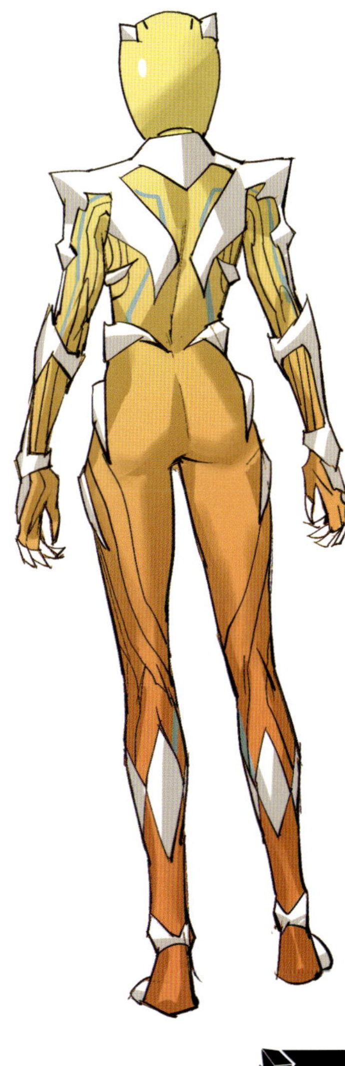

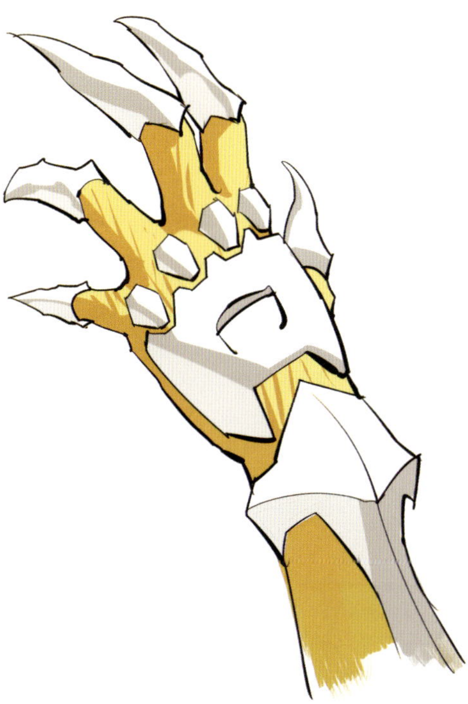

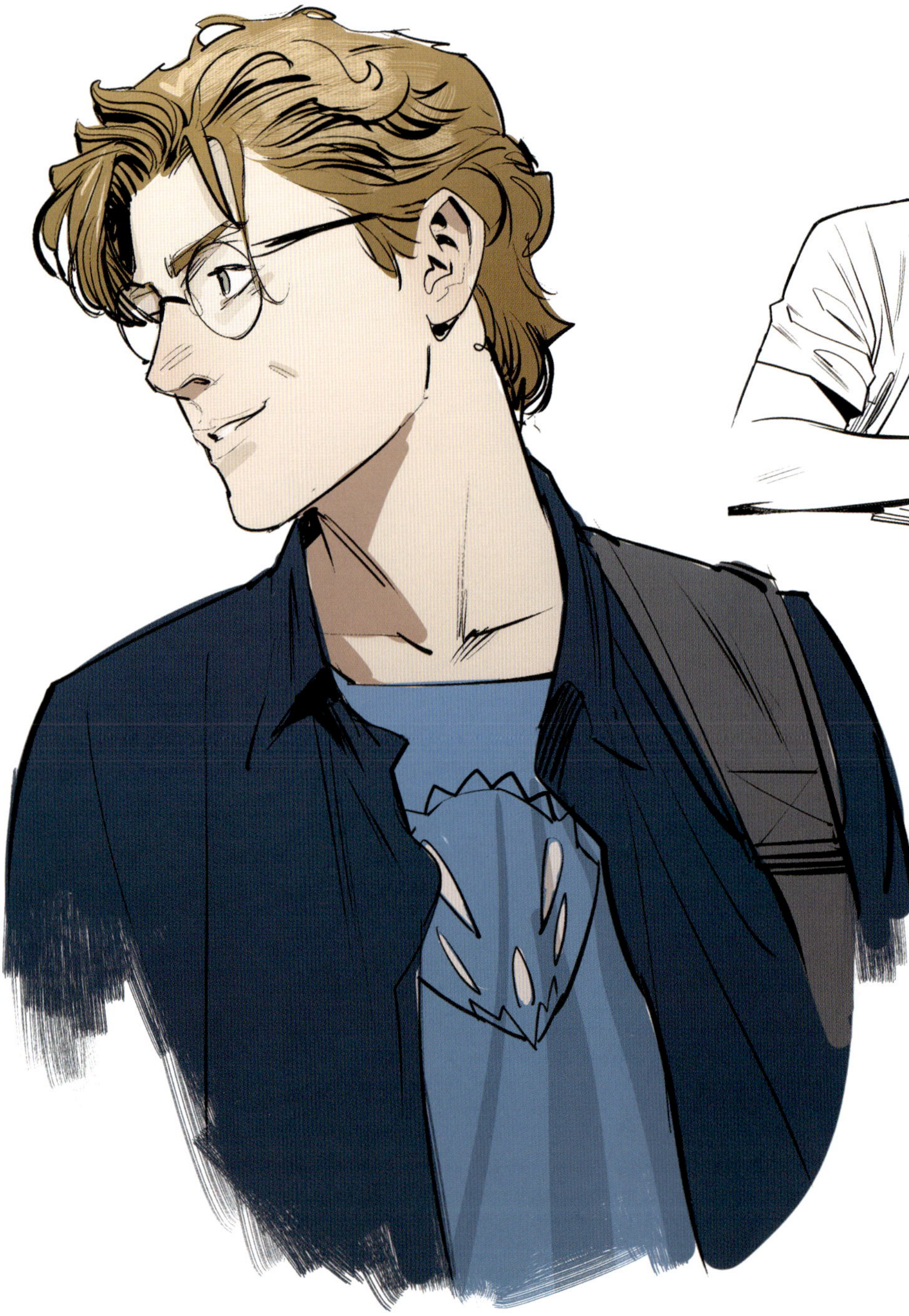

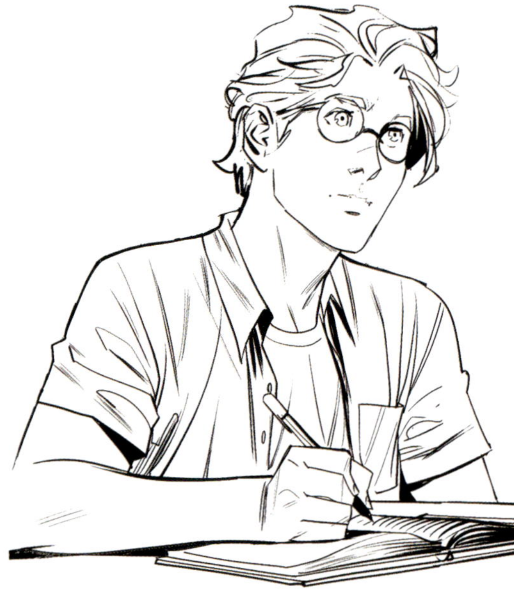

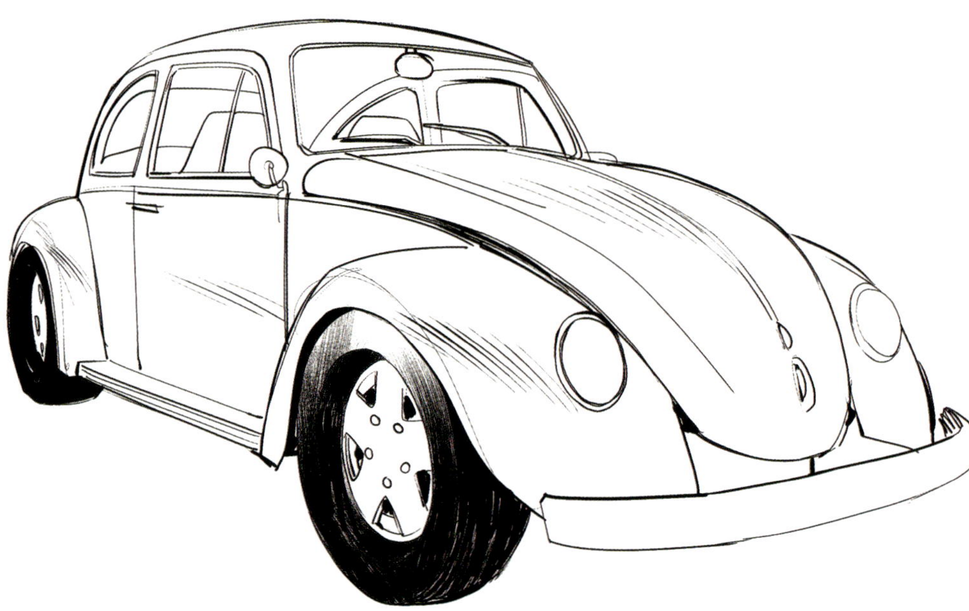

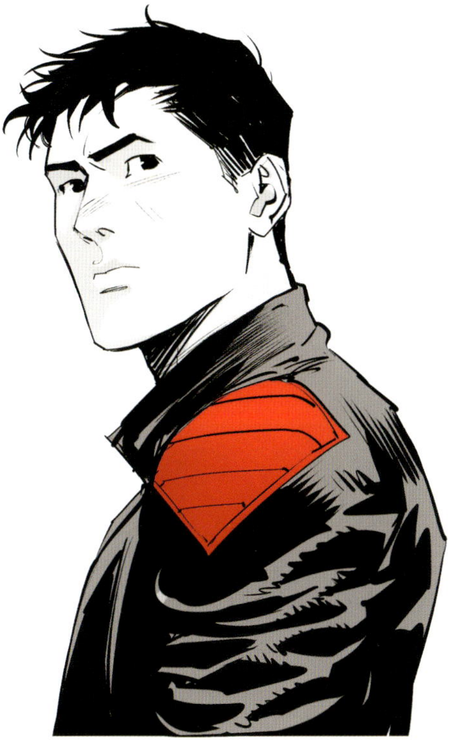

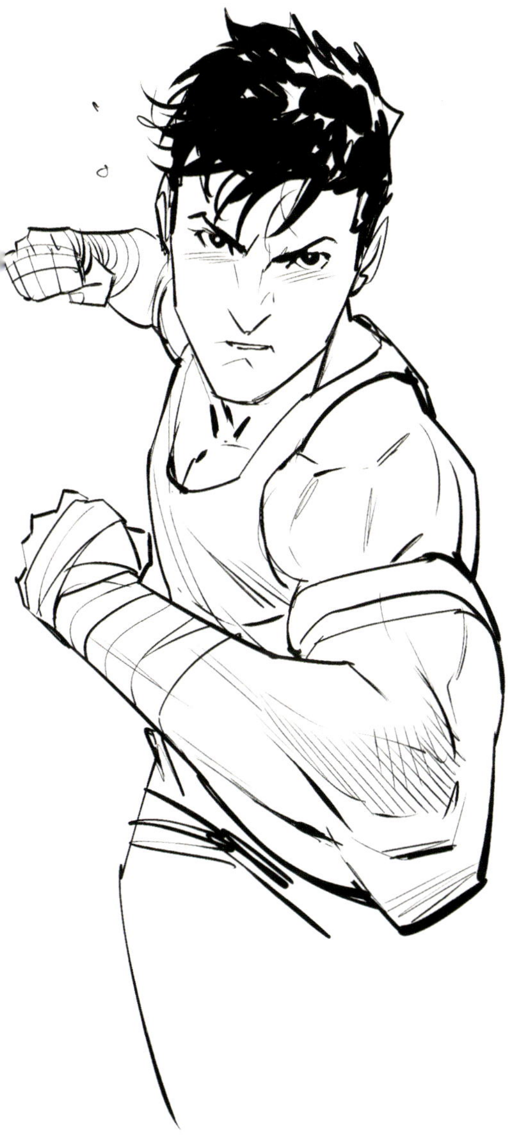

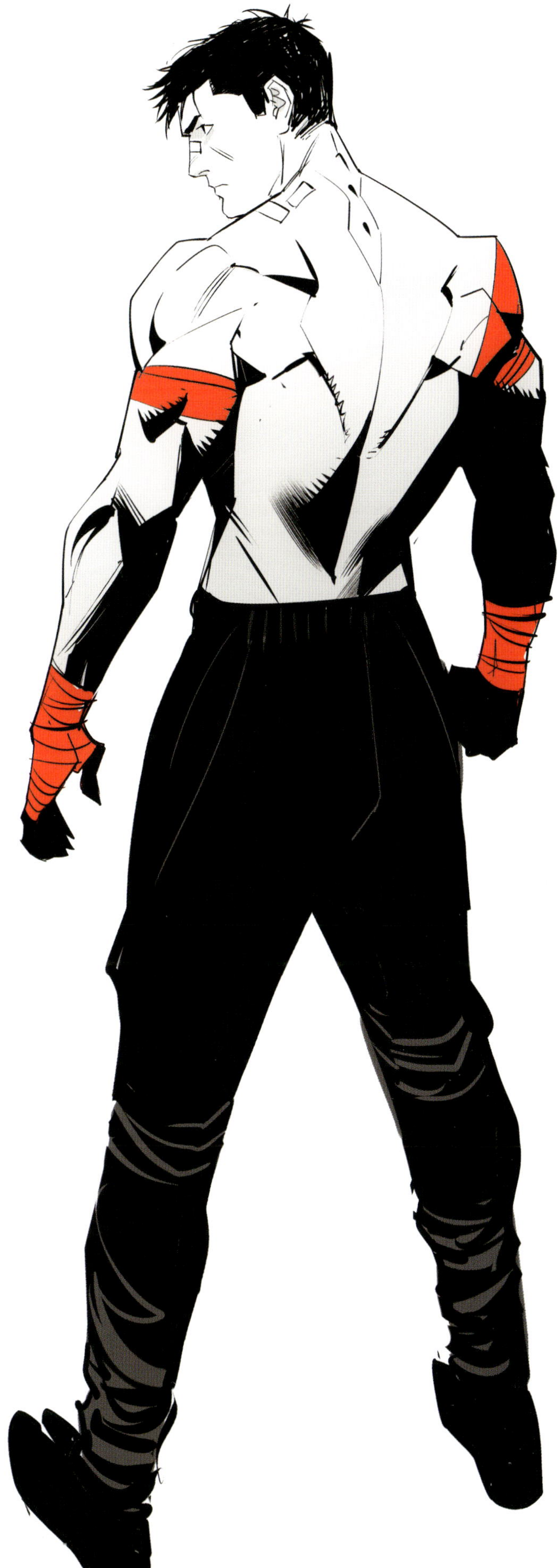

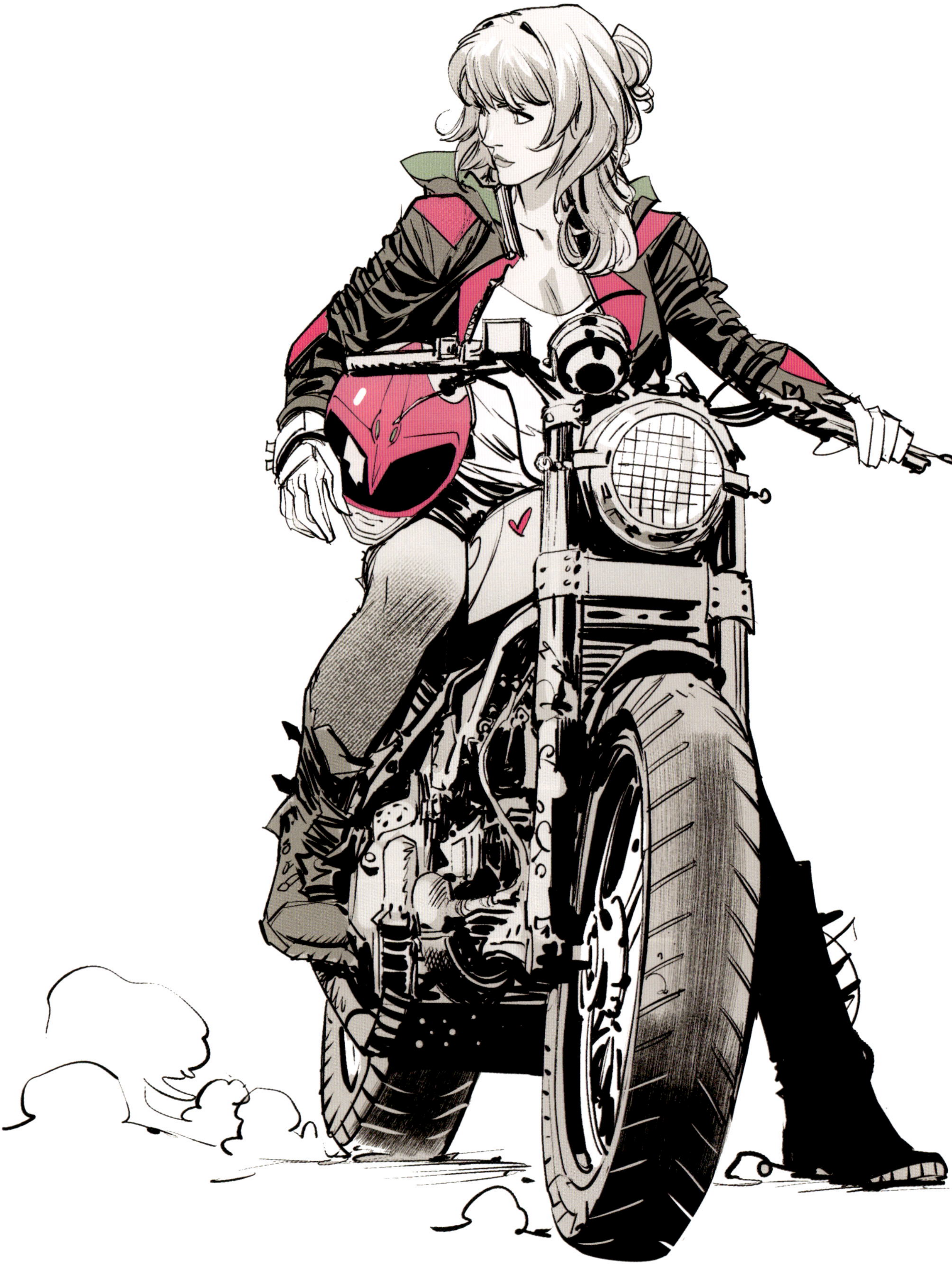

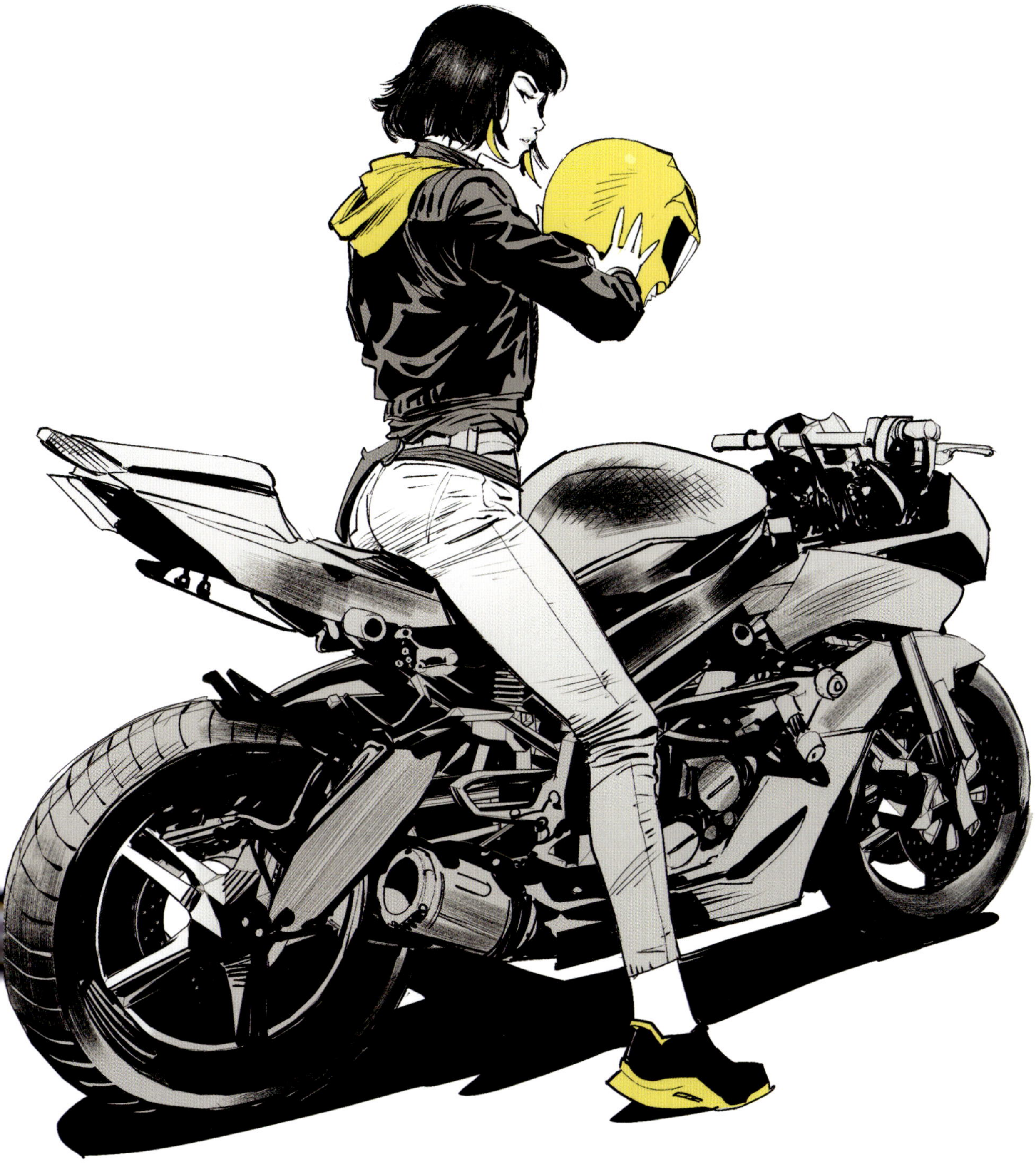

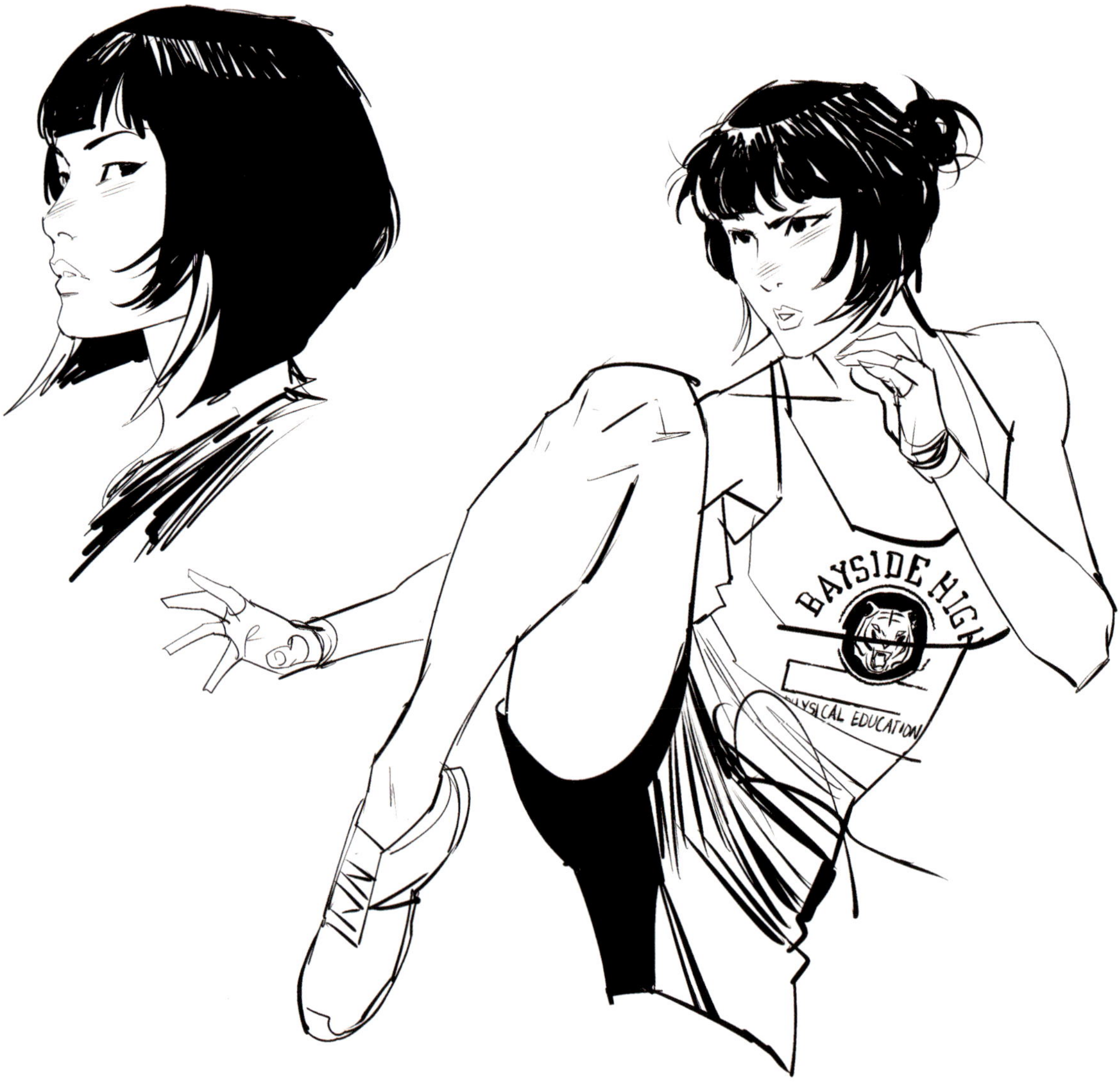
BAYSIDE HIGH
YSICAL EDUCATION

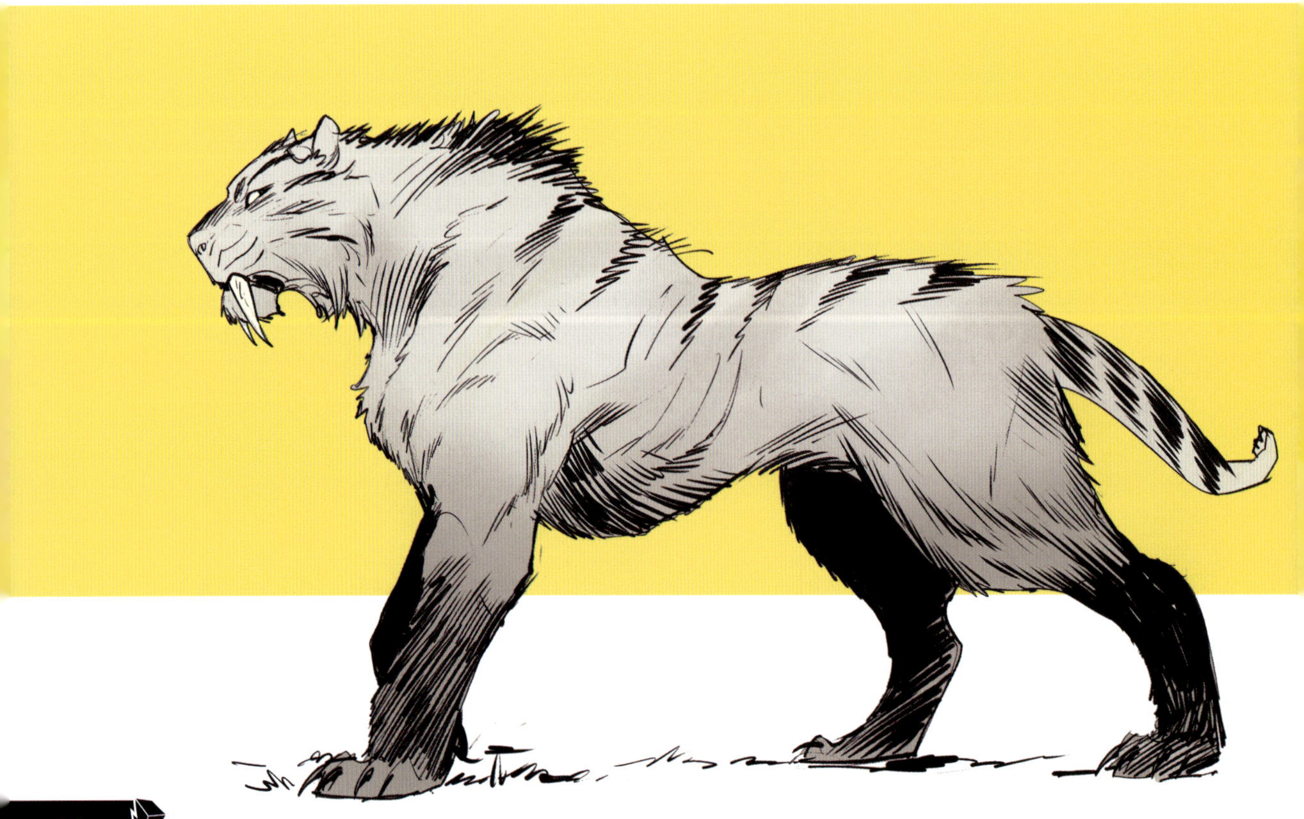

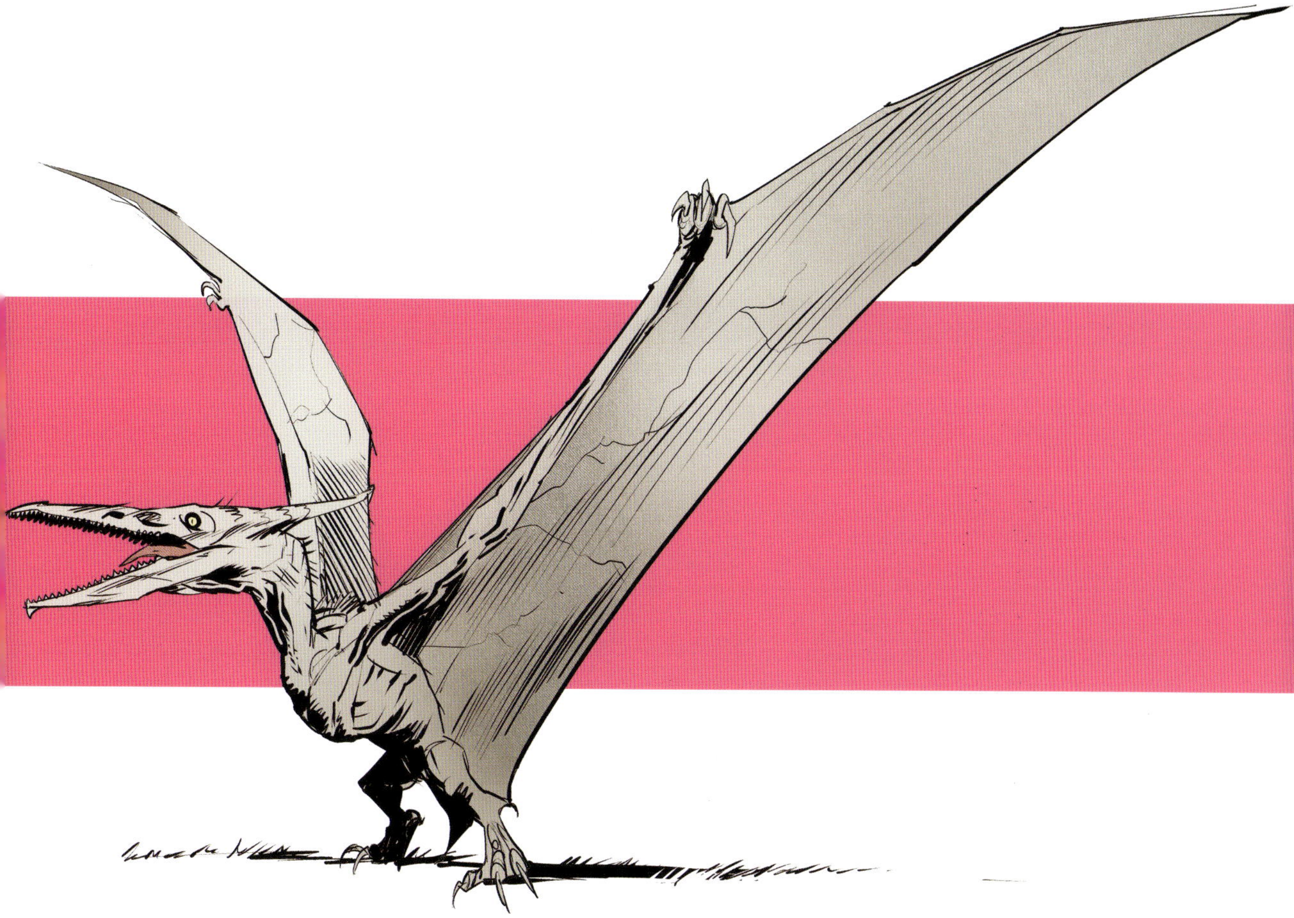

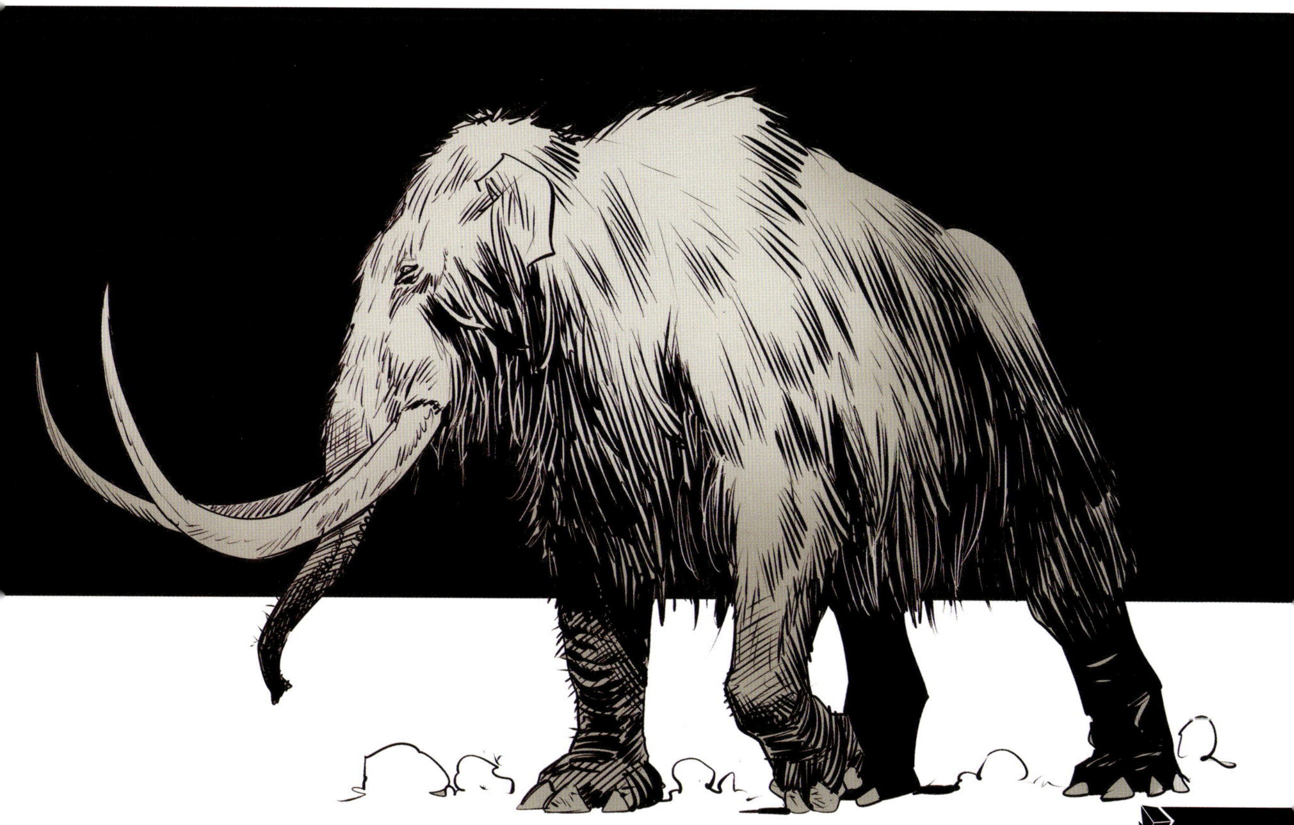

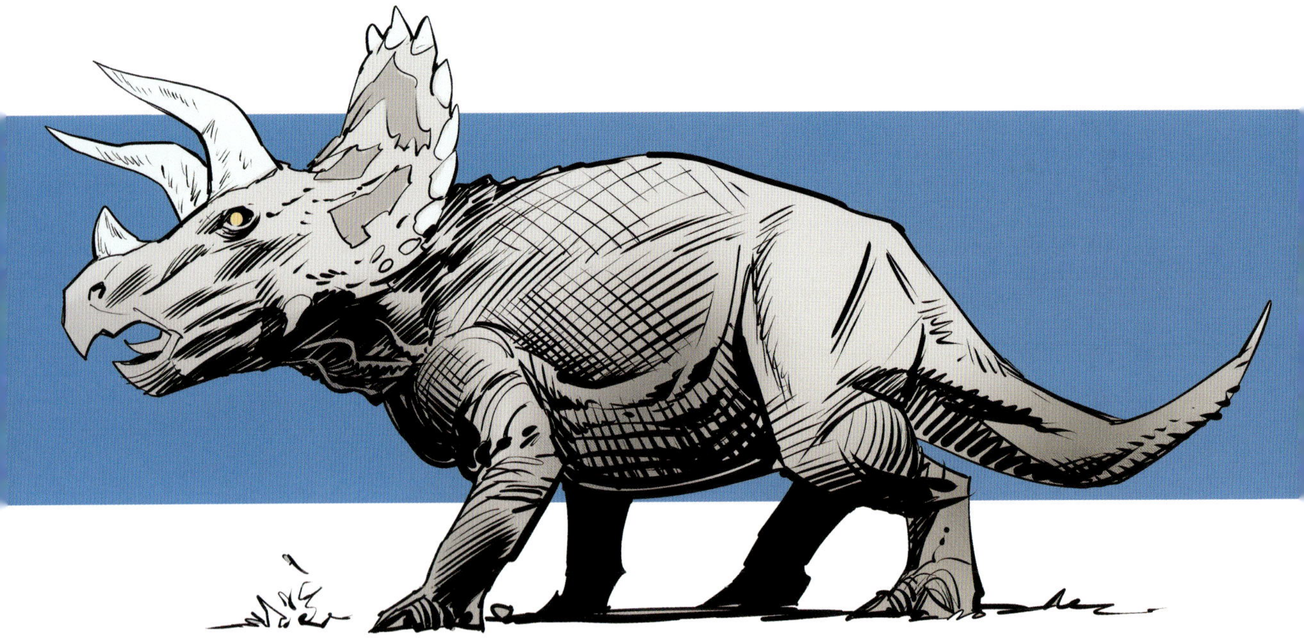

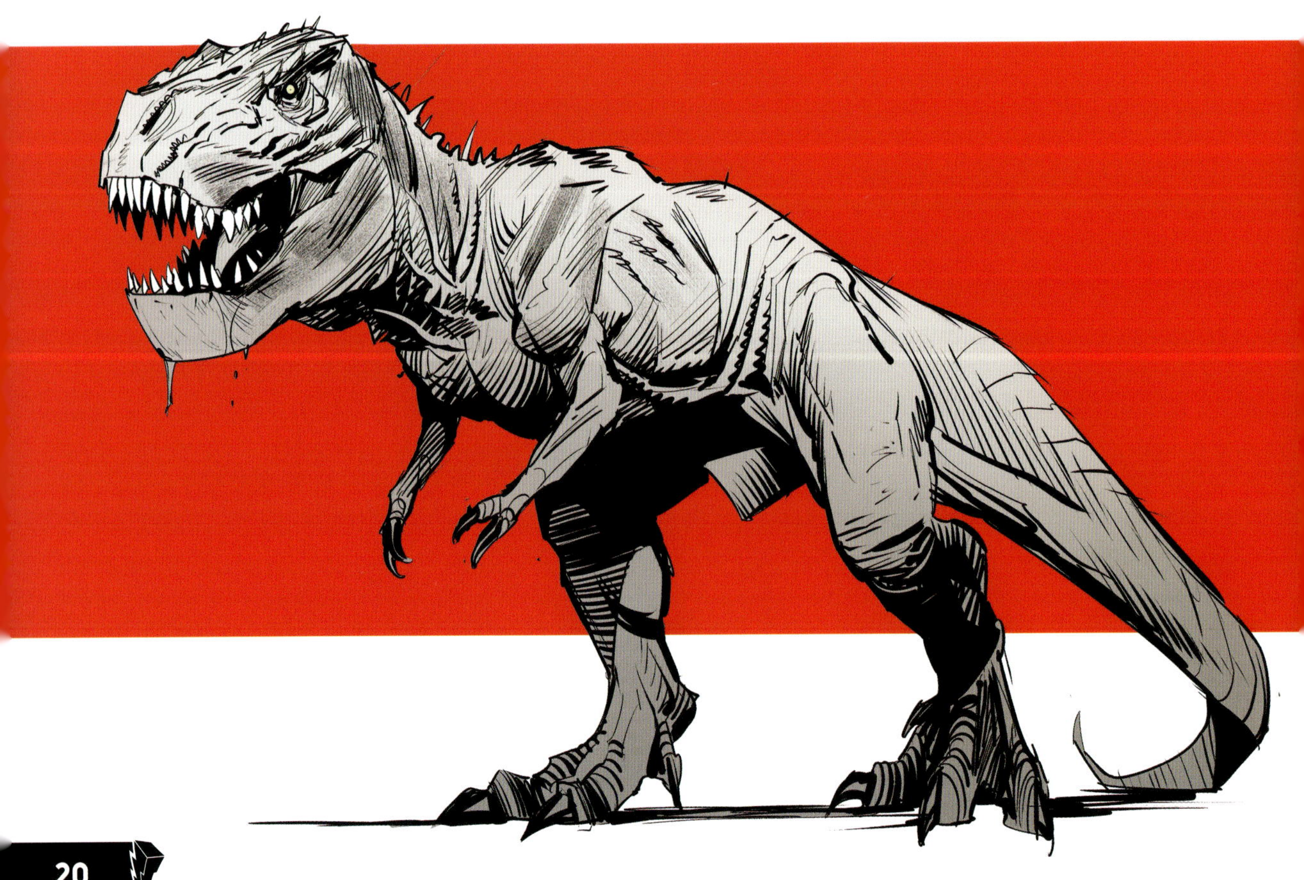

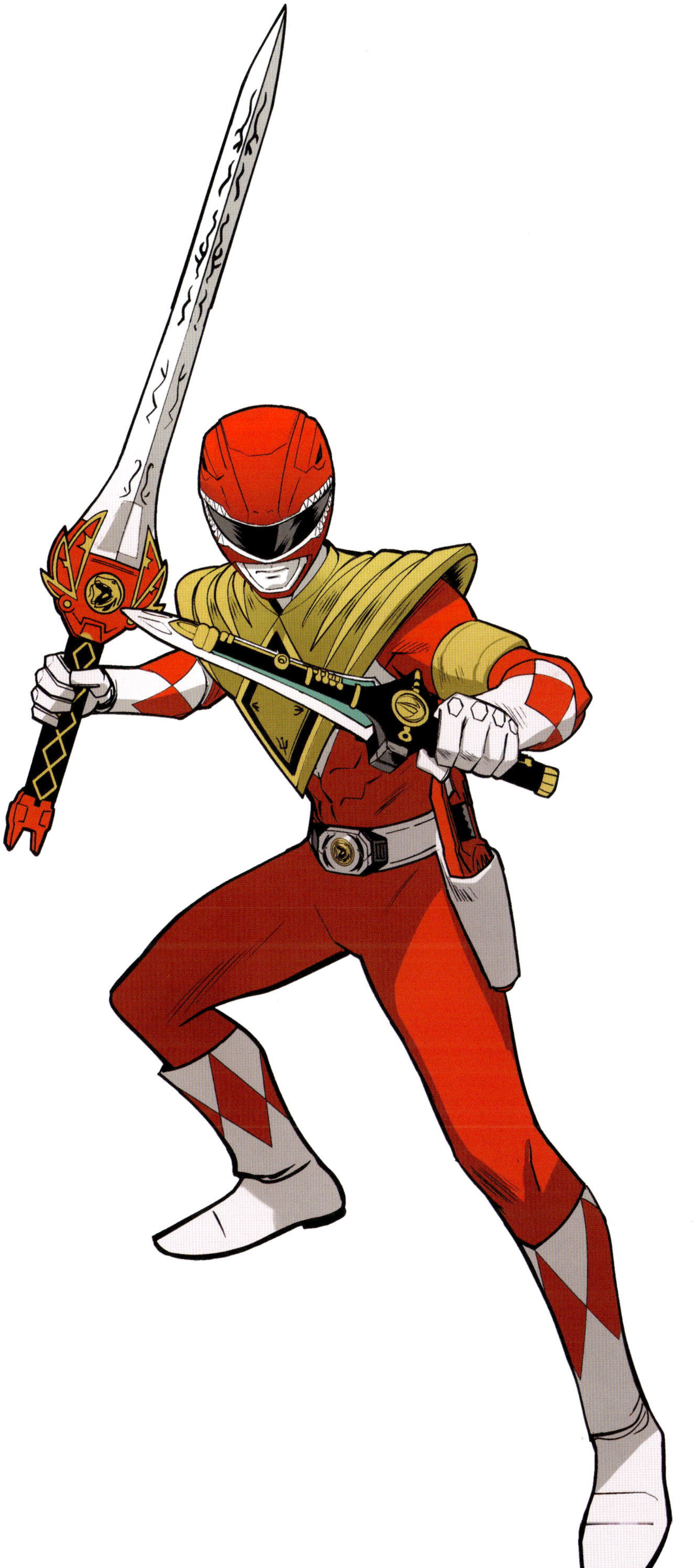

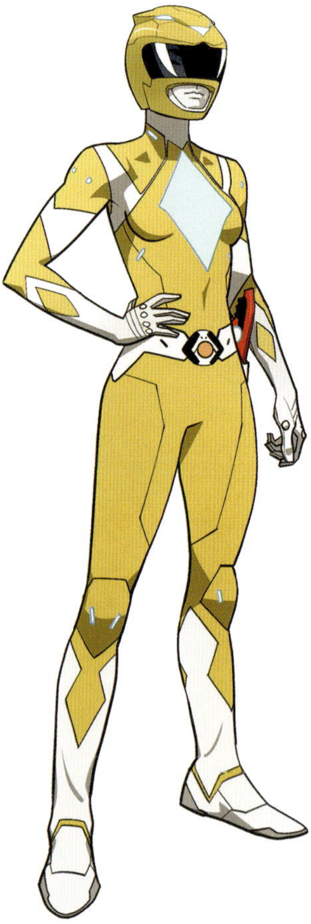

YELLOW RANGER

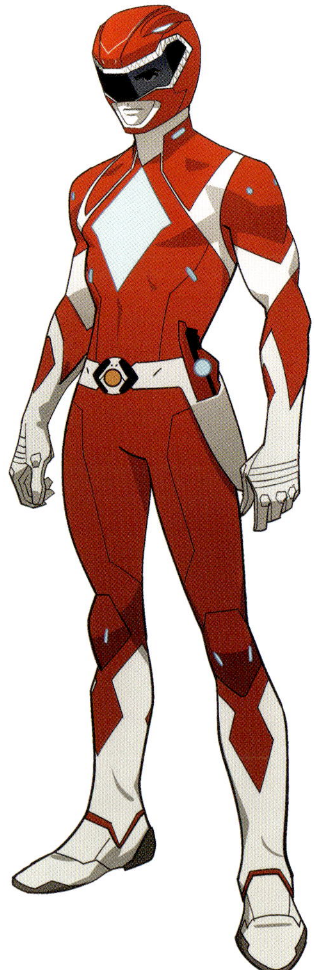

RED RANGER

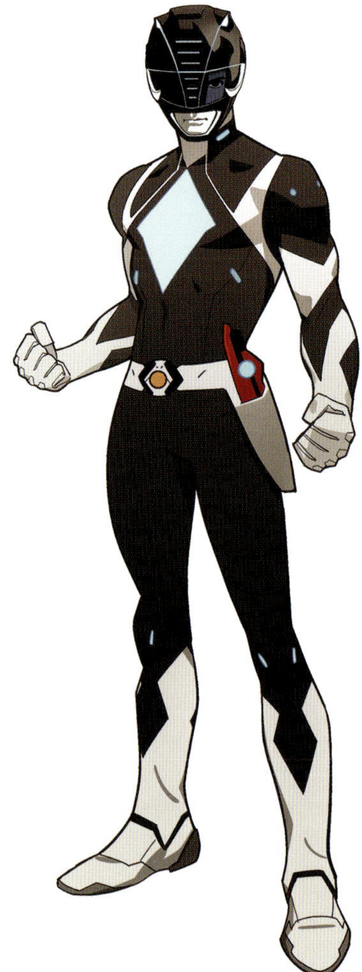

BLACK RANGER

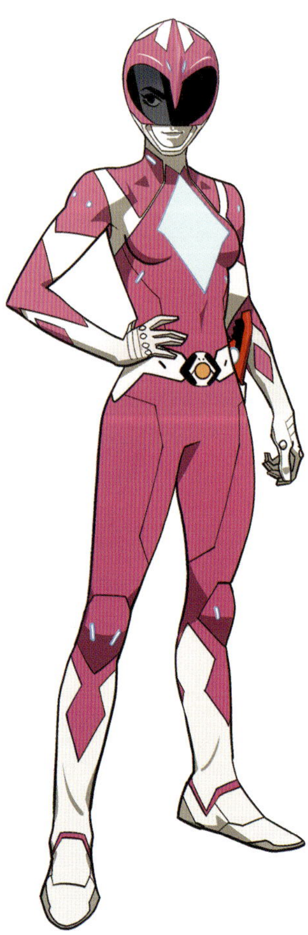

PINK RANGER

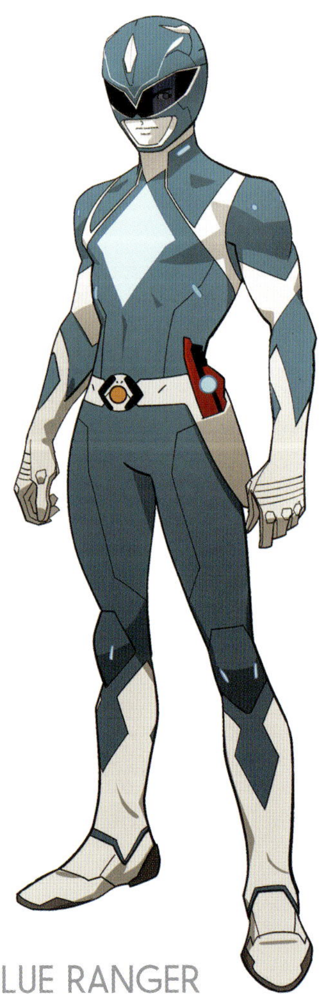

BLUE RANGER

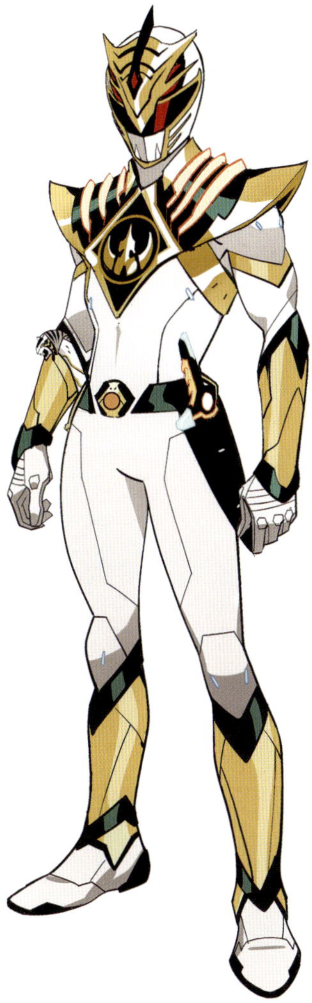

LORD DRAKKON

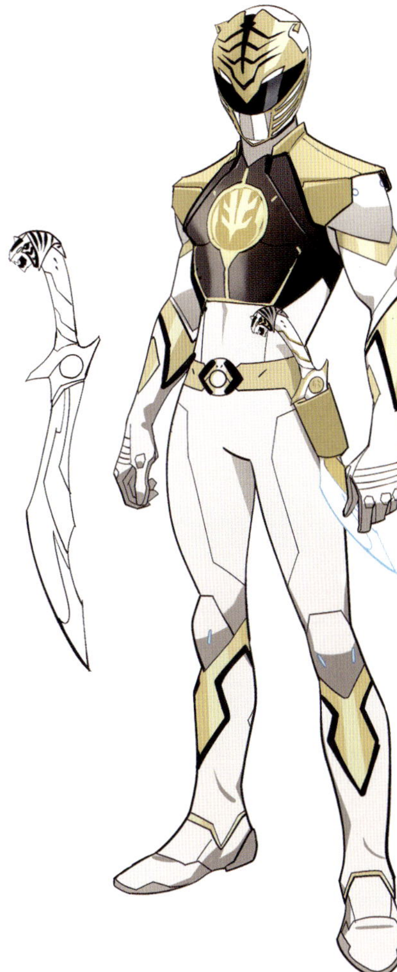

WHITE RANGER

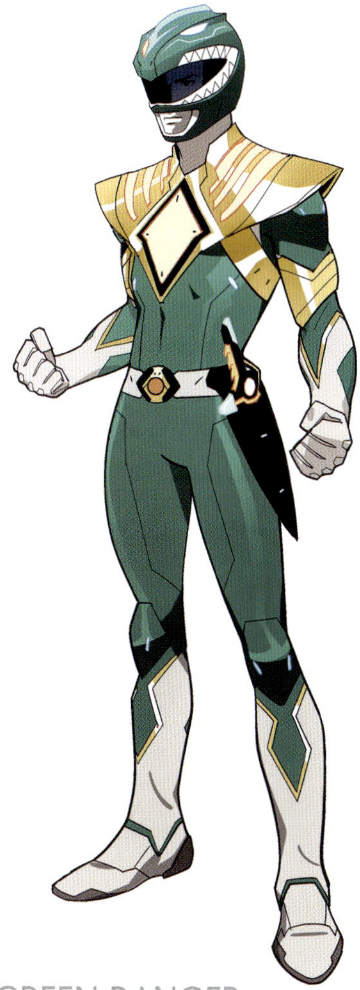

GREEN RANGER

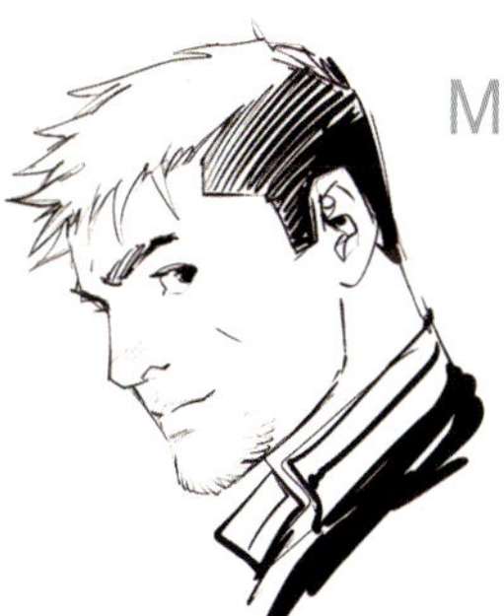

MATT

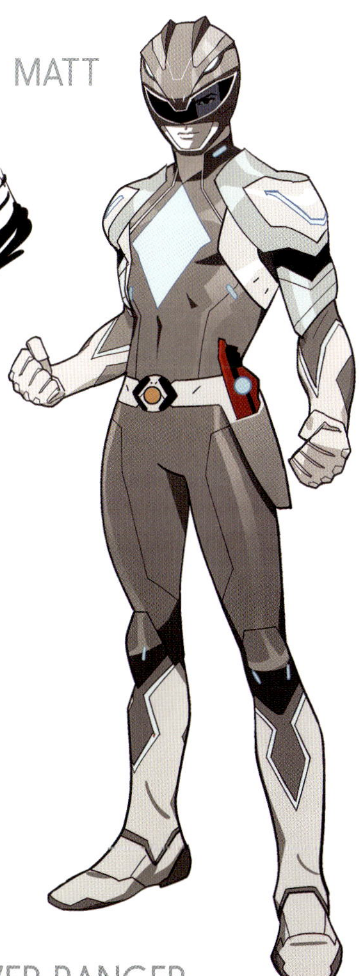

SILVER RANGER

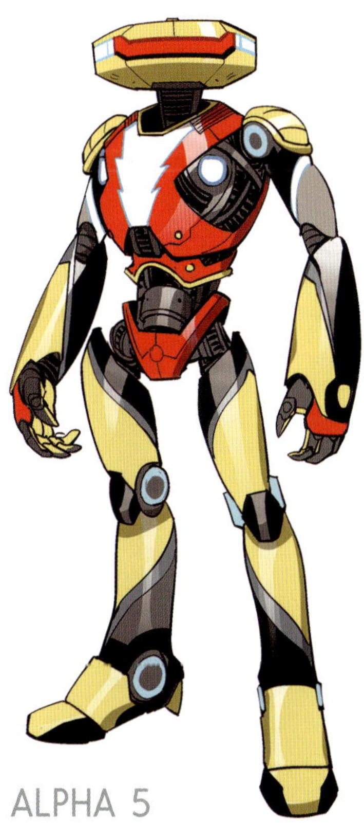

ALPHA 5

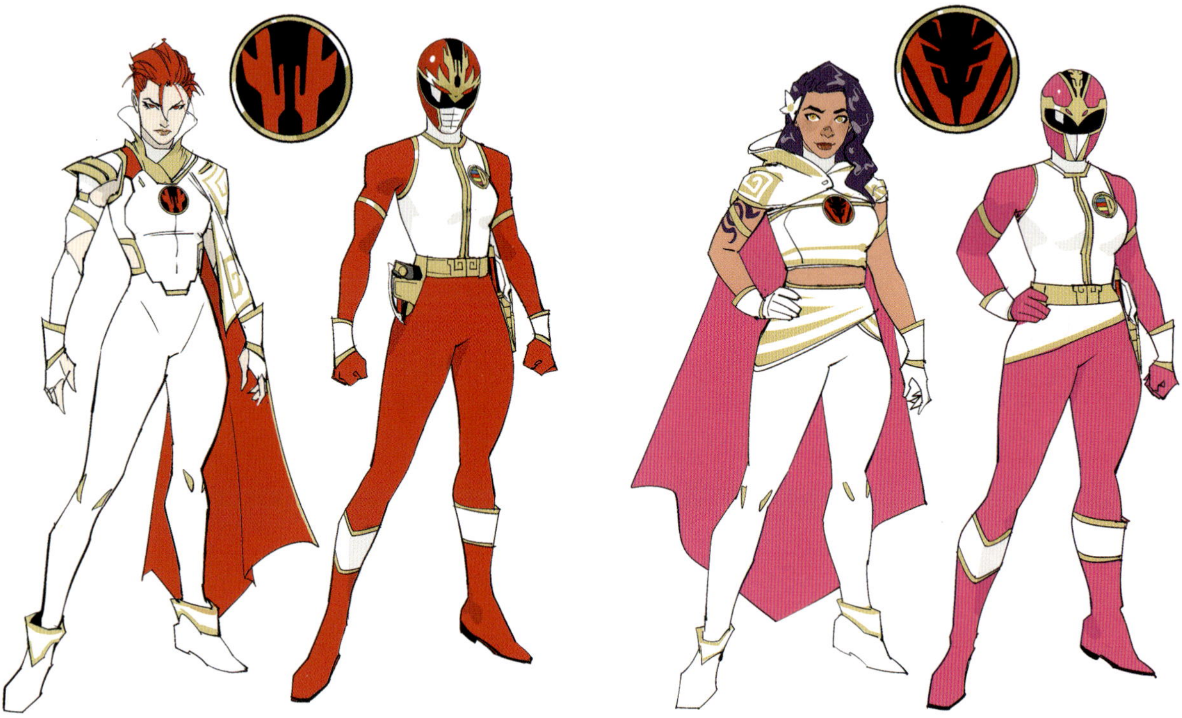

RHIAN

ALEIA

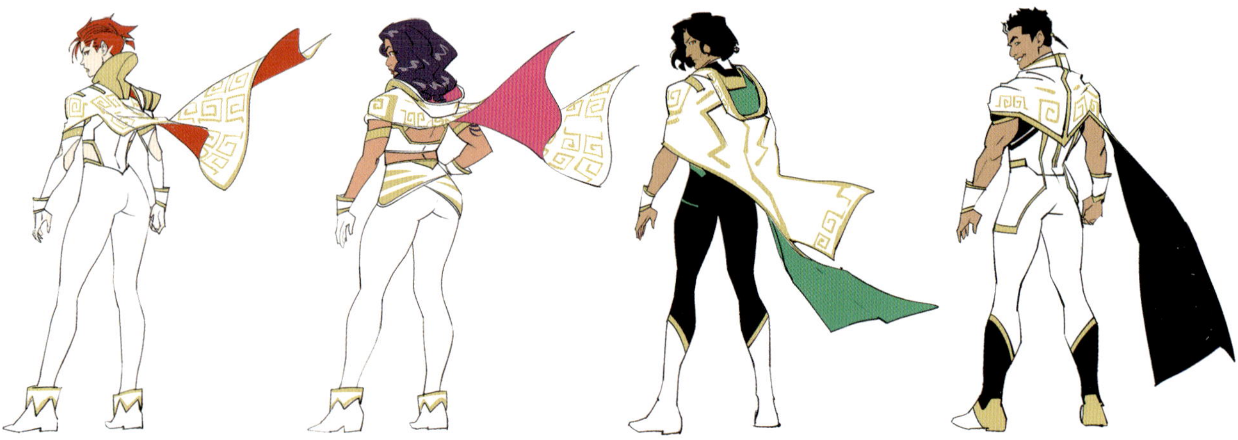

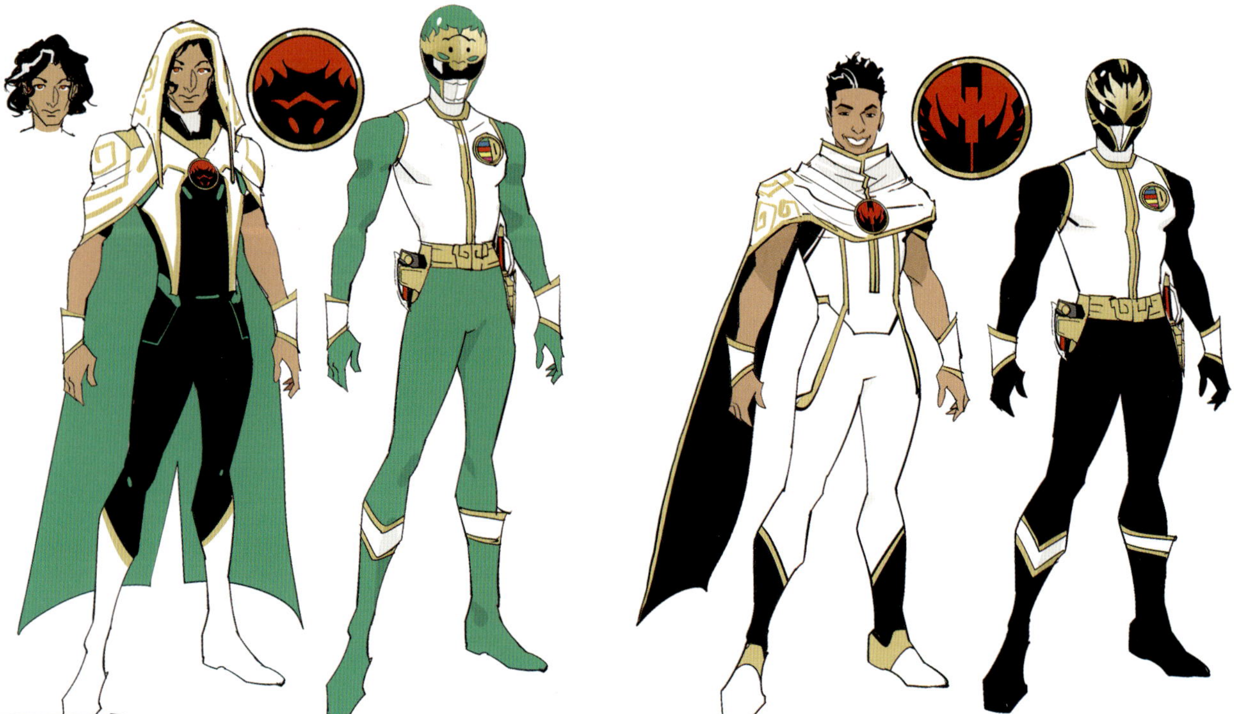

TELOSI

XEV

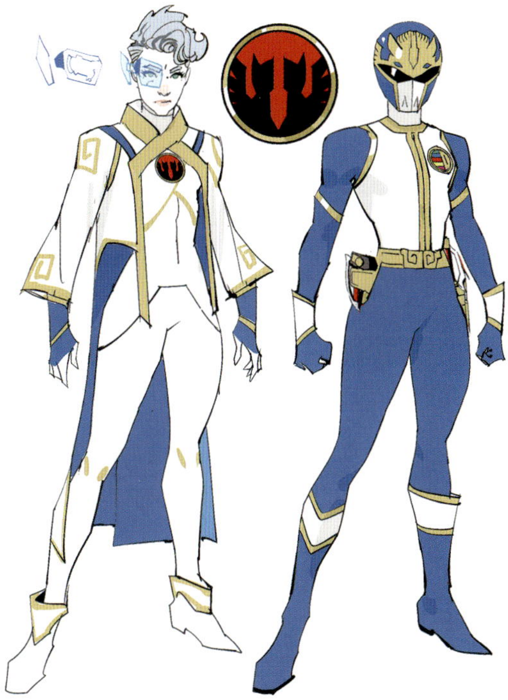

ORISONTH

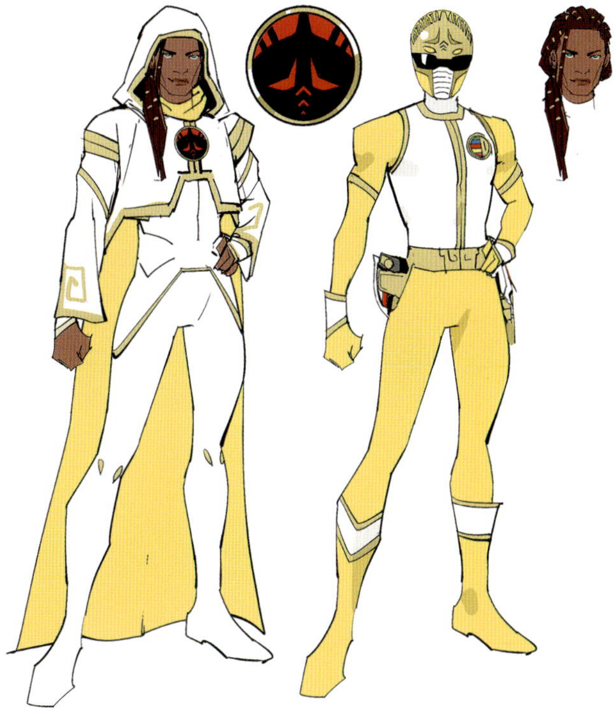

PHIRO

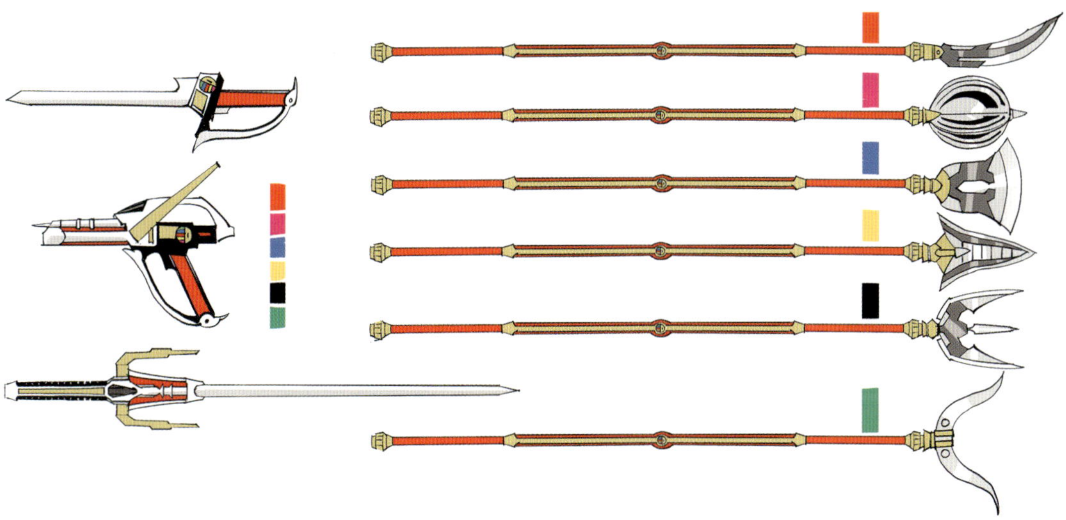

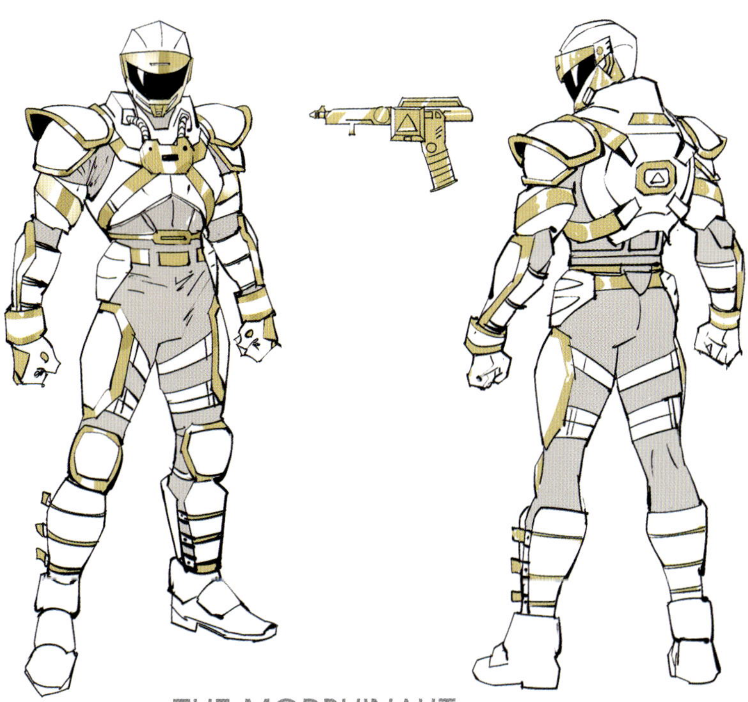

THE MORPHINAUT

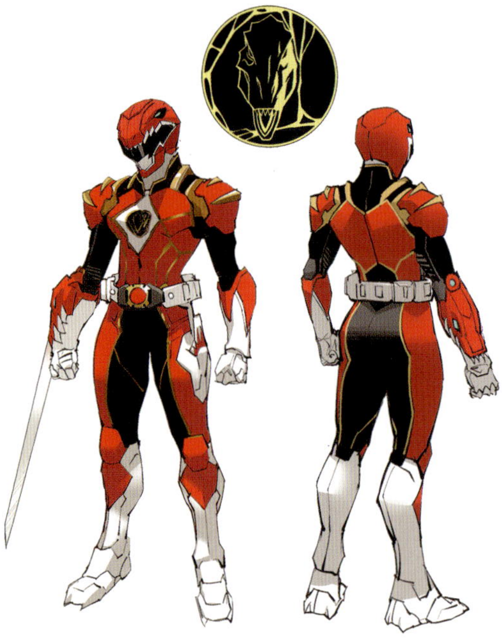

RED RANGER

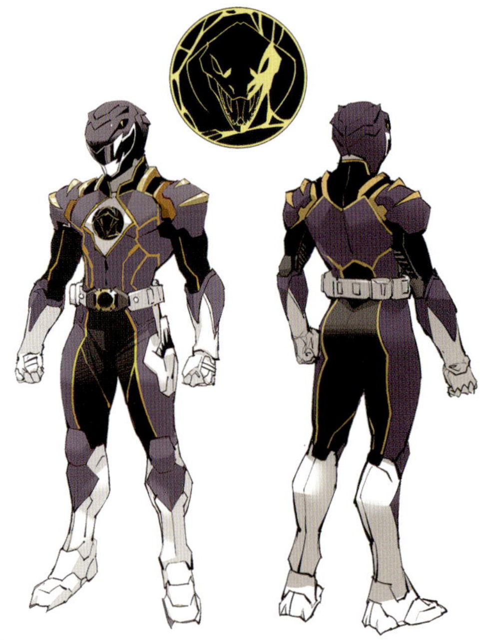

BLACK RANGER

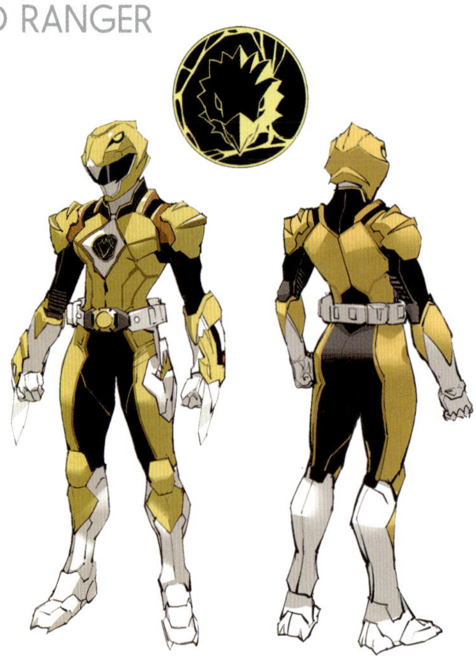

YELLOW RANGER

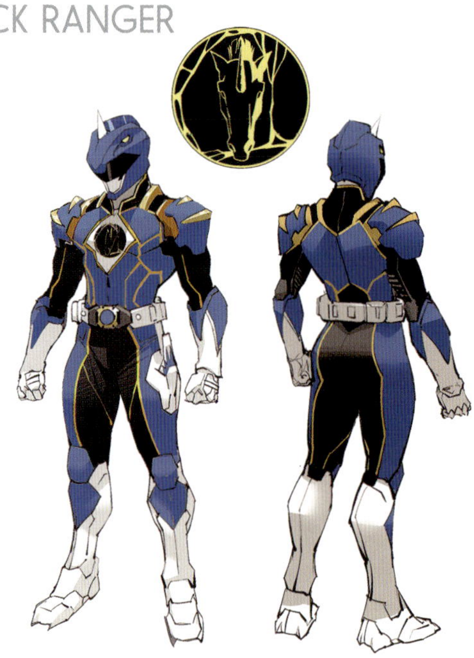

BLUE RANGER

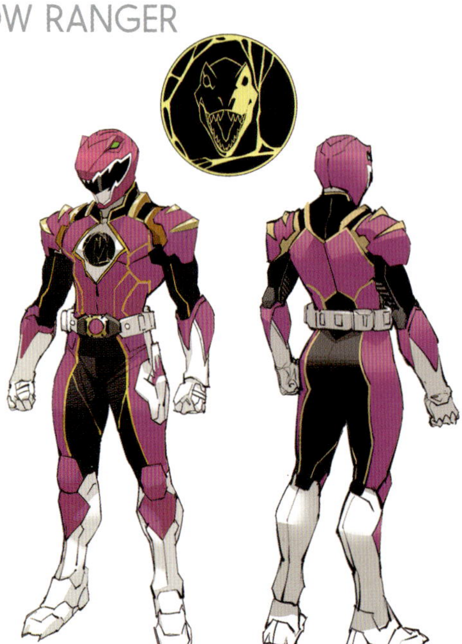

PINK RANGER

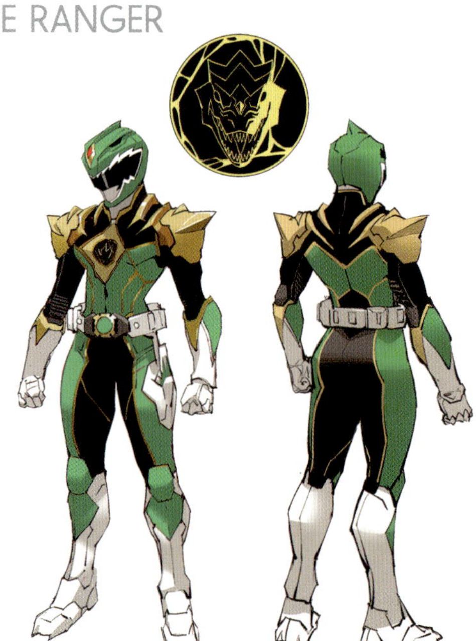

GREEN RANGER

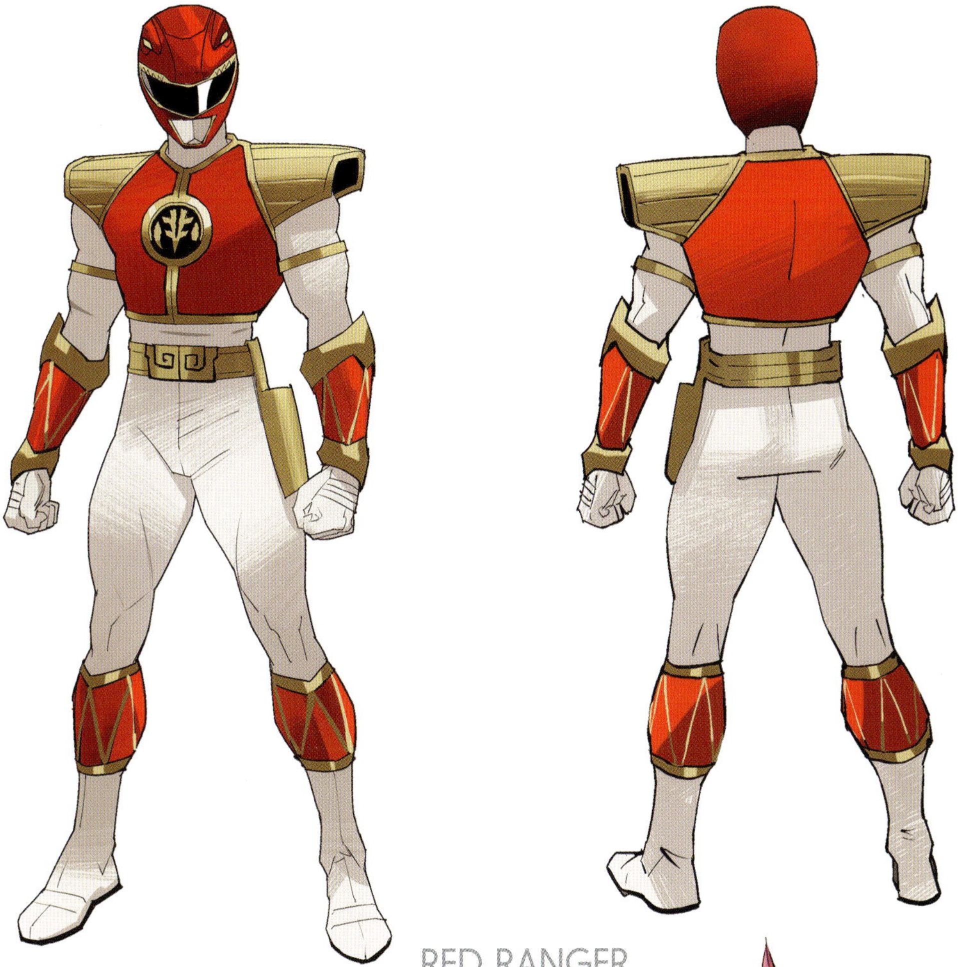

RED RANGER
POWER COIN

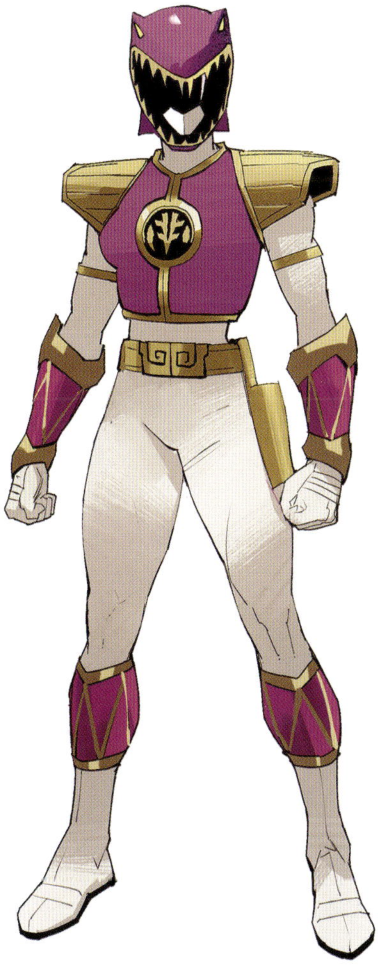

PURPLE RANGER POWER COIN

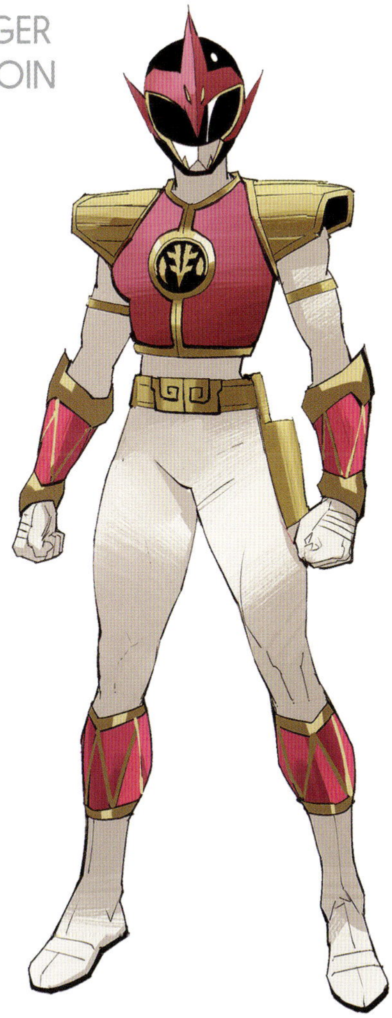

PINK RANGER POWER COIN

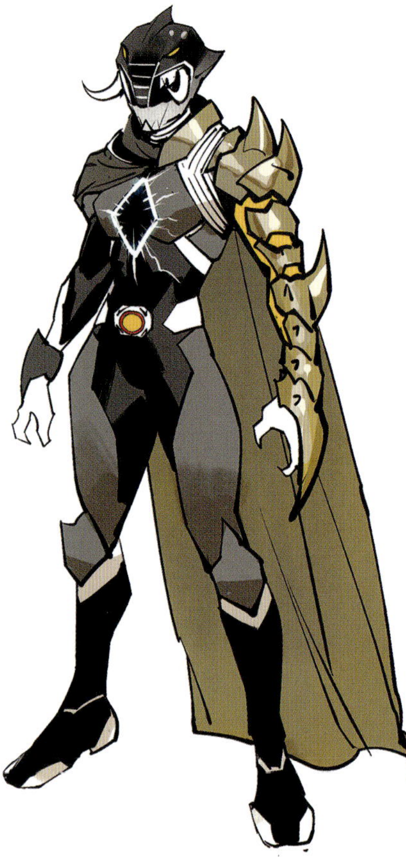

BLACK
DRAKKON RANGER

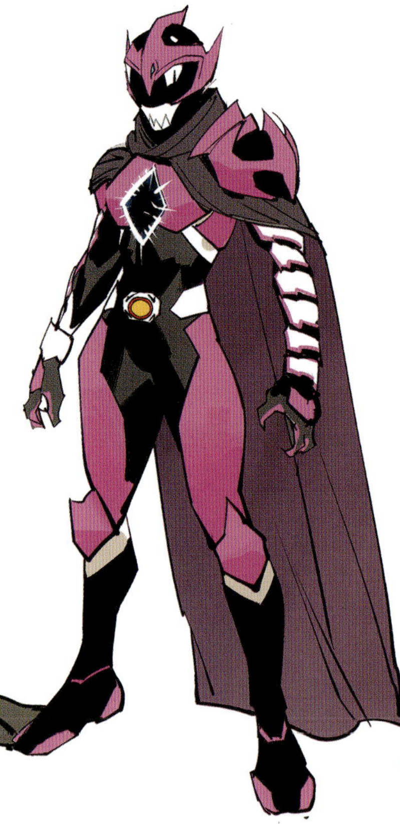

PINK
DRAKKON RANGER

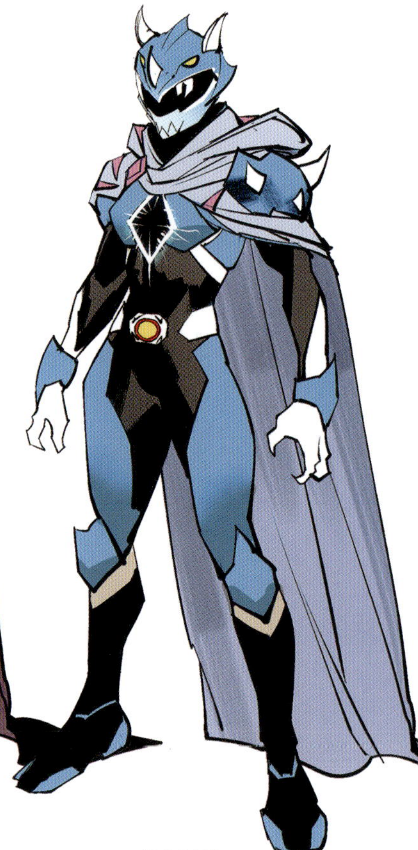

BLUE
DRAKKON RANGER

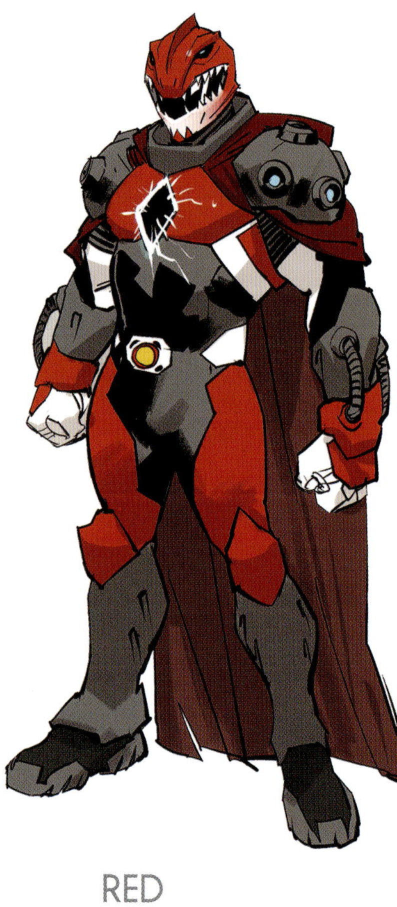

RED
DRAKKON RANGER

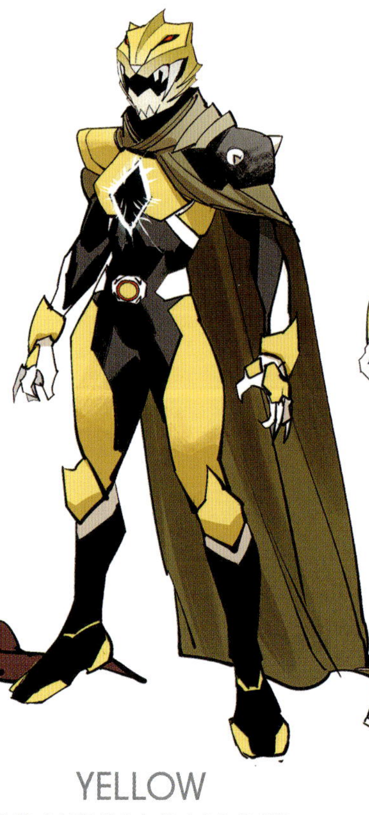

YELLOW
DRAKKON RANGER

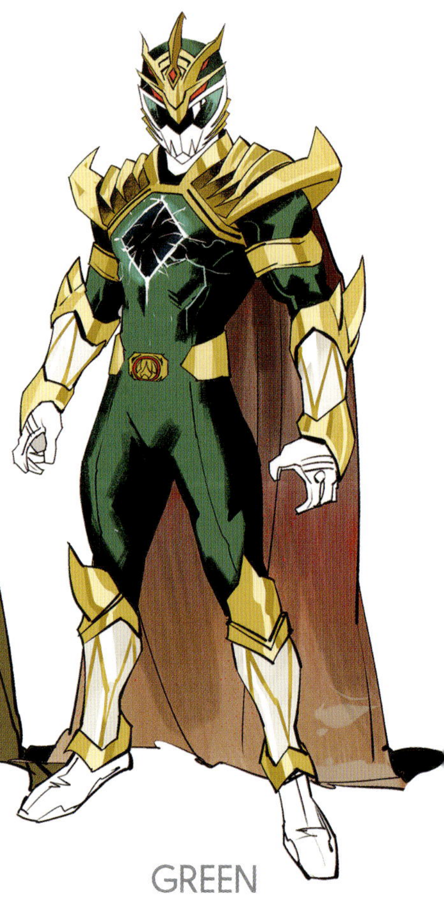

GREEN
DRAKKON RANGER

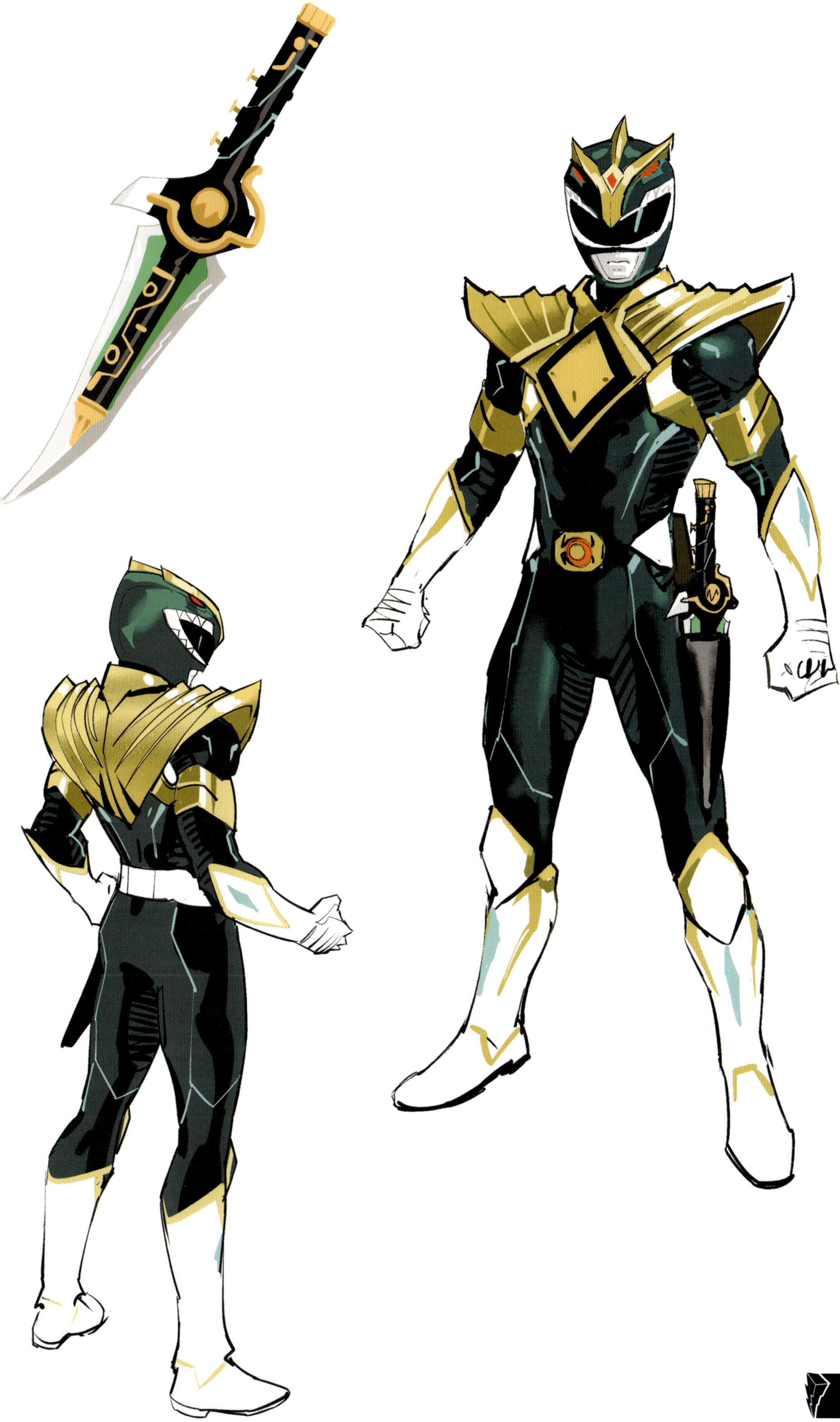

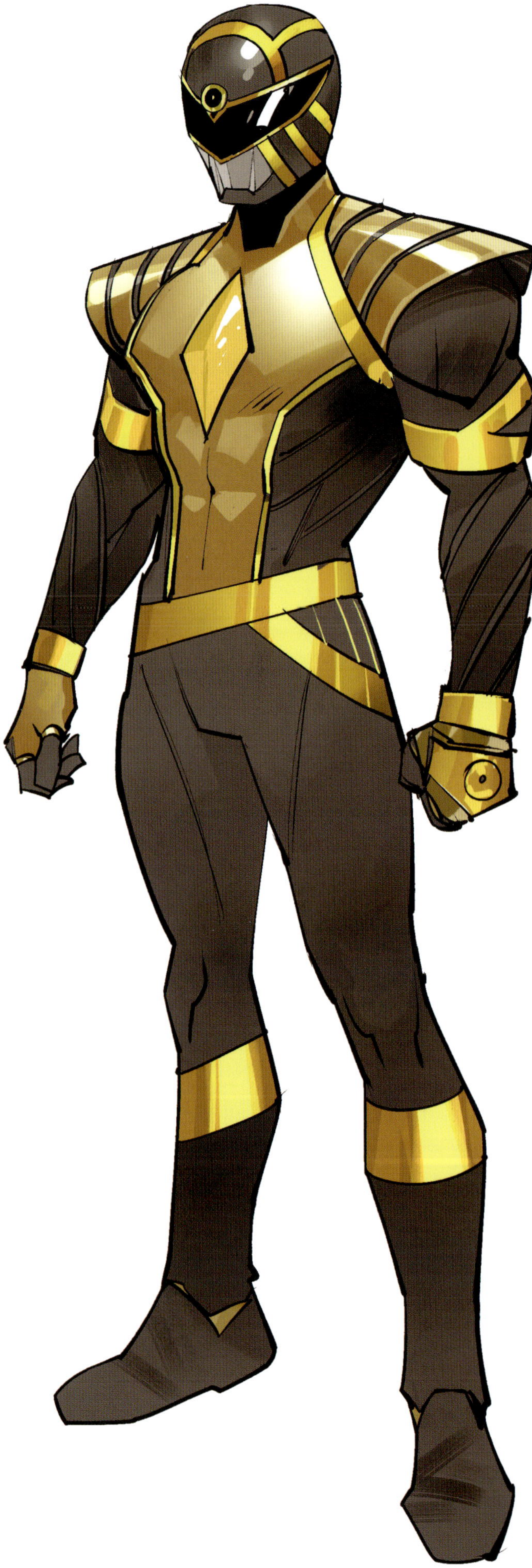

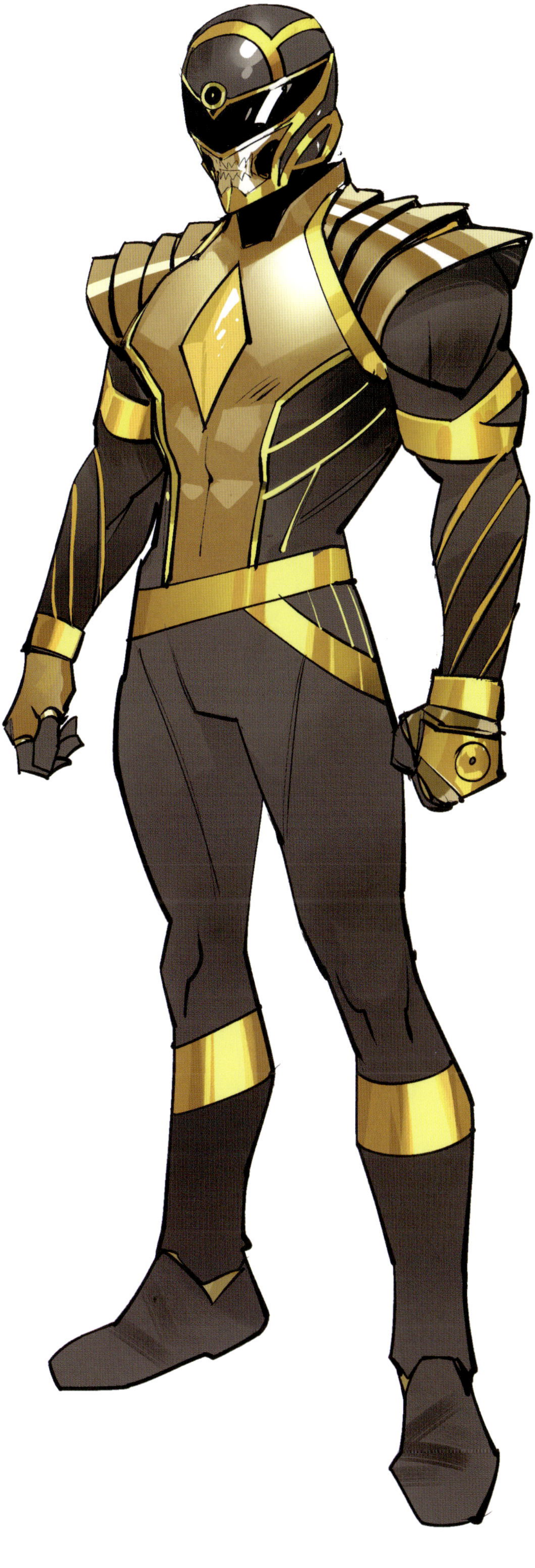

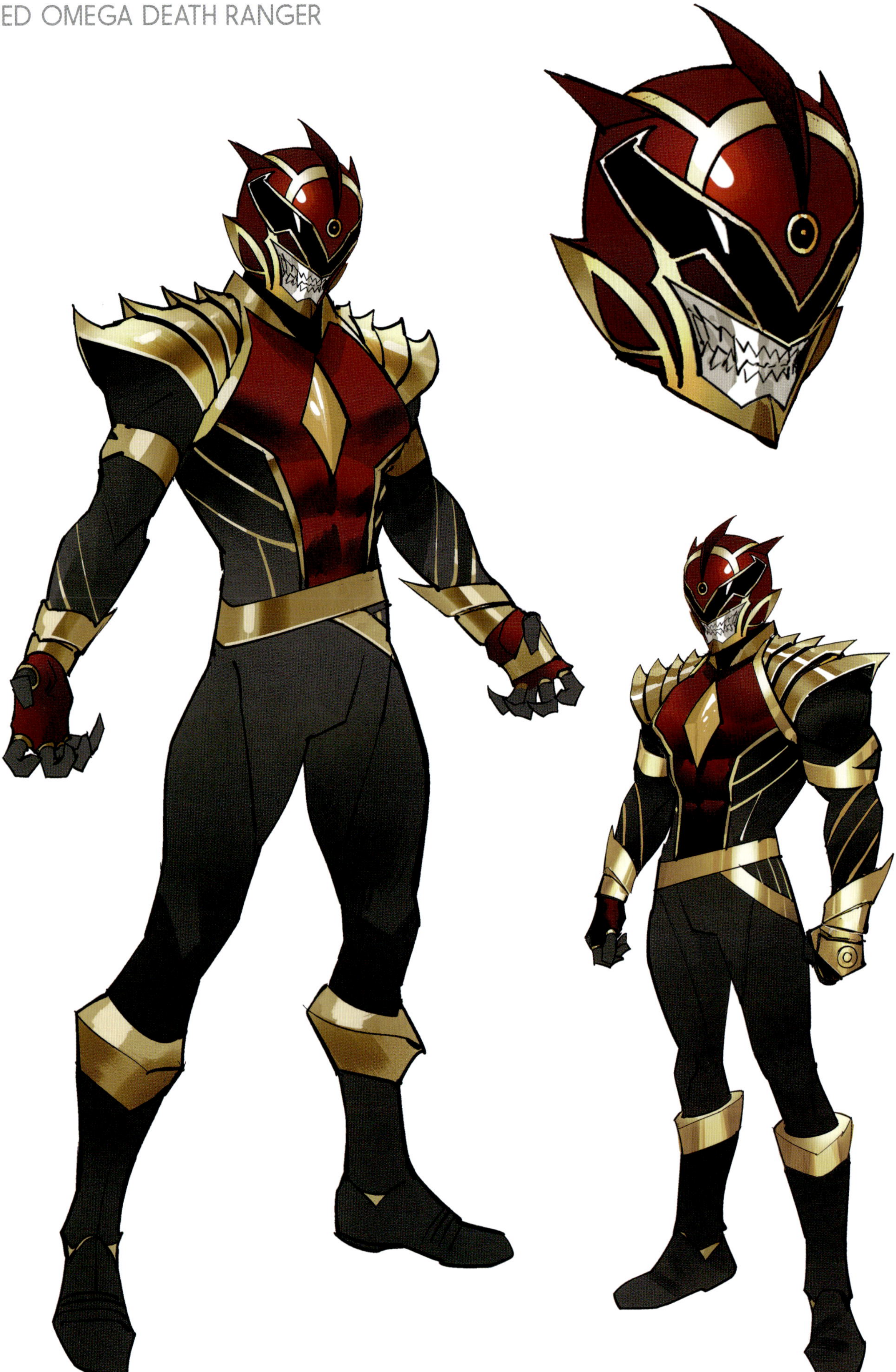

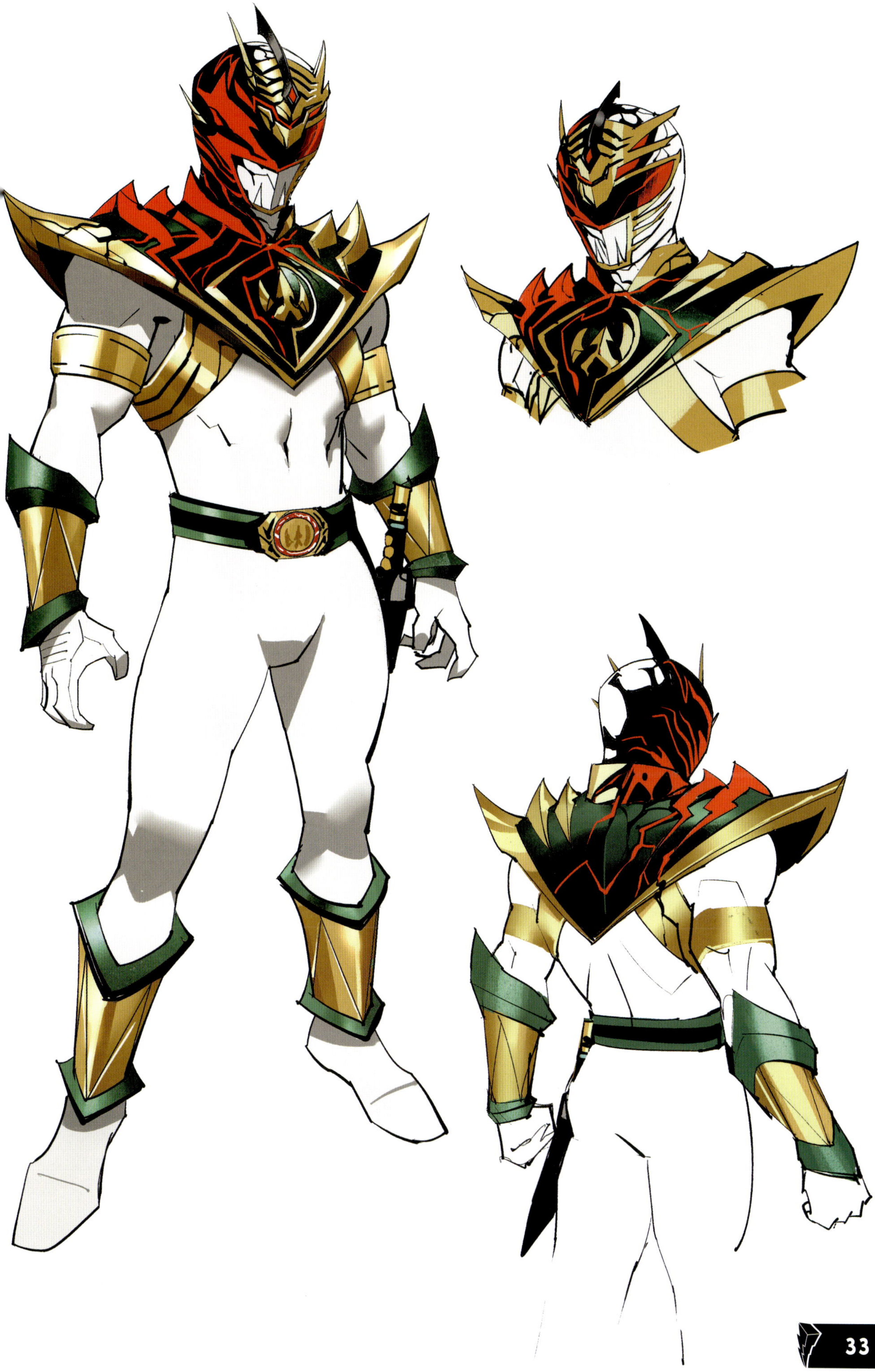

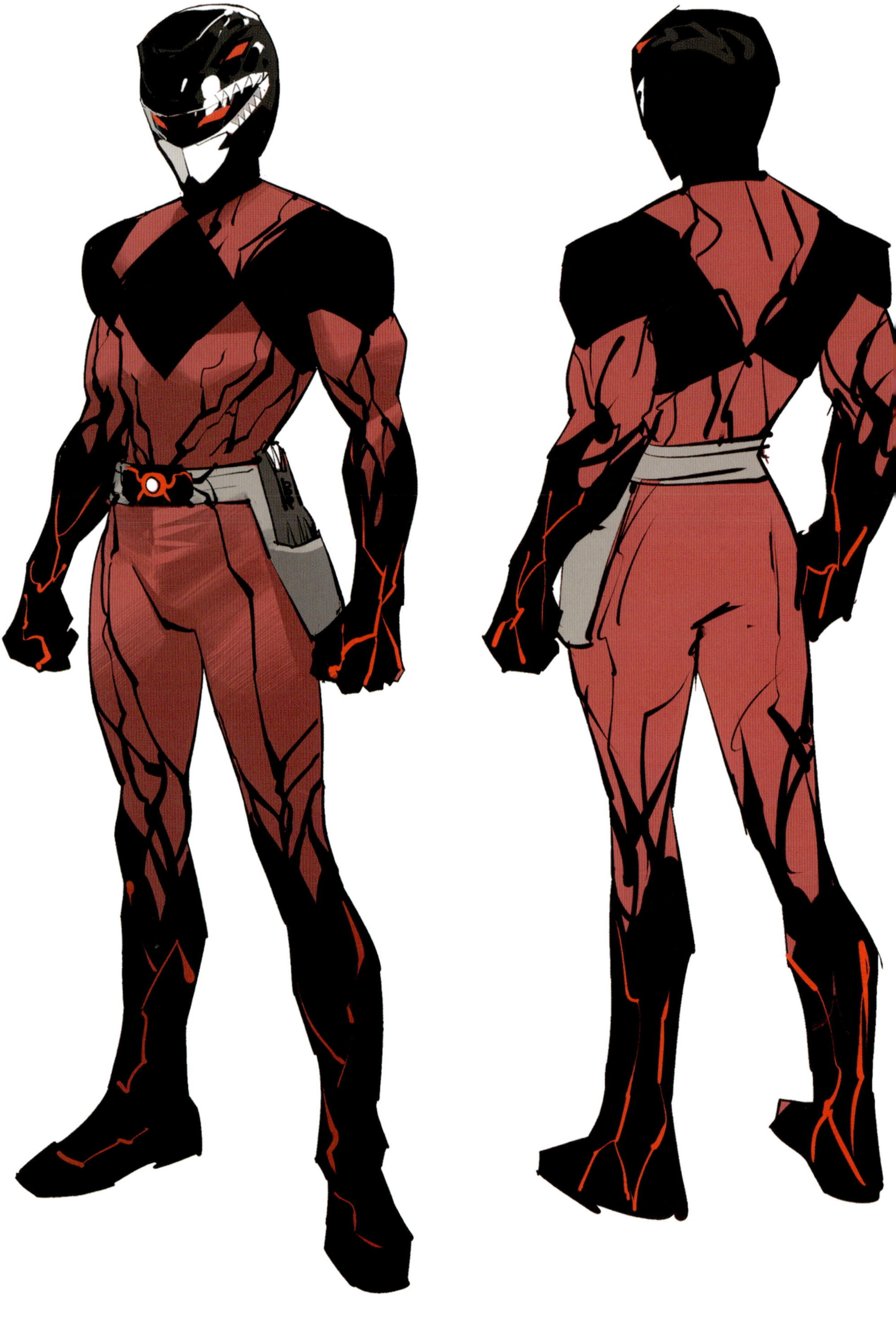

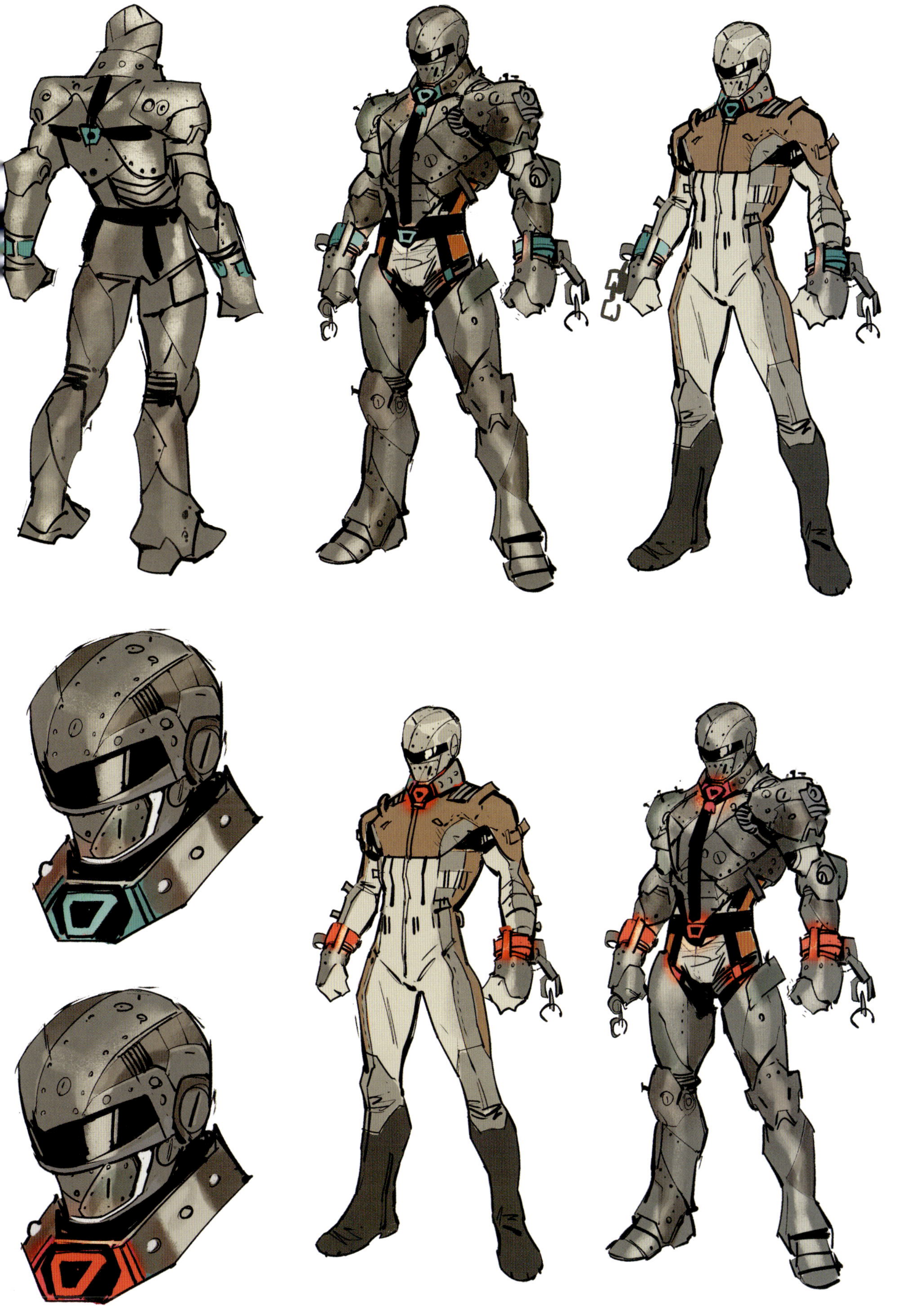

PAGE 38 White Tiger Dragonzord

PAGE 39 Mega Terrorzord

PAGE 40 Dragon Turtlezord

PAGE 41 Red Dragon Thunderzord + Serpentena Zord

PAGE 42 Thunder Mega Dragonzord

PAGE 43 Krang Megazord

PAGE 44 Megazord

PAGE 45 Megazord - Formation

PAGE 46 Megazord - Test Design

PAGE 47 Megazord - Redesign

PAGE 48 Minizords

PAGE 49 Megazord Tigerzord

PAGE 50 Mega Megazord 1

PAGE 51 Mega Megazord 2

PAGE 52 Mega Gravezord A & B

PAGE 53 Thunder Megazord

PAGE 54 Zords · Triceratops · Mastodon

PAGE 55 Zords · Sabertooth Tiger · Tyrannosaurus · Pterodactyl

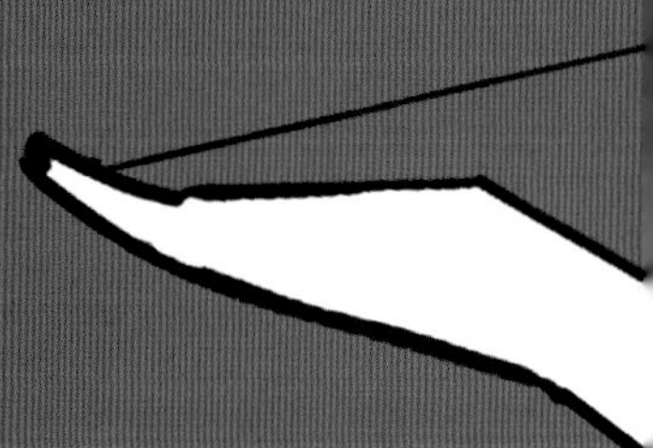

DESIGN LAB: ZORDS

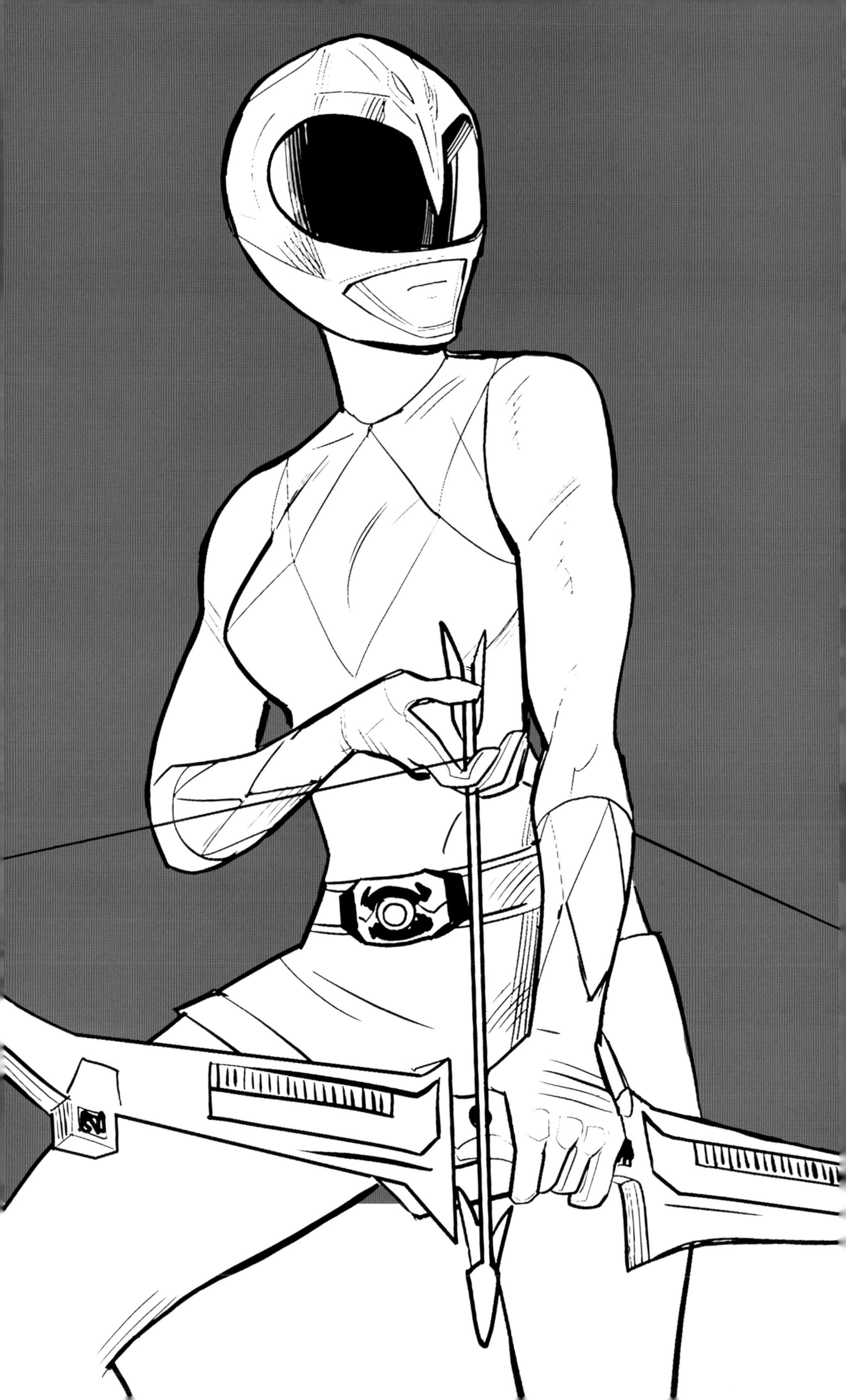

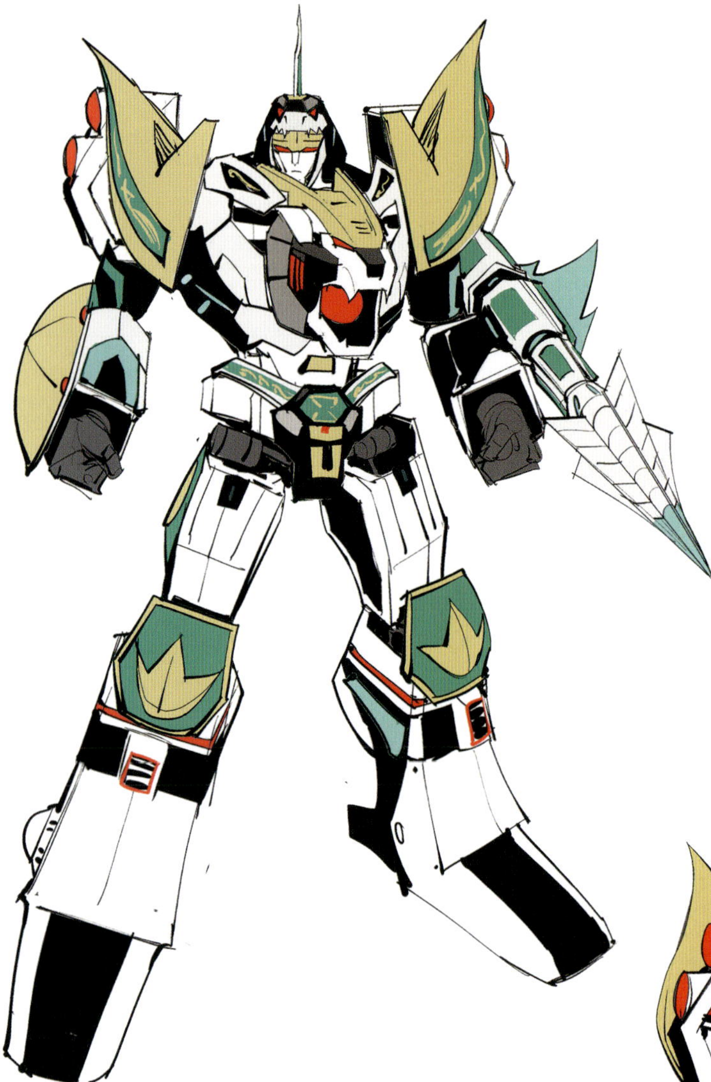

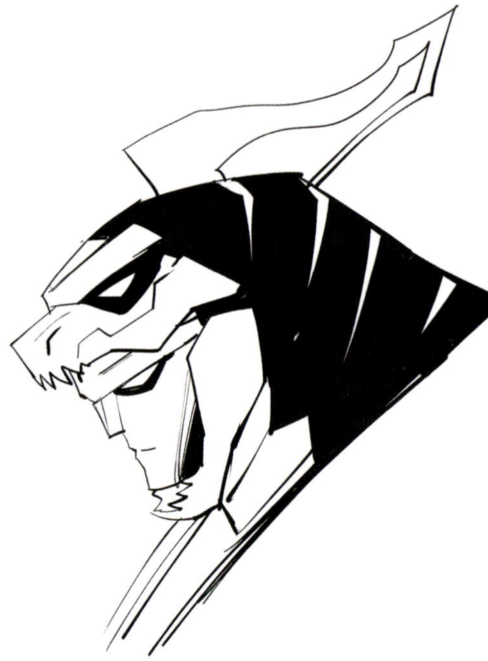

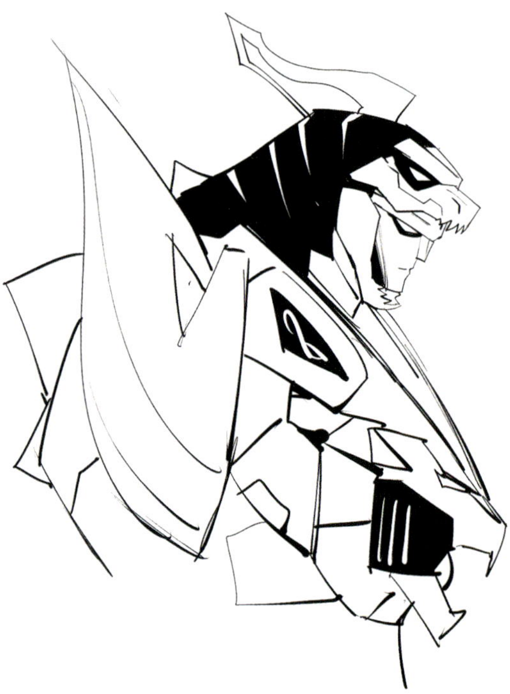

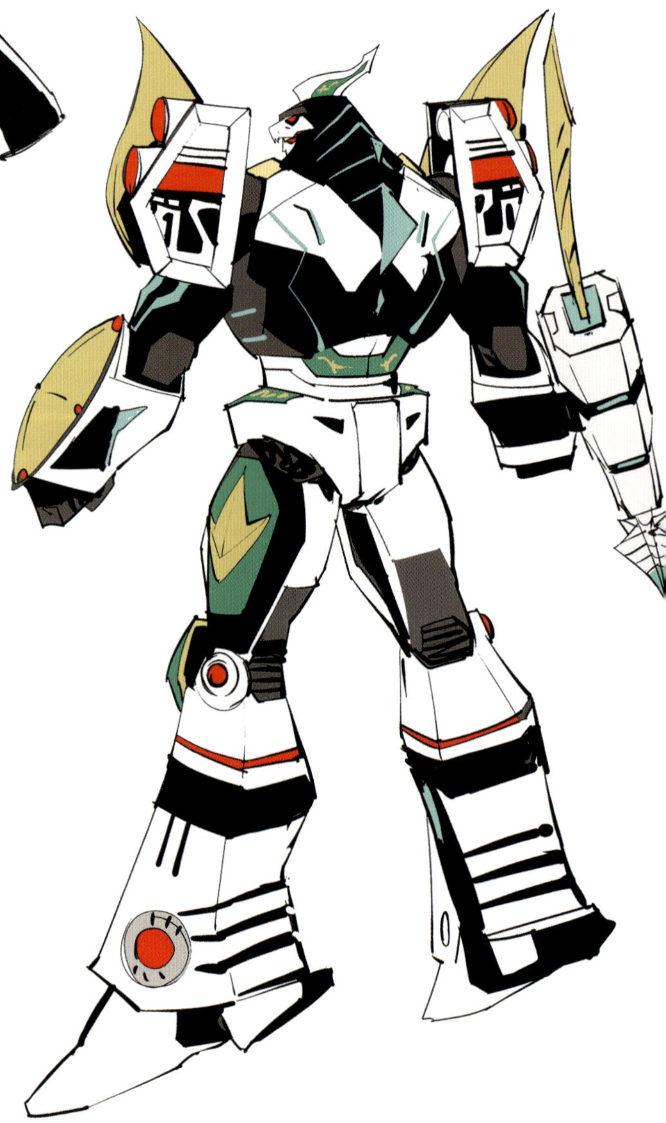

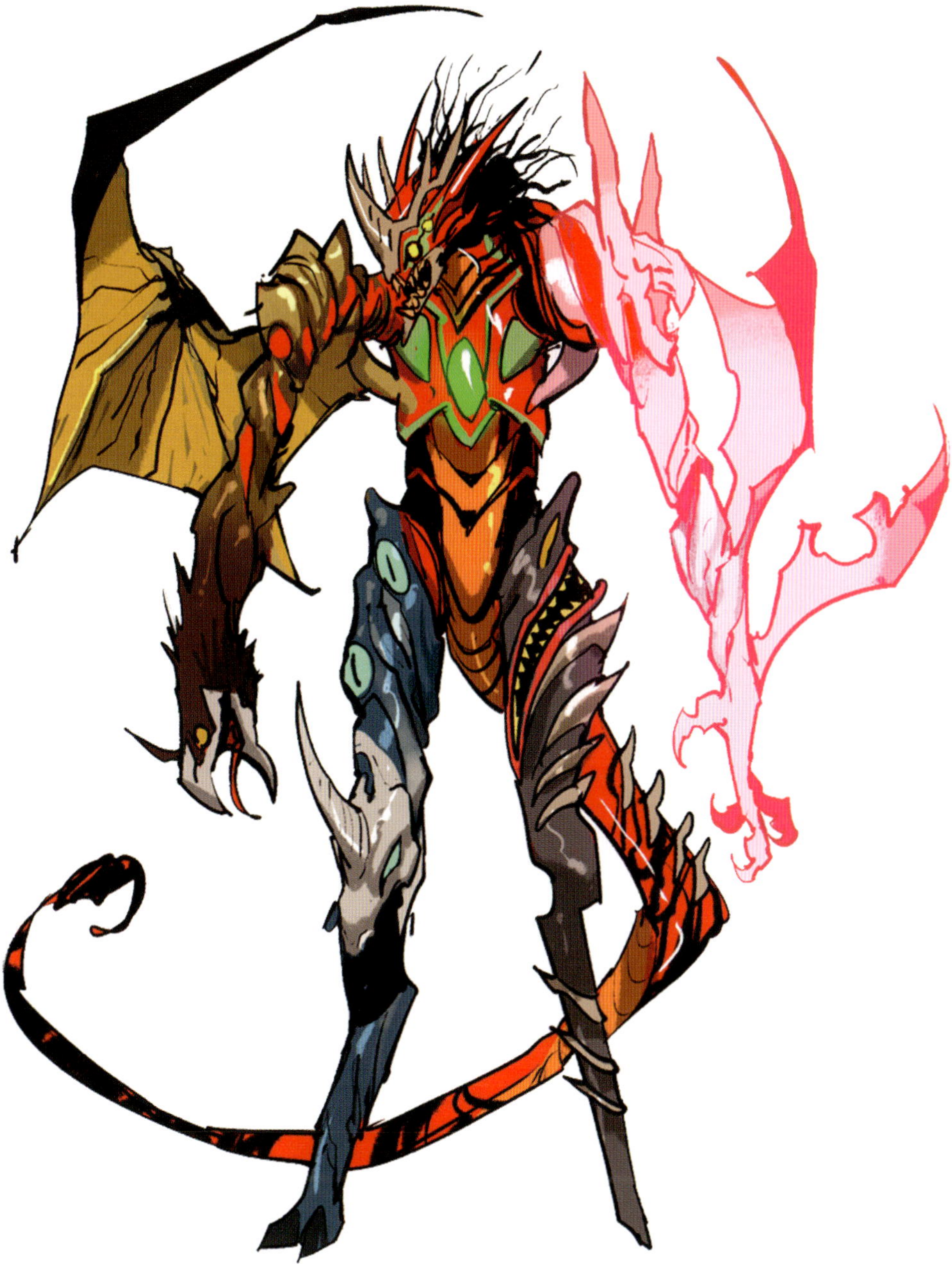

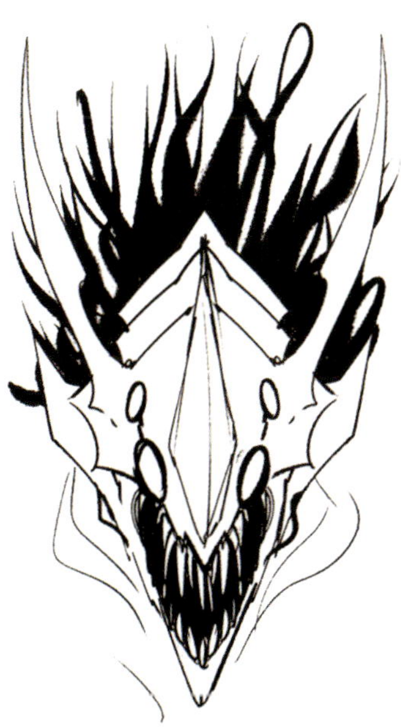

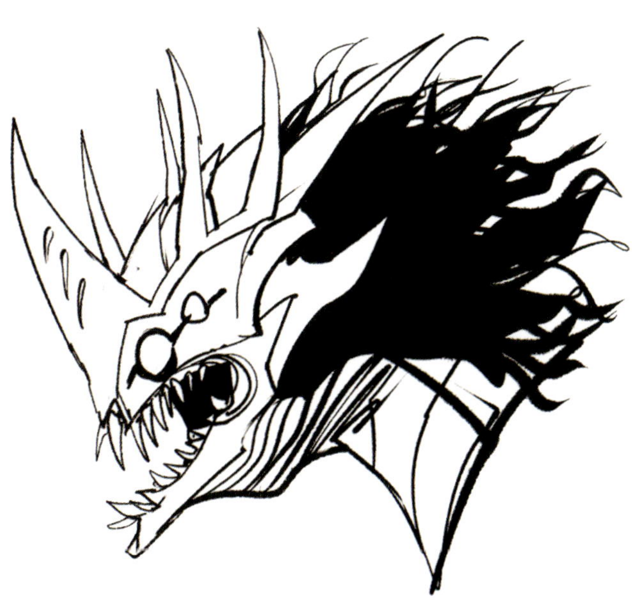

DRAGON TURTLEZORD

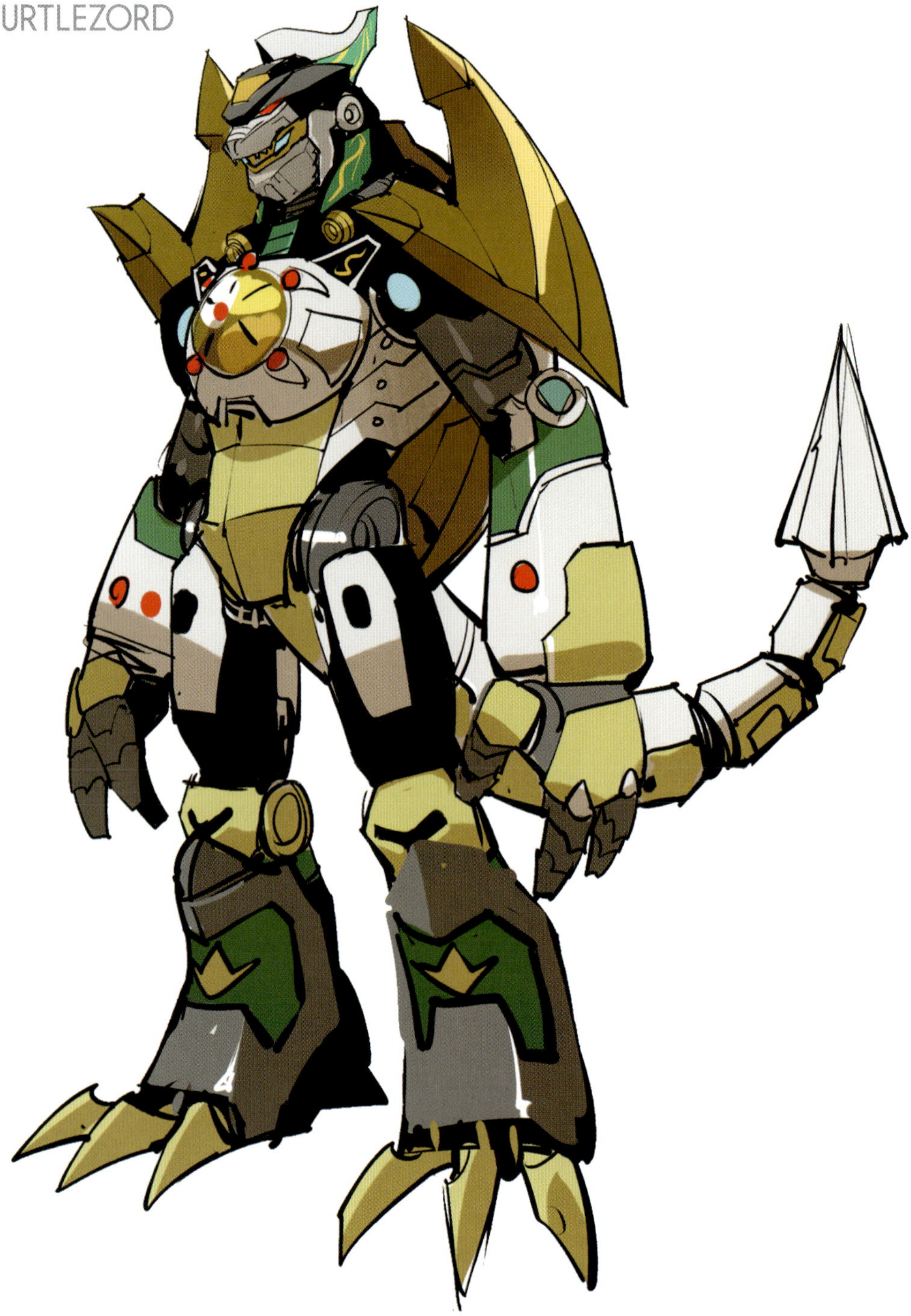

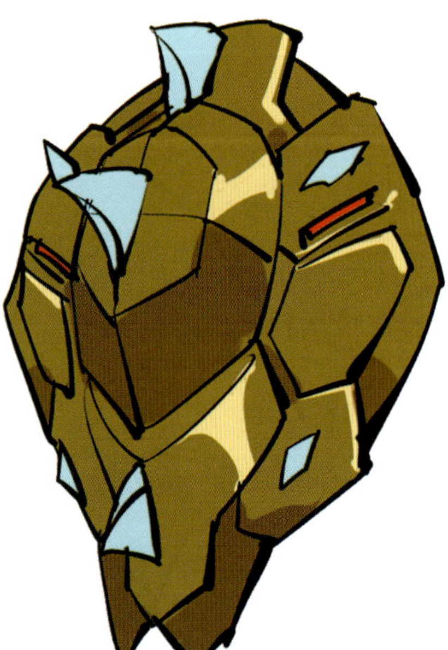

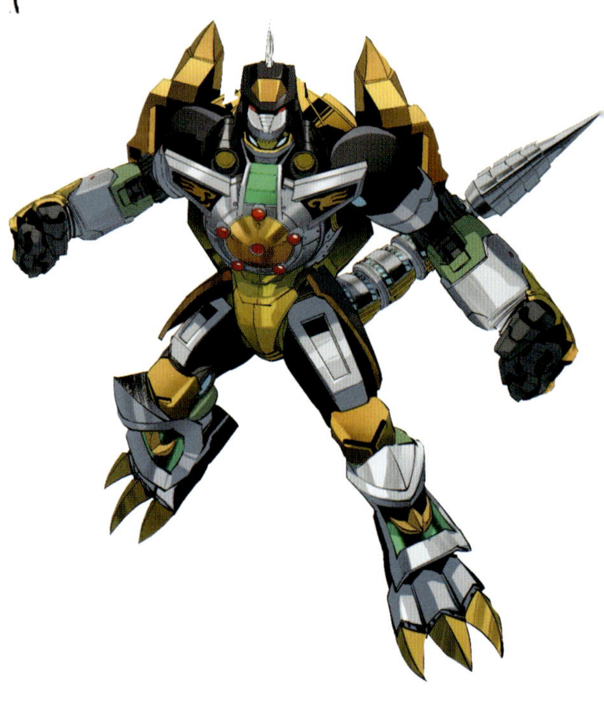

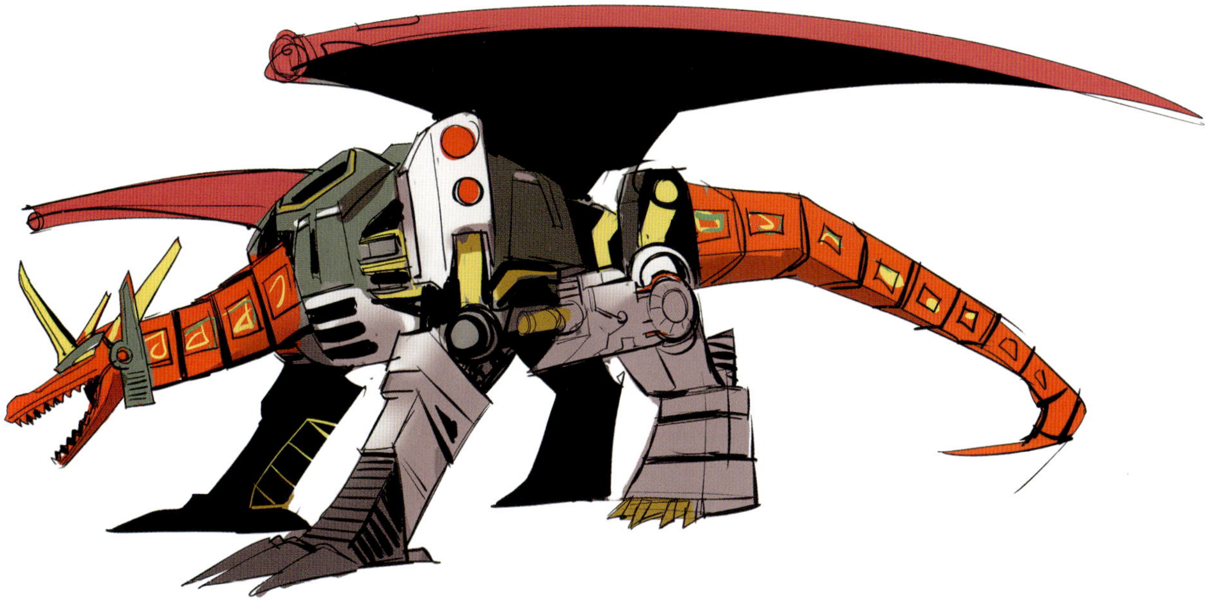

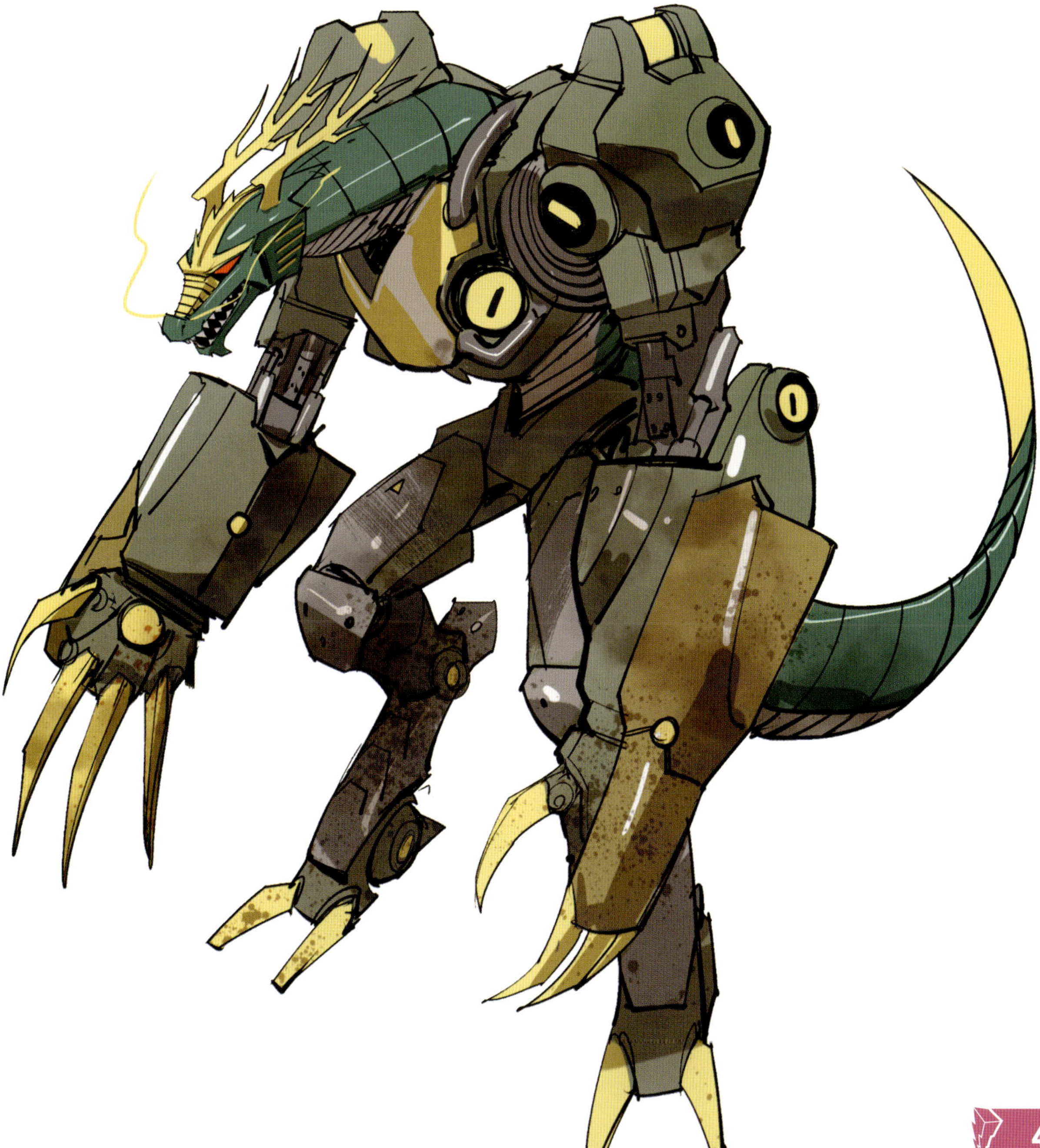

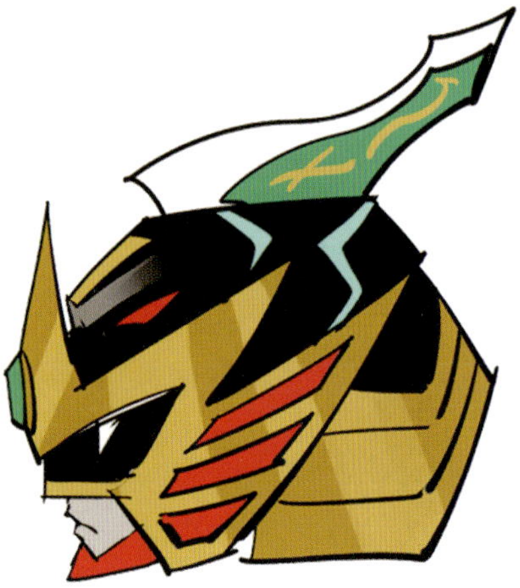

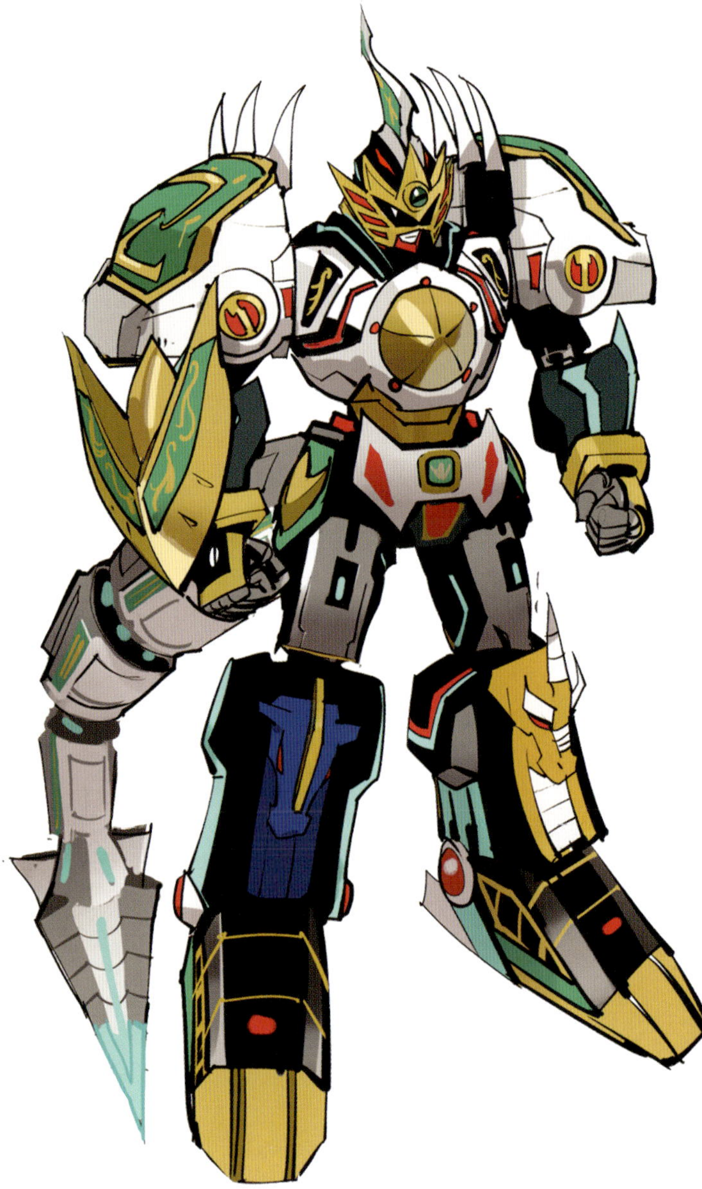

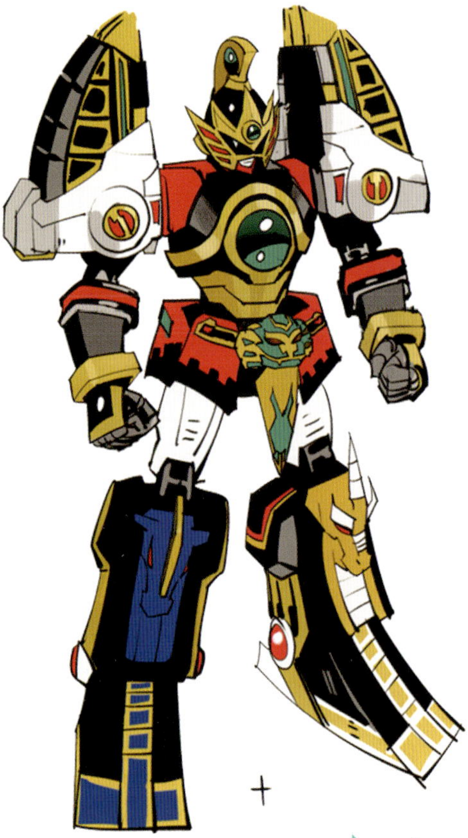

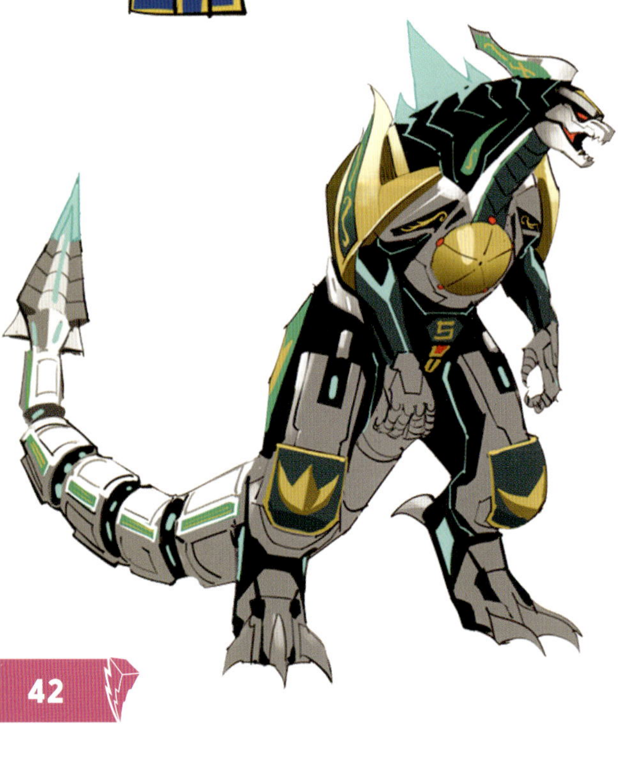

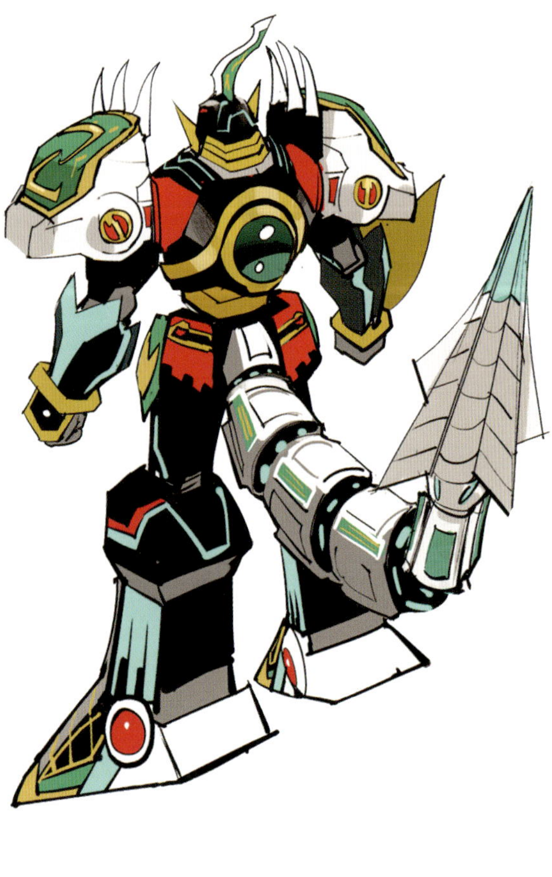

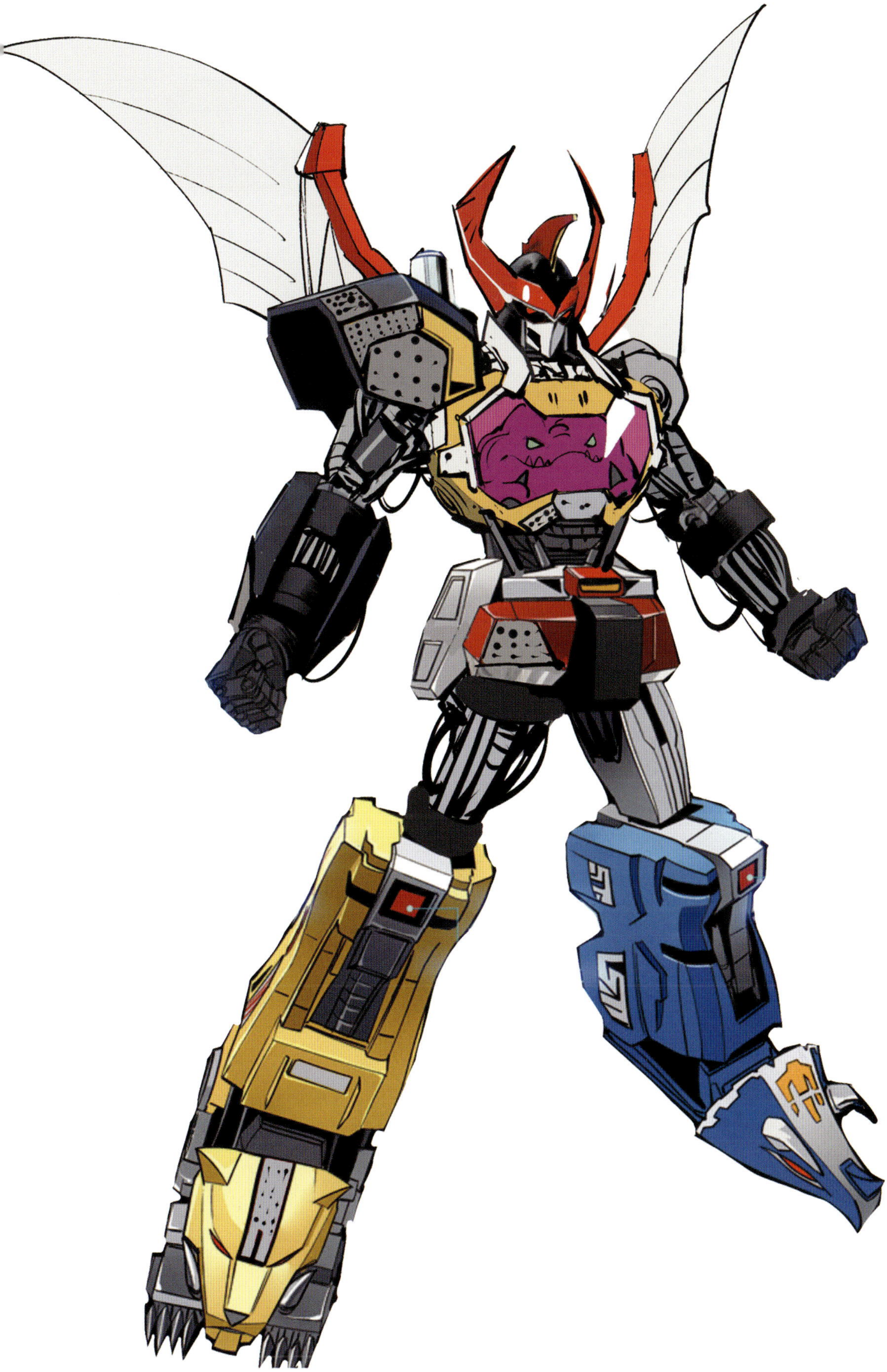

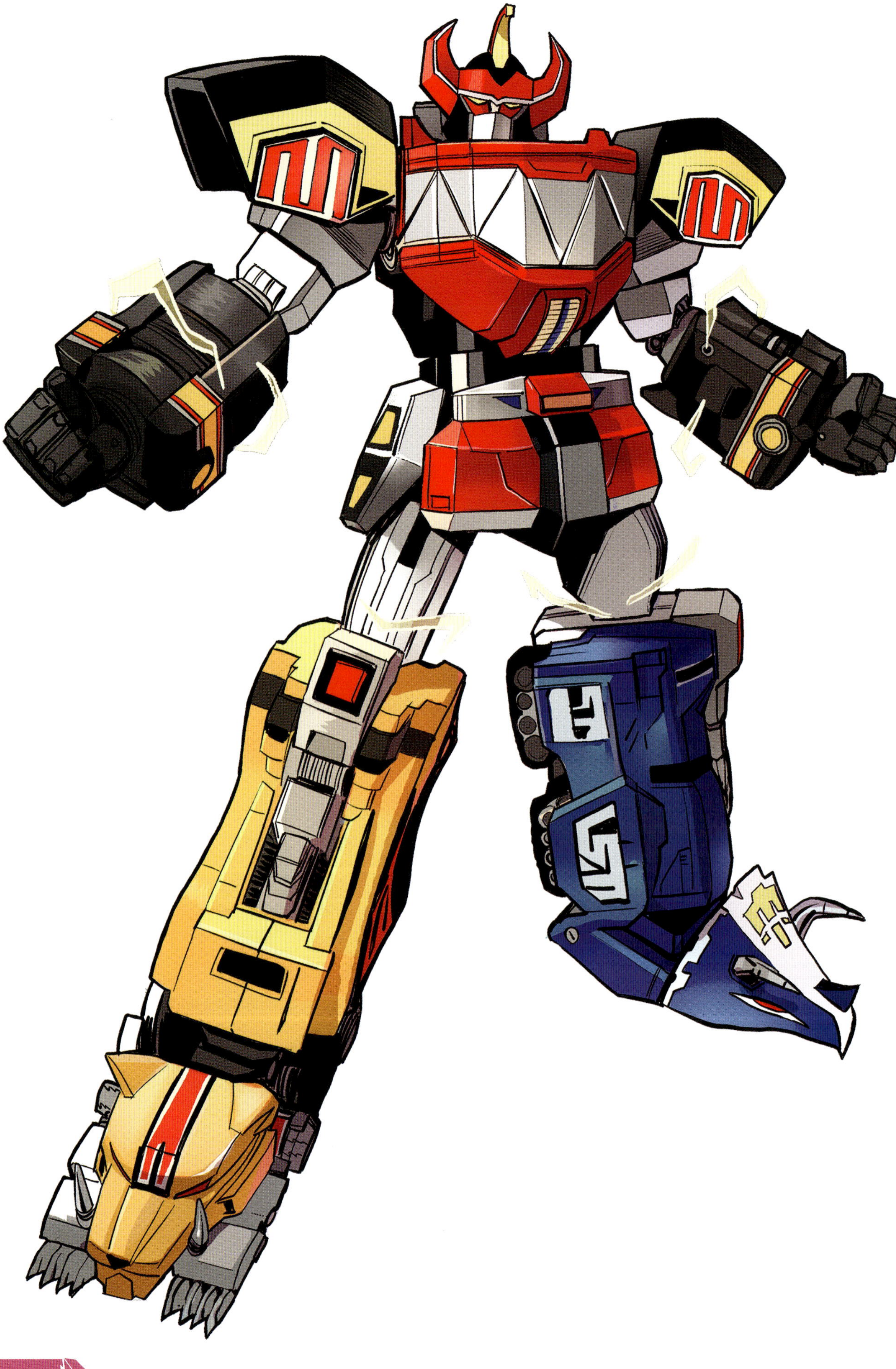

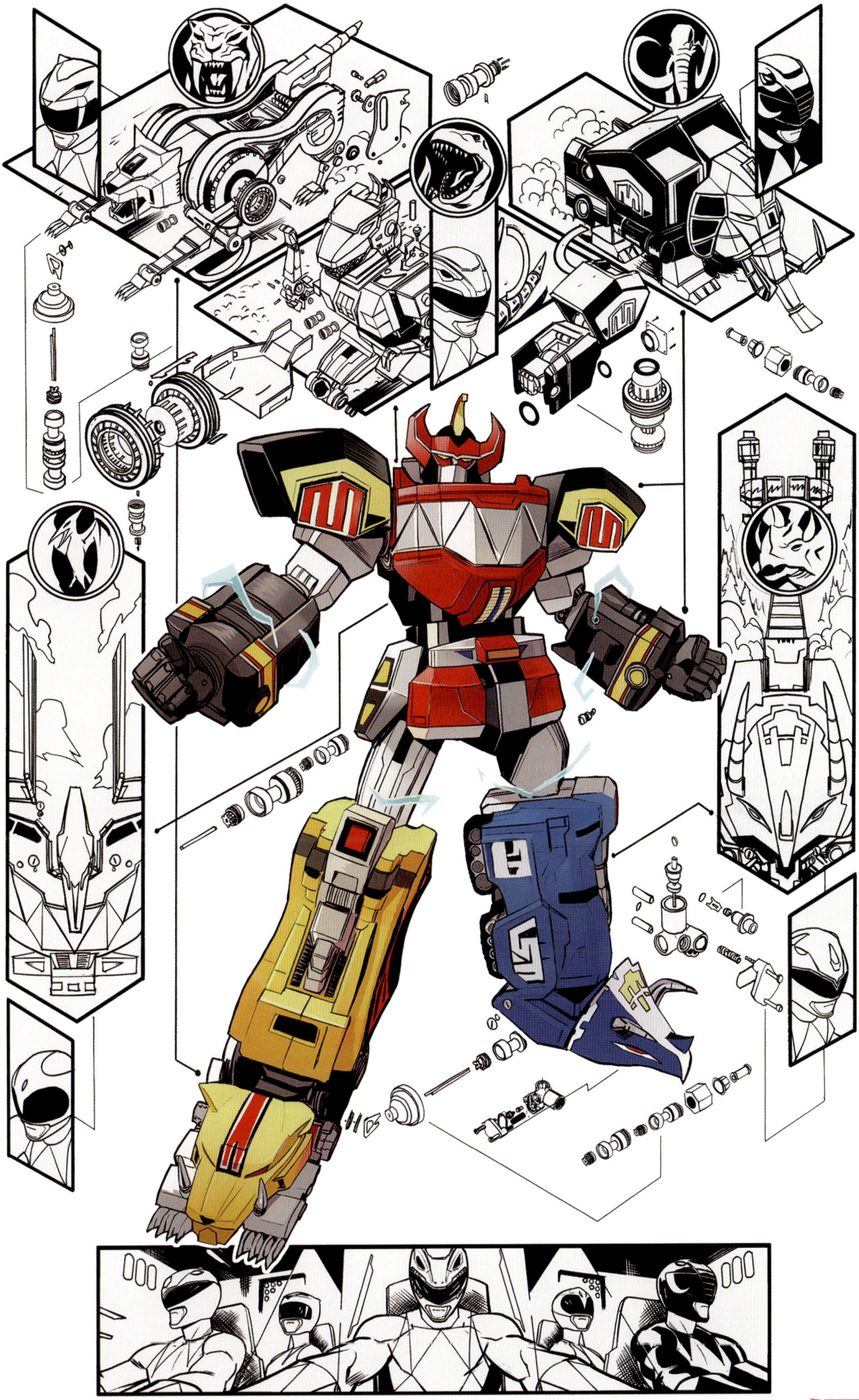

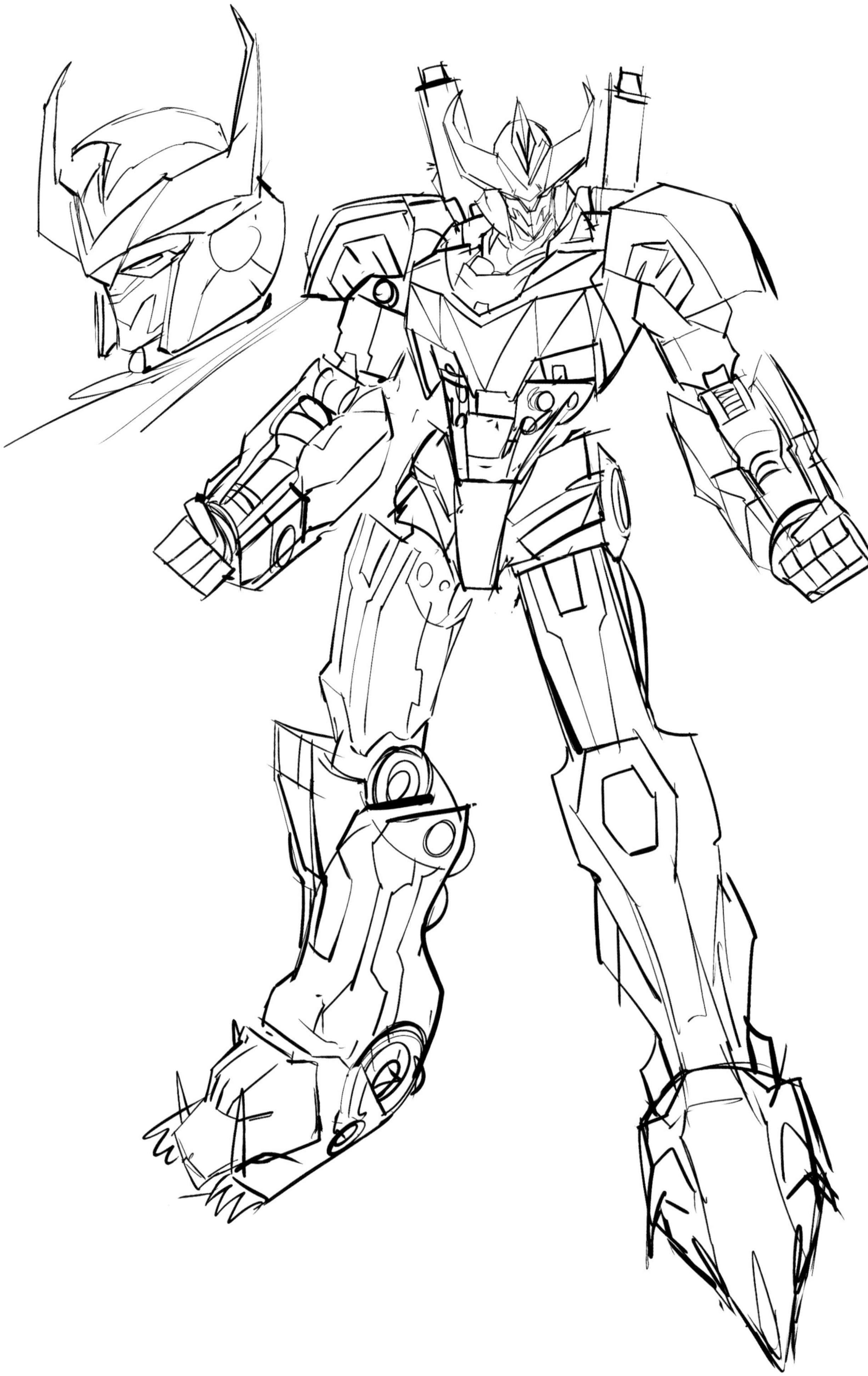

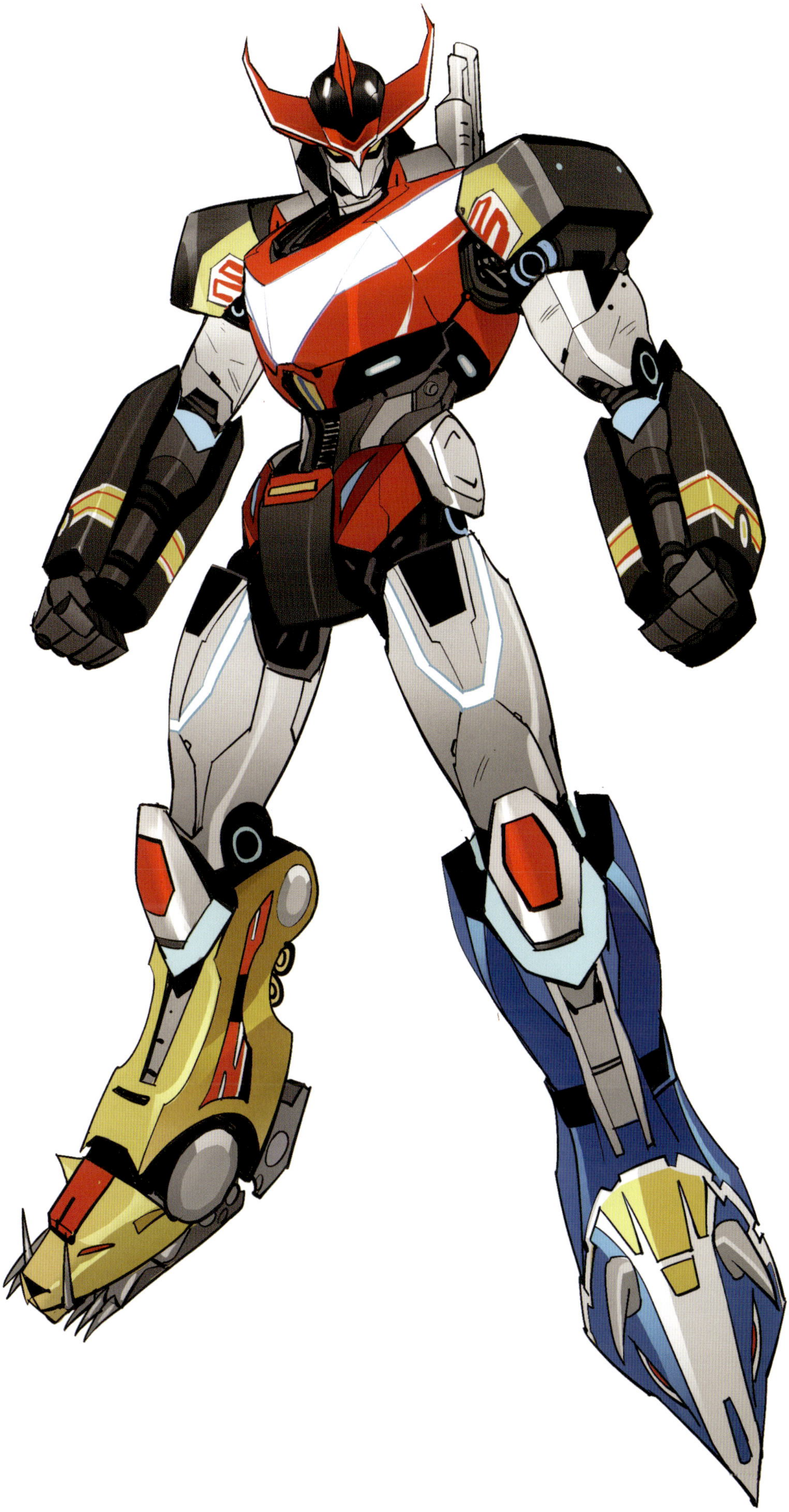

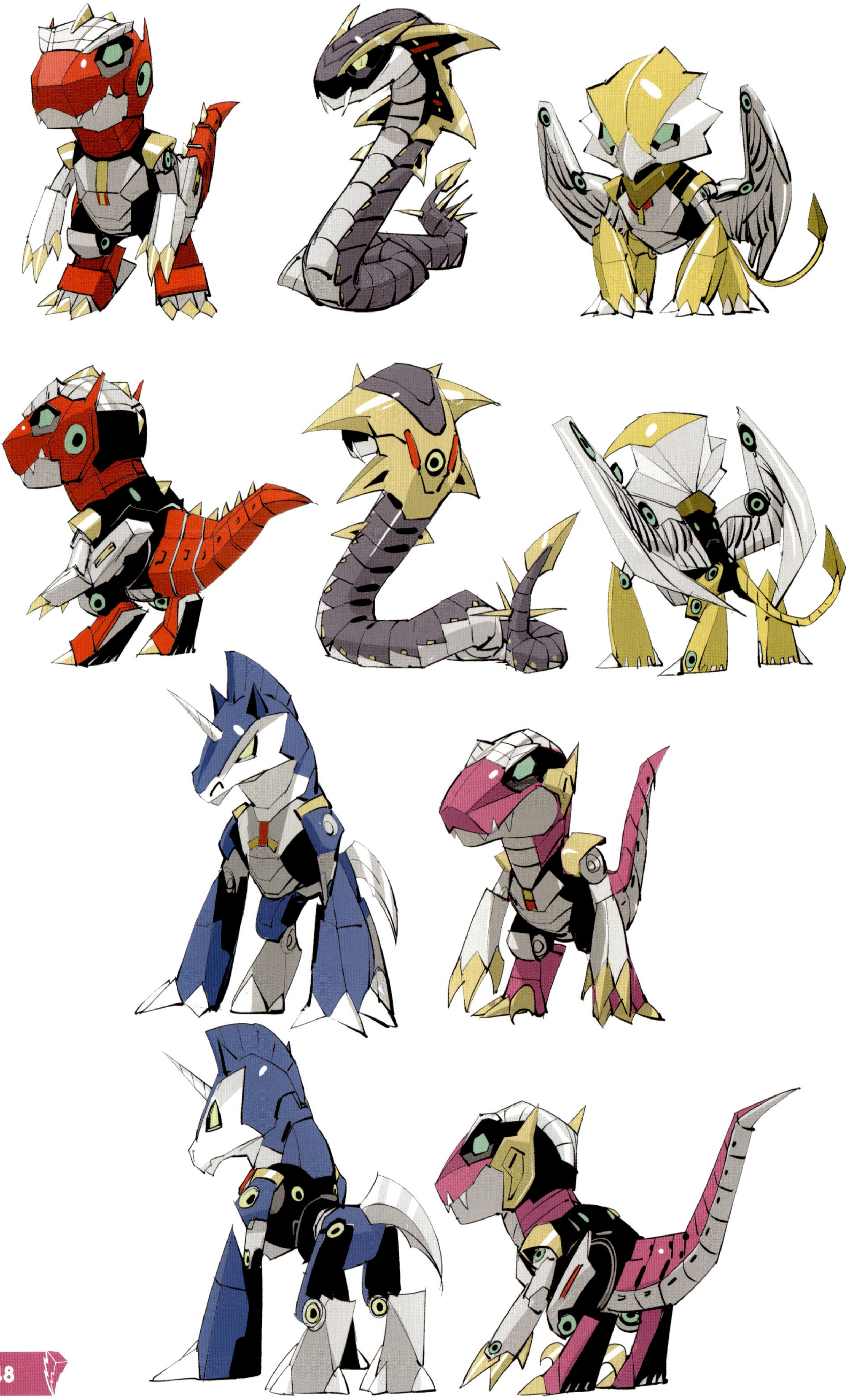

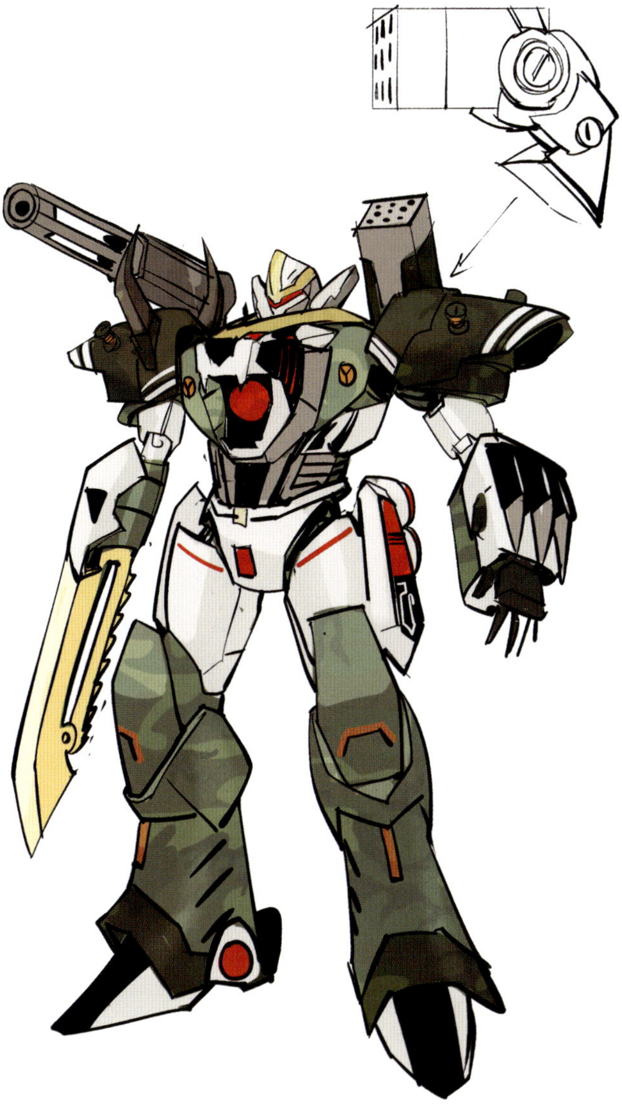

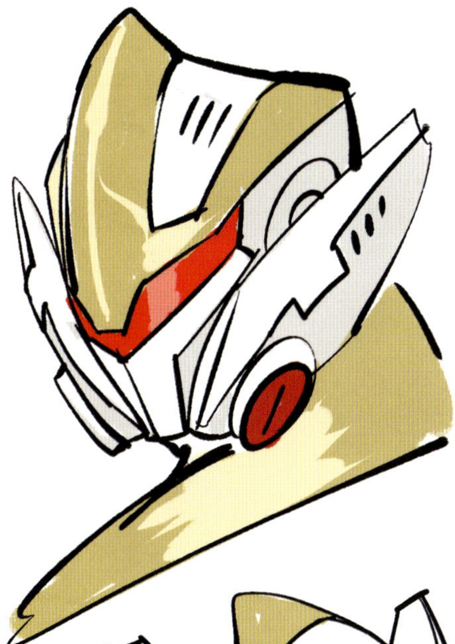

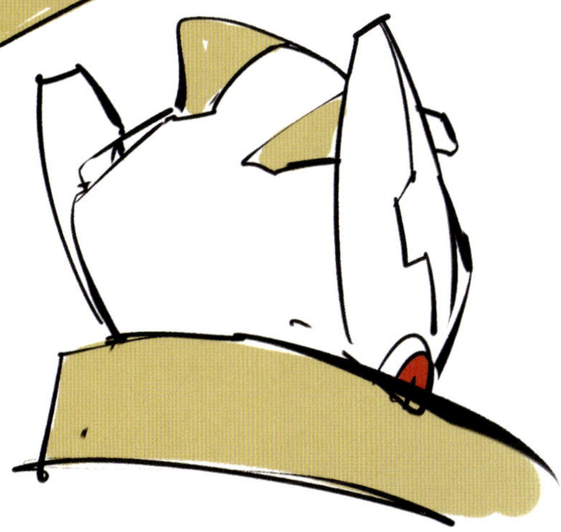

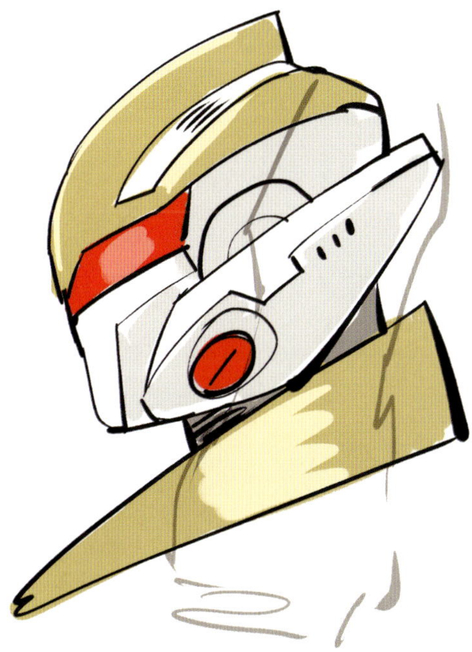

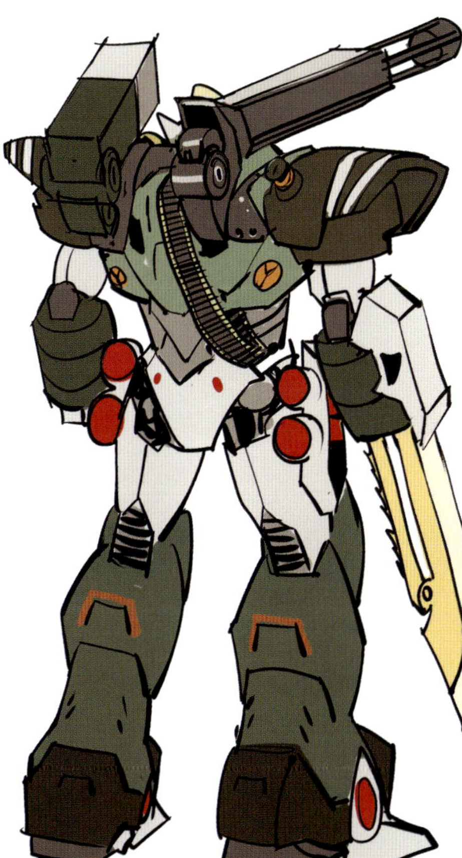

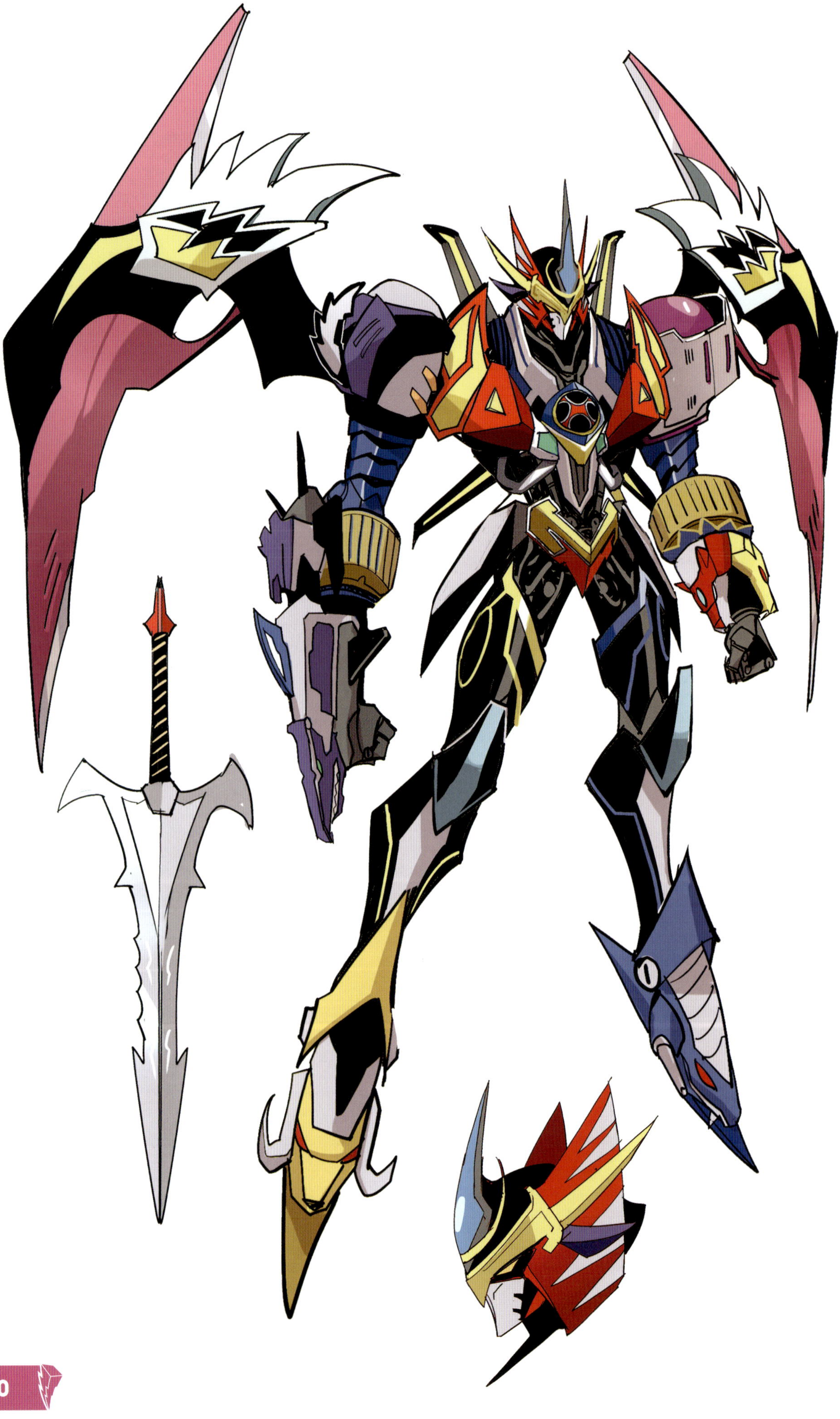

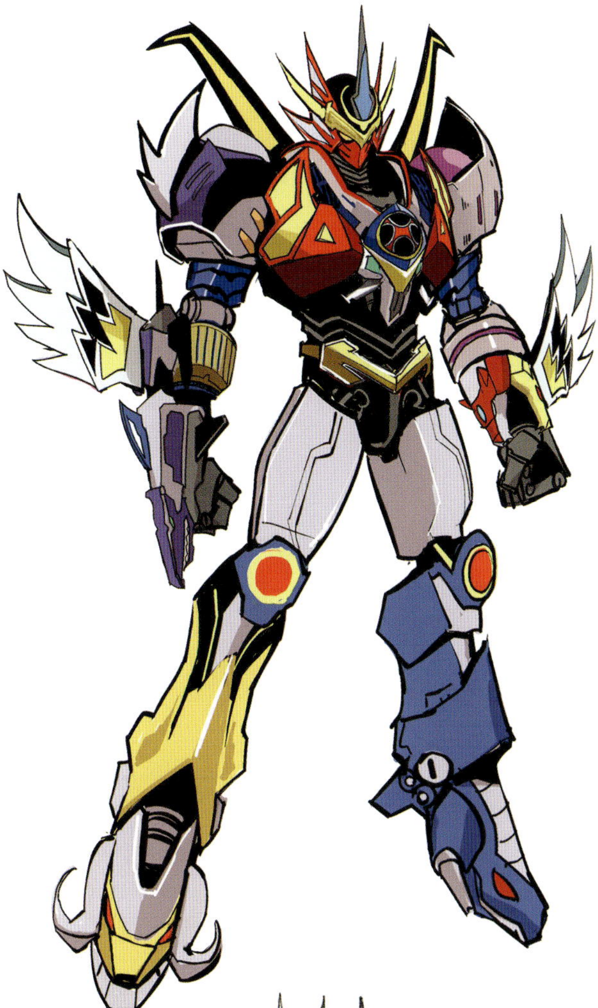

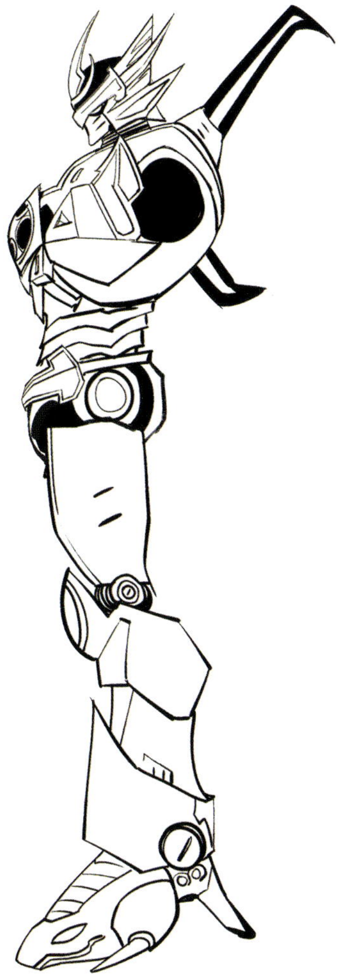

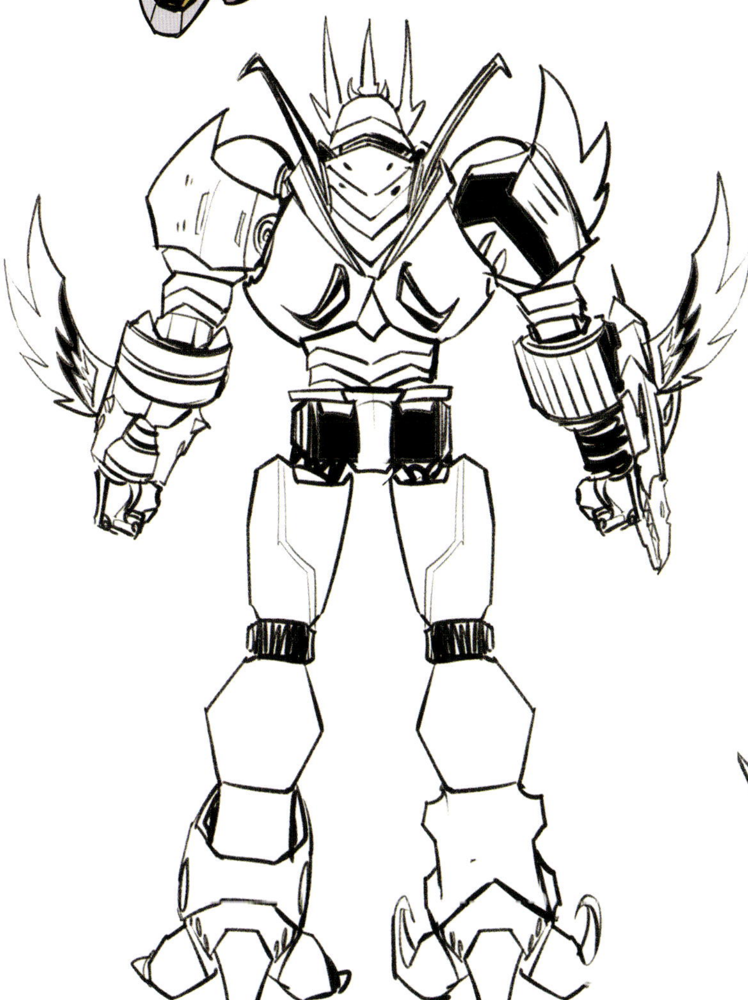

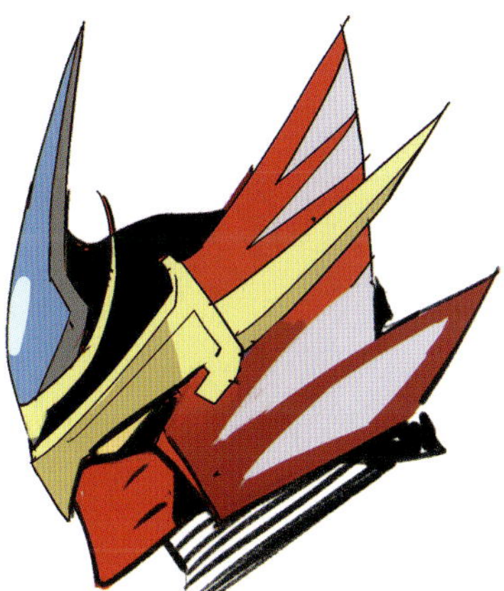

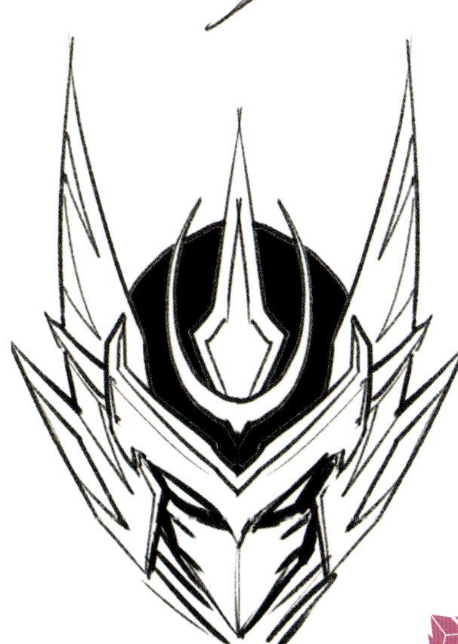

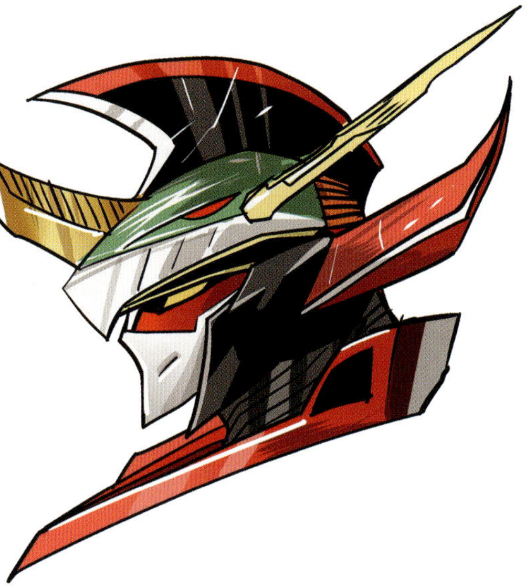

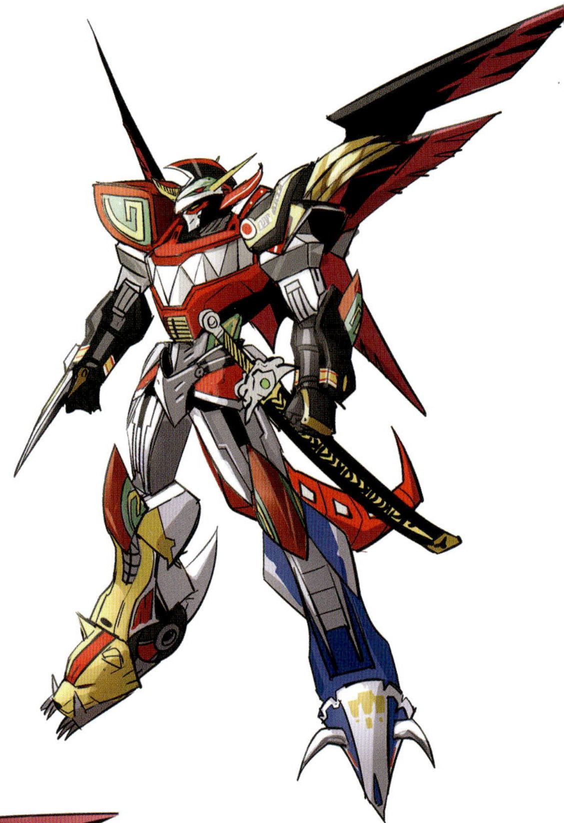

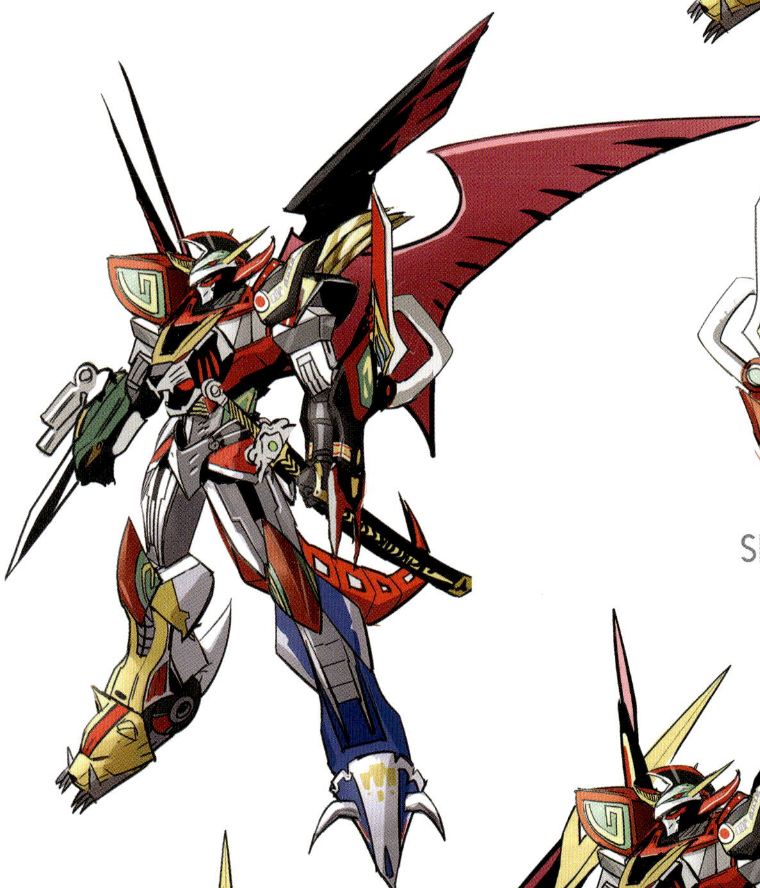

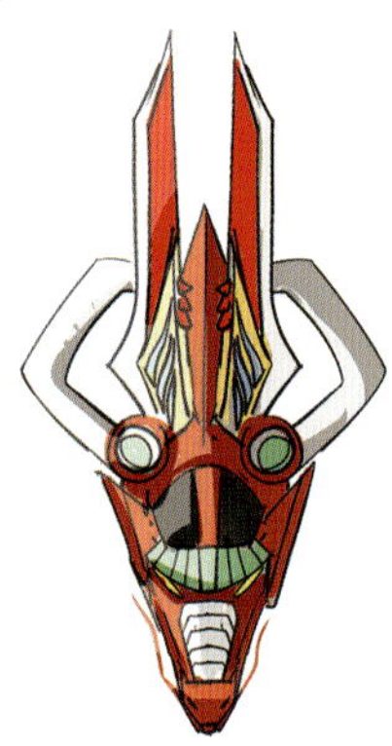

SHIELD

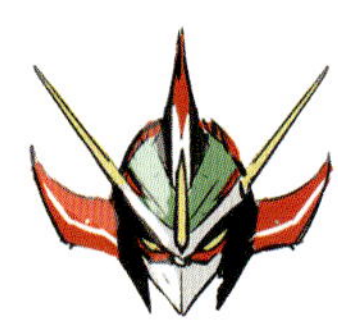

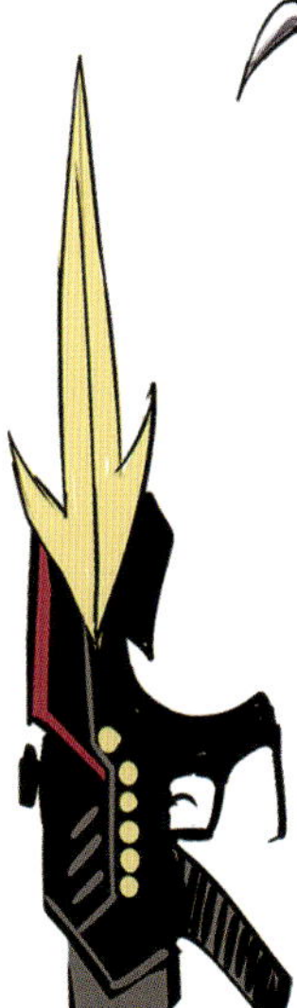

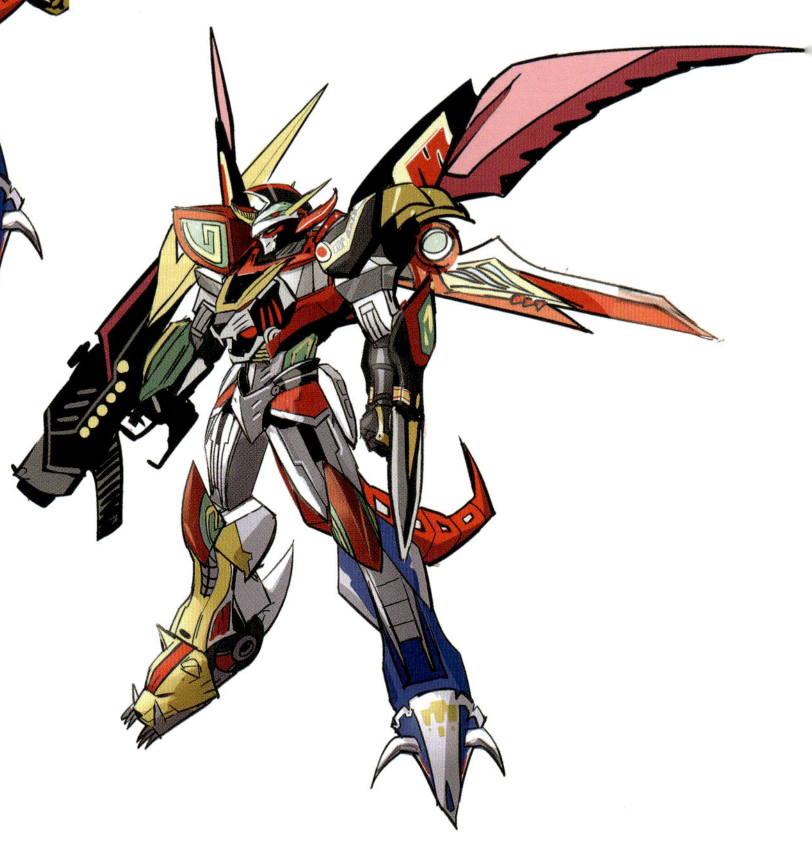

THUNDER MEGAZORD

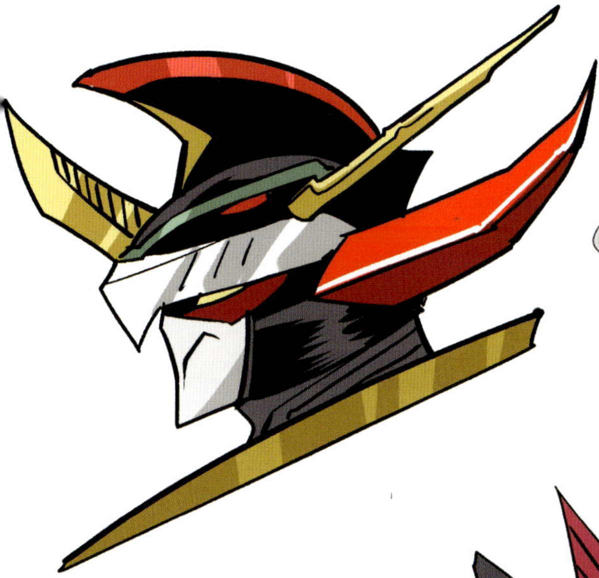

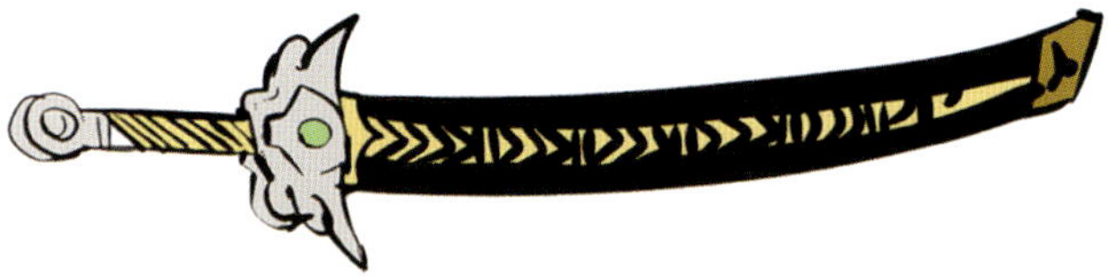

THUNDER MEGAZORD
KATANA

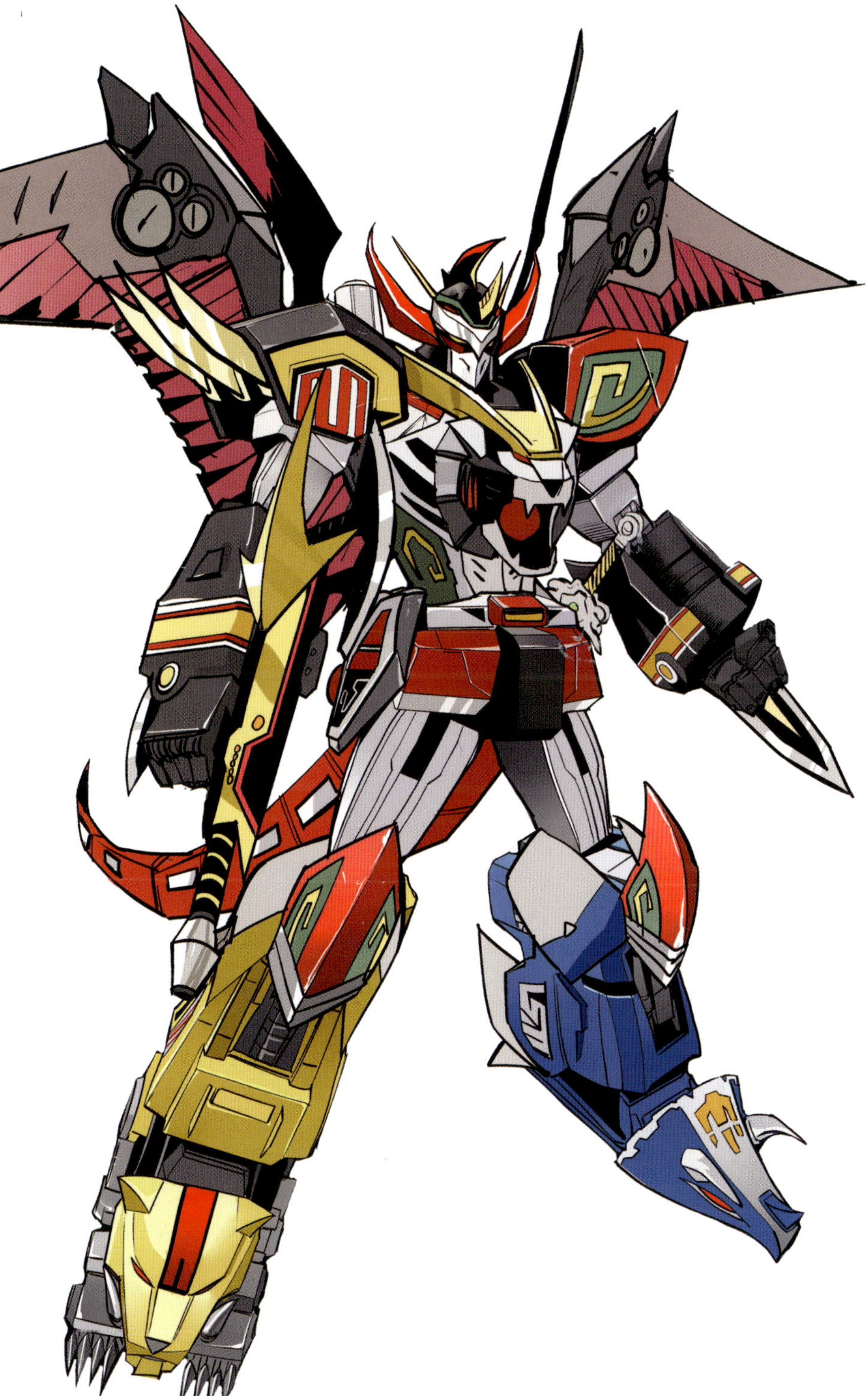

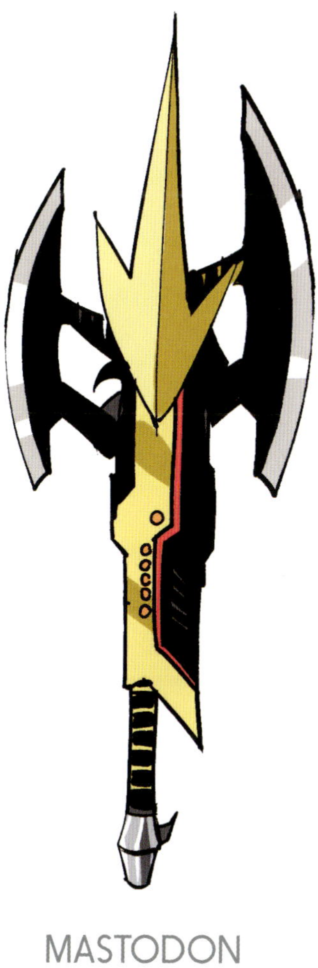

MASTODON
GUN / AXE

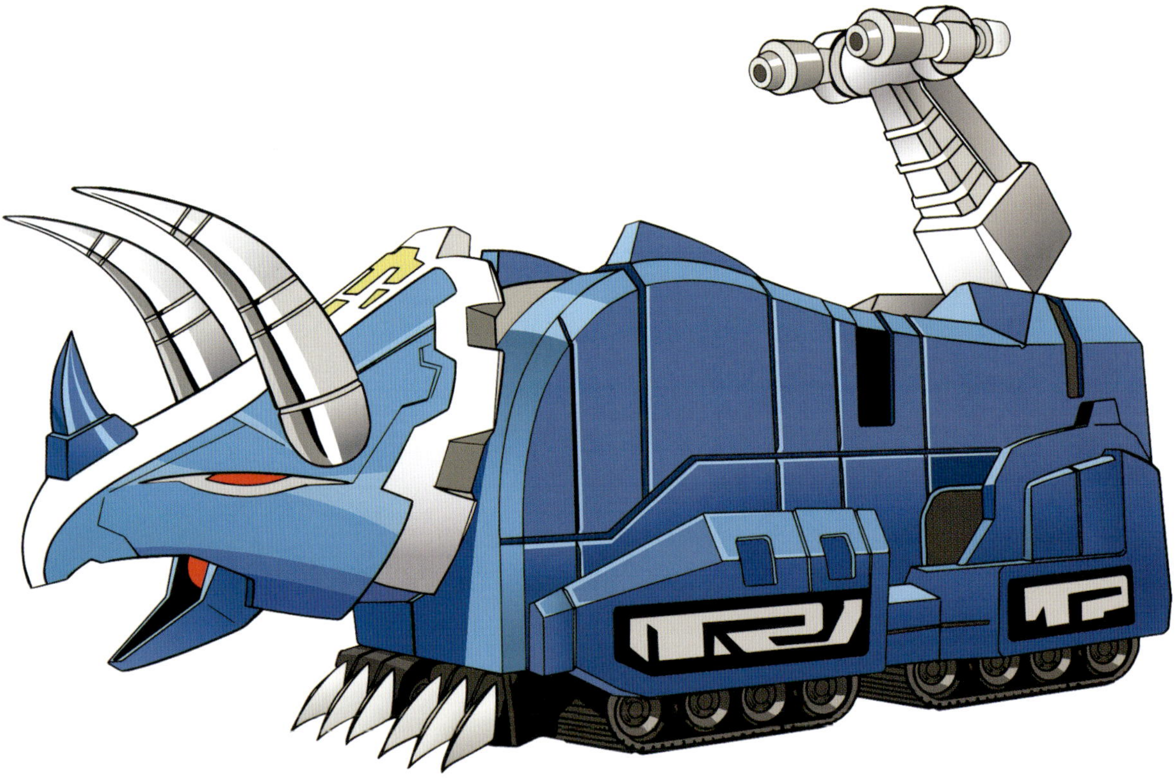

TRICERATOPS DINOZORD

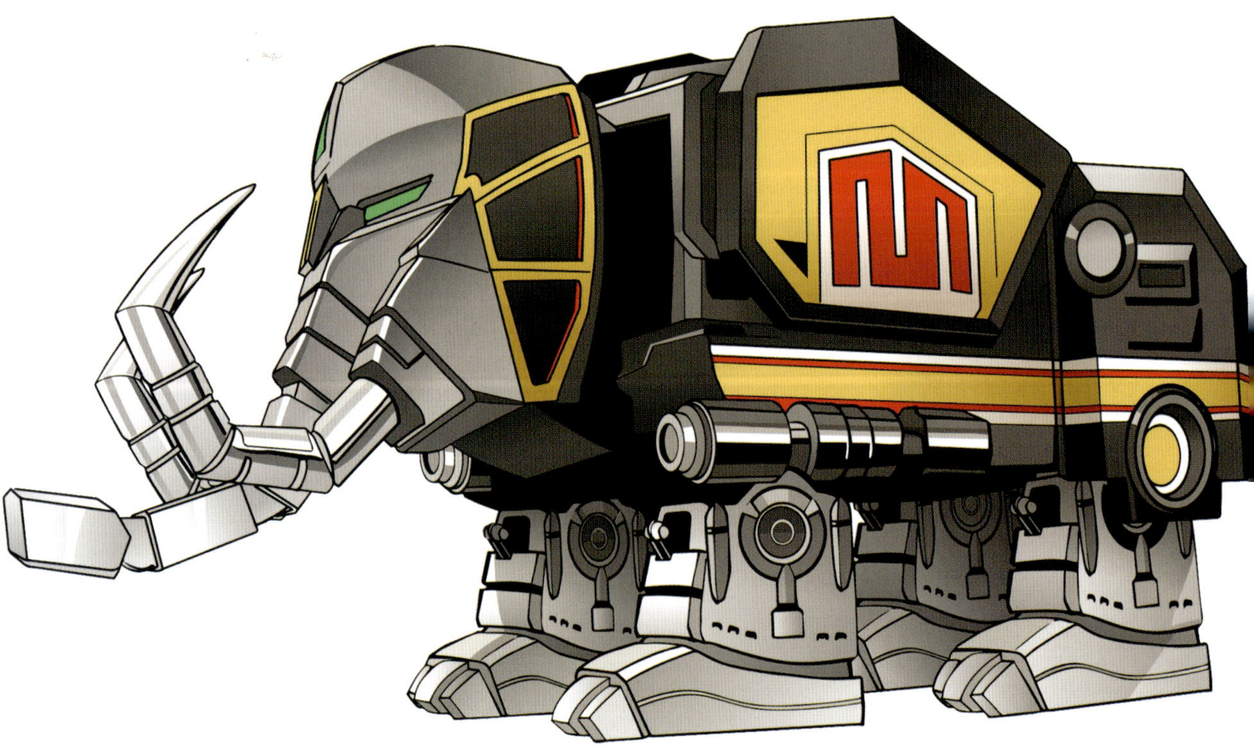

MASTODON DINOZORD

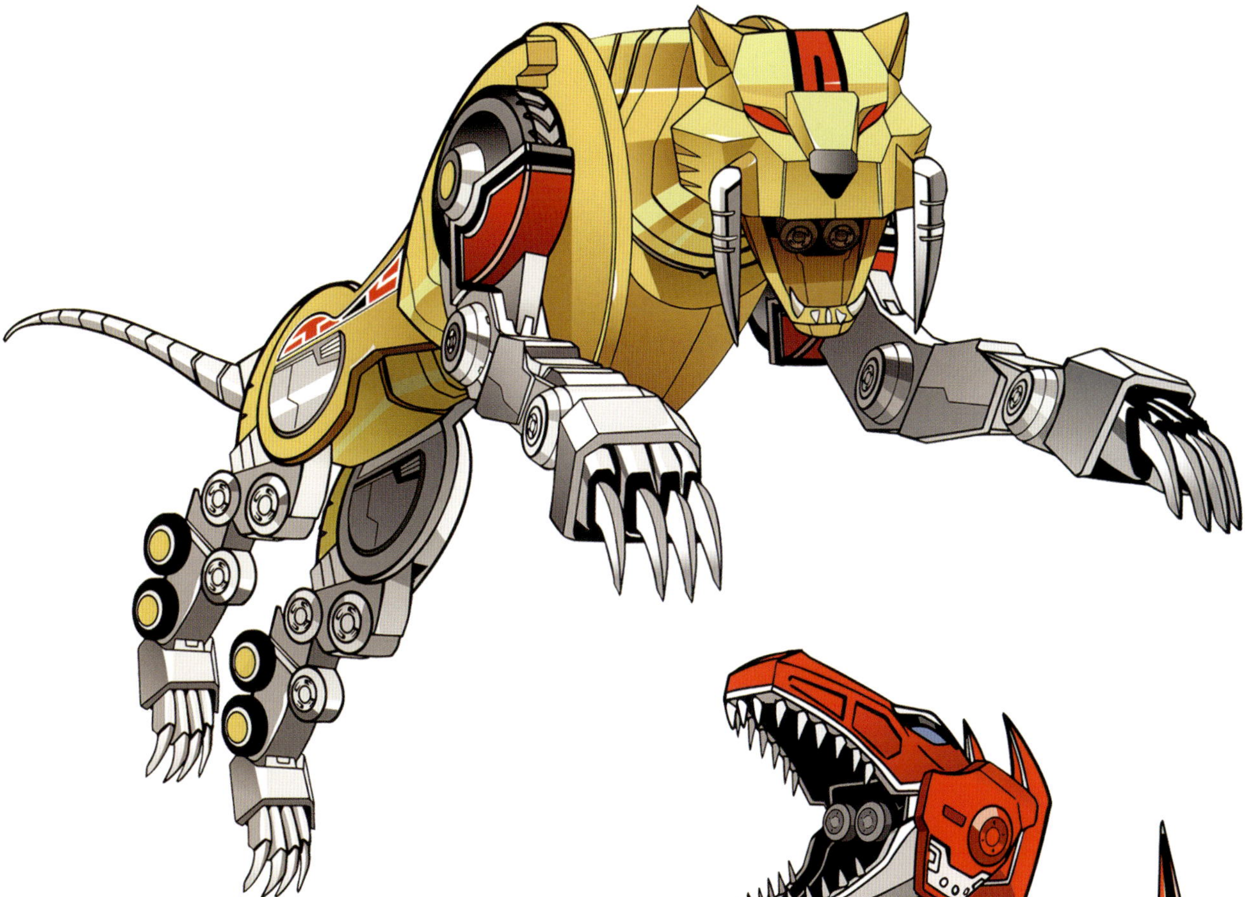

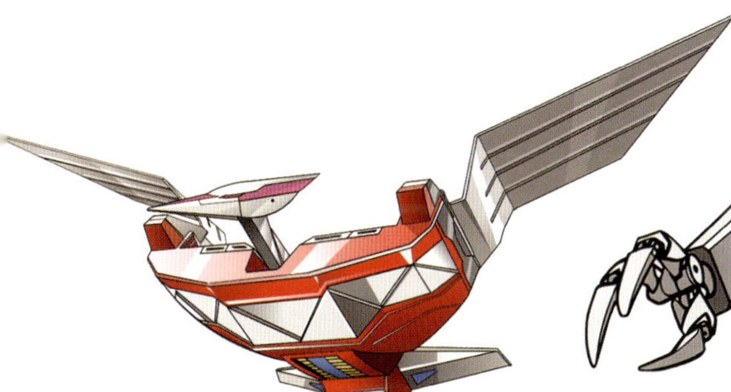

PTERODACTYL
DINOZORD

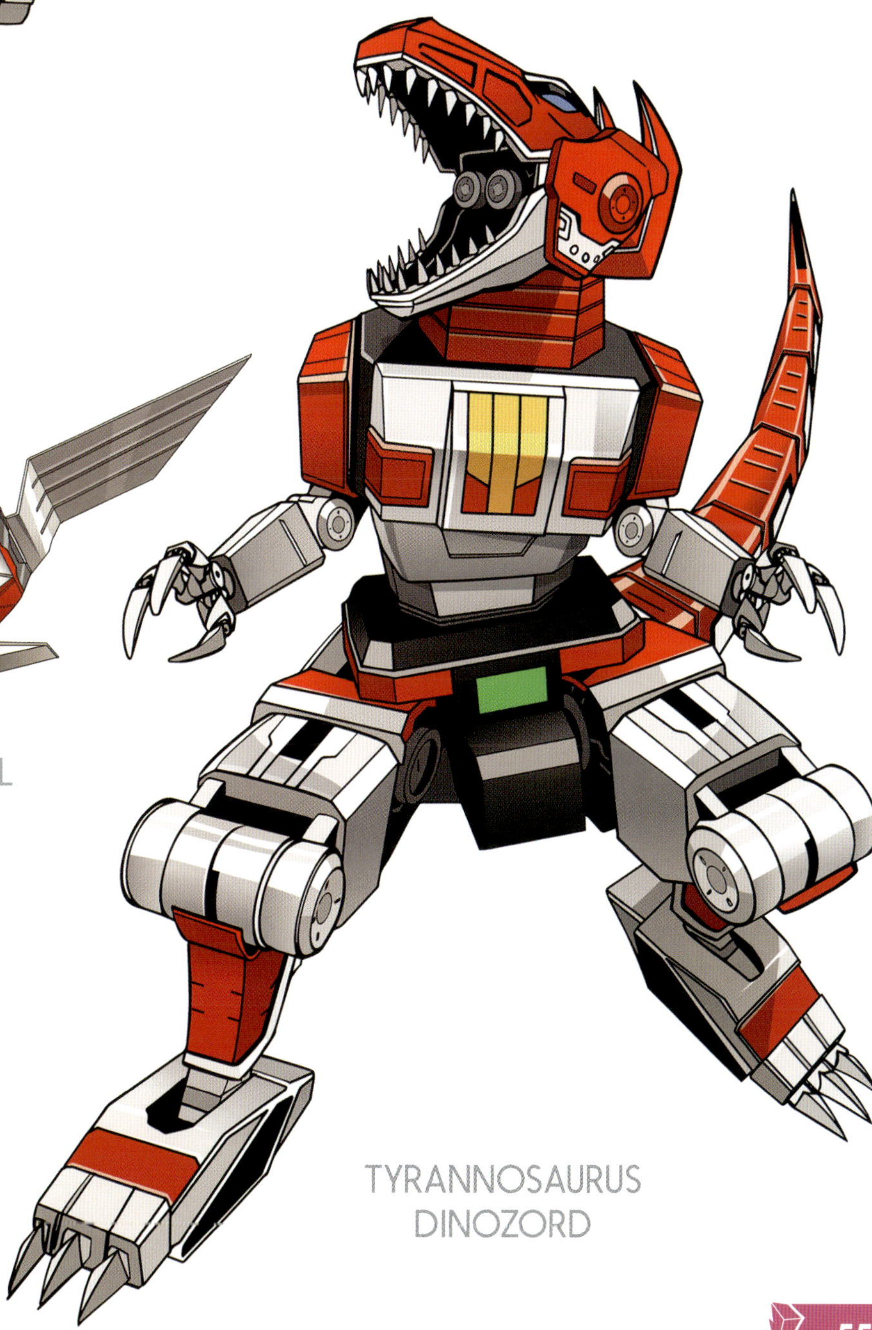

TYRANNOSAURUS
DINOZORD

PAGE 58 The Dark Rangers
PAGE 59 The Terrorzords
PAGE 60 Putty Patroller
PAGE 61 Dark Rangers - Baboo & Squatt
PAGE 62 Armored Zordon
PAGE 63 Eltarian - Zophram
PAGE 64 Bandorian
PAGE 65 Eltarian - Candice
PAGES 66-67 Sentry Force Four
PAGE 68 Feral Rita Repulsa
PAGE 69 Rita Mistress Vile
PAGE 70 New Rita
PAGE 71 Rita Redesign
PAGE 72 Ranger Zedd
PAGE 73 Lord Zedd
PAGE 74 Ranger Slayer
PAGE 75 Drakkon
PAGE 76 Ecliptor
PAGE 77 Ecliptra
PAGE 78 Vessel Blue
PAGE 79 Vessel Red
PAGE 80 Goldar
PAGE 81 Goldar in action
PAGE 82 Young Astronema
PAGE 83 Evil Andros

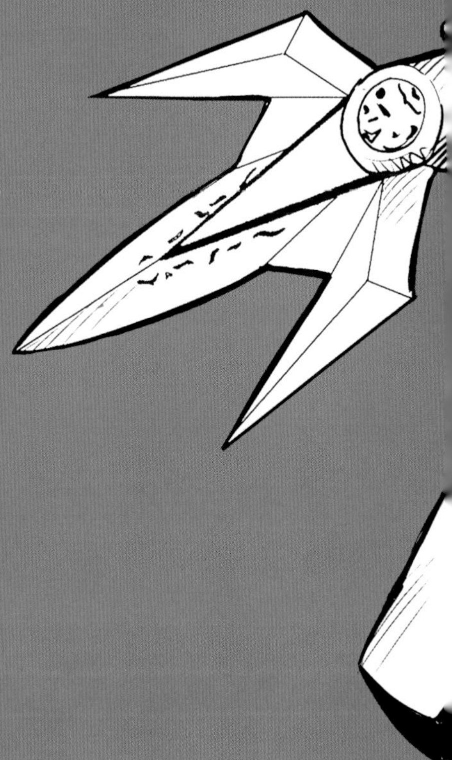

DESIGN LAB:

VILLAINS AND

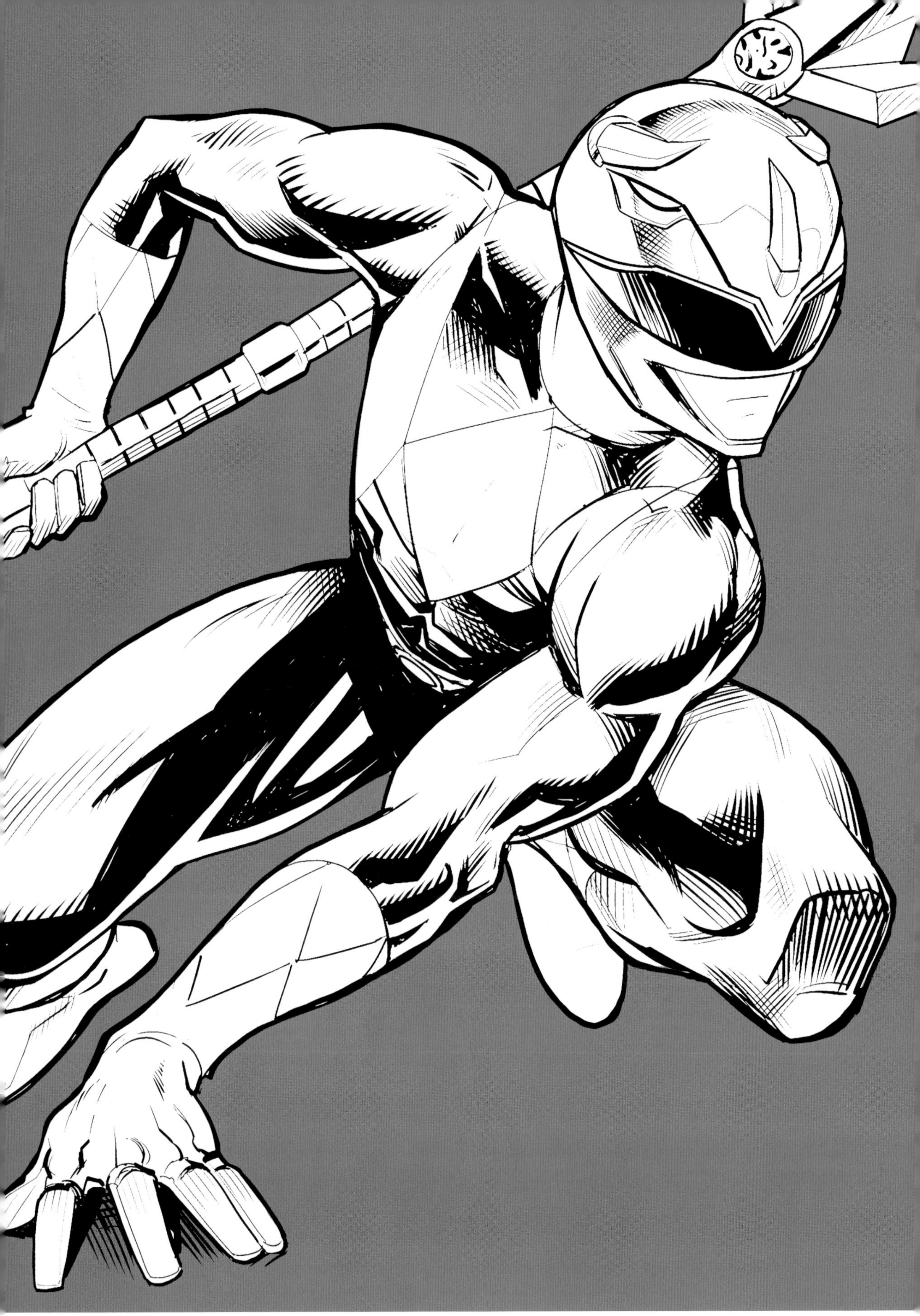

ALIENS

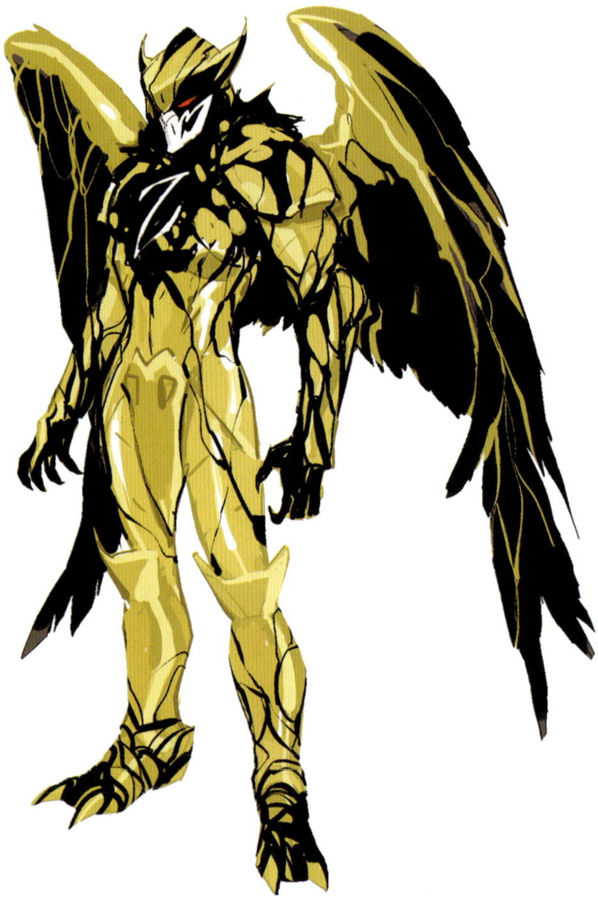

YELLOW DARK RANGER

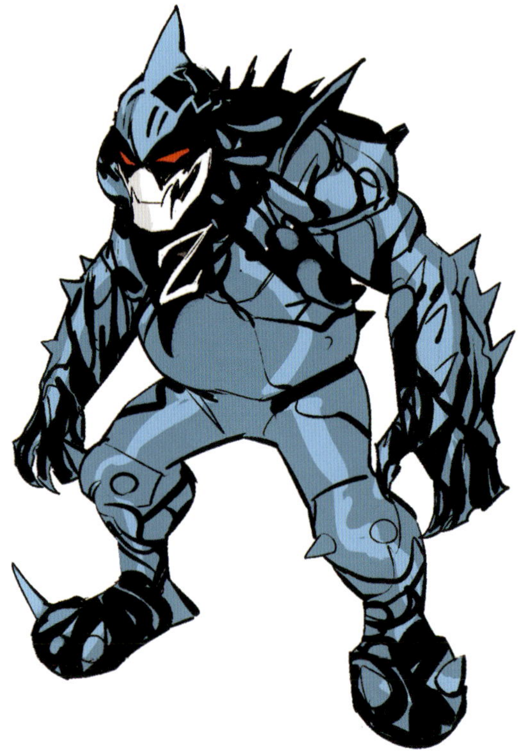

BLUE DARK RANGER

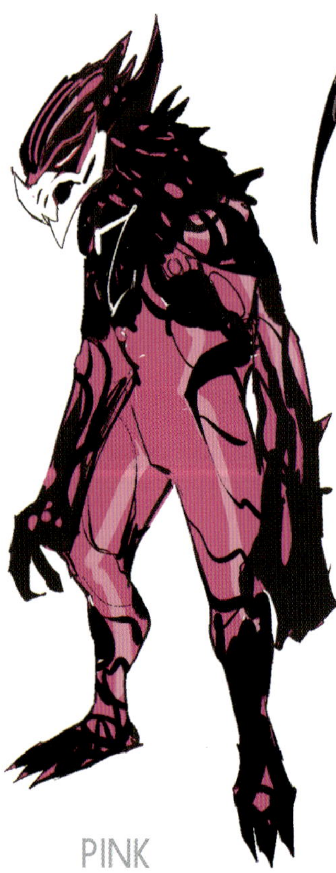

PINK
DARK RANGER

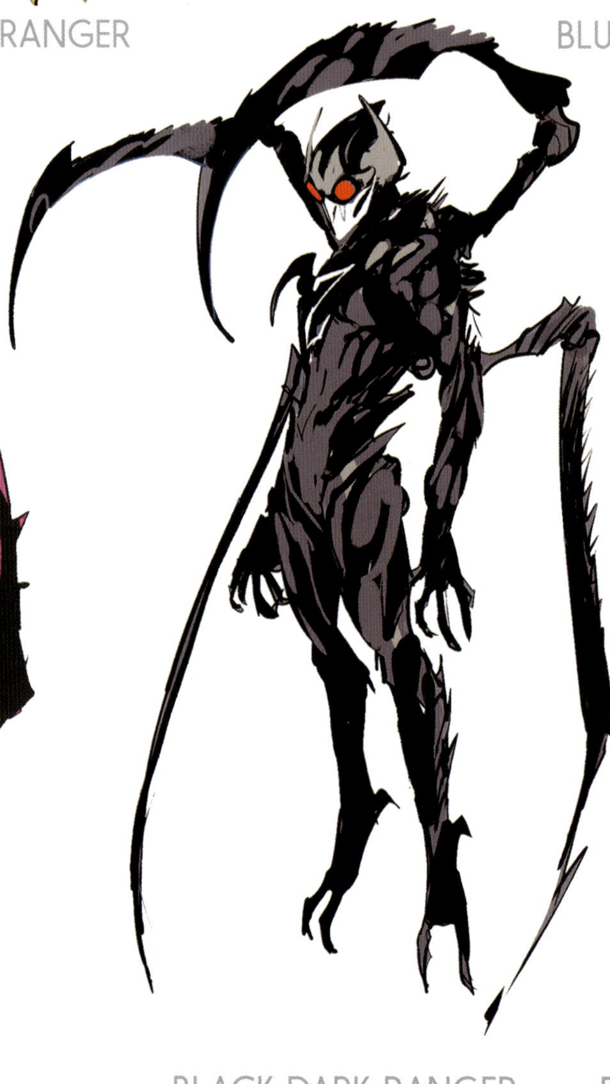

BLACK DARK RANGER

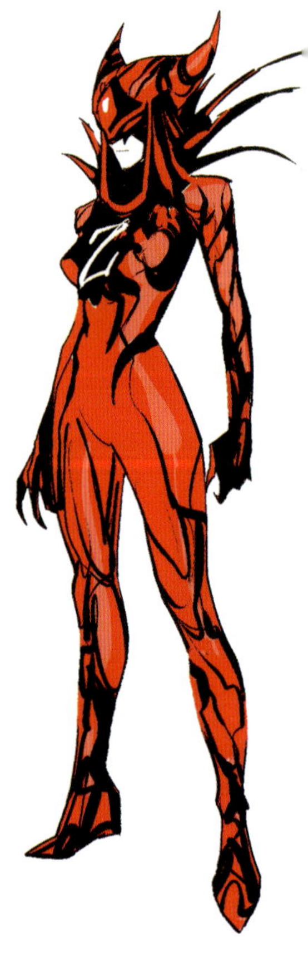

RED DARK RANGER

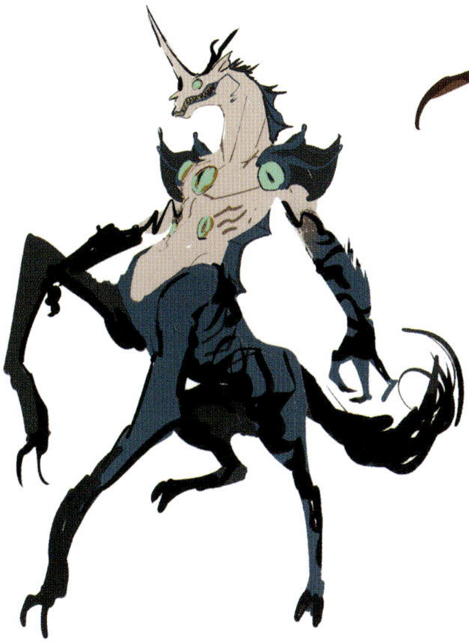

BLUE TERRORZORD

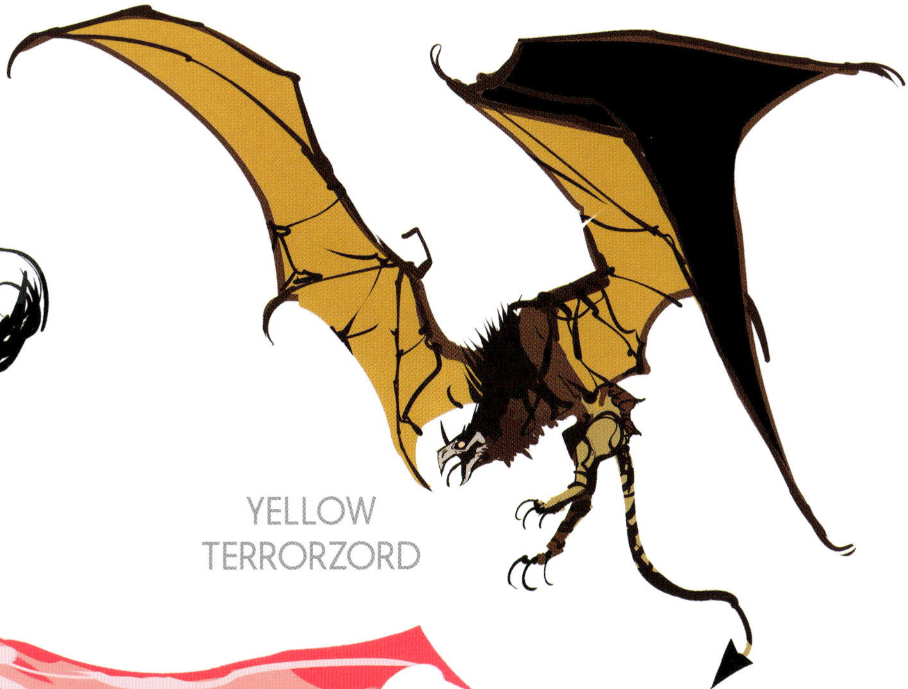

YELLOW TERRORZORD

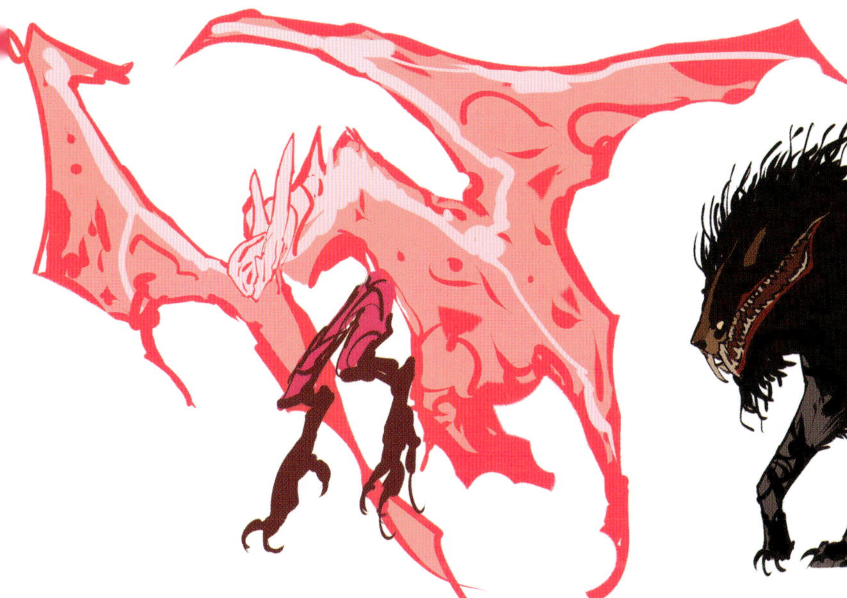

PINK TERRORZORD

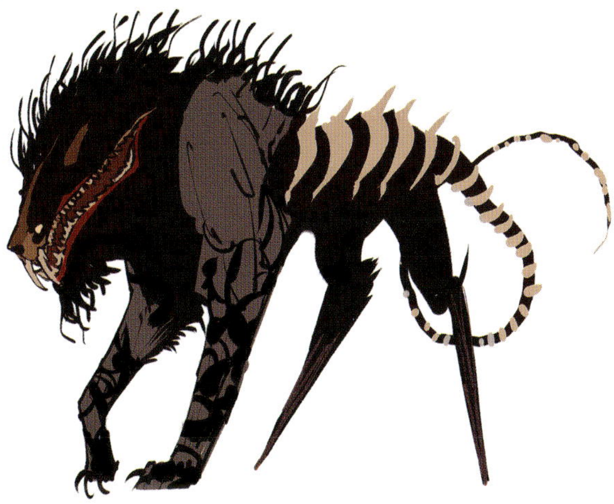

BLACK TERRORZORD

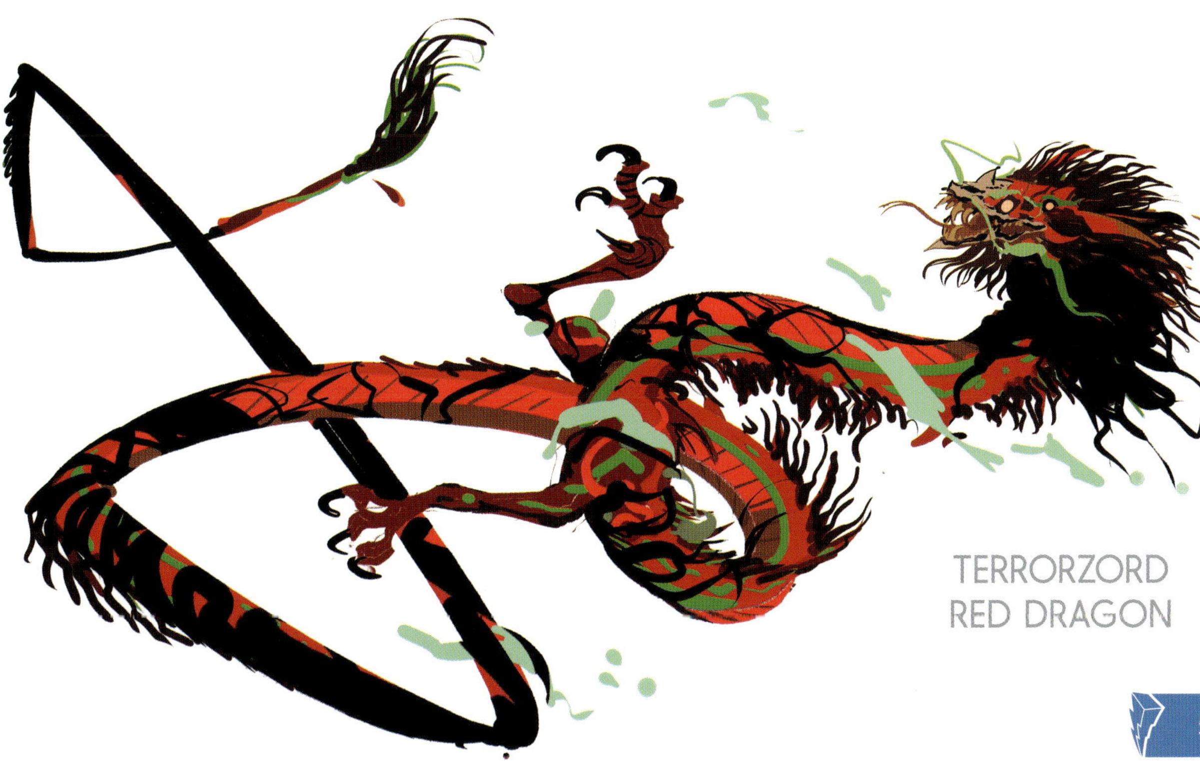

TERRORZORD RED DRAGON

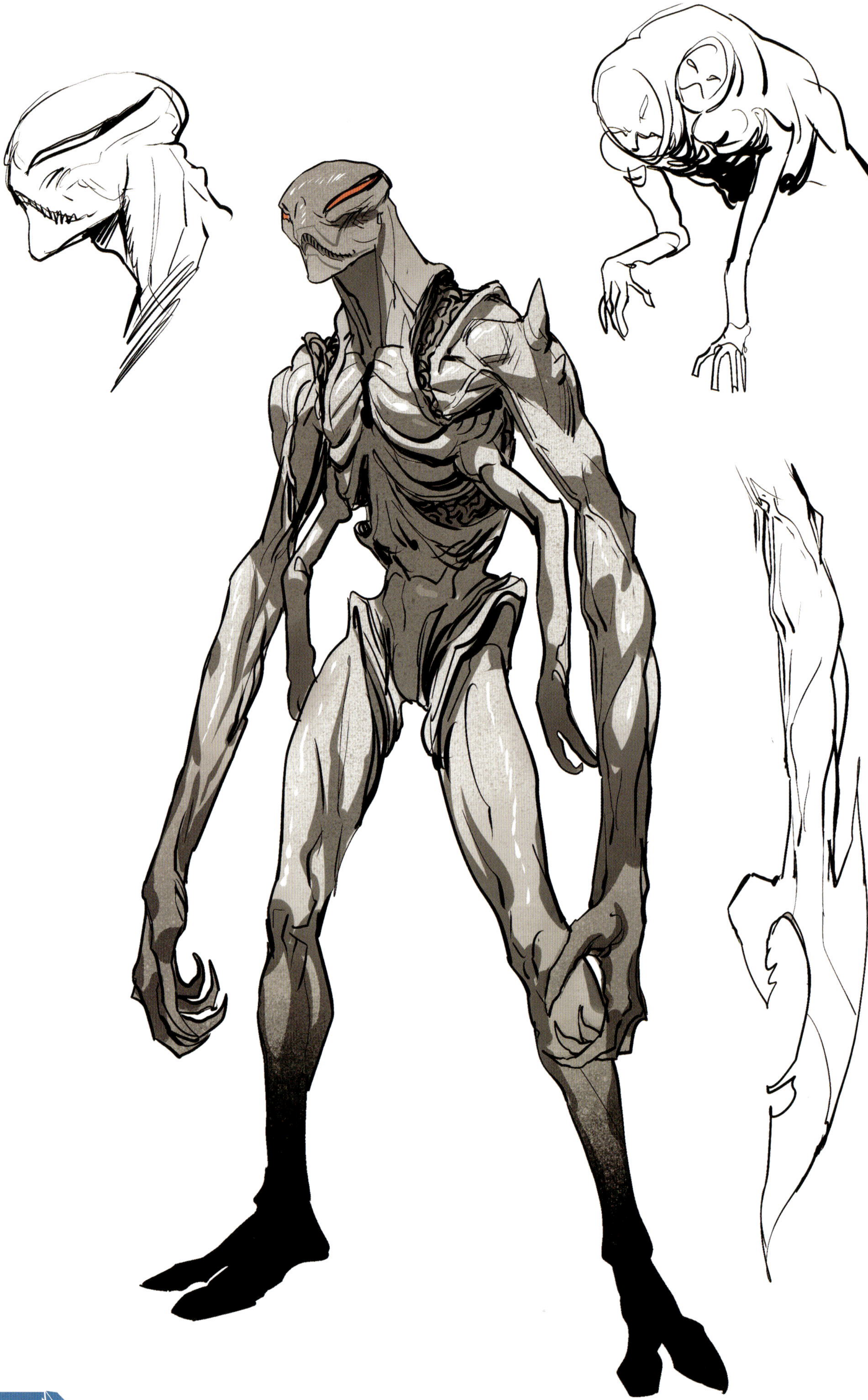

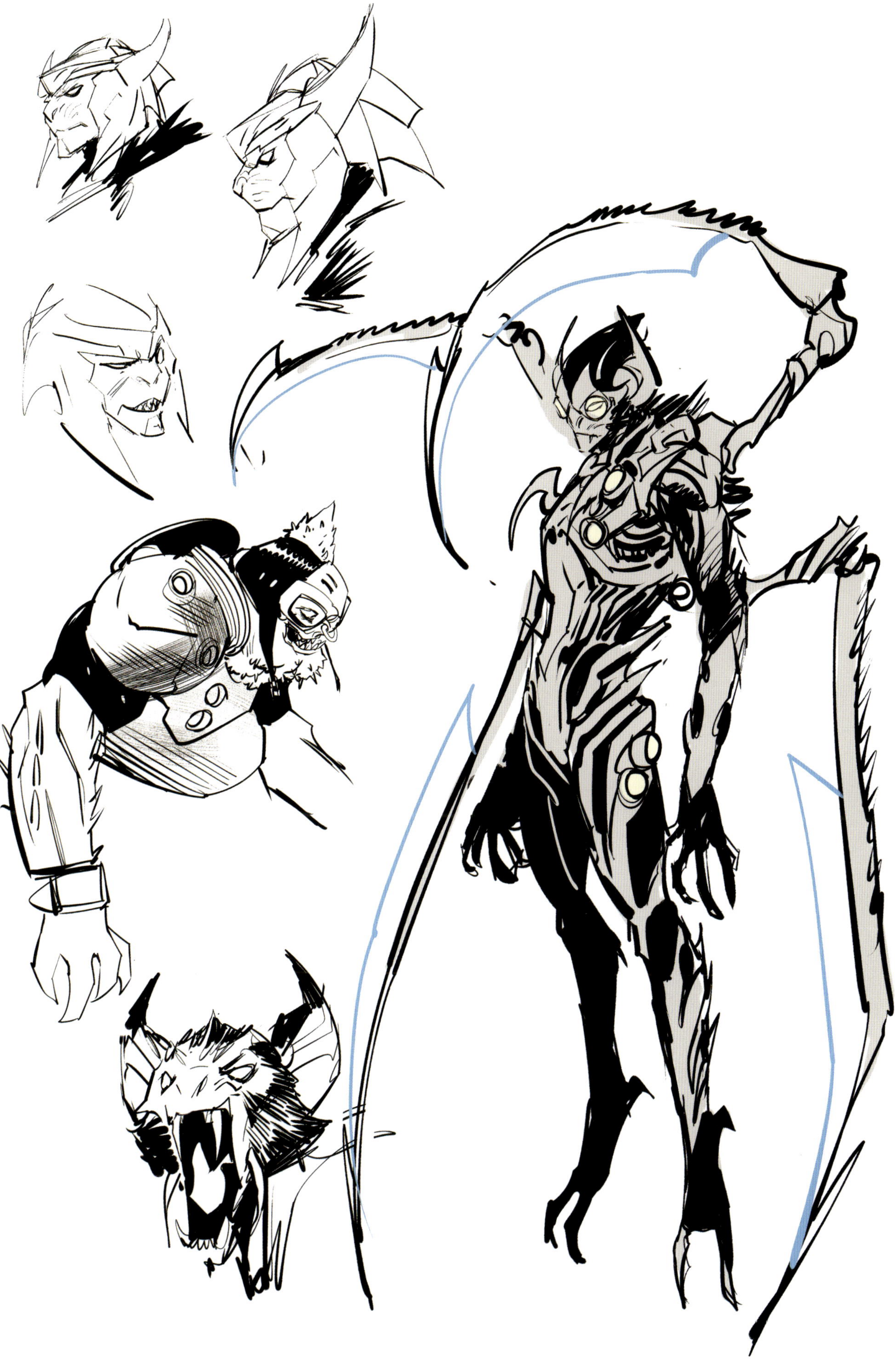

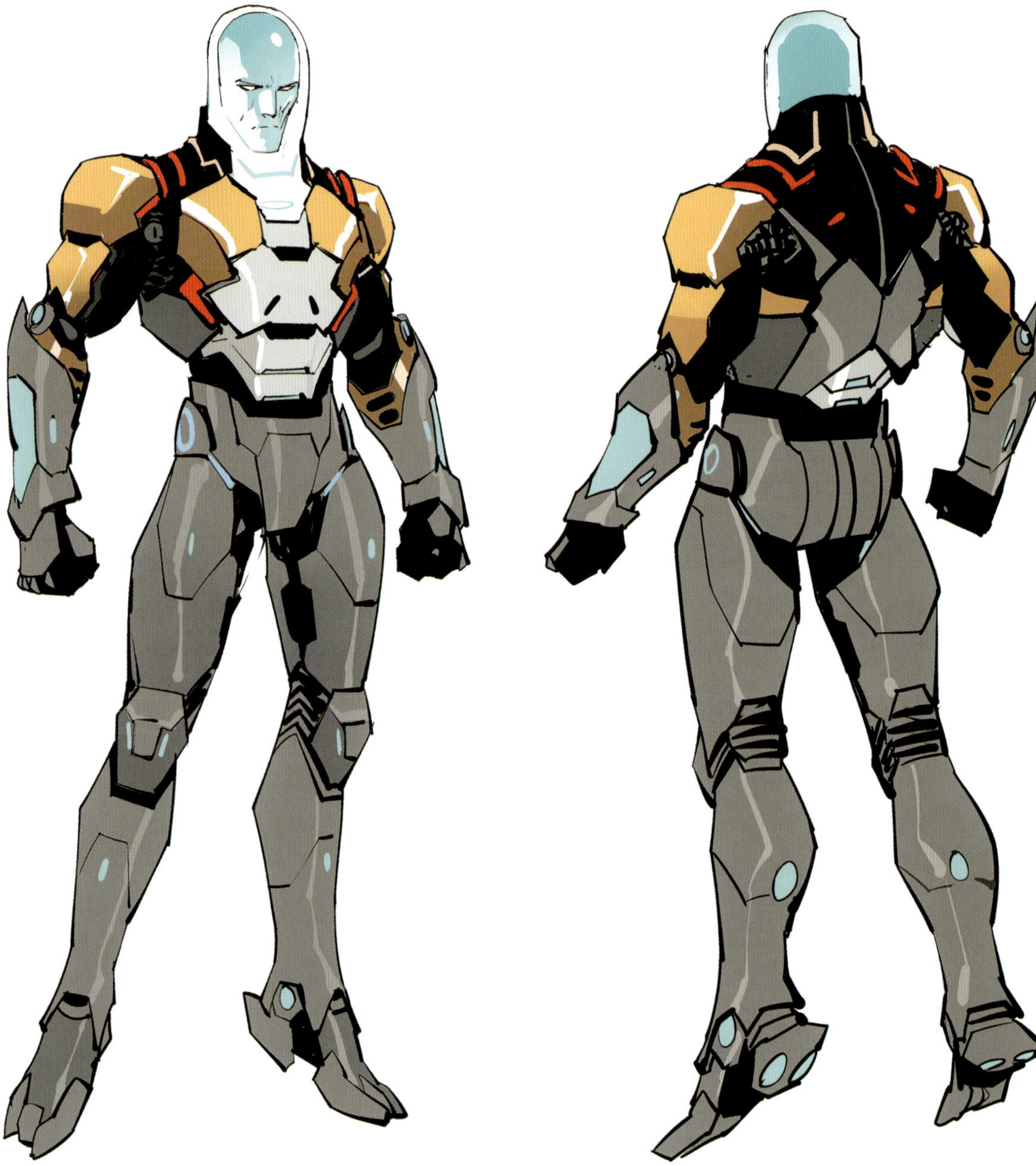

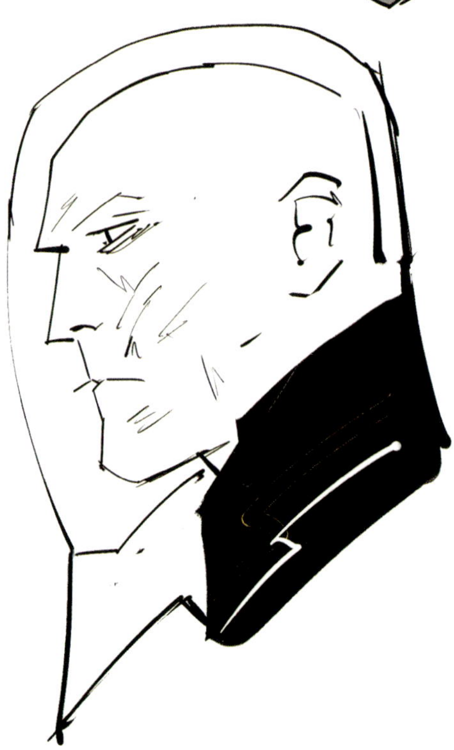

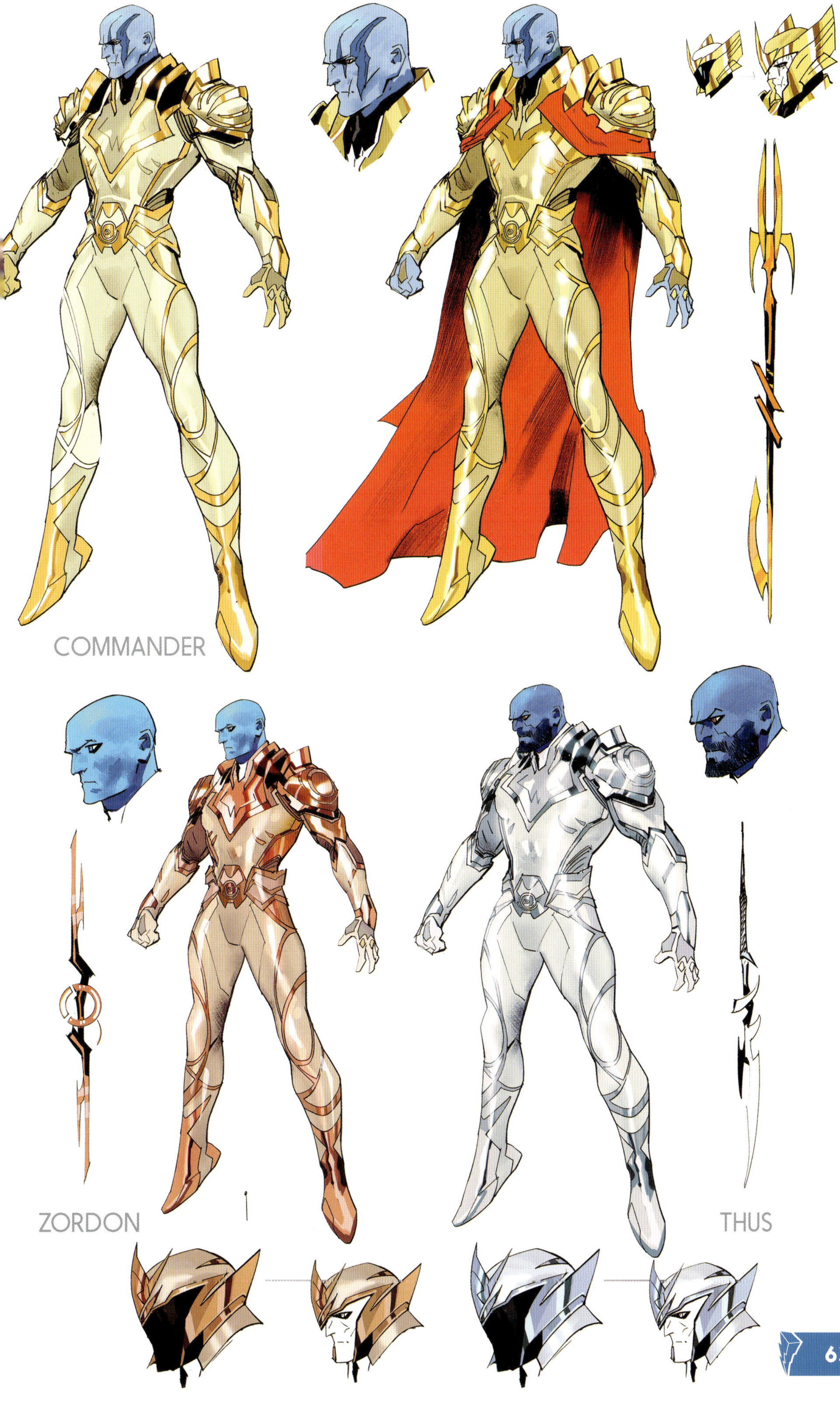
COMMANDER
ZORDON
THUS

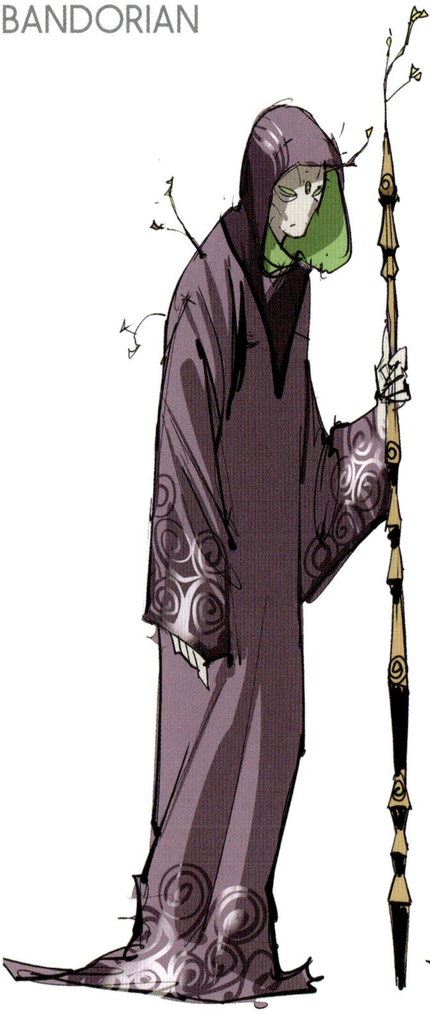

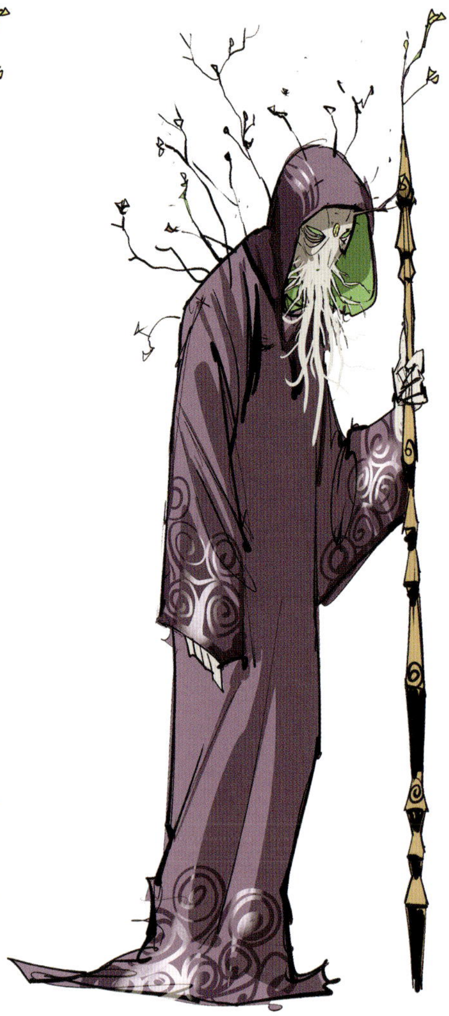

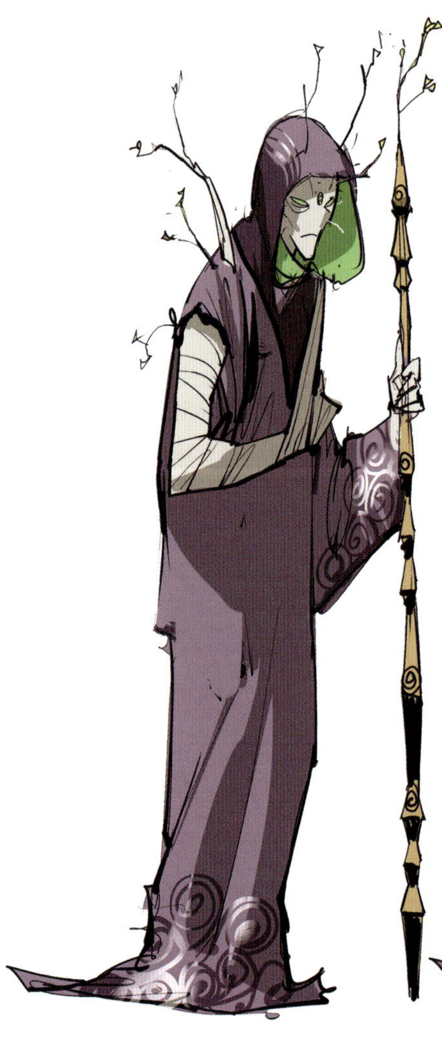

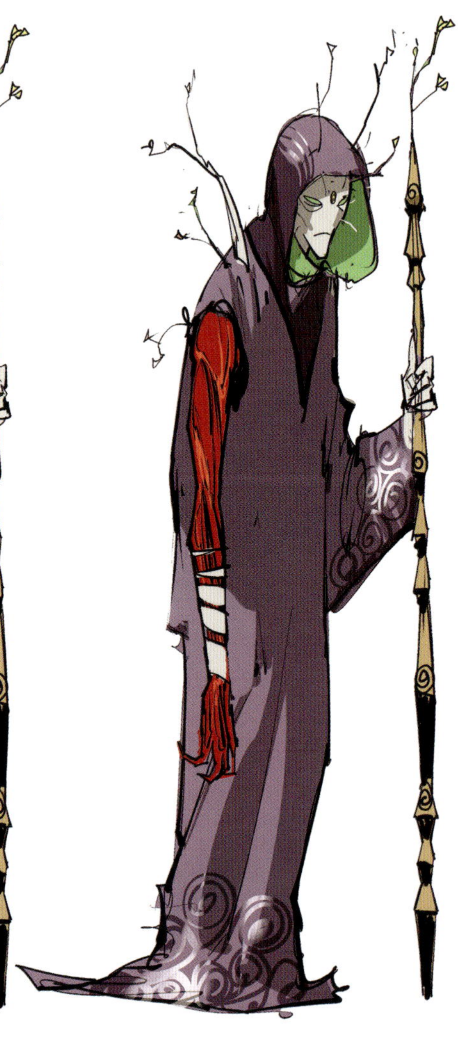

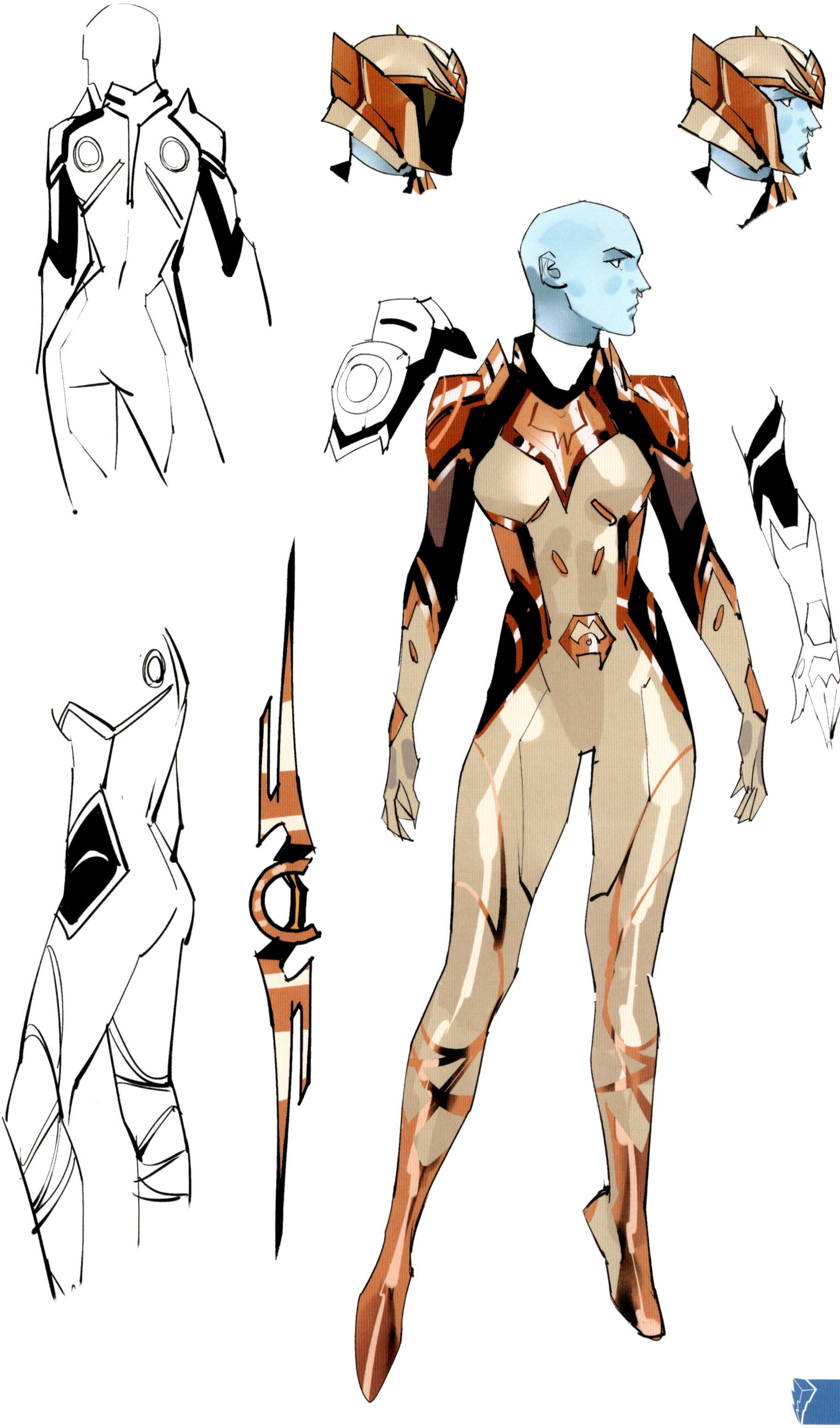

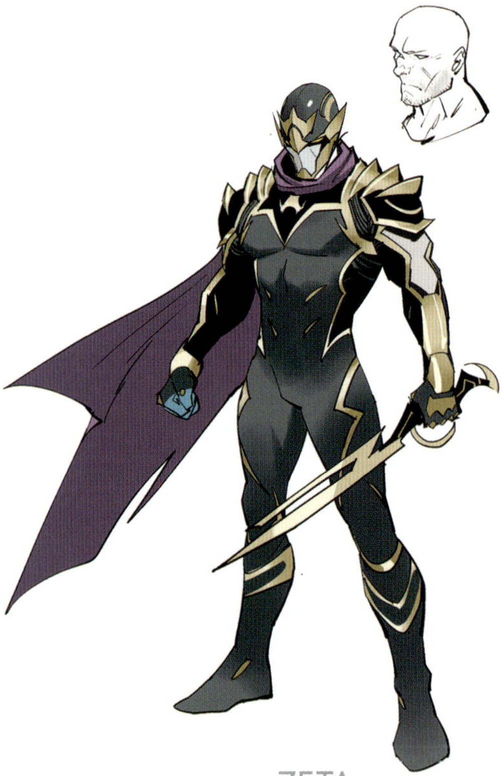

ZETA

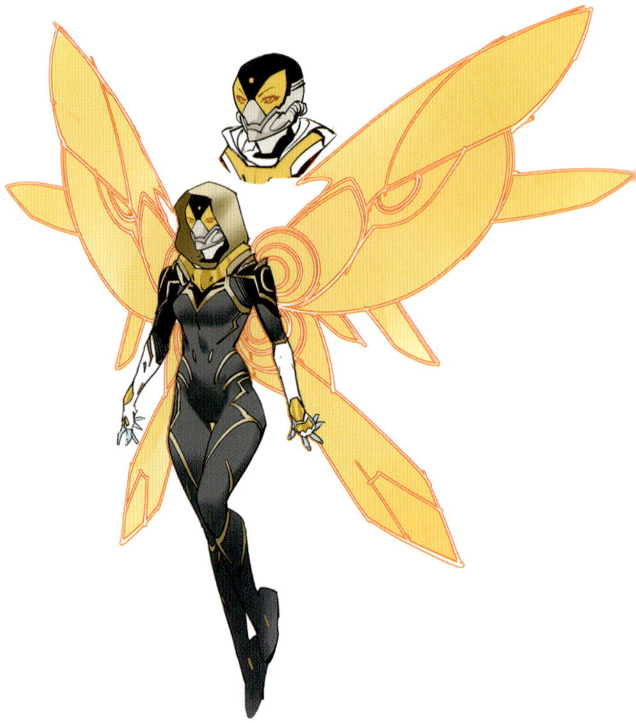

ZENITH

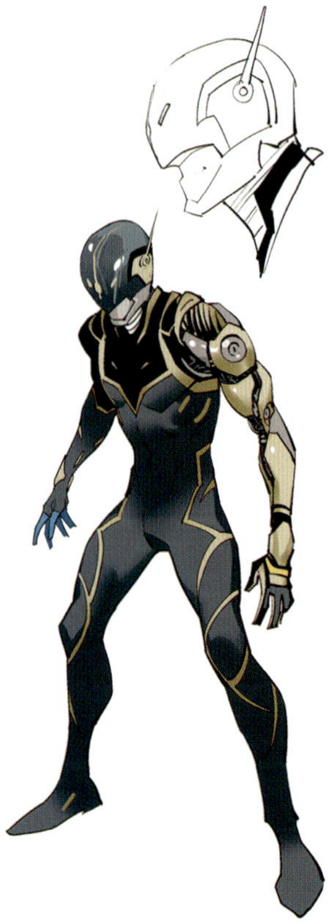

ZAG

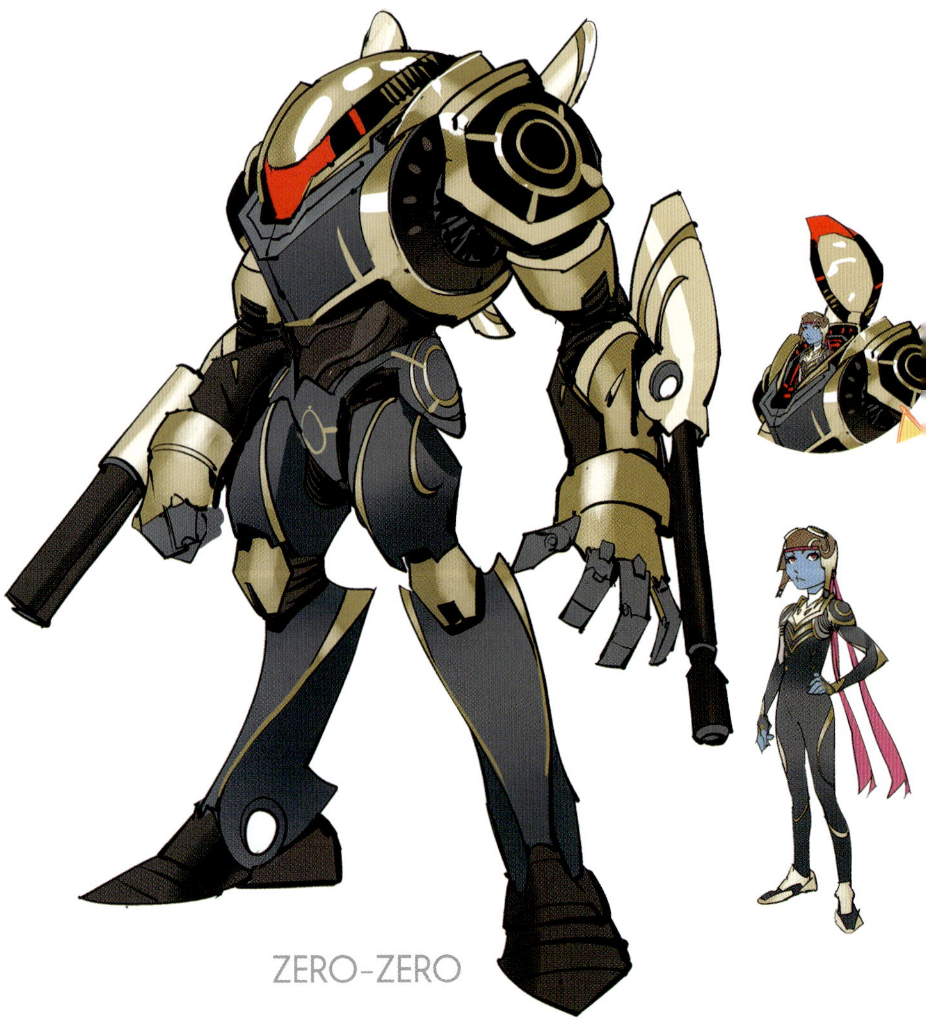

ZERO-ZERO

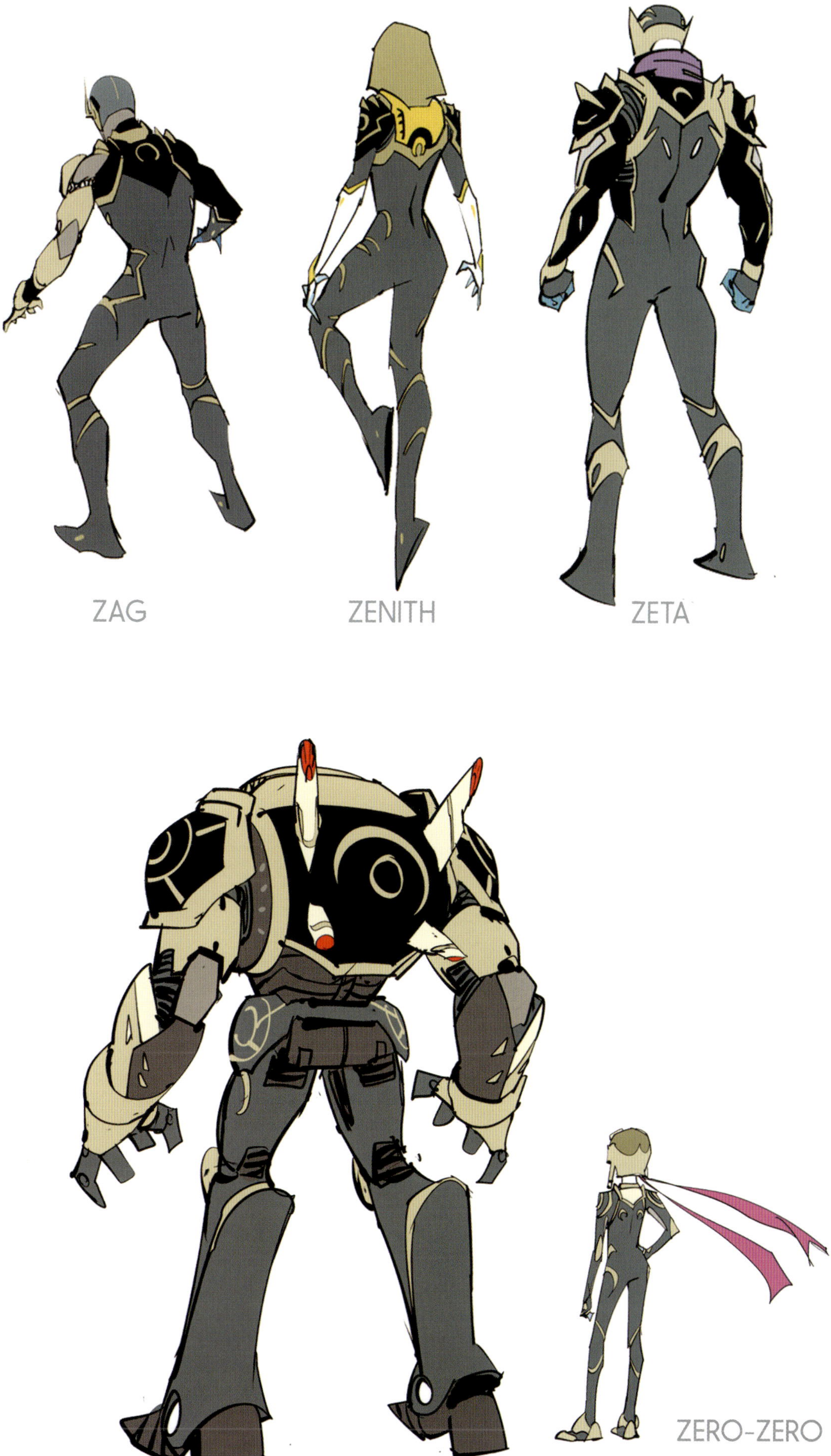
ZAG
ZENITH
ZETA
ZERO-ZERO

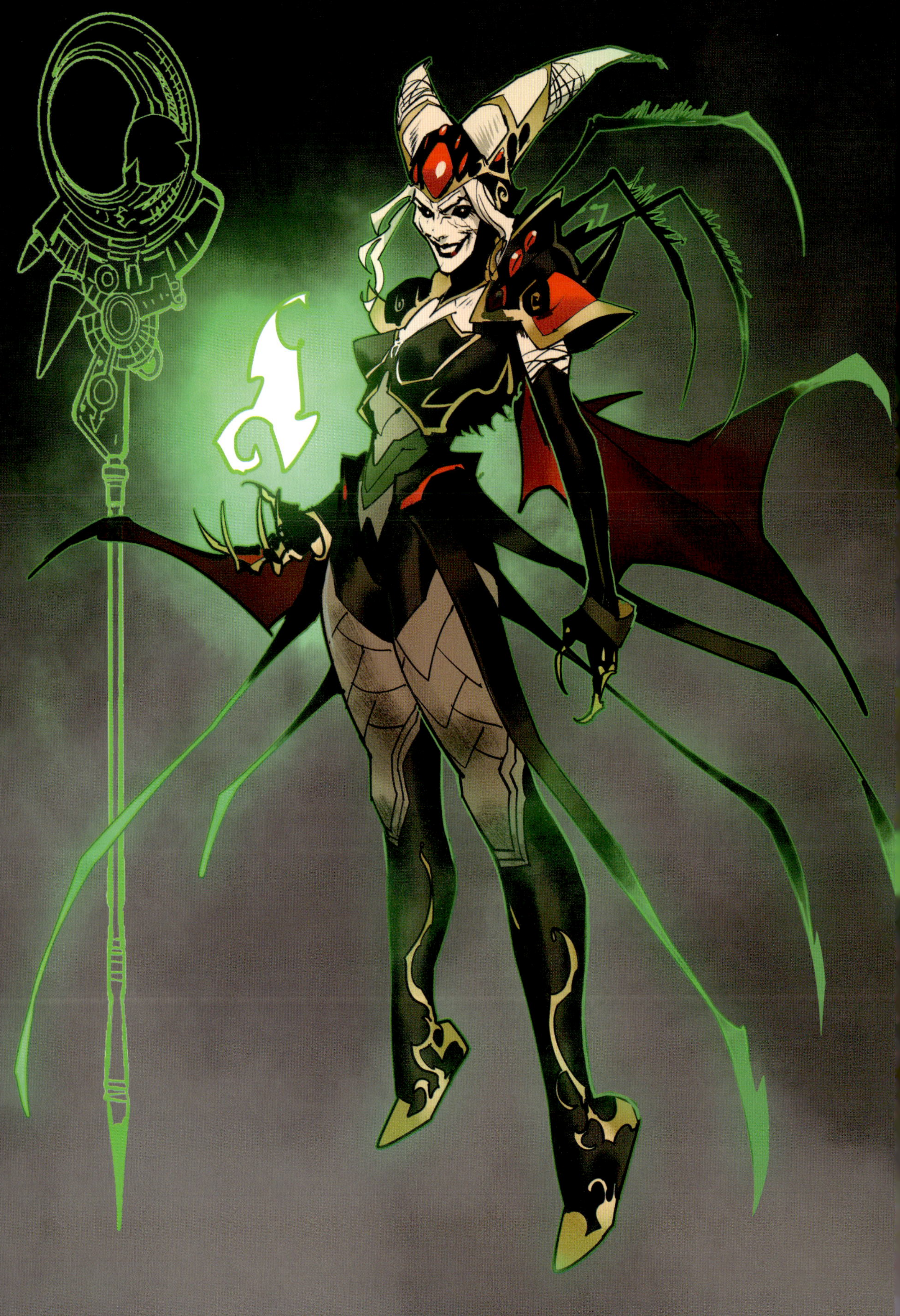

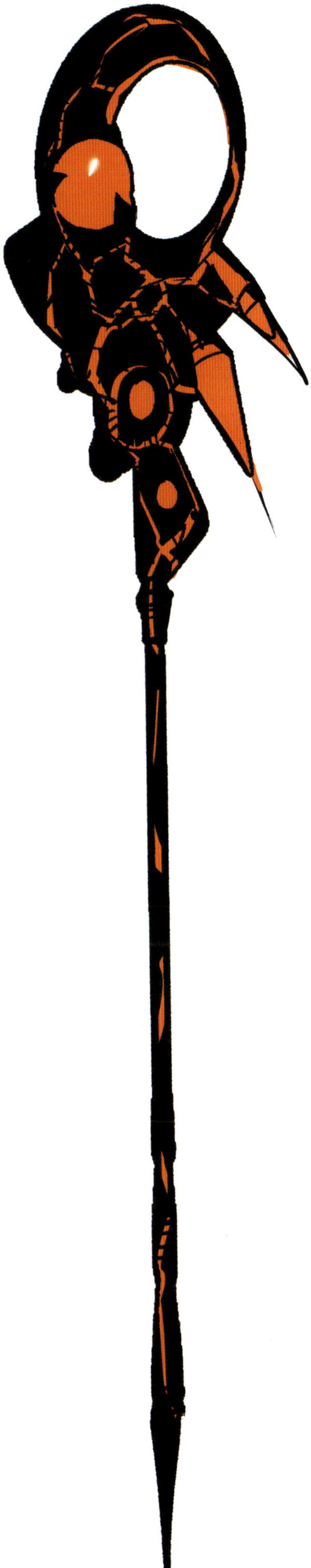

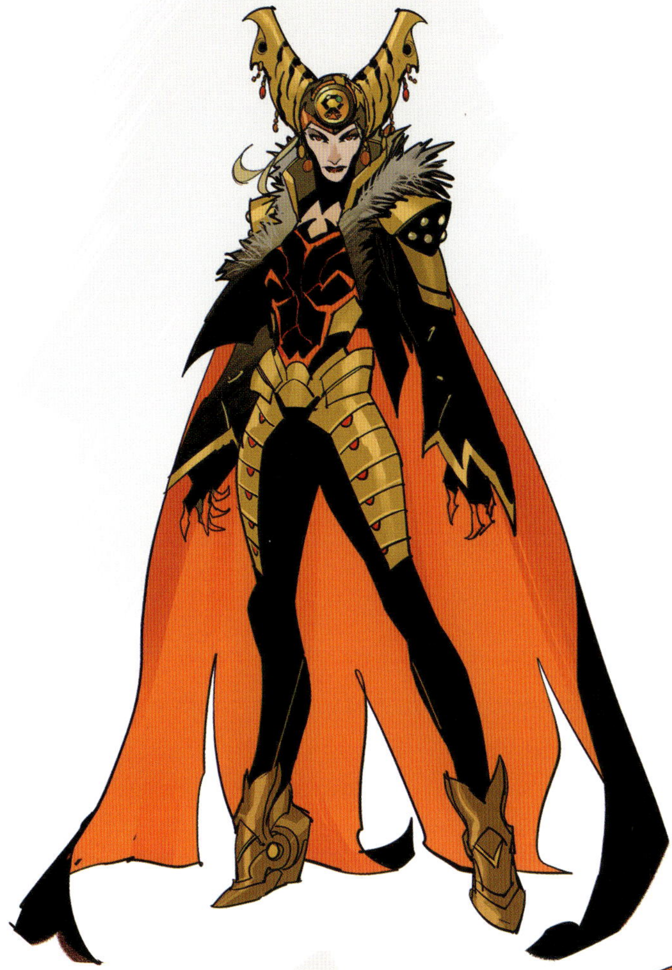

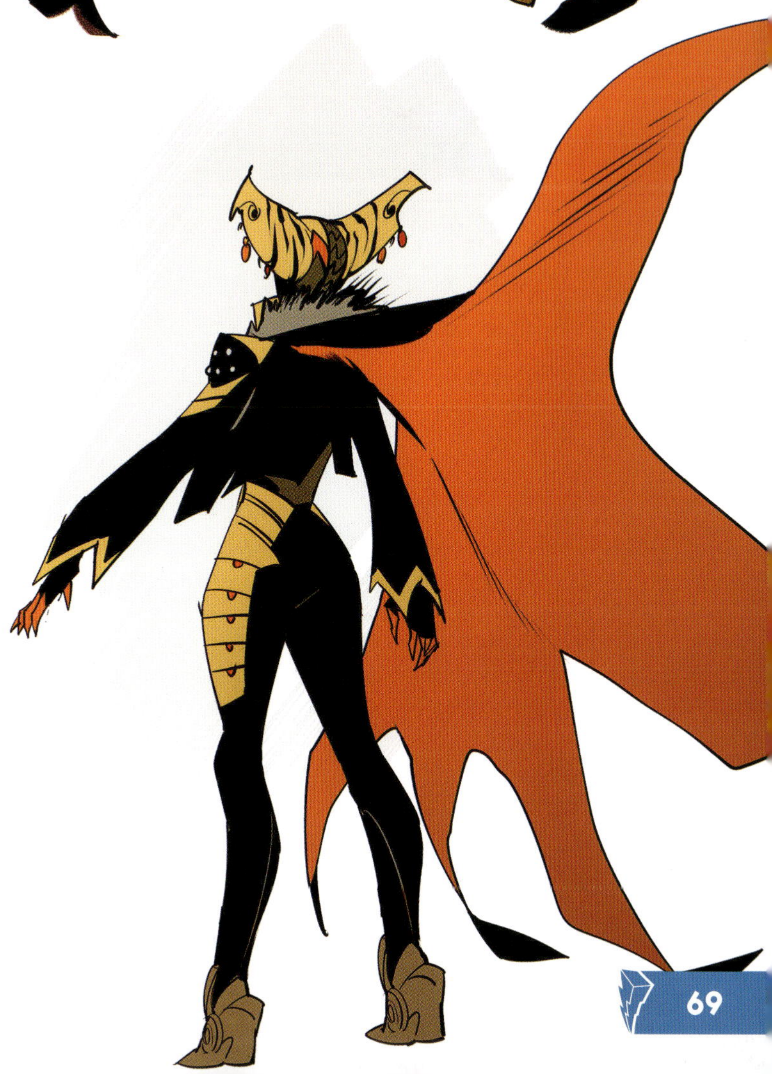

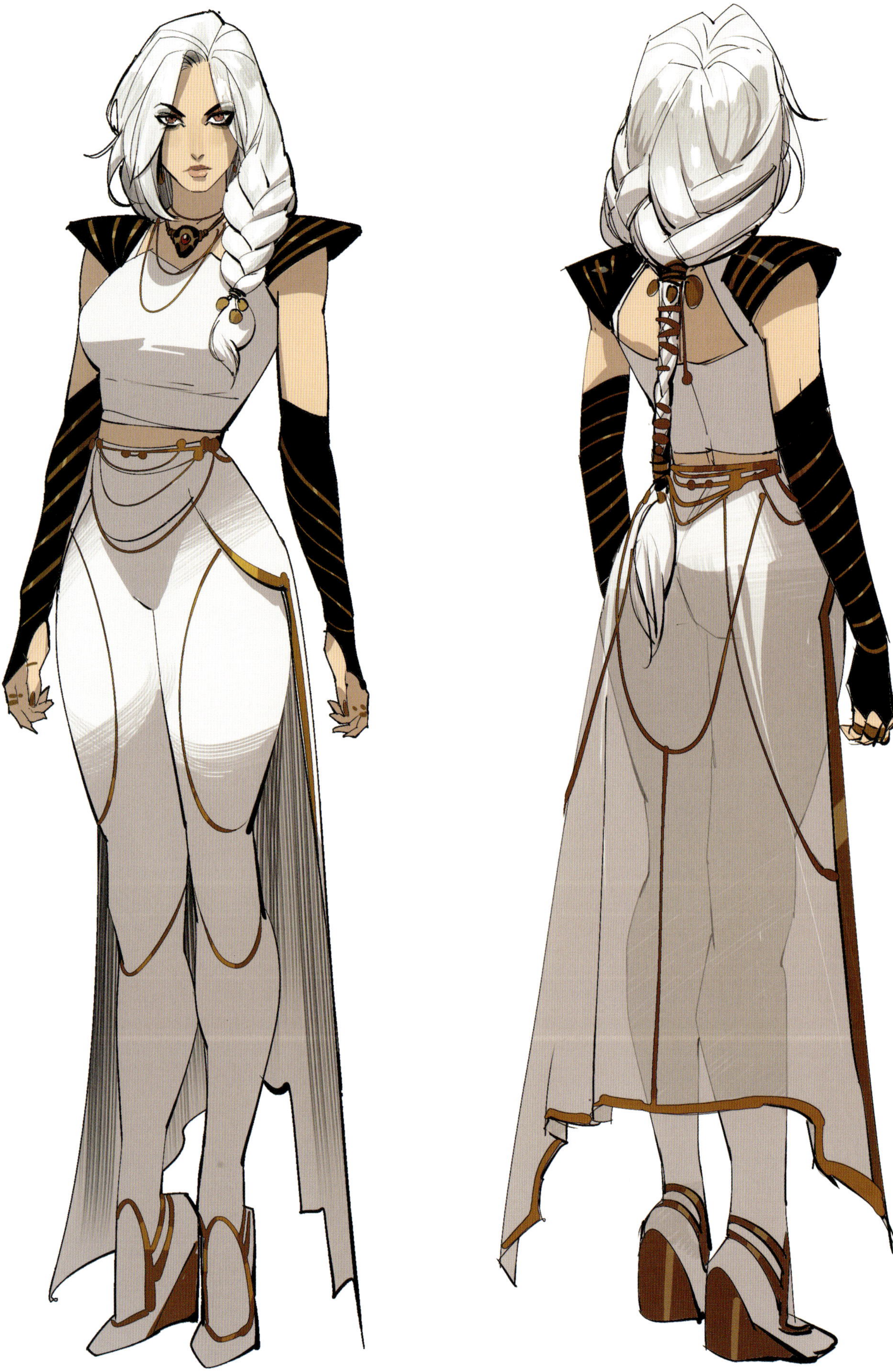

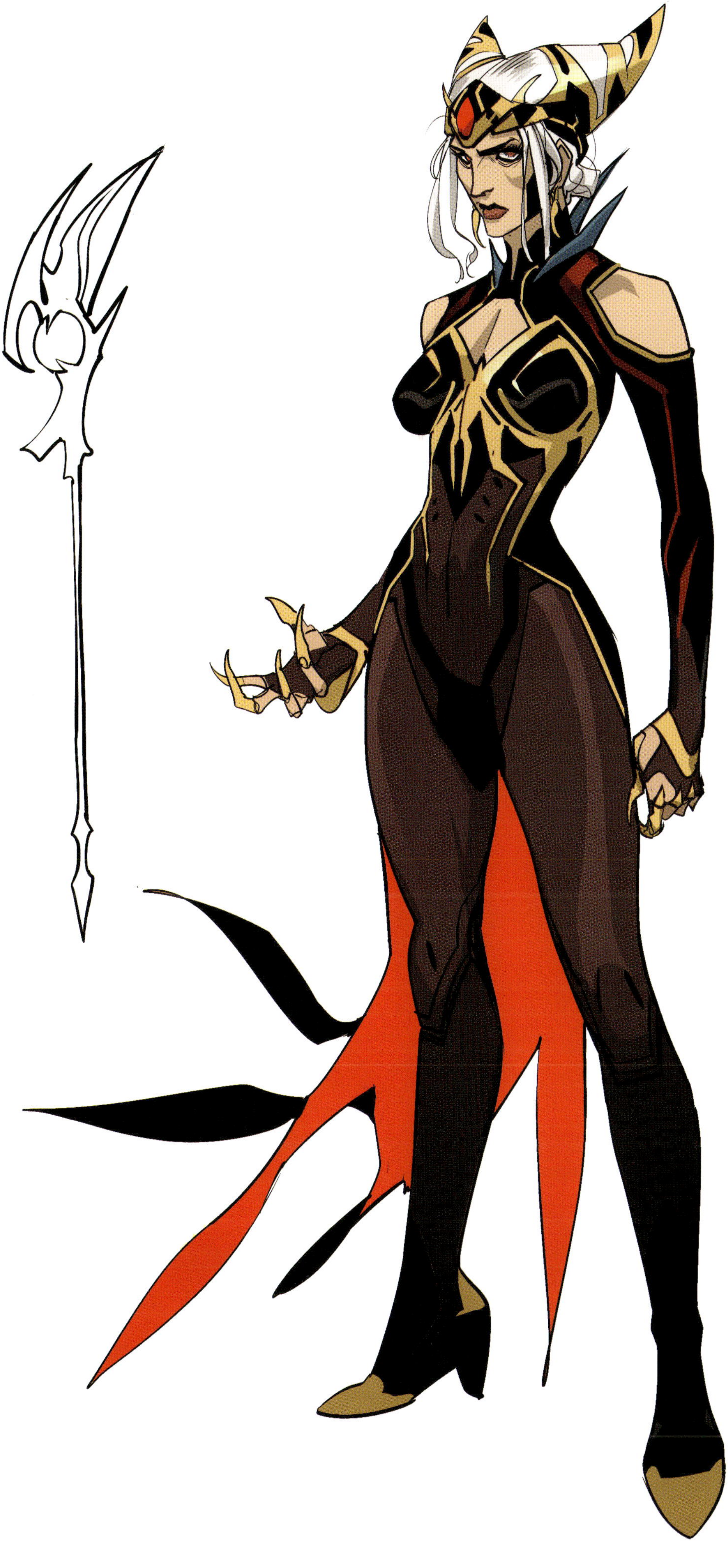

RANGER ZEDD

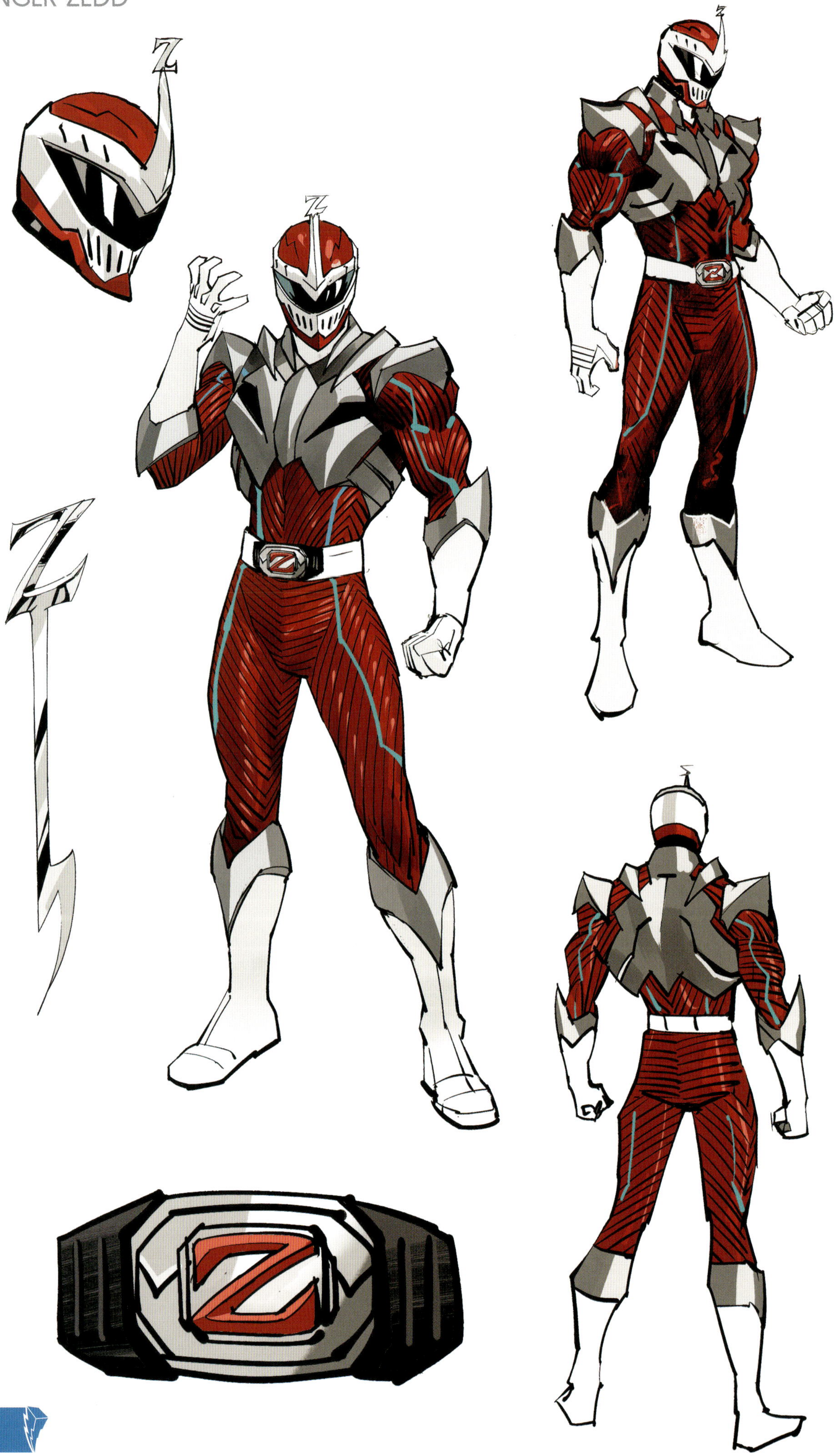

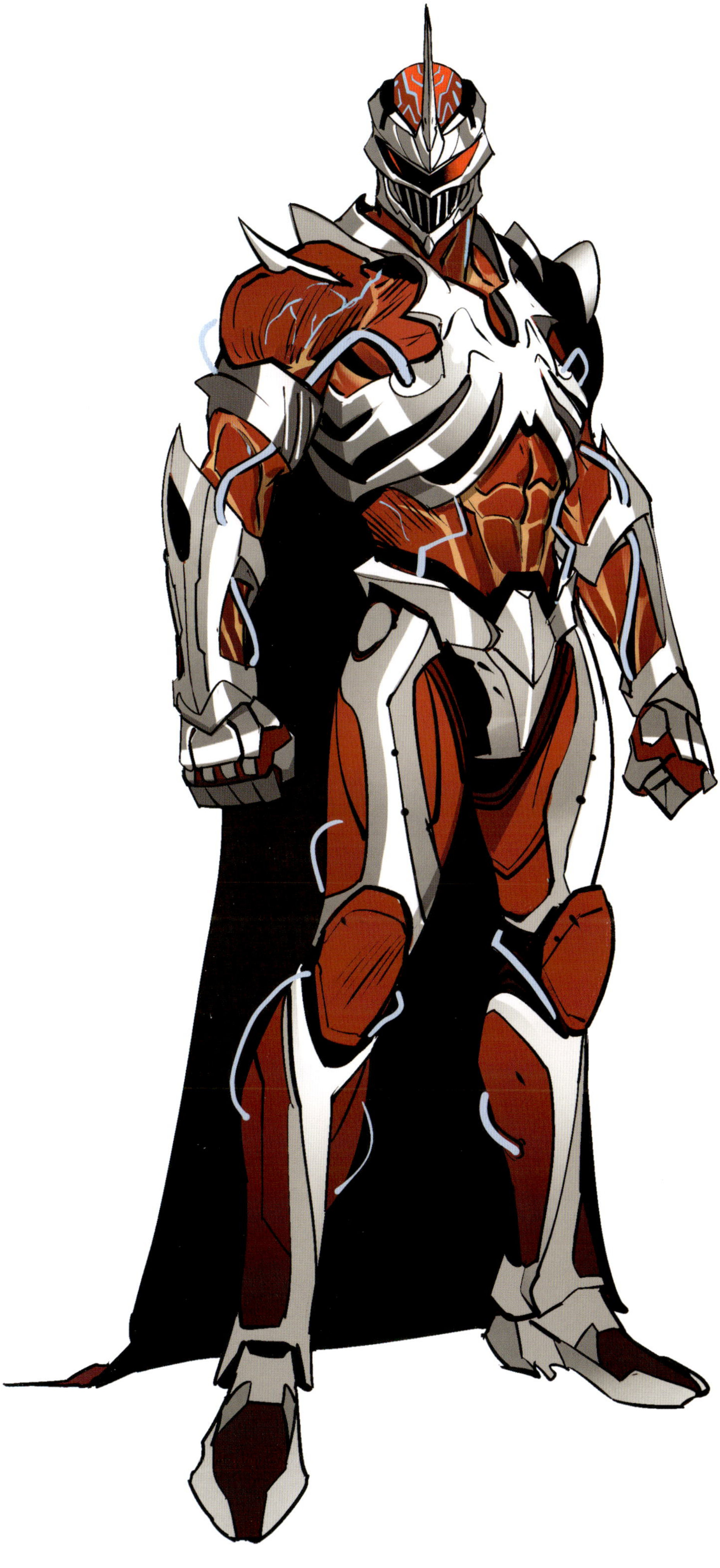

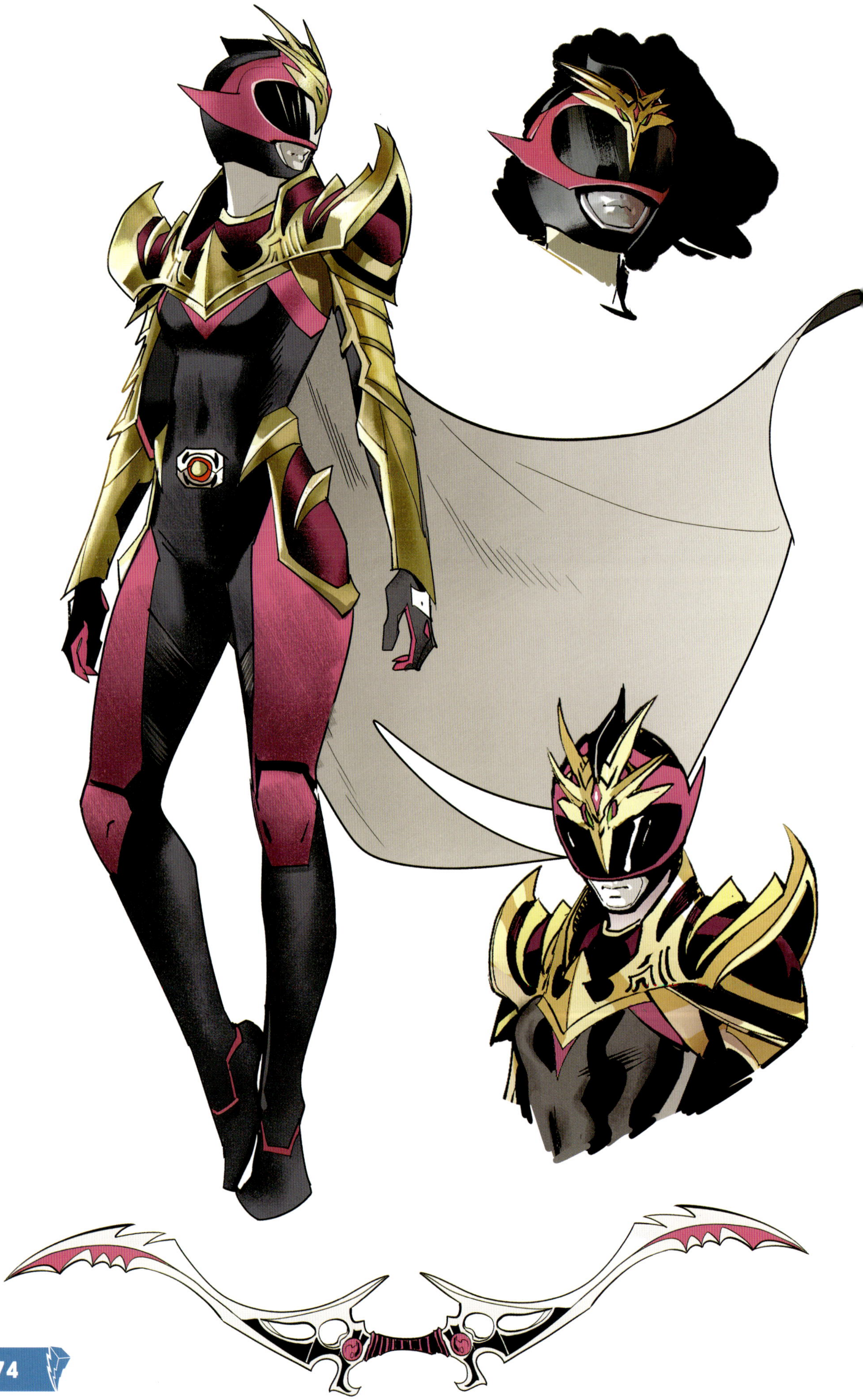

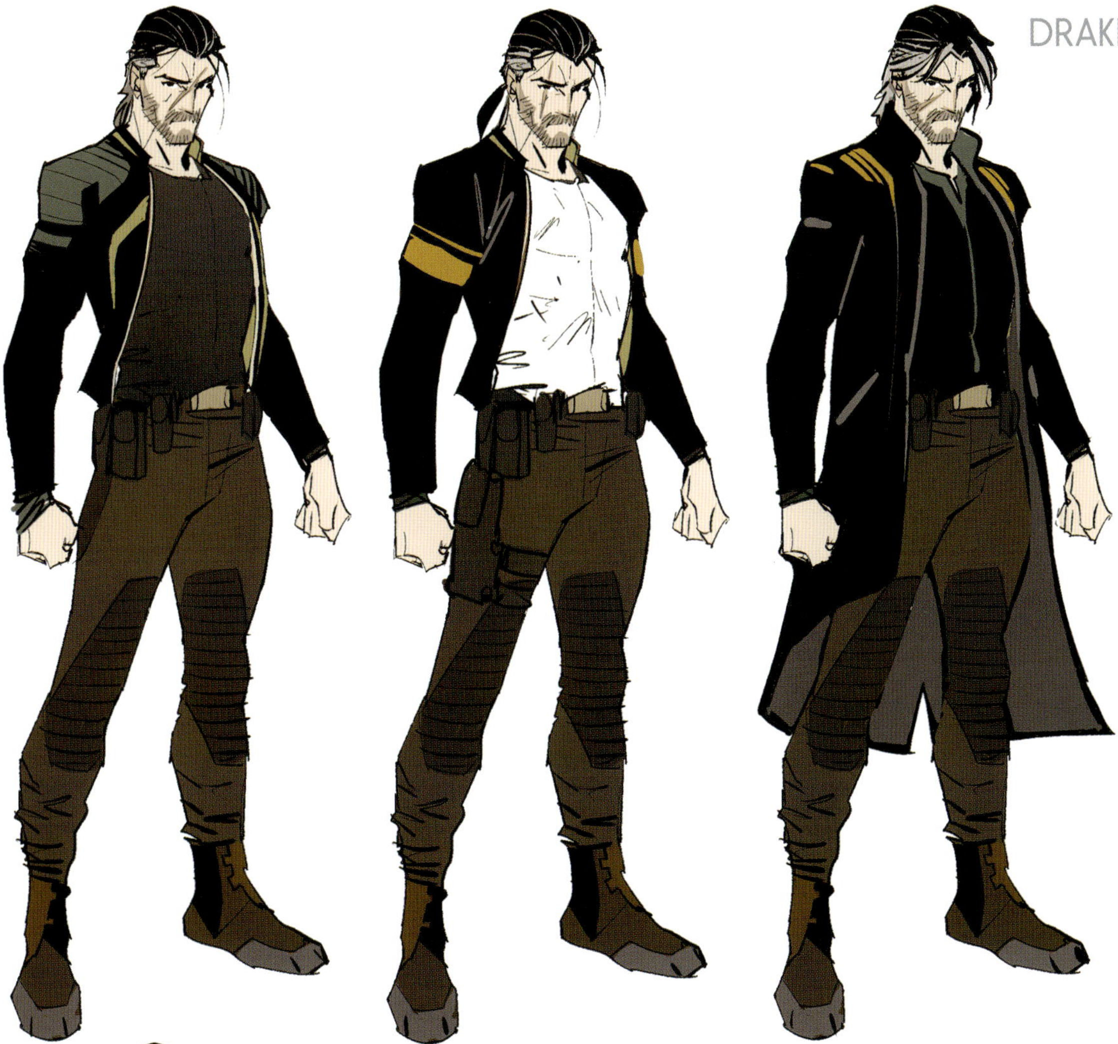

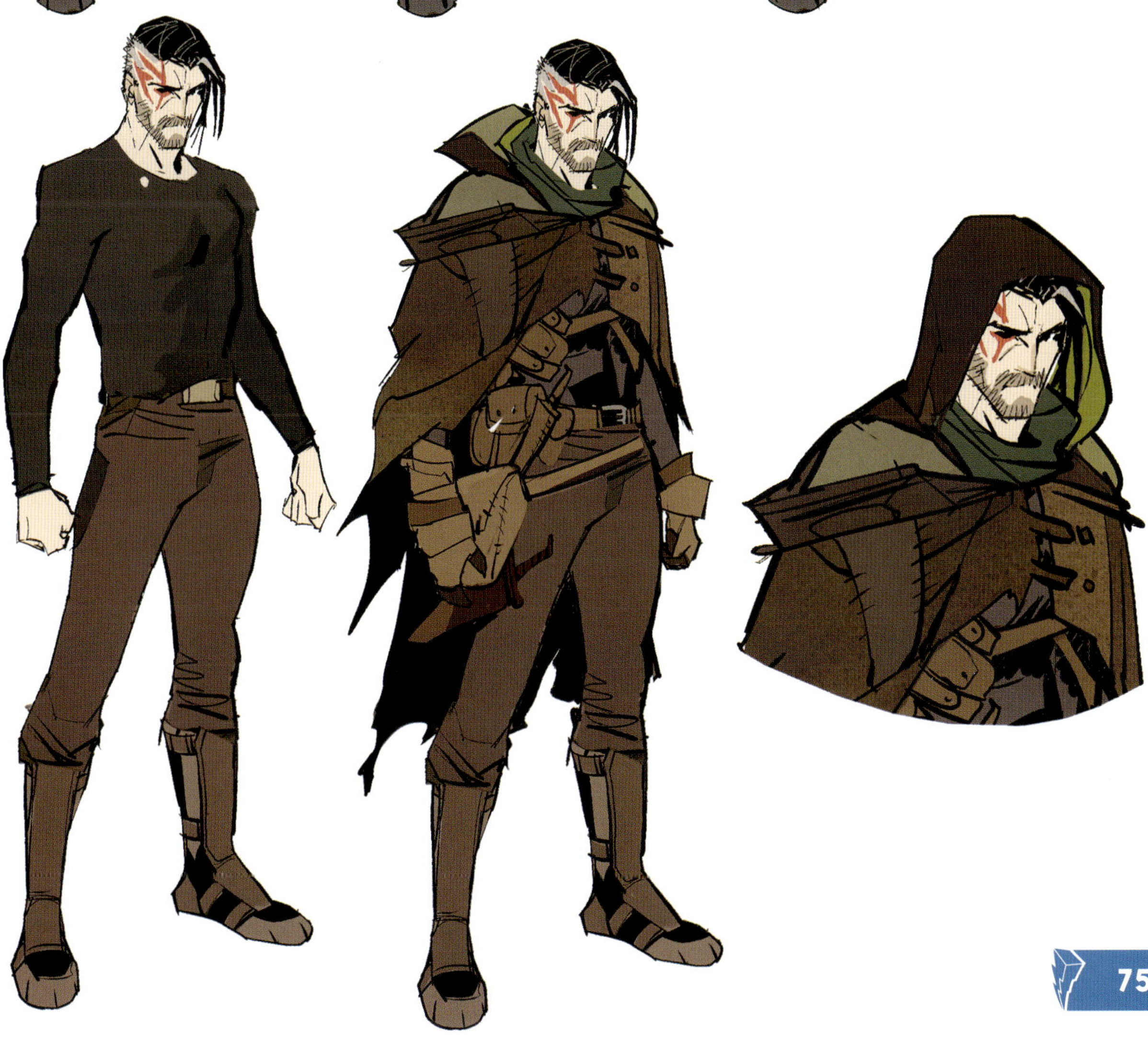

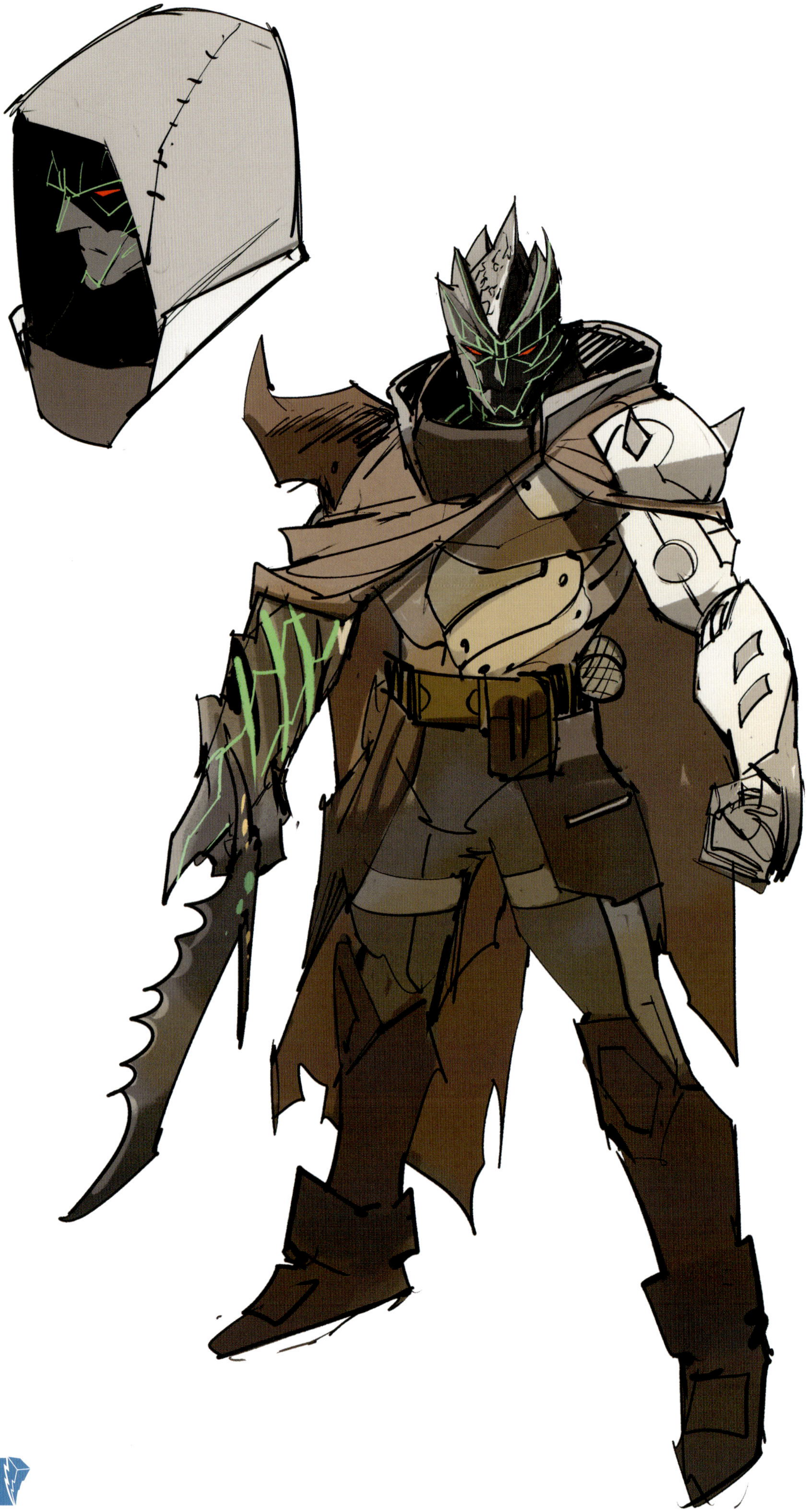

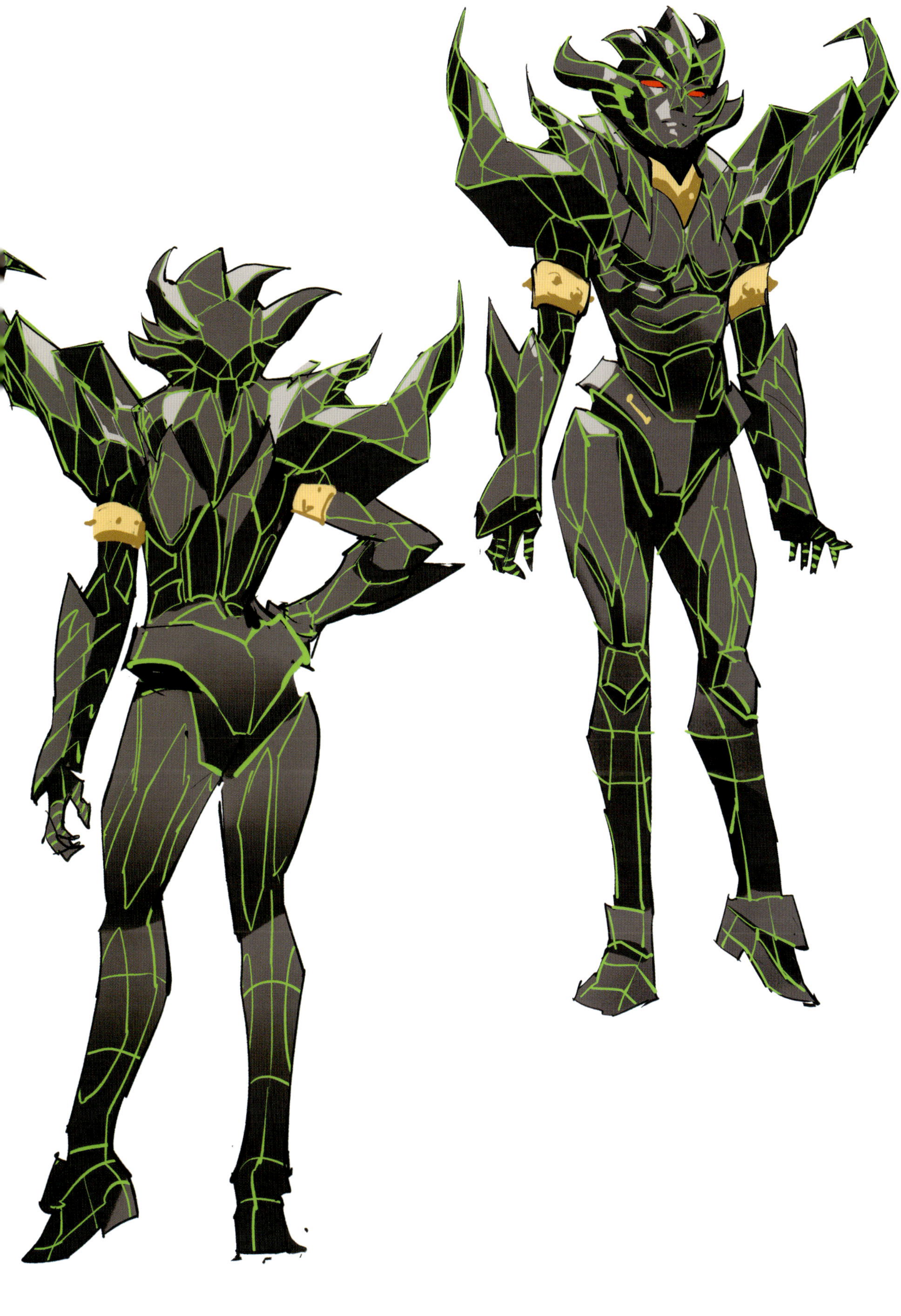

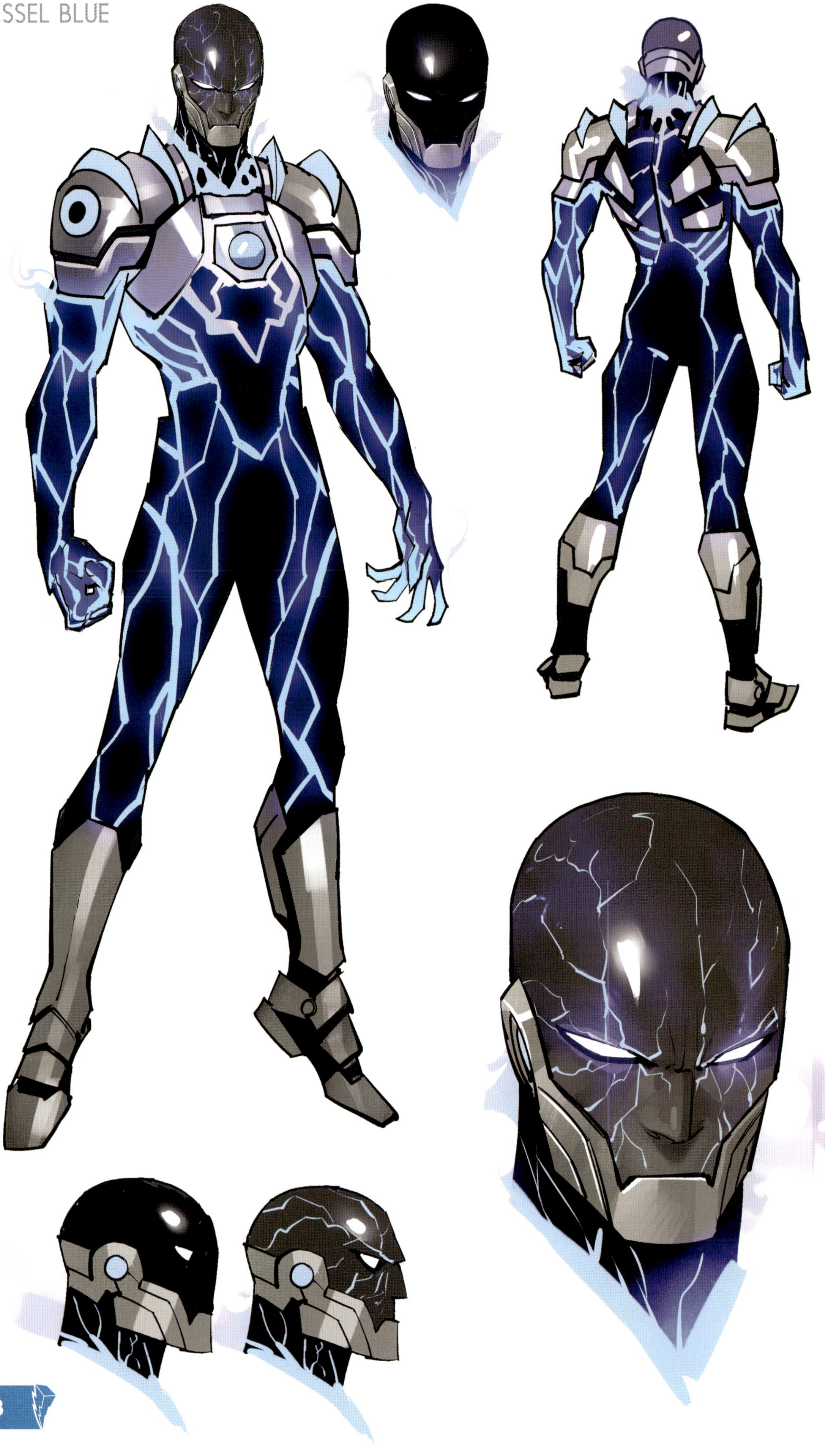

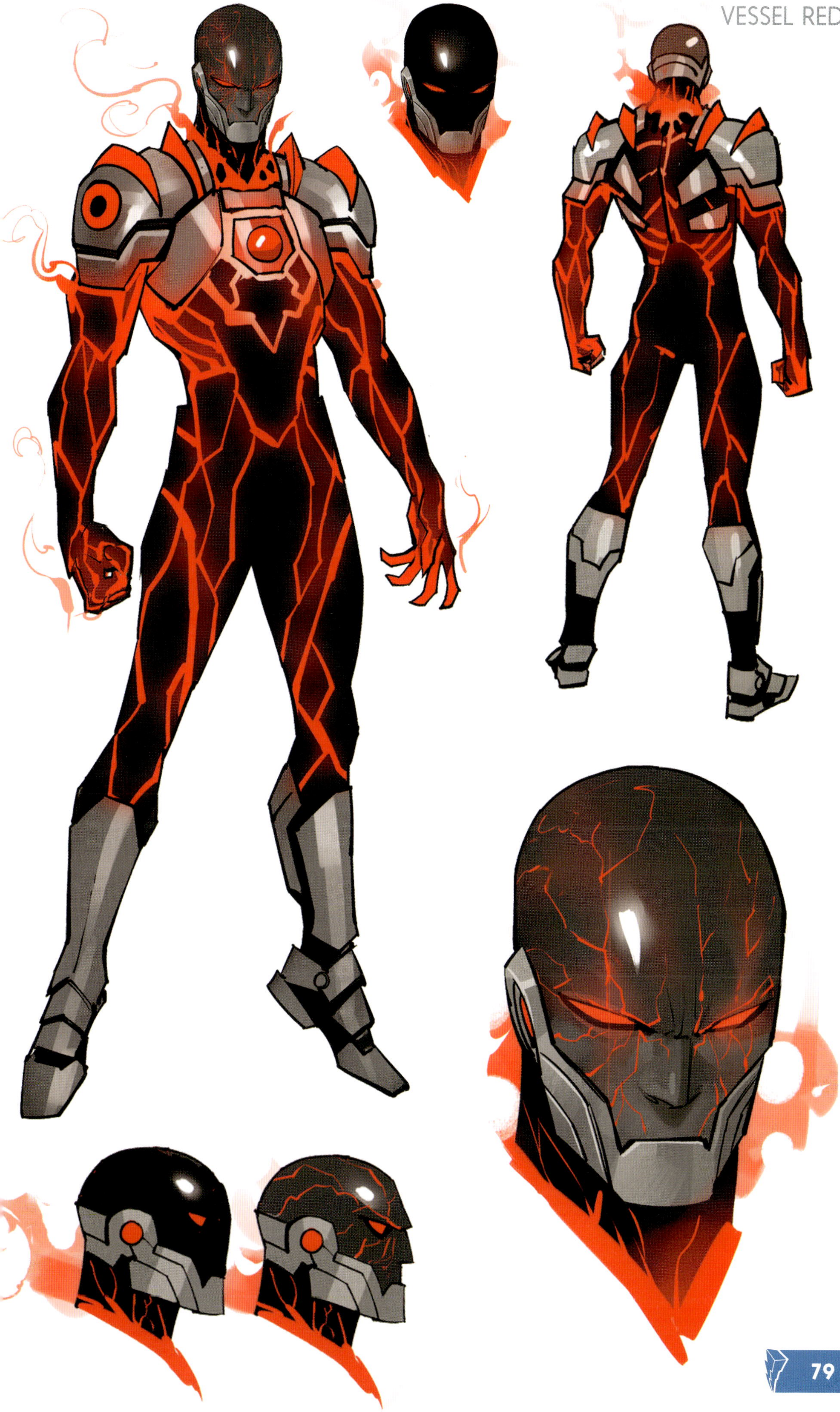

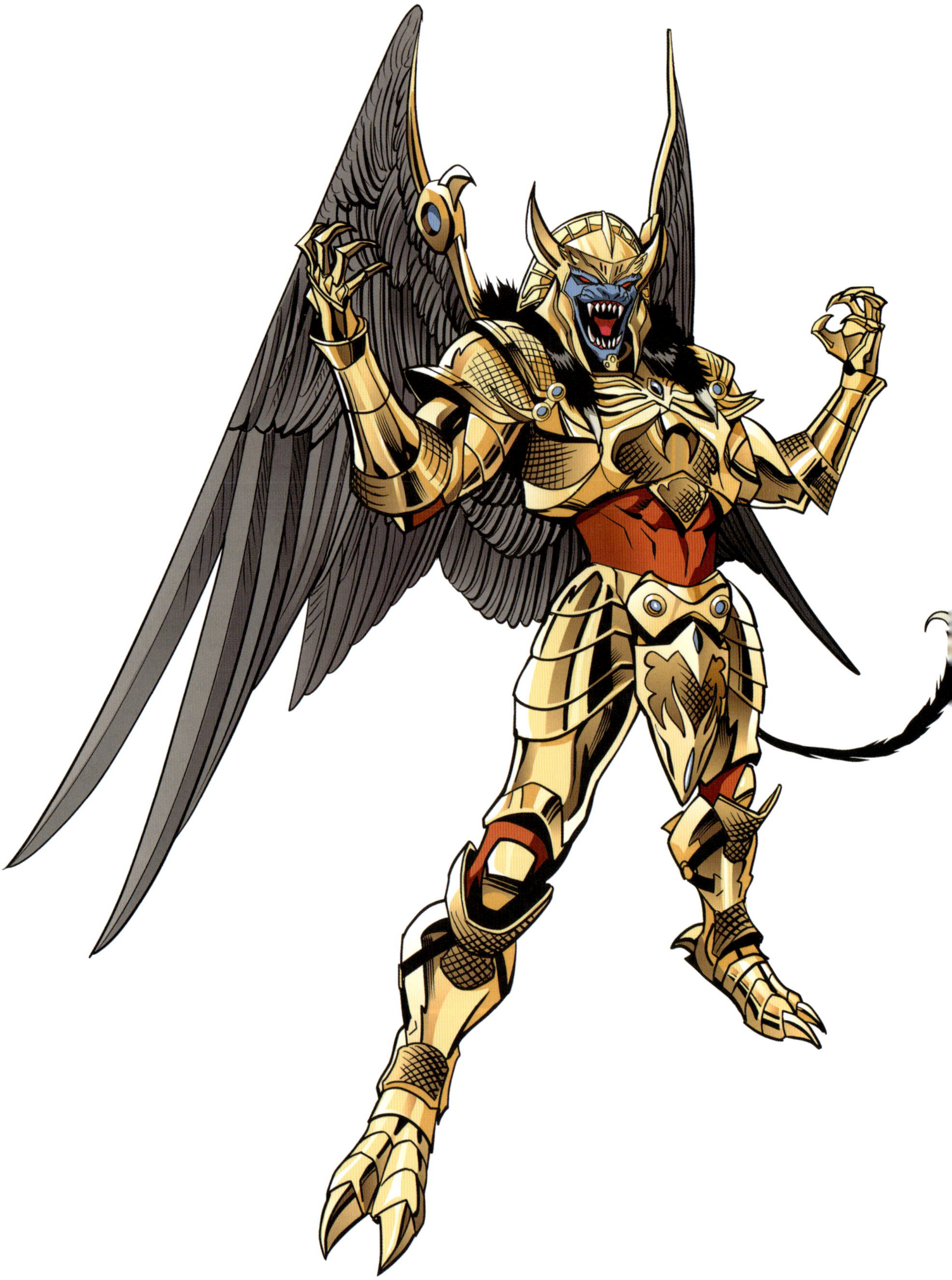

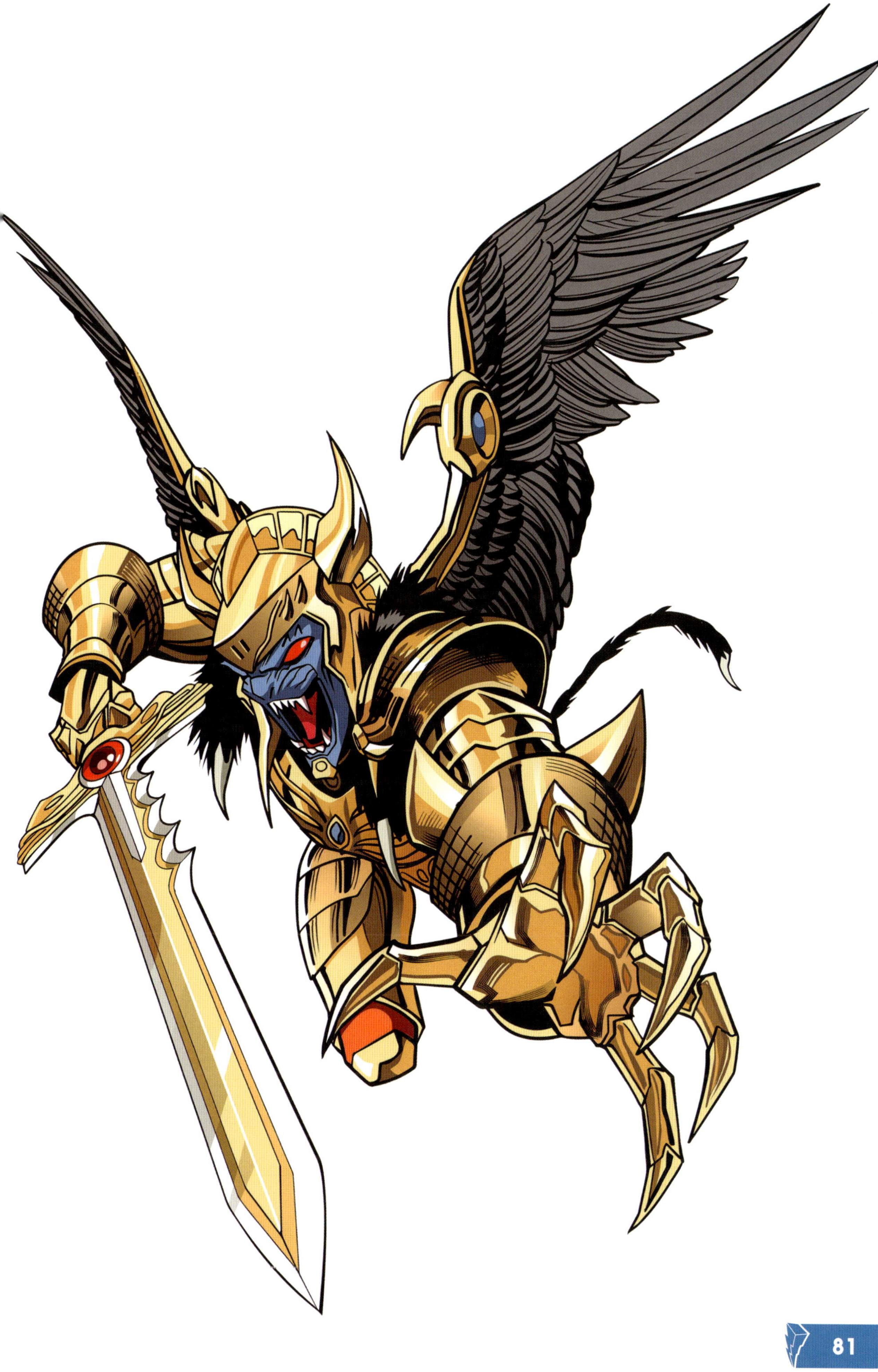

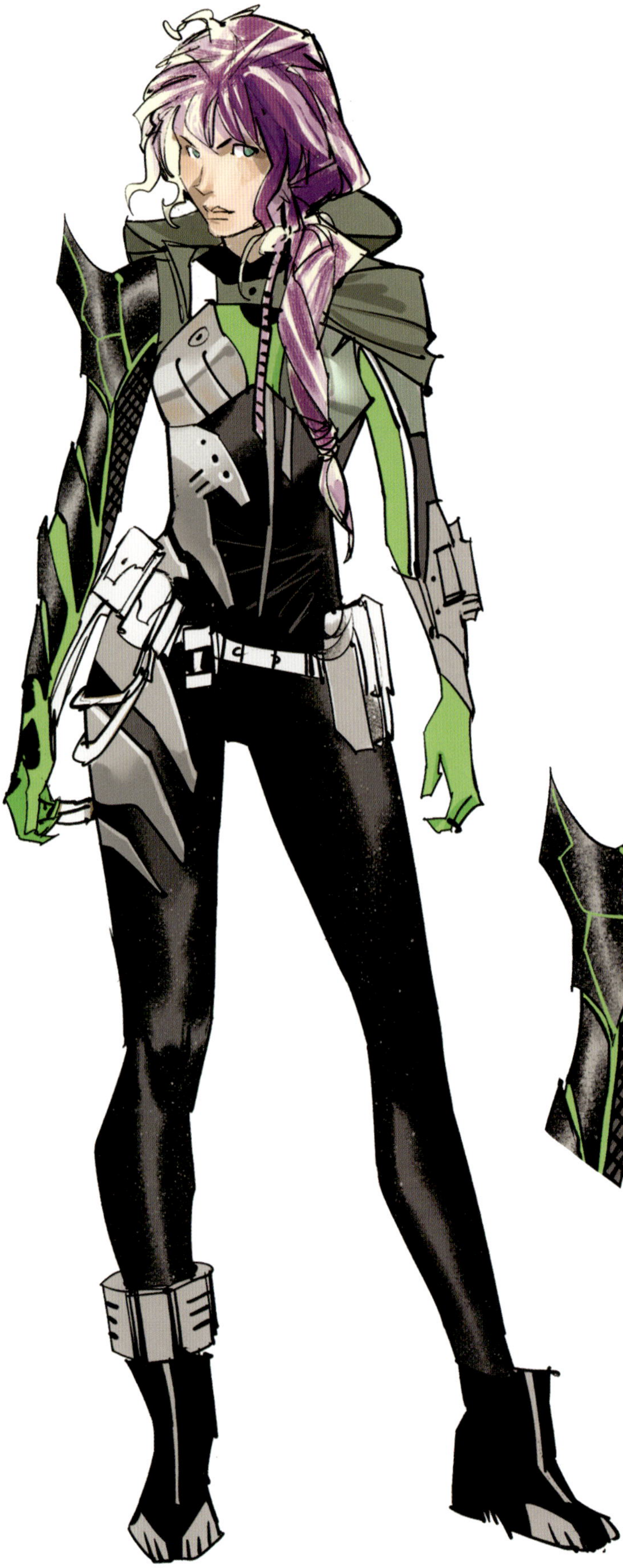

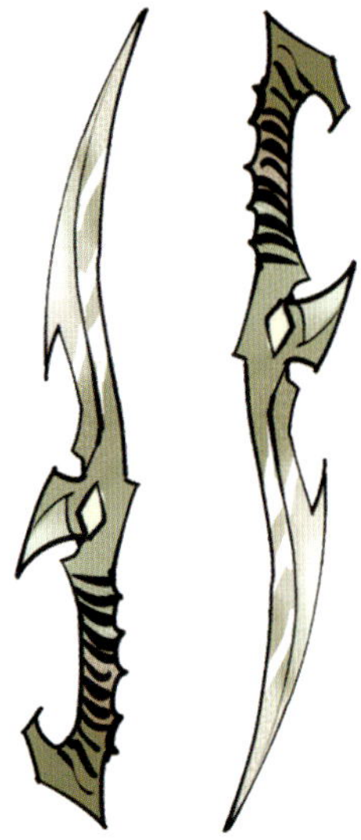

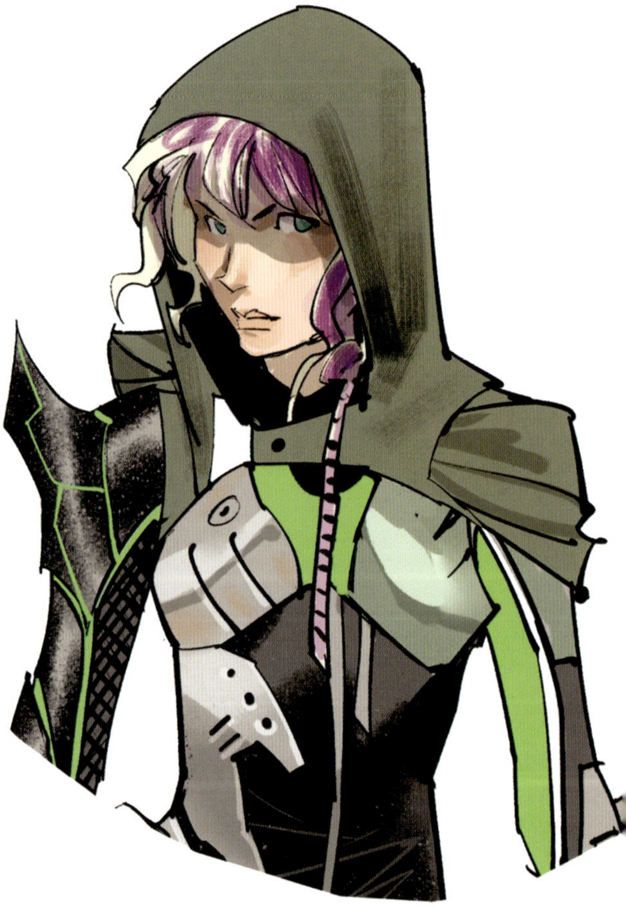

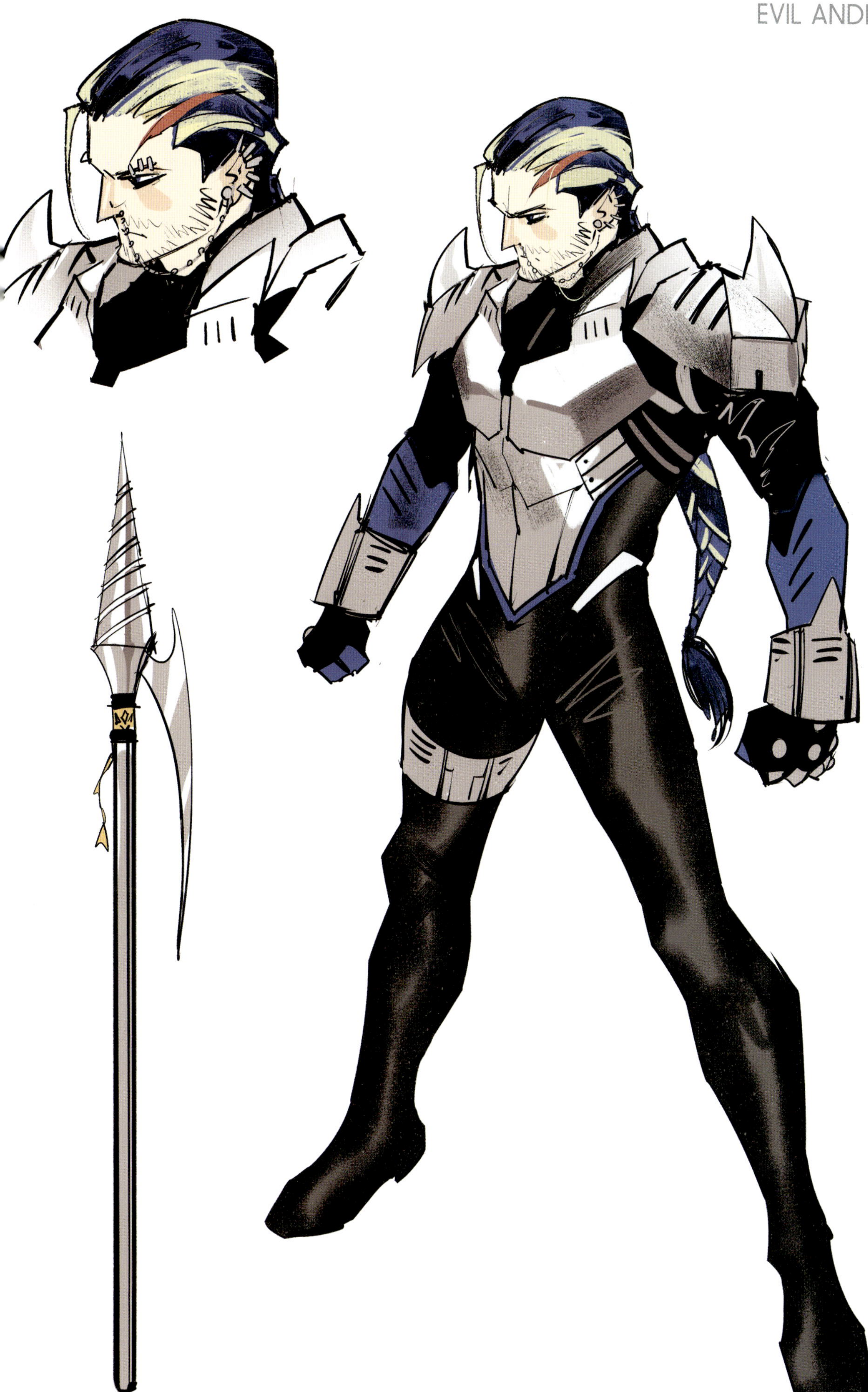

PAGE 86 Mighty Morphin #1 "Every Ranger Ever" Variant Cover

PAGE 87 Power Rangers #1 "Every Ranger Ever" Variant Cover

PAGE 88 Mighty Morphin #2 "Every Ranger Ever" Variant Cover

PAGE 89 Power Rangers #2 "Every Ranger Ever" Variant Cover

PAGES 90-93 Go Go Power Rangers #1 San Diego Comic-Con Connecting Exclusive Cover

PAGE 94 Go Go Power Rangers #1 Cover

PAGE 95 Go Go Power Rangers #2 Cover

PAGE 96 Go Go Power Rangers #3 Cover

PAGE 97 Go Go Power Rangers #4 Cover

PAGE 98 Go Go Power Rangers #5 Cover

PAGE 99 Go Go Power Rangers #6 Cover

PAGE 100 Go Go Power Rangers #7 Cover

PAGE 101 Go Go Power Rangers #8 Cover

PAGE 102 Go Go Power Rangers #9 Cover

PAGE 103 Go Go Power Rangers #10 Cover

PAGE 104 Go Go Power Rangers #11 Cover

PAGE 105 Go Go Power Rangers #12 Cover

PAGE 106 Go Go Power Rangers #13 Cover

PAGE 107 Go Go Power Rangers #14 Cover

PAGE 108 Go Go Power Rangers #15 Cover

PAGE 109 Go Go Power Rangers #16 Cover

PAGE 110 Go Go Power Rangers #8 Variant Cover

PAGE 111 Go Go Power Rangers: Back To School #1 Cover

PAGES 112-113 Go Go Power Rangers: Forever Rangers #1 Cover

PAGE 114 Power Rangers Prime #1 Cover

PAGE 115 Power Rangers Prime #1 Unlockable Variant Cover

PAGE 116 Power Rangers Prime #2 Cover

PAGE 117 Power Rangers Prime #3 Cover

PAGE 118 Power Rangers Prime #4 Cover

PAGE 119 Power Rangers Prime #4 Variant Cover

PAGE 120 Power Rangers Prime #5 Cover

PAGE 121 Power Rangers Prime #6 Cover

PAGE 122 Power Rangers Prime #7 Cover

PAGE 123 Power Rangers Prime #8 Cover

PAGE 124 Mighty Morphin Power Rangers #18 Versus Variant Cover

PAGE 125 Mighty Morphin Power Rangers #19 Versus Variant Cover

PAGE 126 Mighty Morphin Power Rangers #20 Versus Variant Cover

PAGE 127 Mighty Morphin Power Rangers #21 Versus Variant Cover

PAGE 128 Mighty Morphin Power Rangers #22 Versus Variant Cover

PAGE 129 Mighty Morphin Power Rangers #23 Versus Variant Cover

PAGE 130 Mighty Morphin Power Rangers #24 Versus Variant Cover

COVERS

PAGE 131 Power Rangers Universe #1 Cover

PAGE 132 Power Rangers Universe #2 Cover

PAGE 133 Power Rangers Universe #3 Cover

PAGE 134 Power Rangers Universe #4 Cover

PAGE 135 Power Rangers Universe #5 Cover

PAGE 136 Power Rangers Universe #6 Cover

PAGE 137 Power Rangers: Drakkon New Dawn #1 Variant

PAGE 138 Mighty Morphin Power Rangers #17 Versus Variant Cover

PAGE 139 Mighty Morphin Power Rangers: The Return #1 Variant Cover

PAGE 140 Power Rangers Unlimited: Heir to Darkness #1 Cover

PAGE 141 Power Rangers Unlimited: The Coinless #1 Cover

PAGE 142 Mighty Morphin #10 Variant Cover

PAGE 143 Power Rangers Unlimited: Edge of Darkness #1 Cover

PAGE 144 Ranger Academy #5 Variant Cover

PAGE 145 Mighty Morphin Power Rangers 30th Anniversary Special #1 Cover

PAGE 146 Mighty Morphin Power Rangers: Darkest Hour #1 FOC Reveal Variant Cover

PAGE 147 Mighty Morphin Power Rangers 2017 Annual #1 Variant Cover

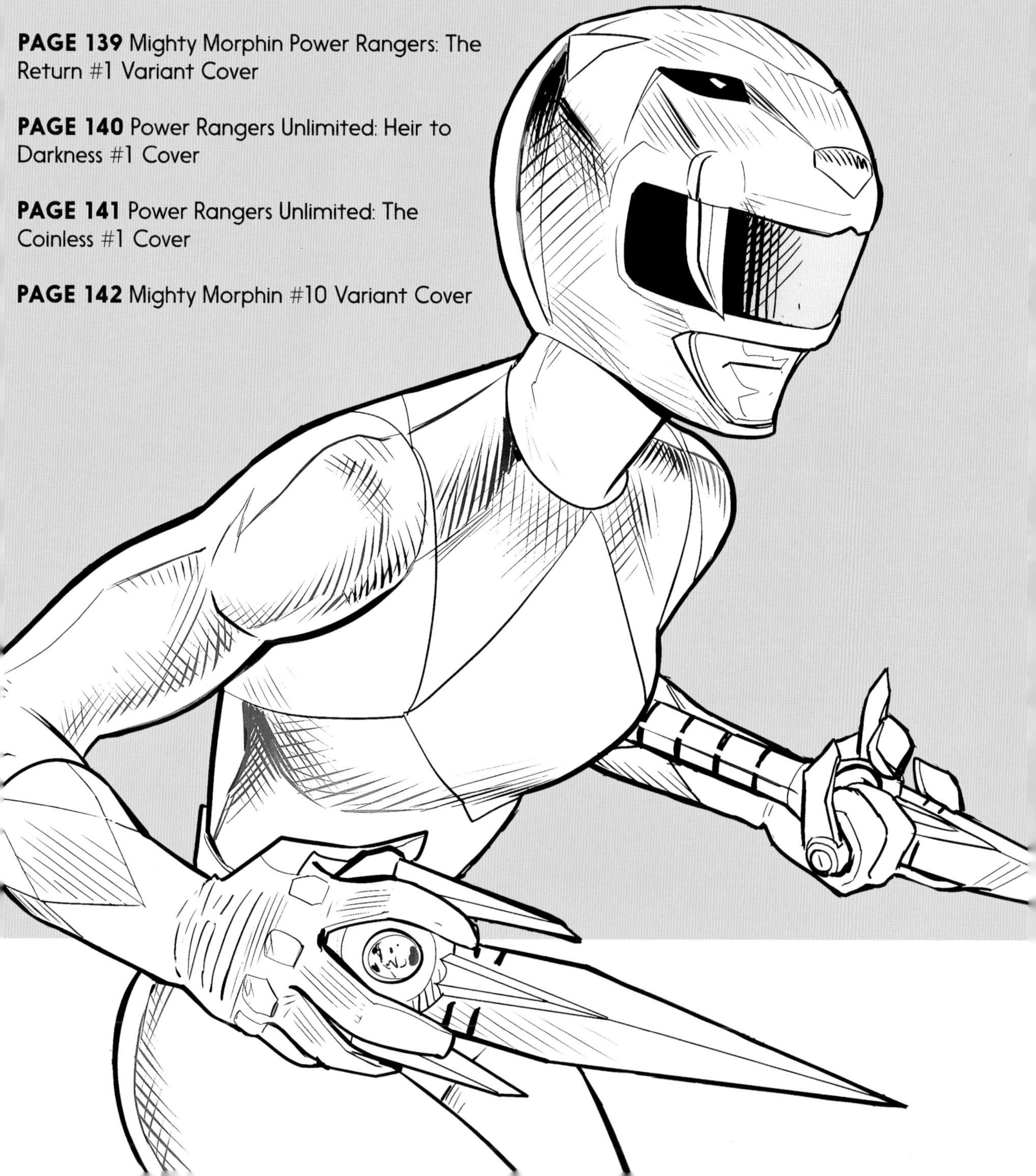

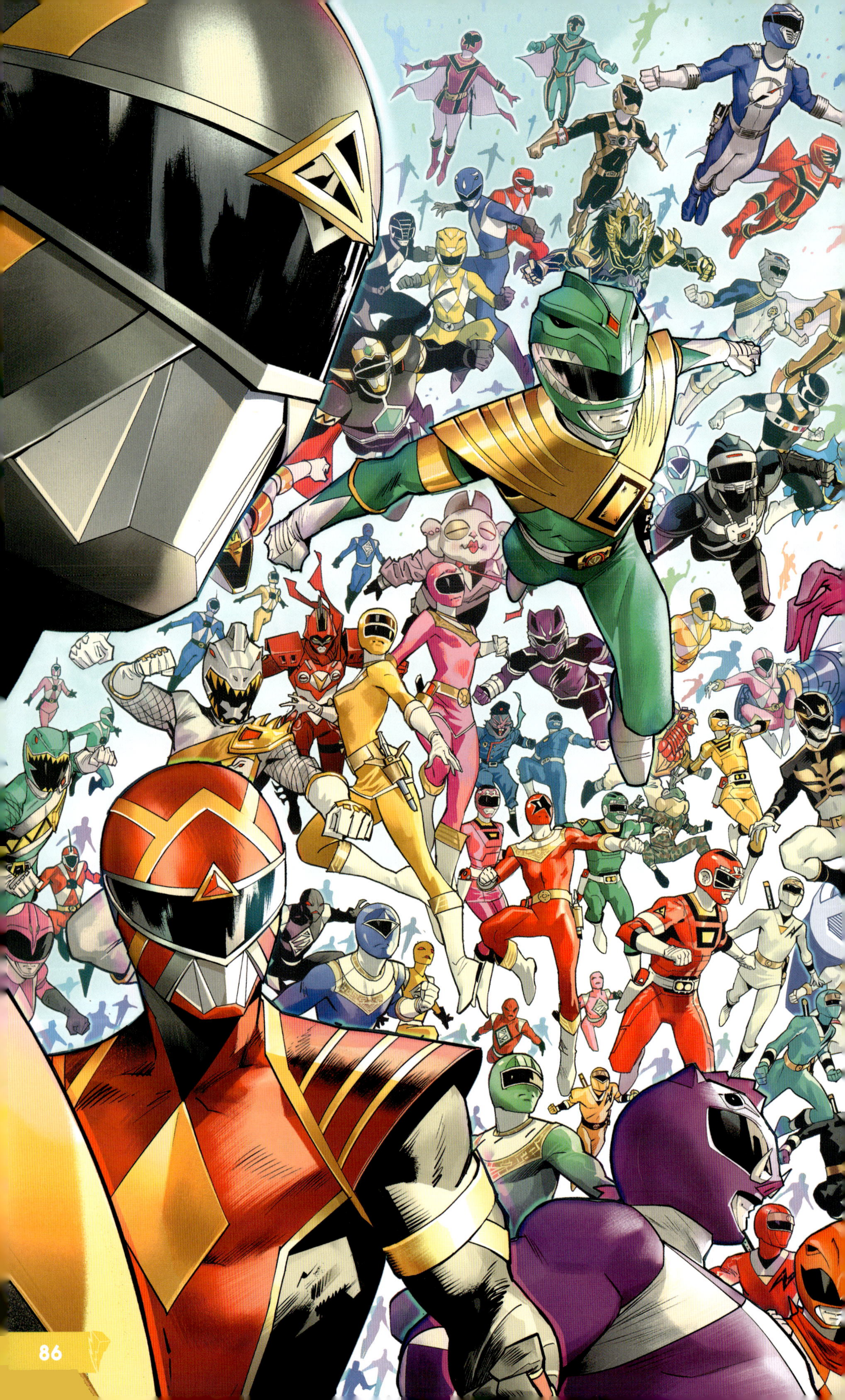

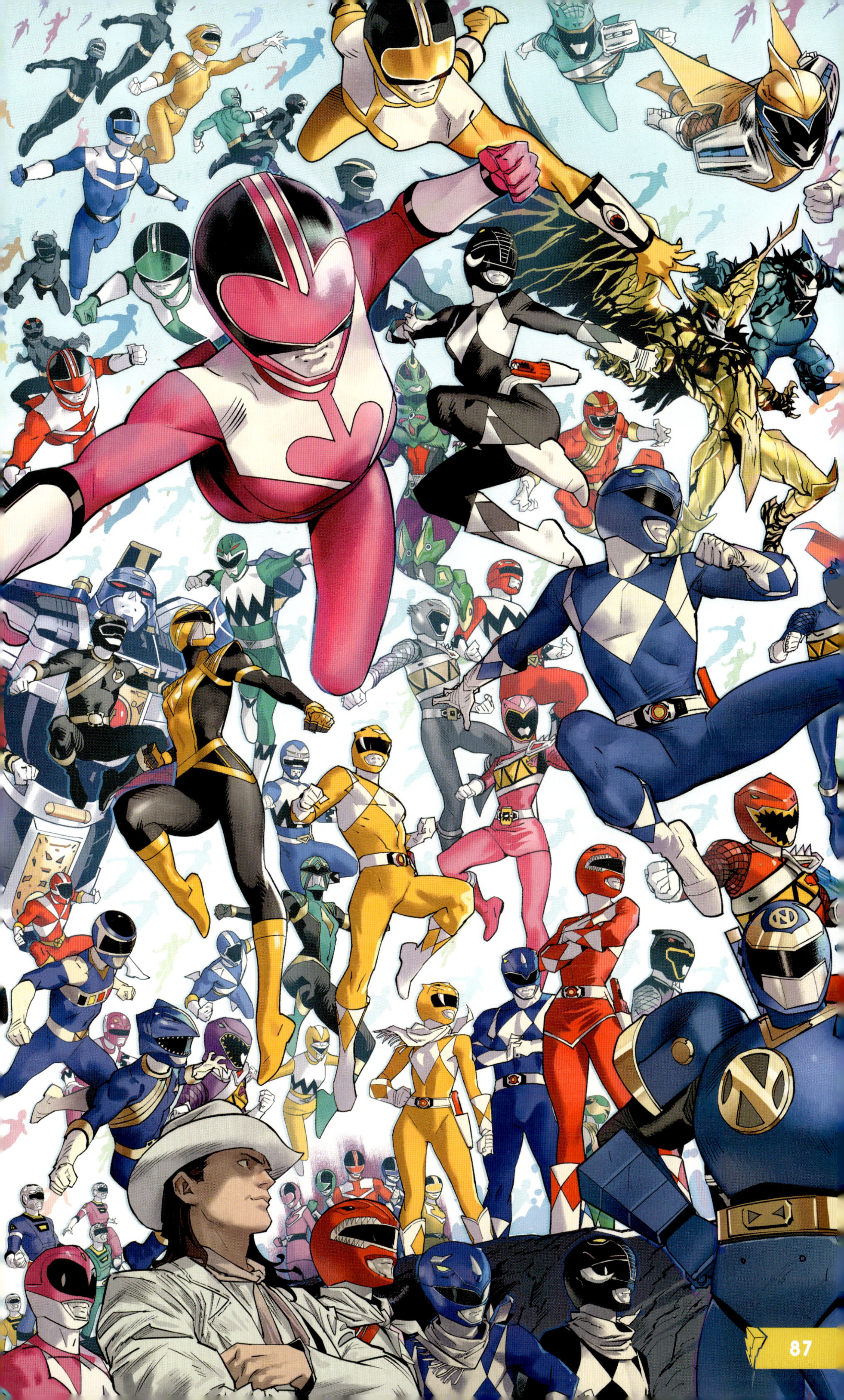

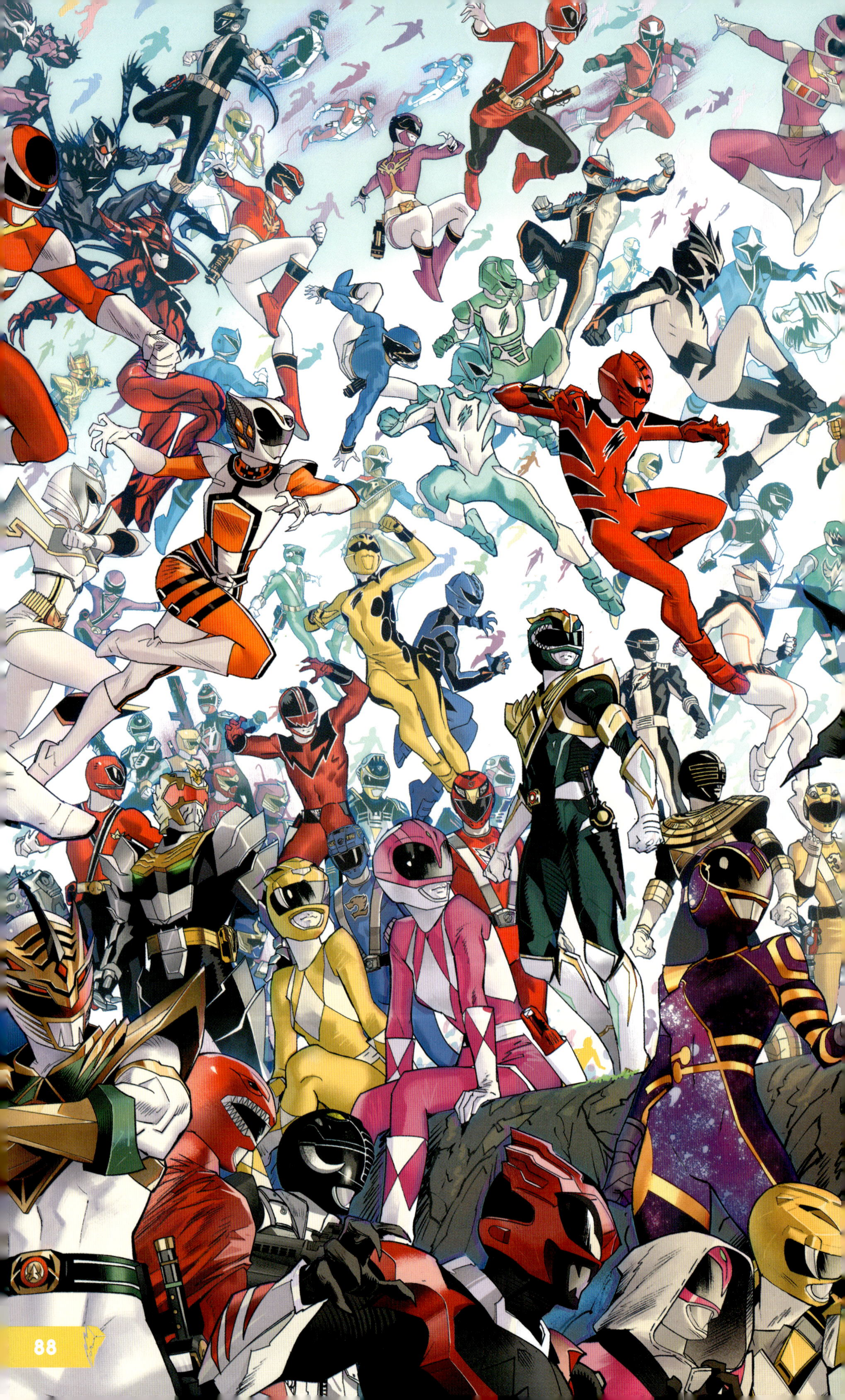

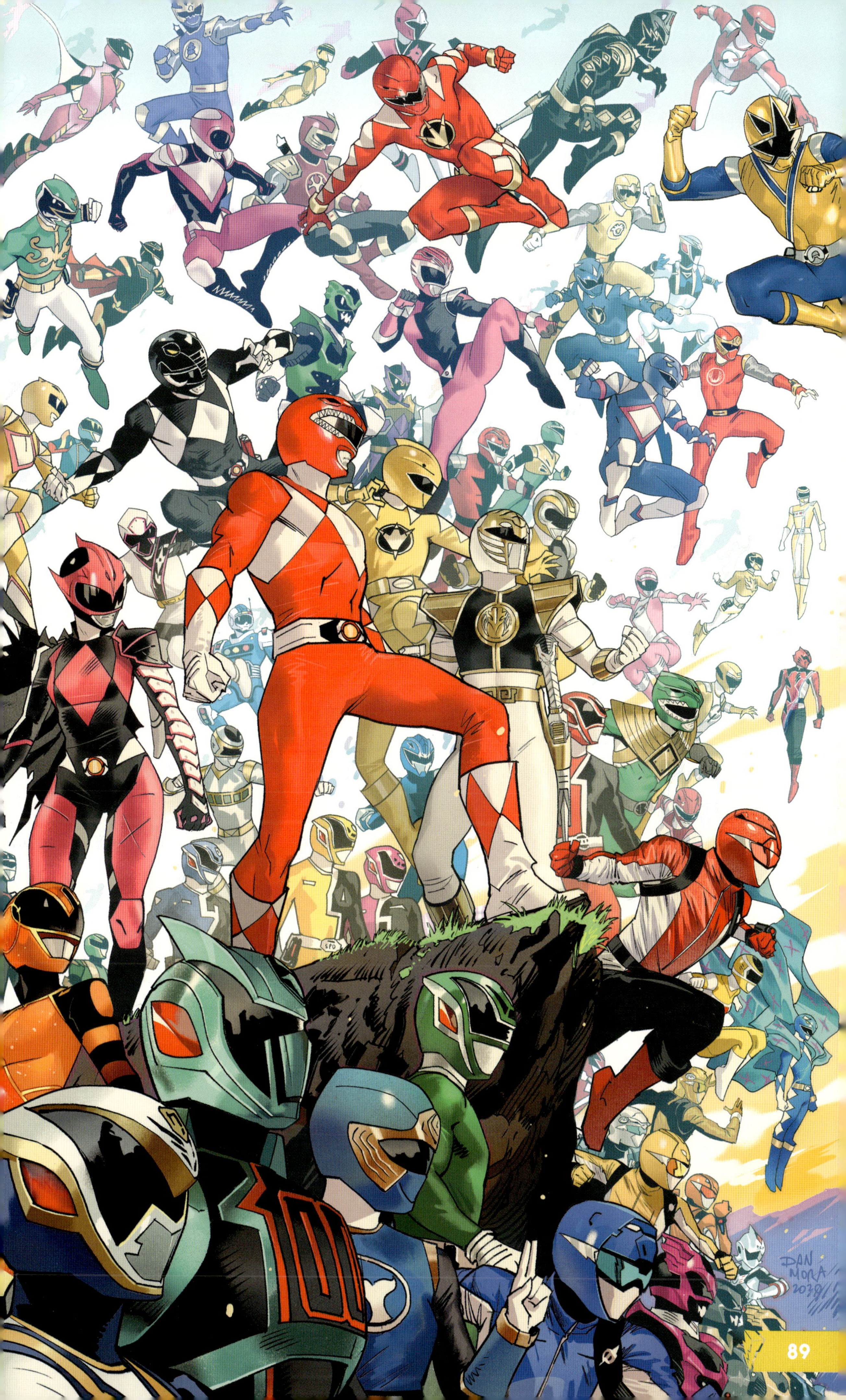
DAN
MORA
2018

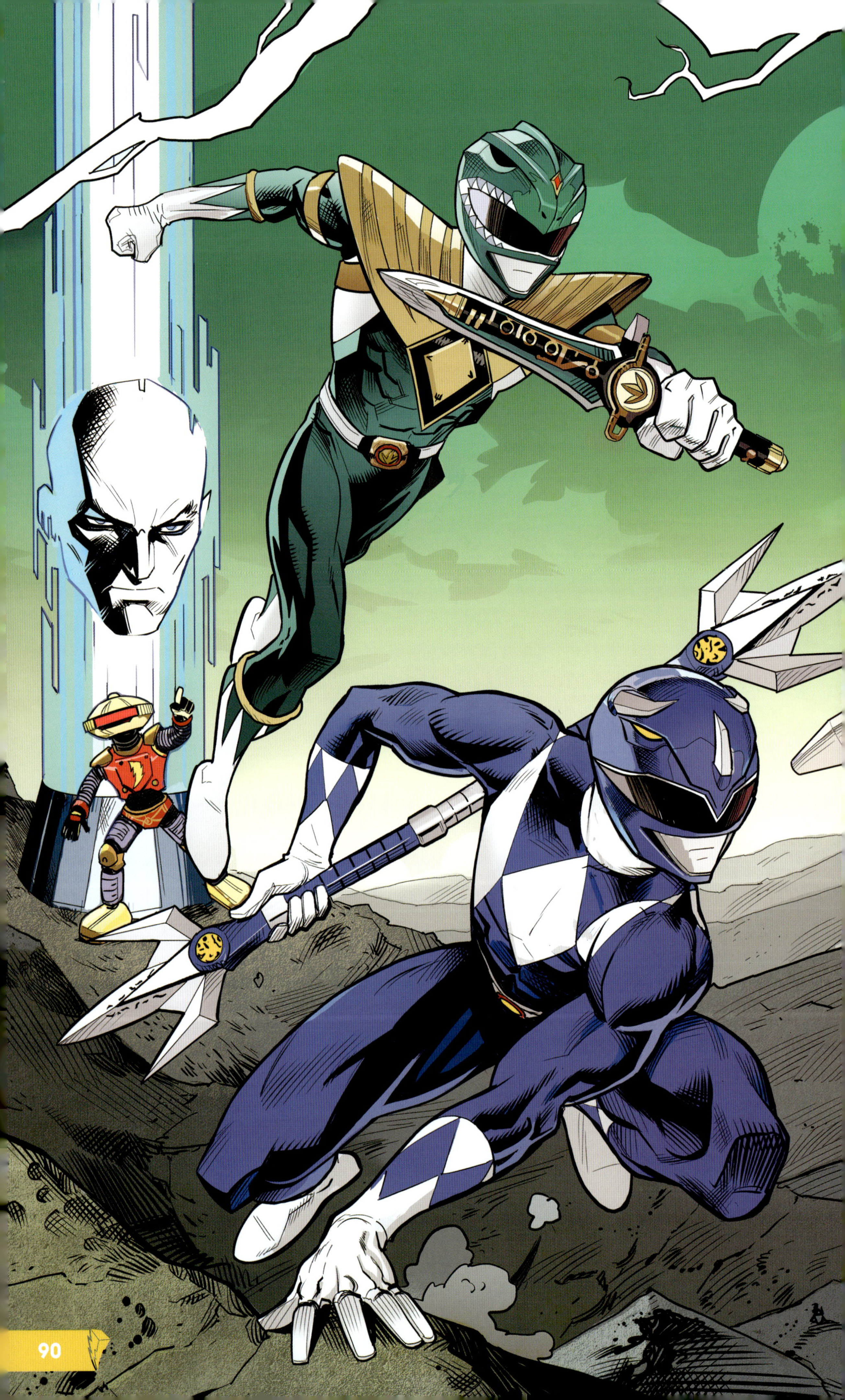

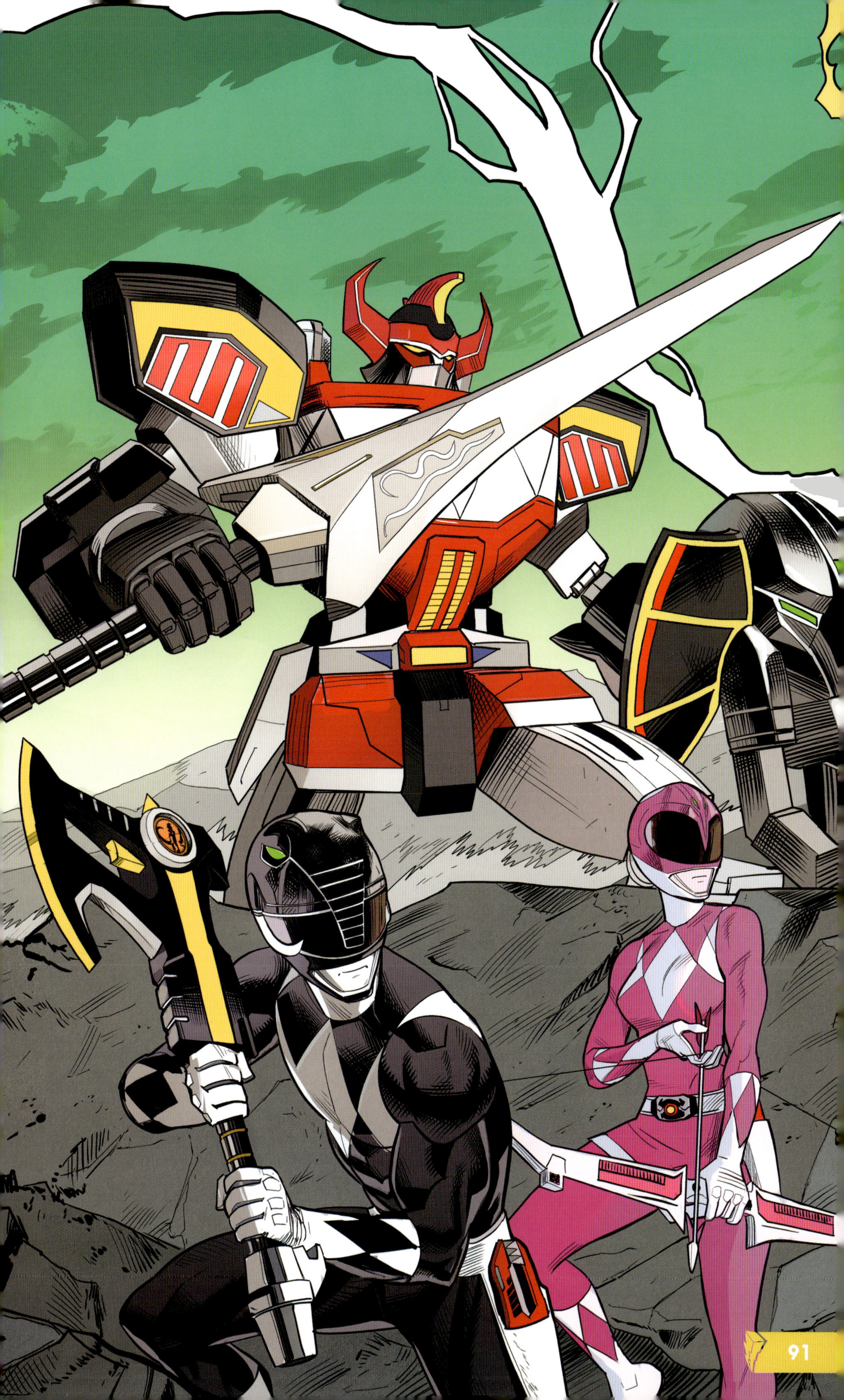

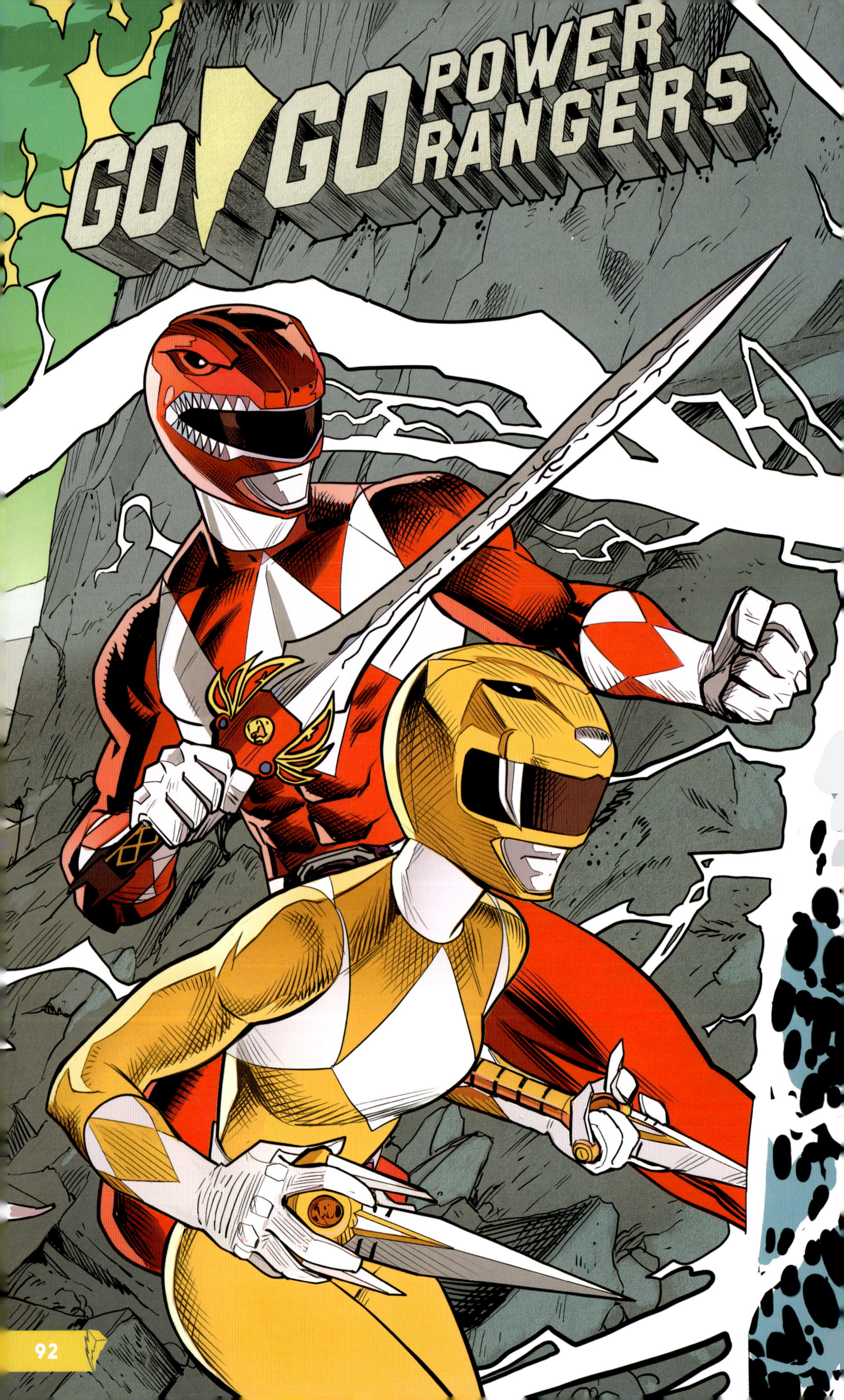
GO GO POWER RANGERS

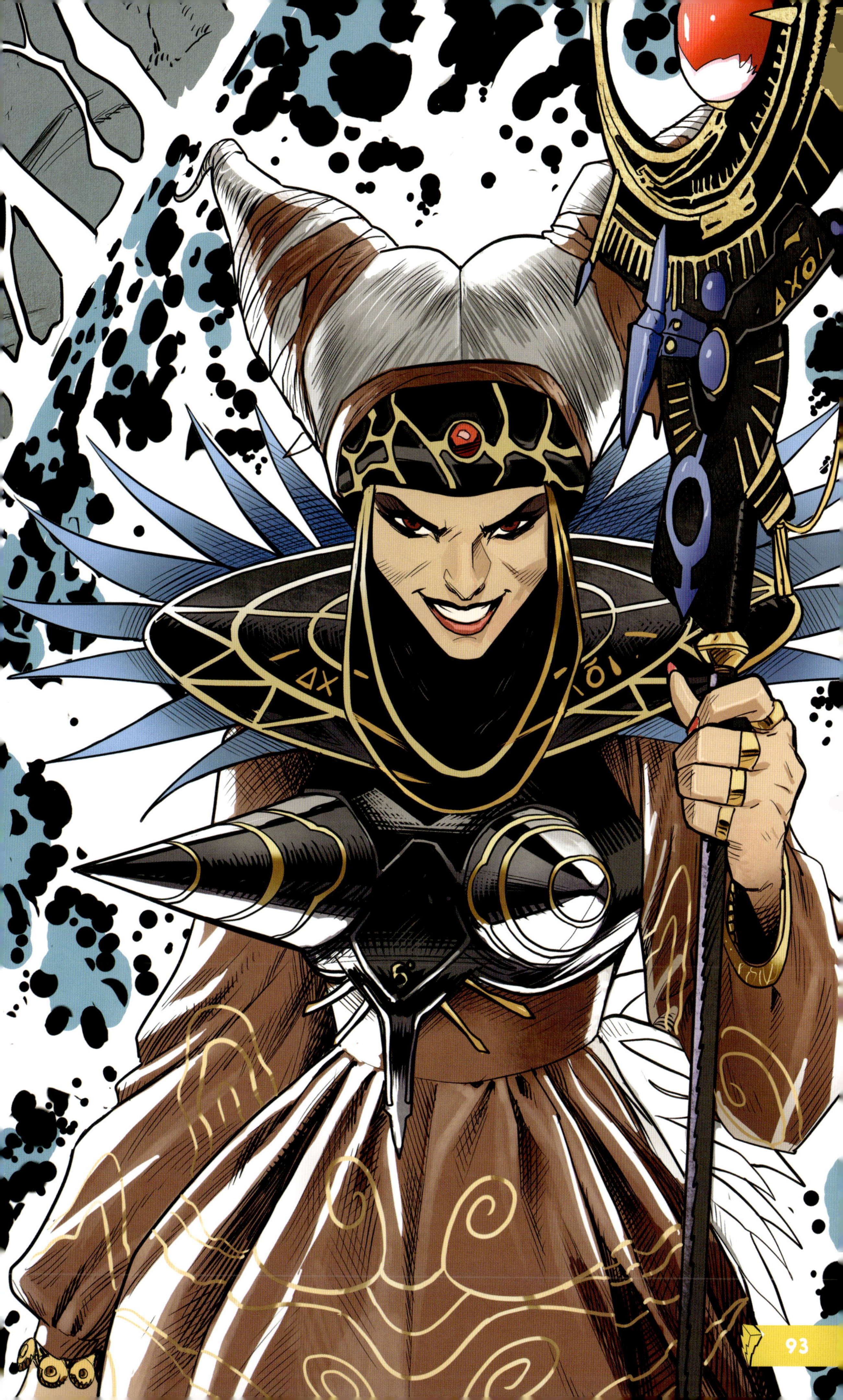

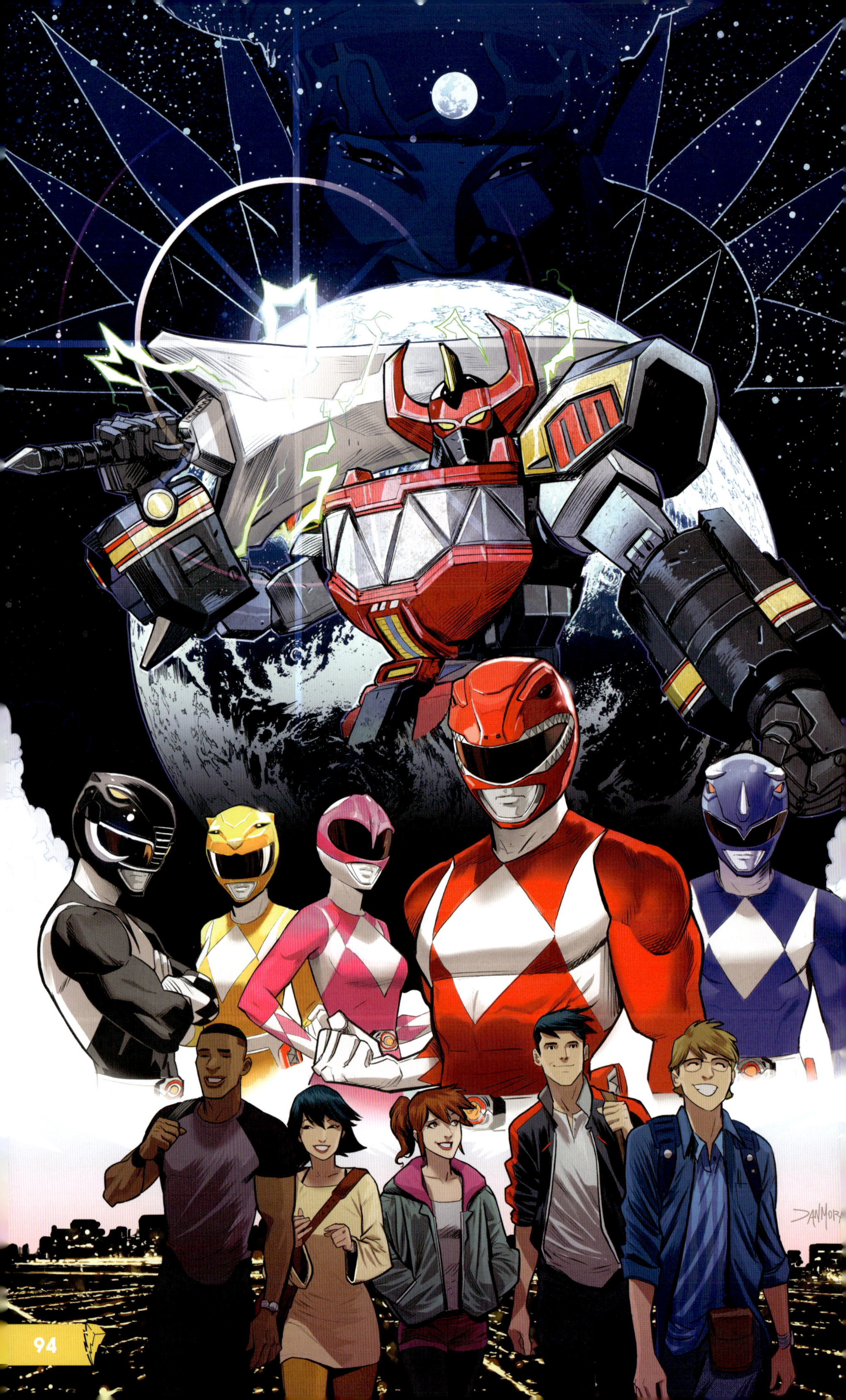
DANMORA

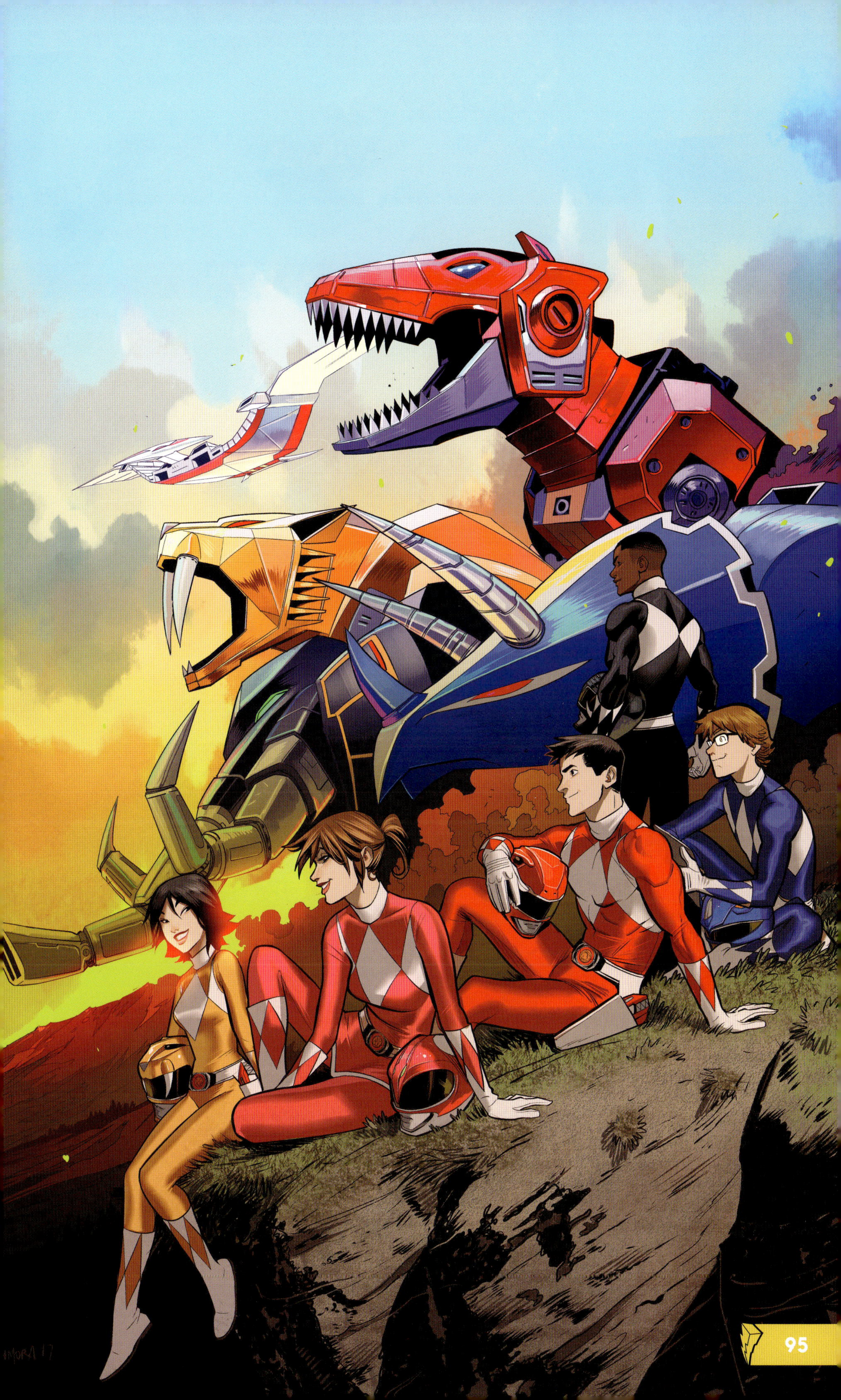

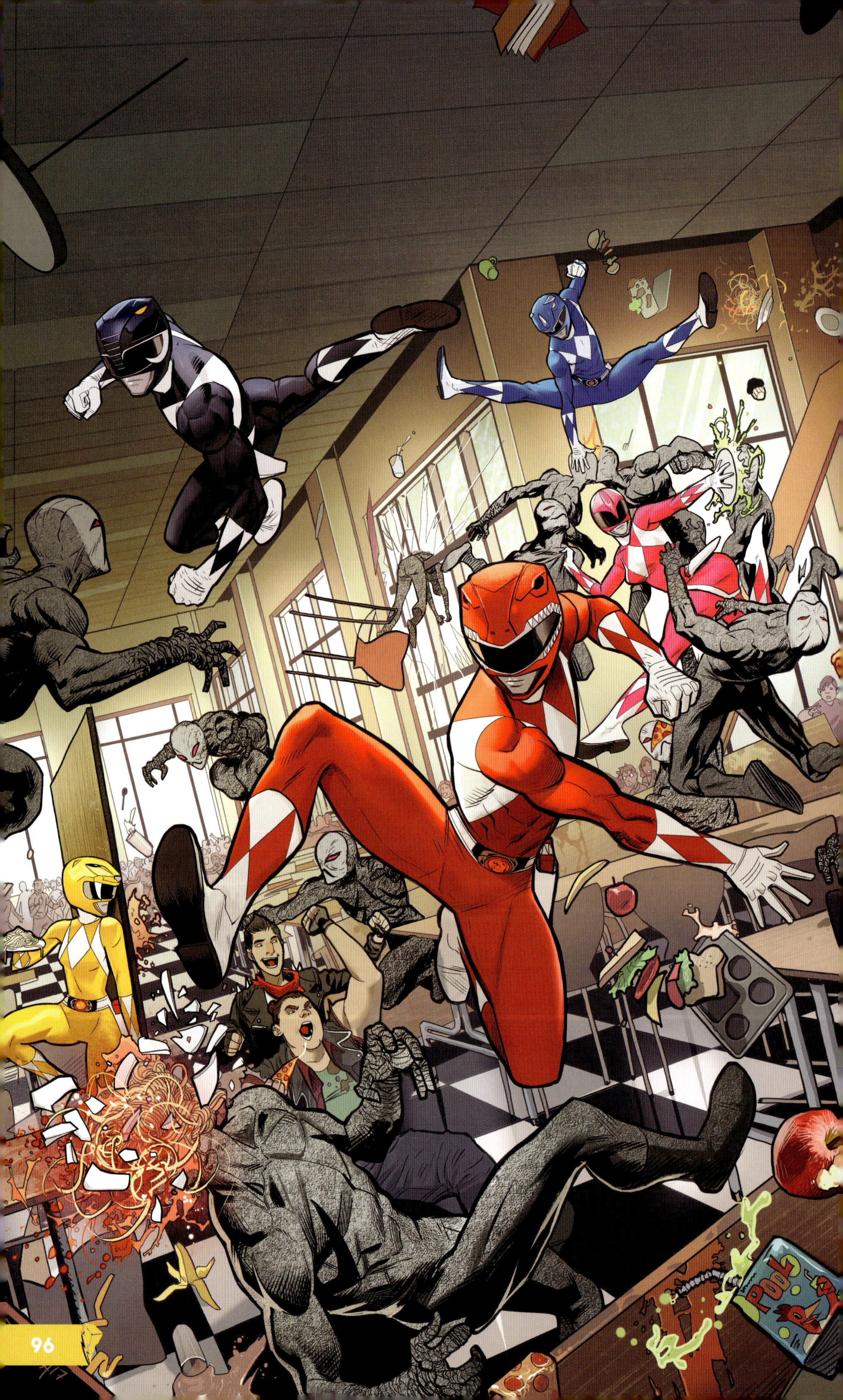

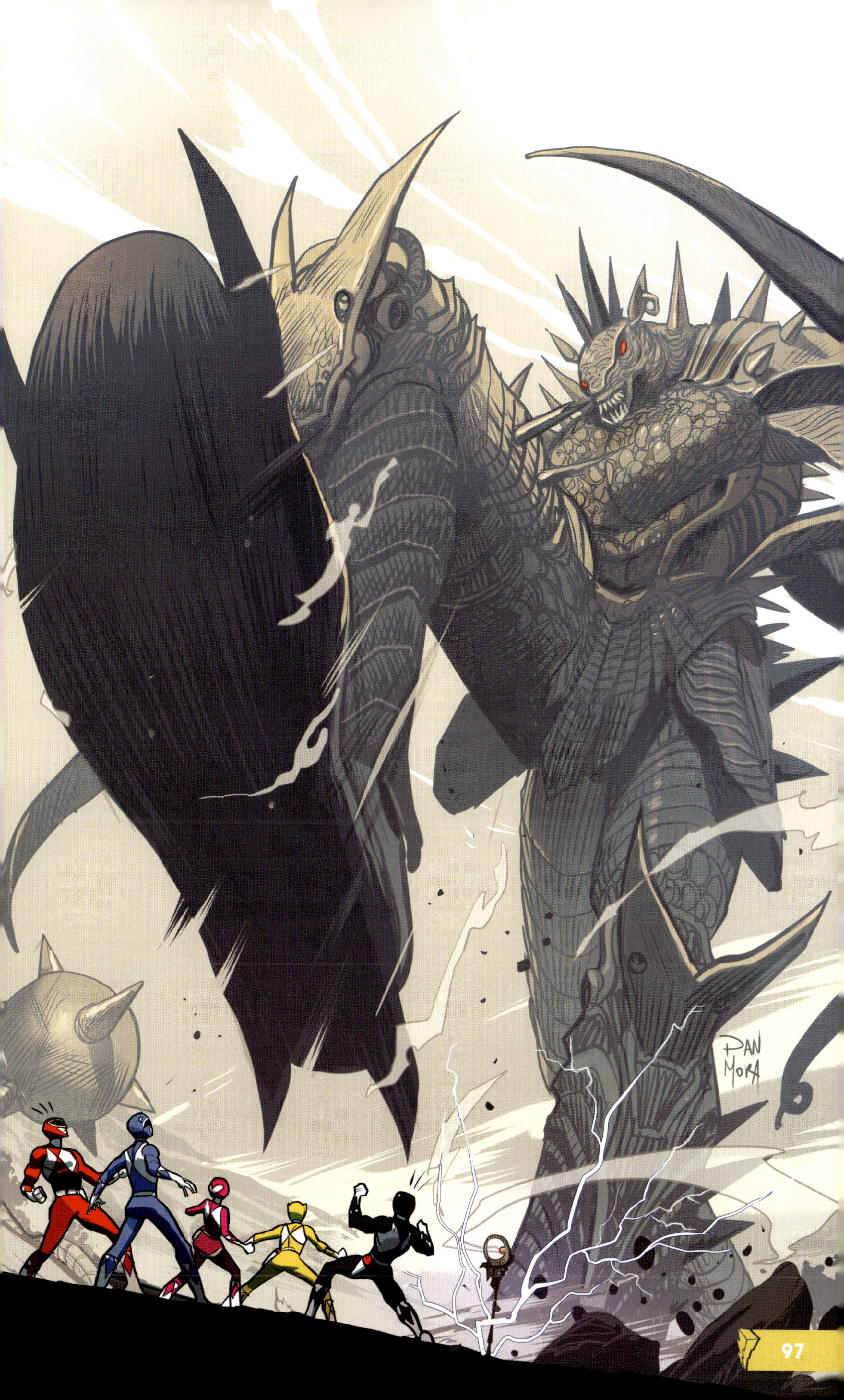
DAN
MORA

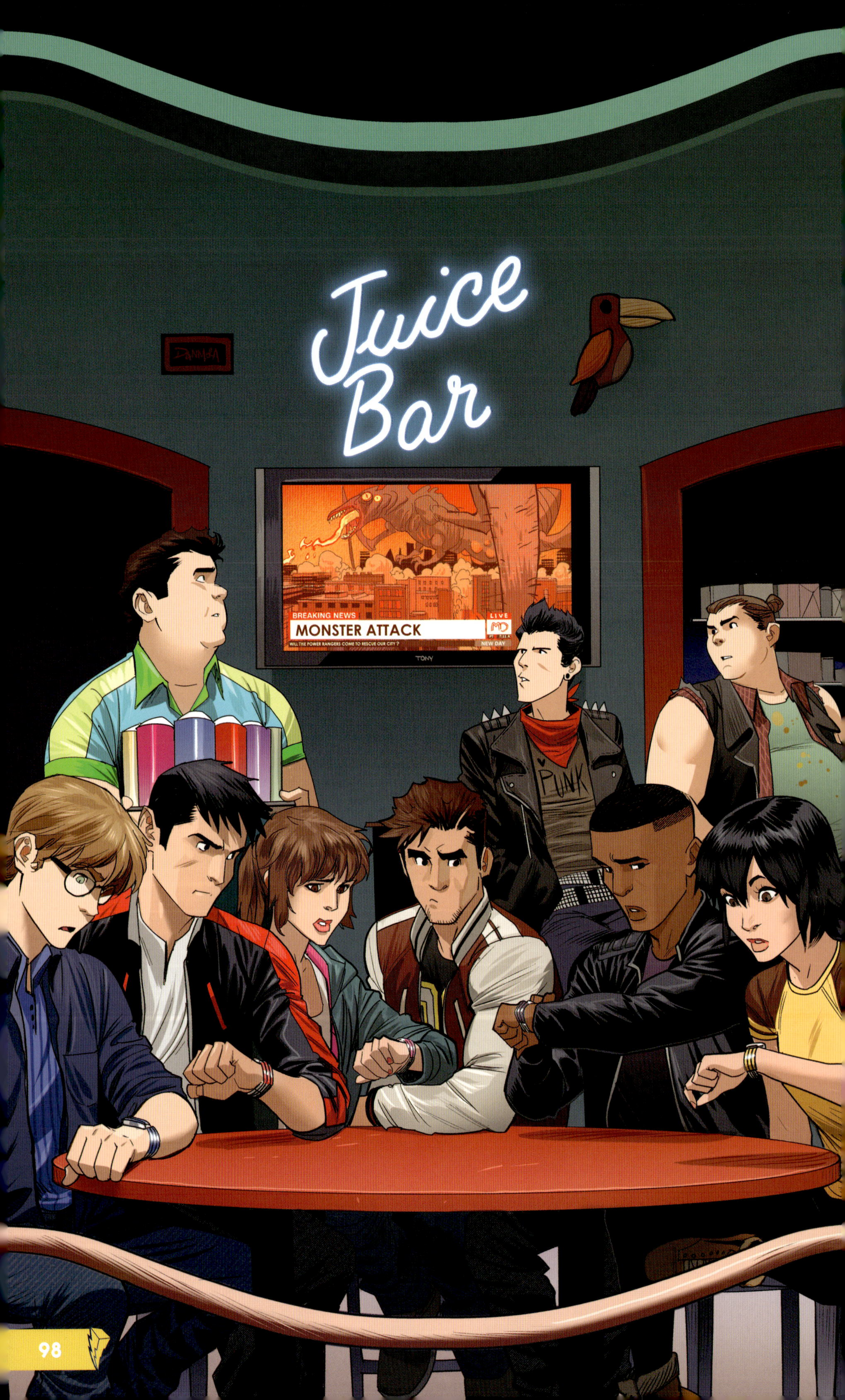
Juice Bar
BREAKING NEWS
MONSTER ATTACK
LIVE
MD
WILL THE POWER RANGERS COME TO RESCUE OUR CITY ?
NEW DAY
TONY
PUNK

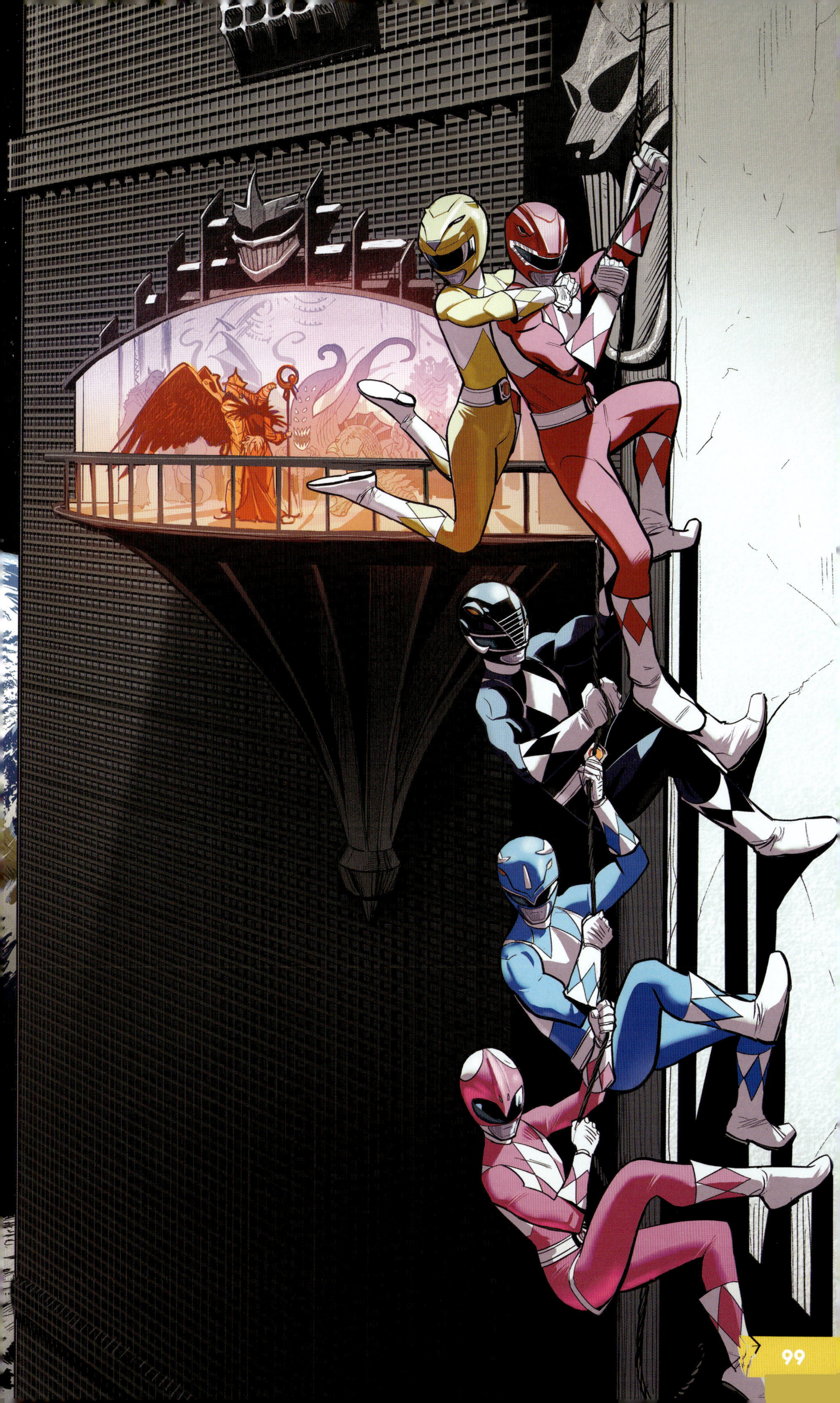

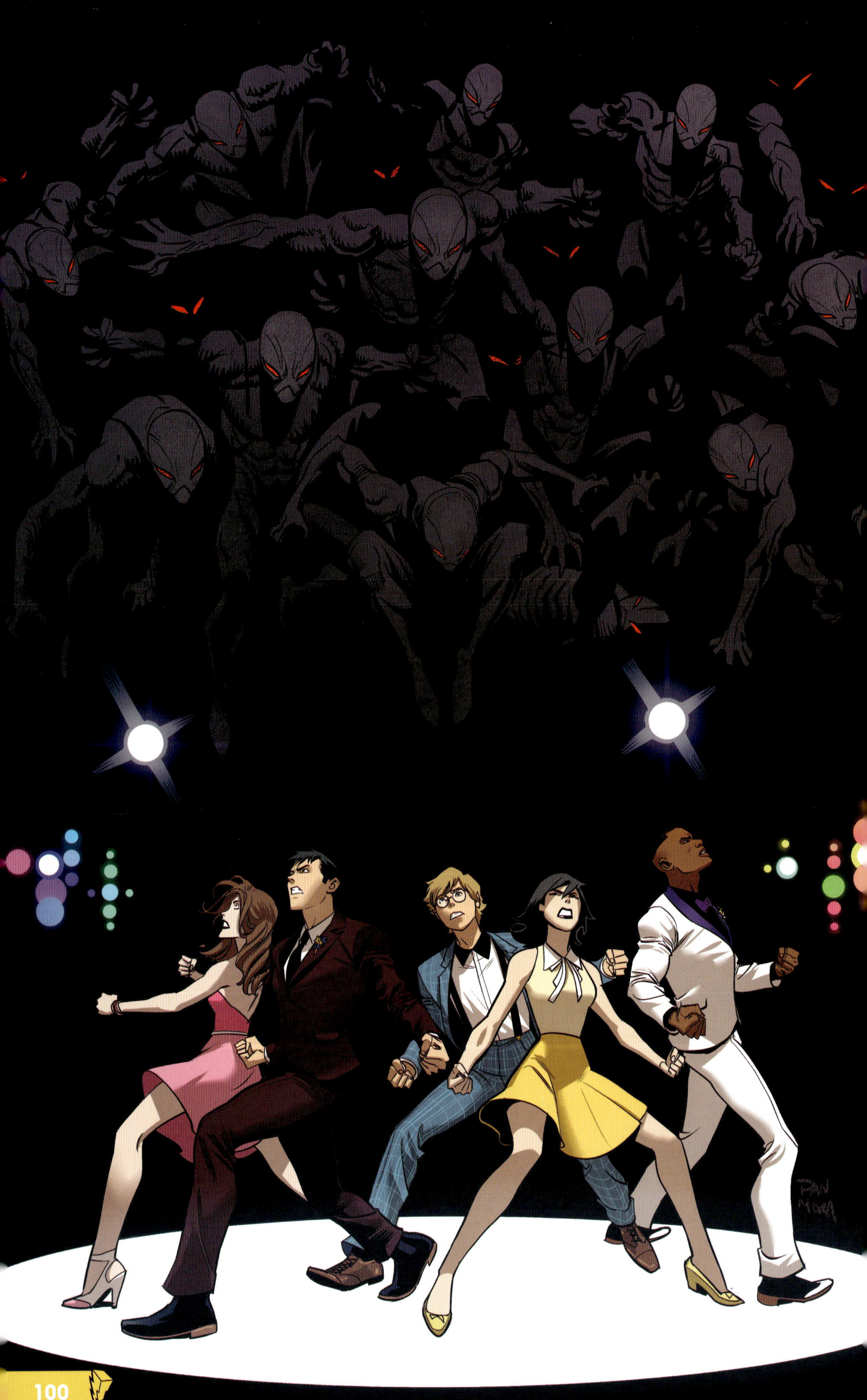

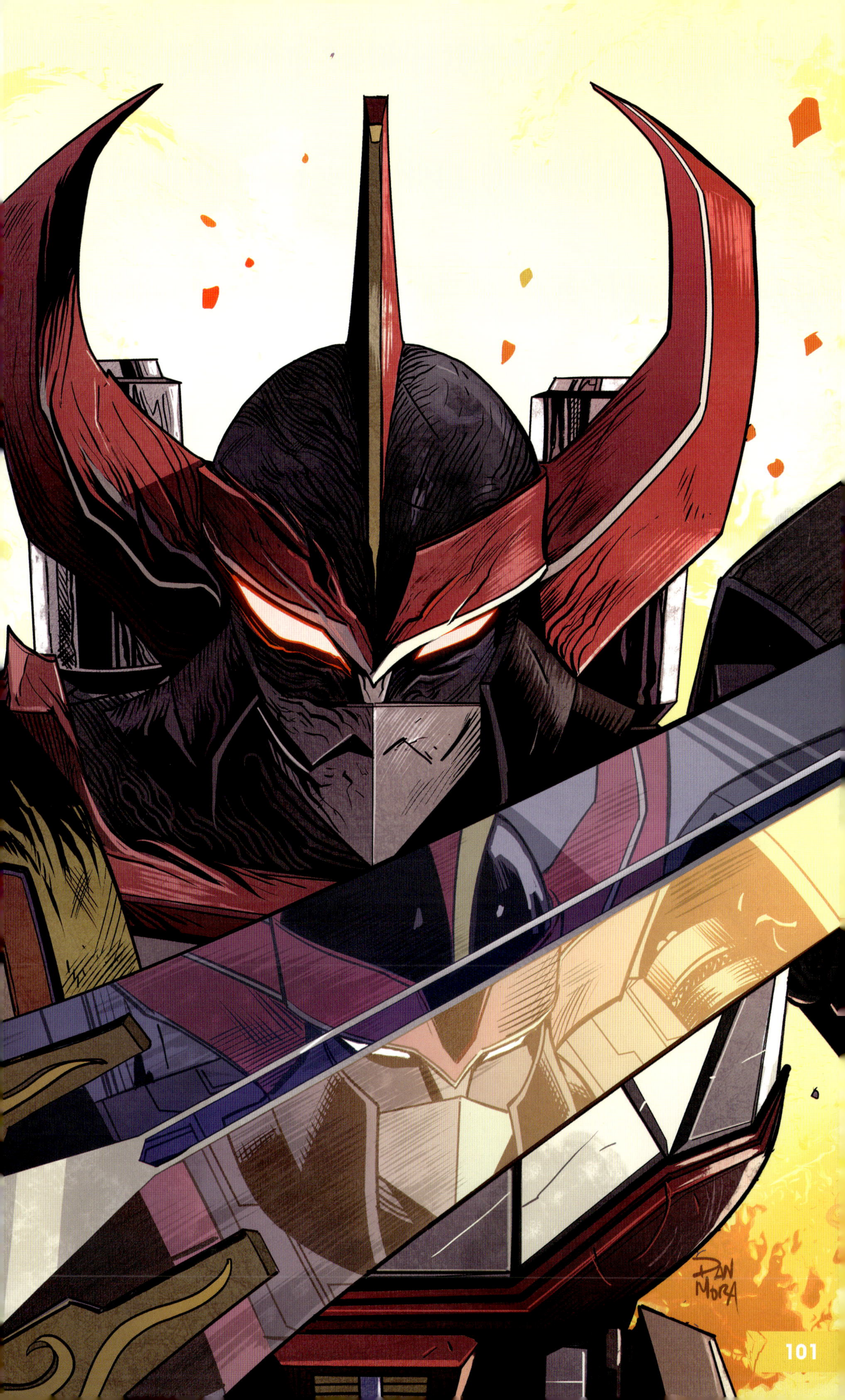
DAN MORA

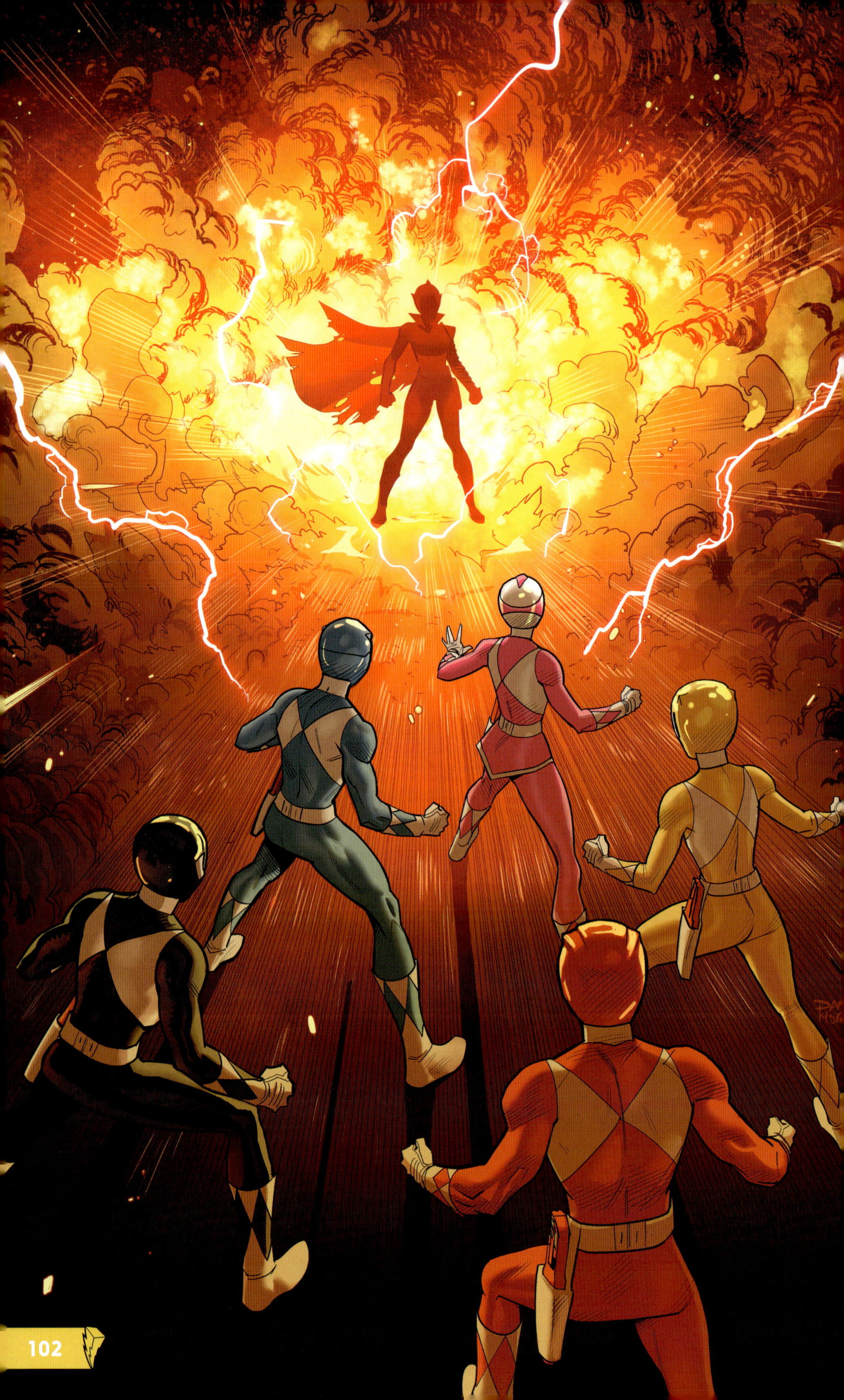

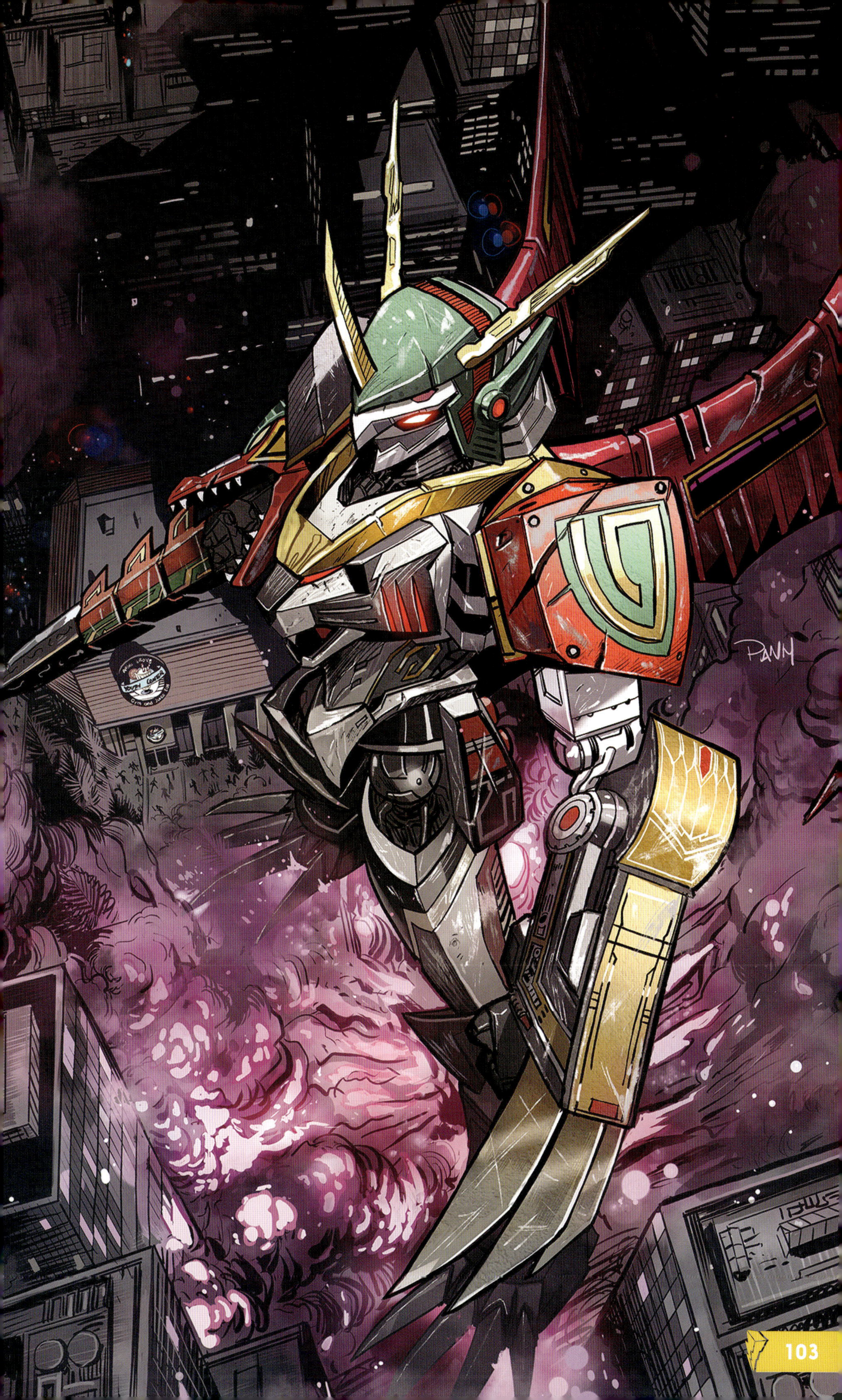

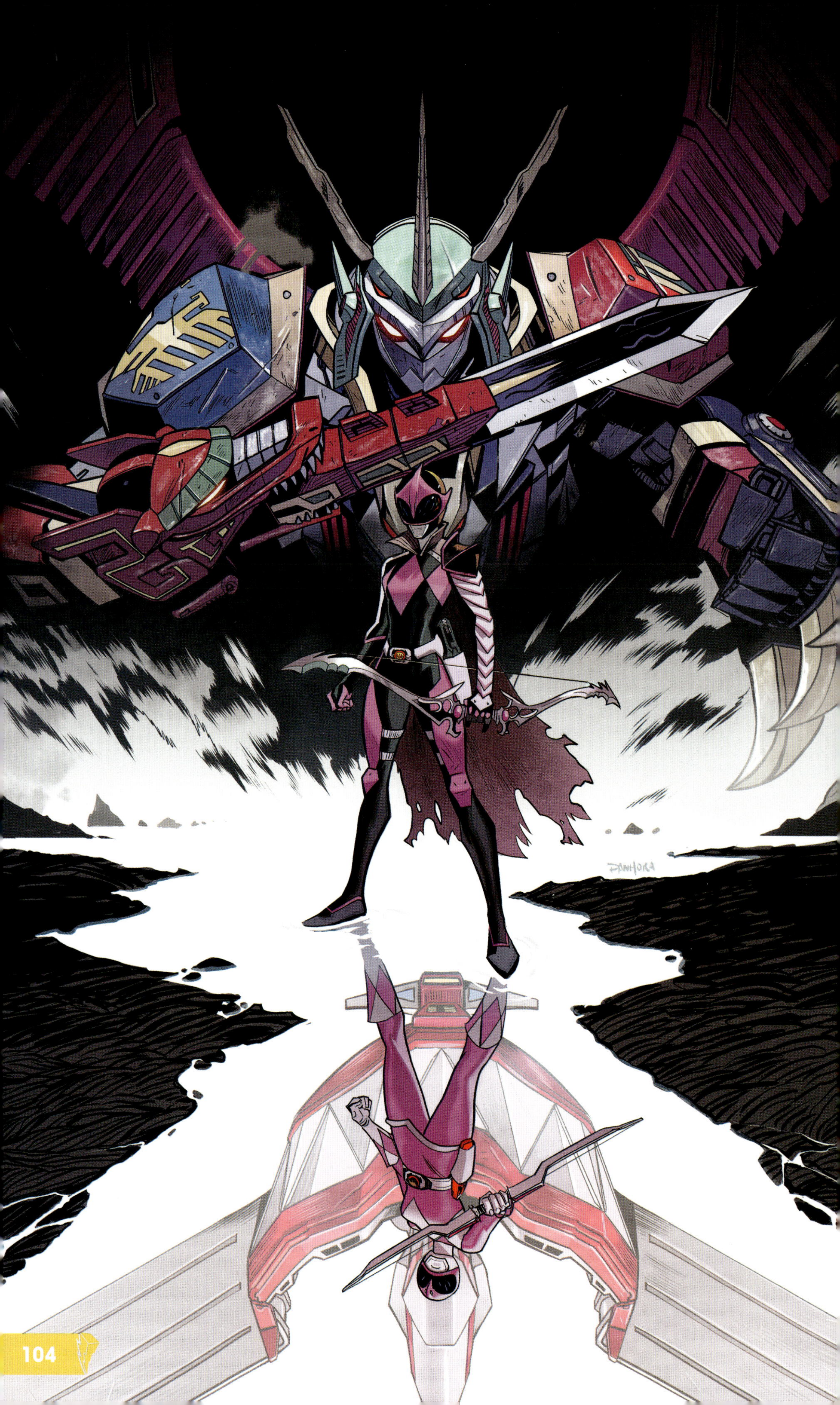

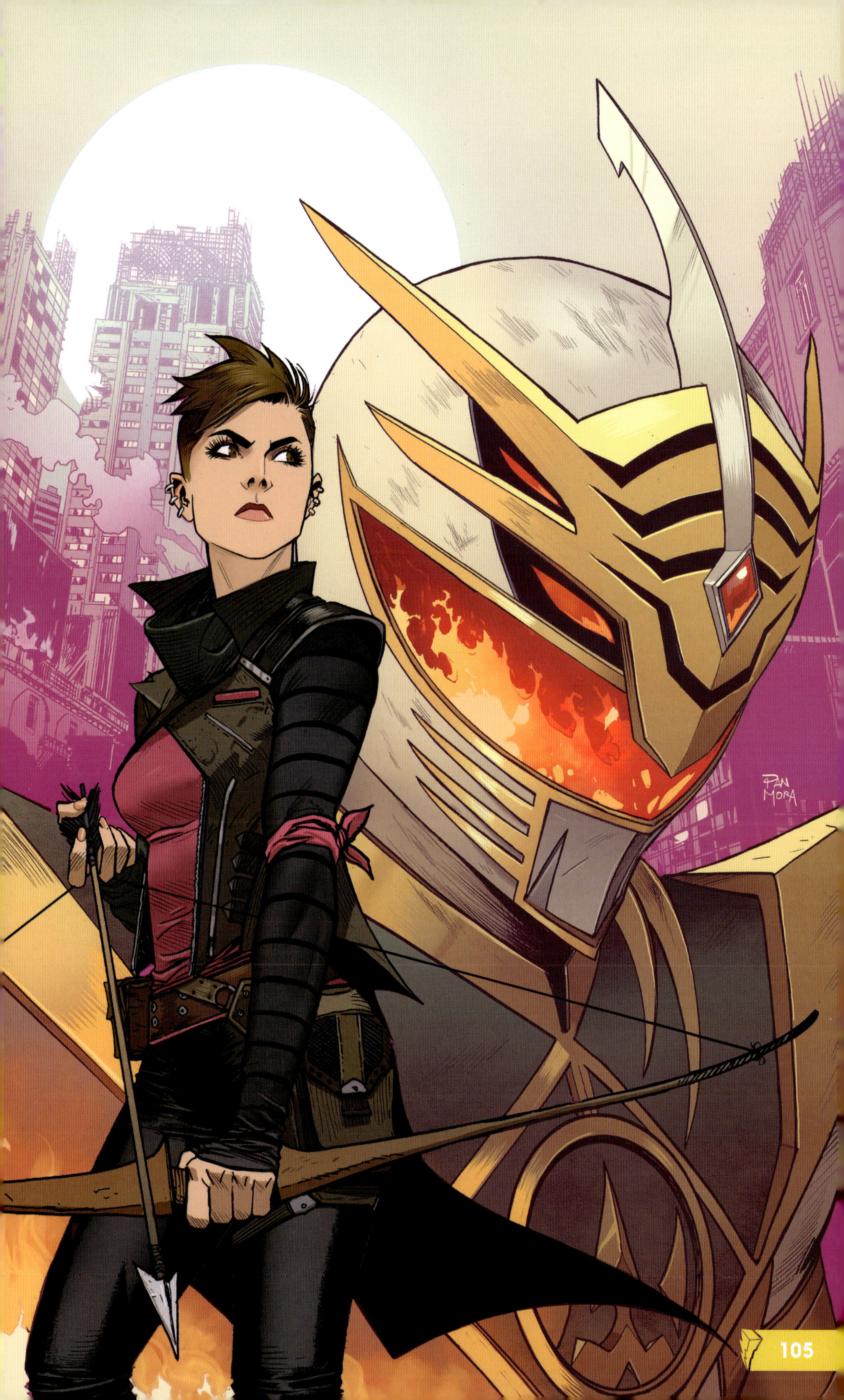
DAN MORA

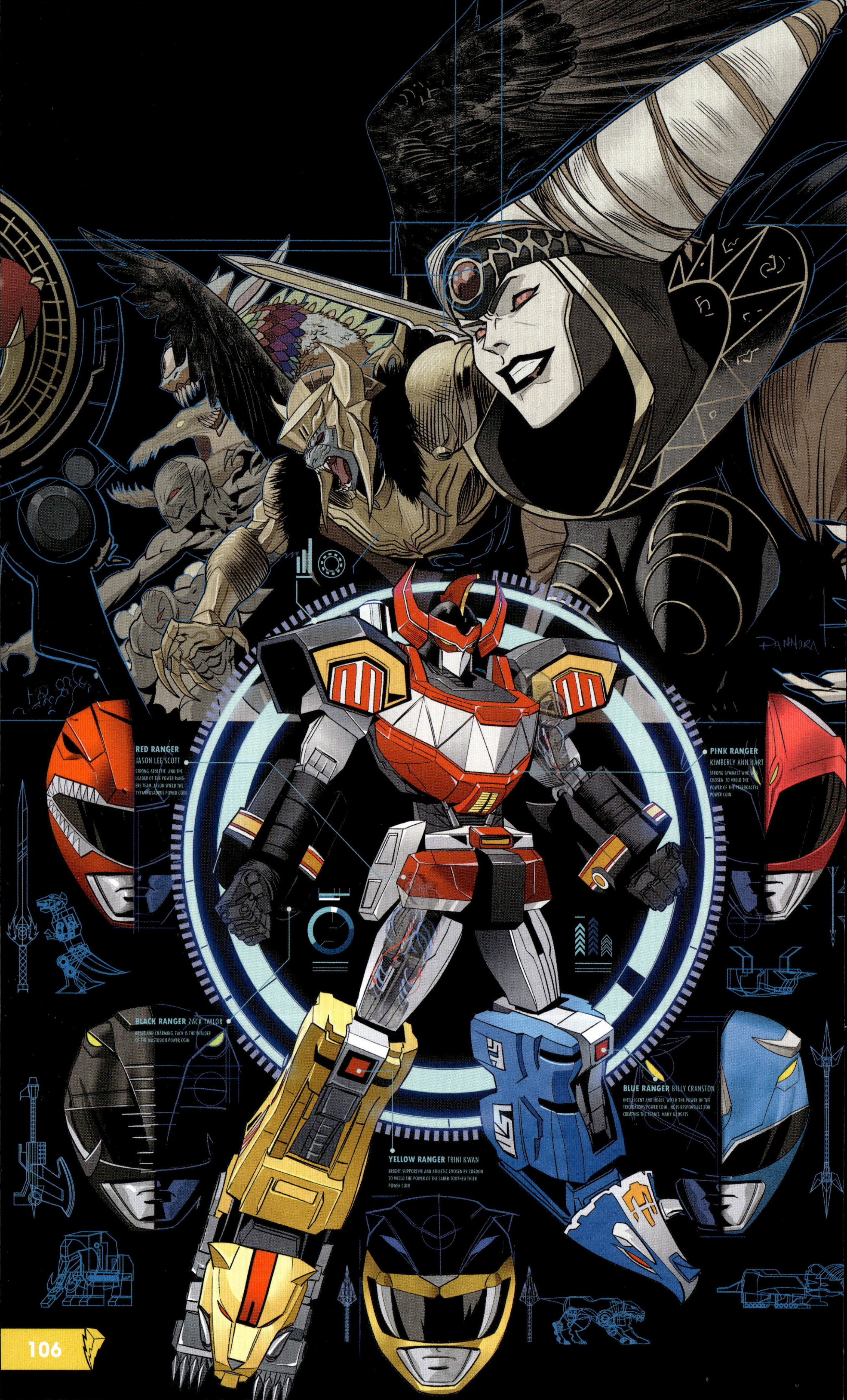
RED RANGER
JASON LEE SCOTT
STRONG, ATHLETIC AND THE LEADER OF THE POWER RANGERS TEAM, JASON WIELD THE TYRANNOSAURUS POWER COIN
PINK RANGER
KIMBERLY ANN HART
STRONG GYMNAST WHO
CHOSEN TO WIELD THE POWER OF THE PTERODACTYL POWER COIN
BLACK RANGER ZACK TAYLOR
BRAVE AND CHARMING, ZACK IS THE WIELDER OF THE MASTODON POWER COIN
BLUE RANGER BILLY CRANSTON
INTELLIGENT AND NOBLE, WIELD THE POWER OF THE TRICERATOPS POWER COIN , HE IS RESPONSIBLE FOR CREATING THE TEAM'S MANY GADGETS
YELLOW RANGER TRINI KWAN
BRIGHT, SUPPORTIVE AND ATHLETIC CHOSEN BY ZORDON TO WIELD THE POWER OF THE SABER-TOOTHED TIGER POWER COIN

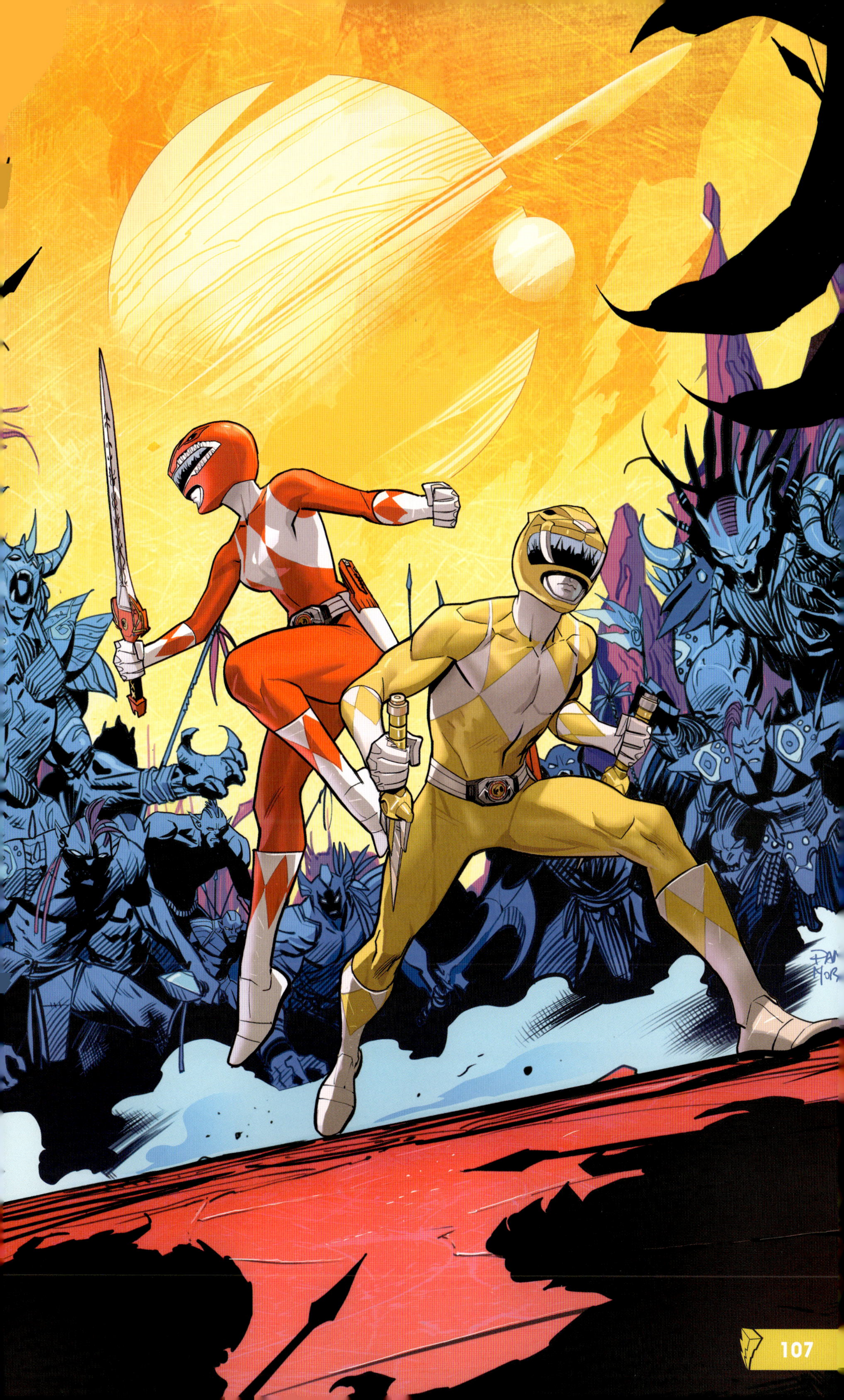

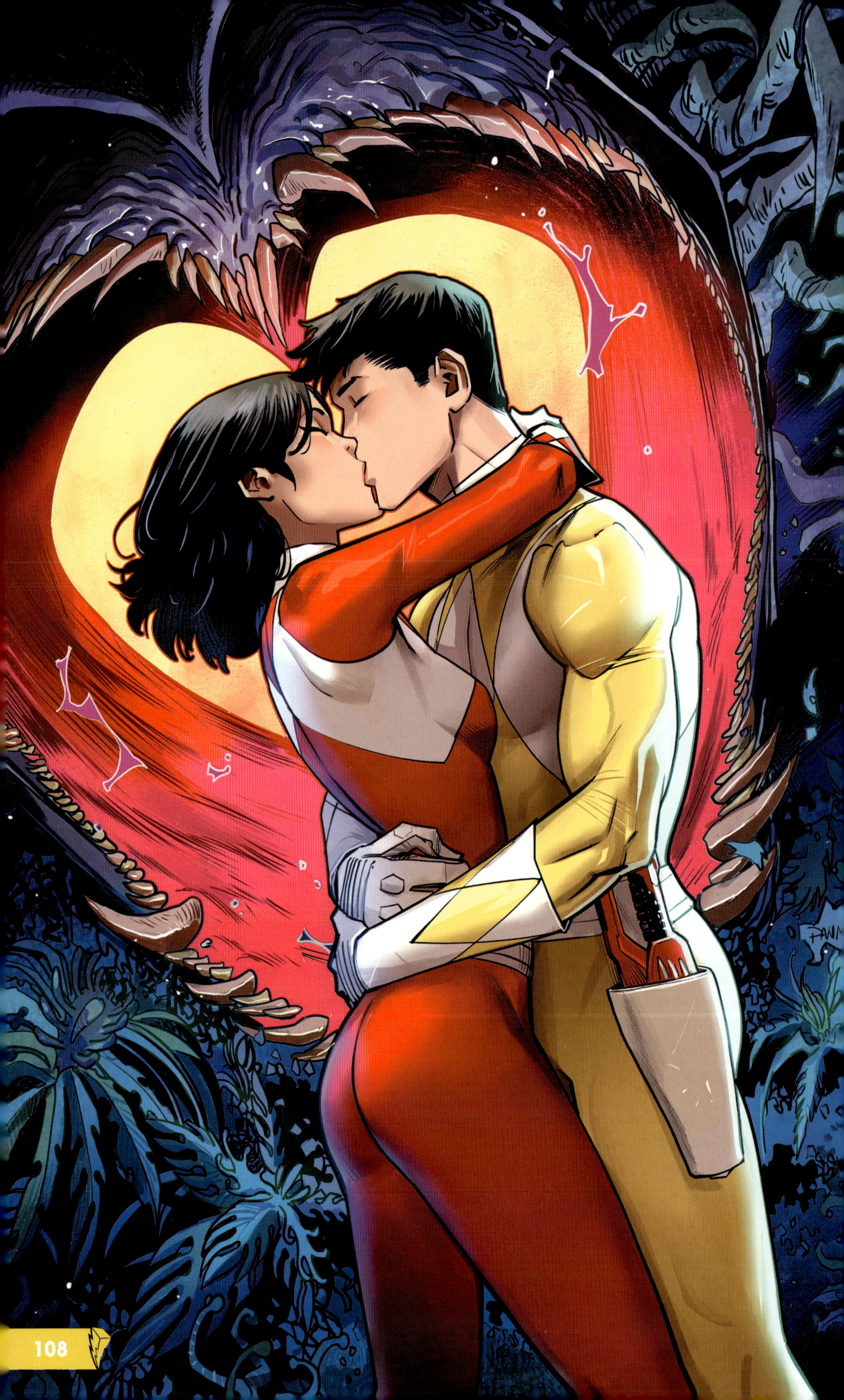

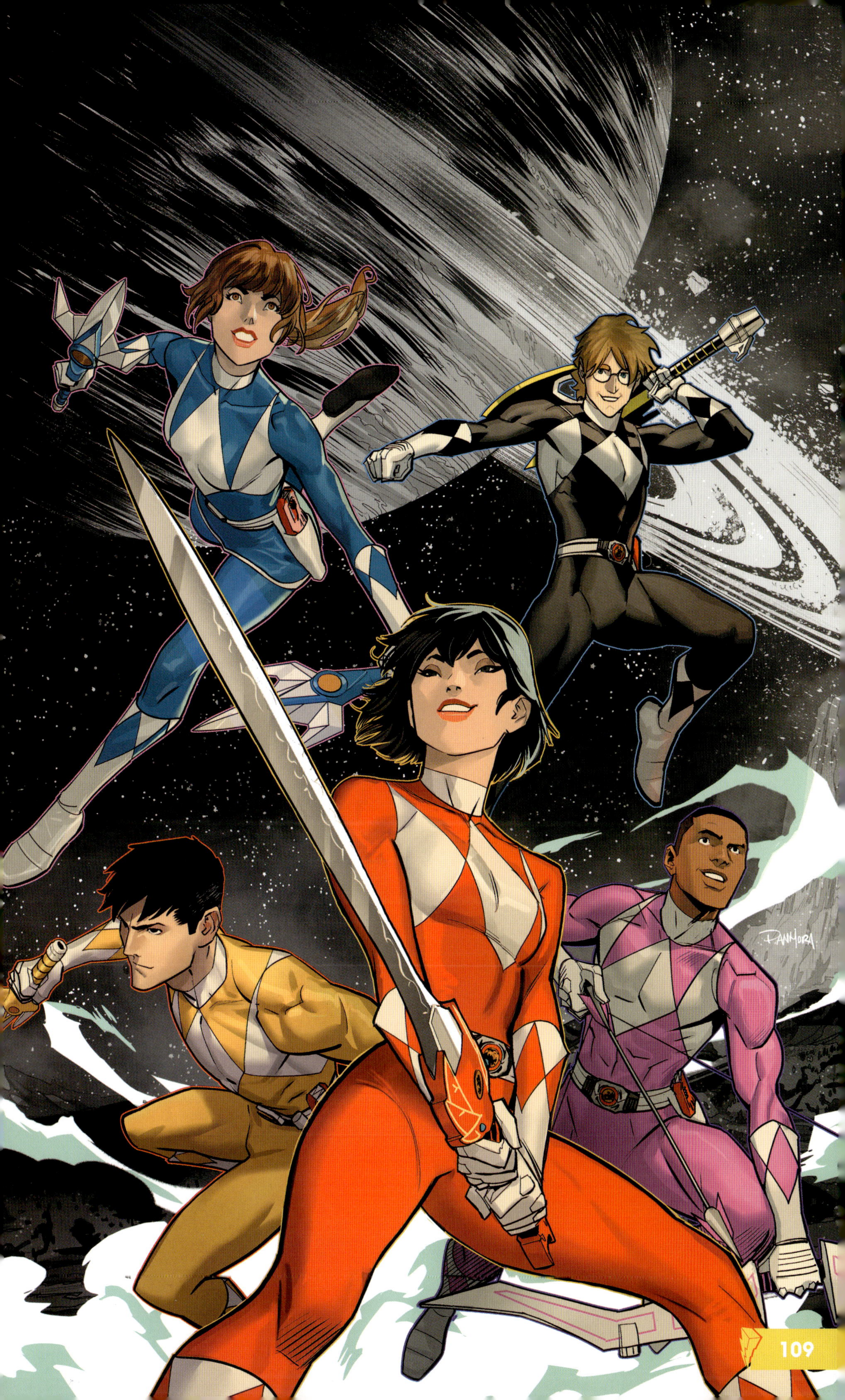
DANMORA

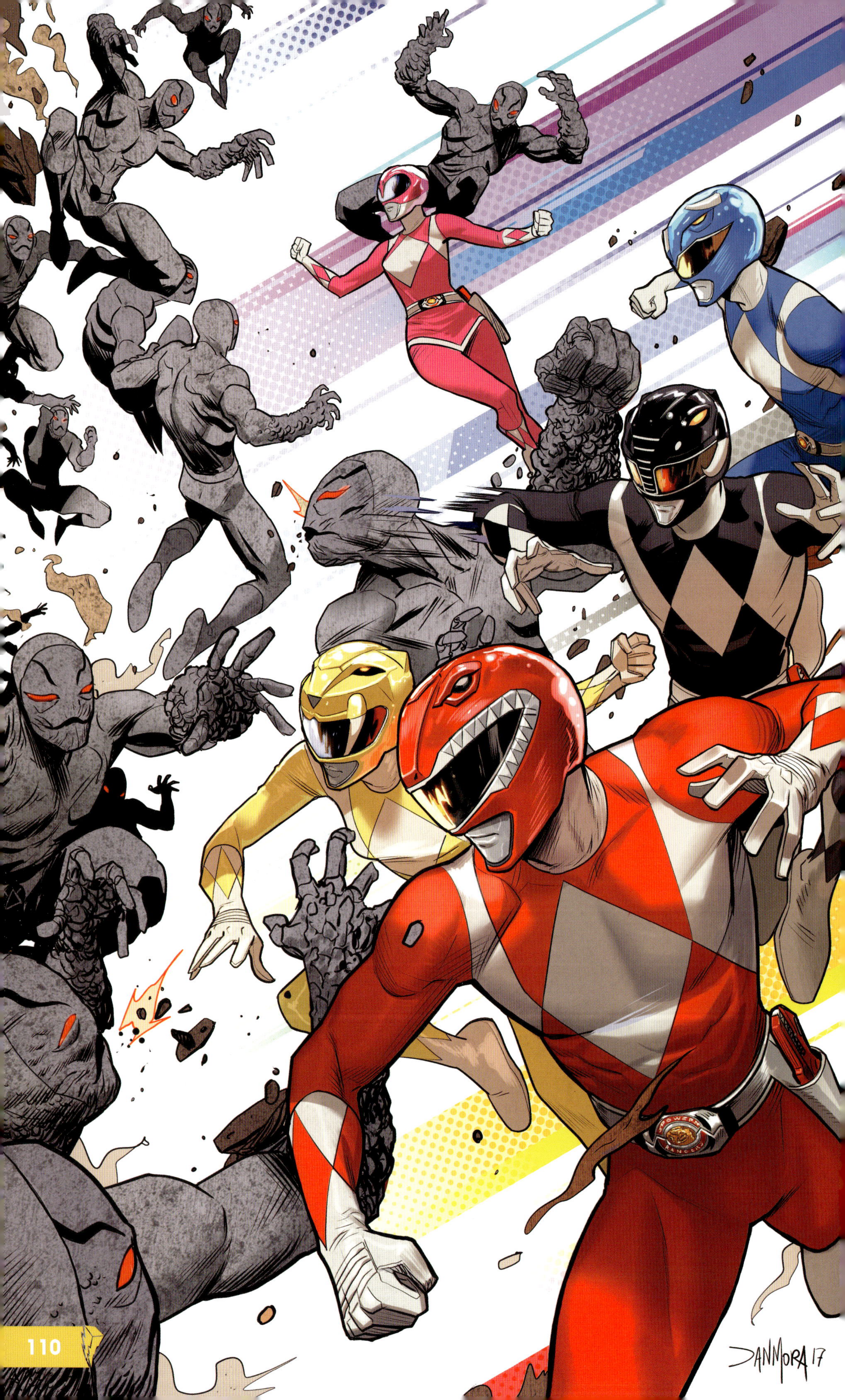
DANMORA 17

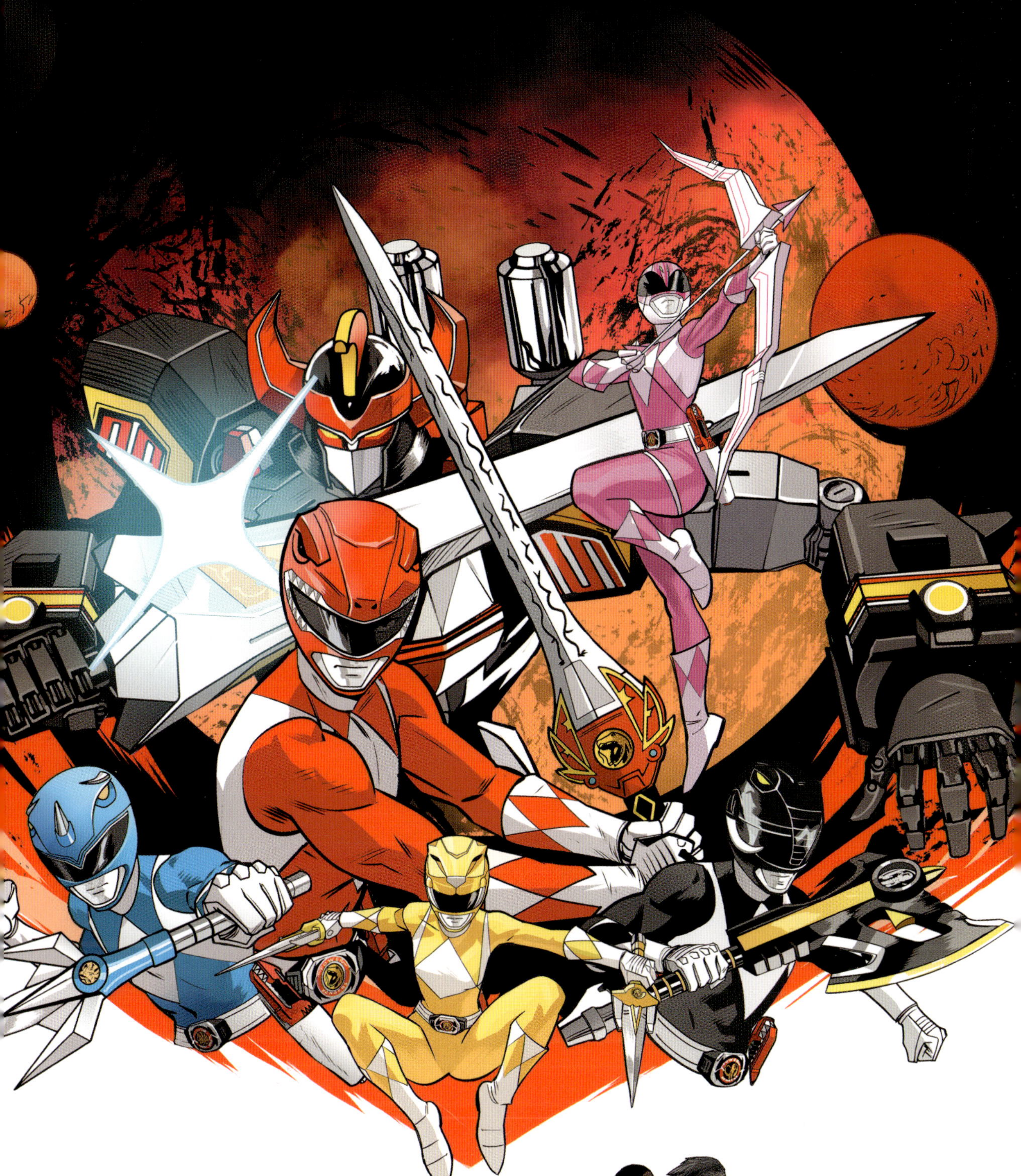

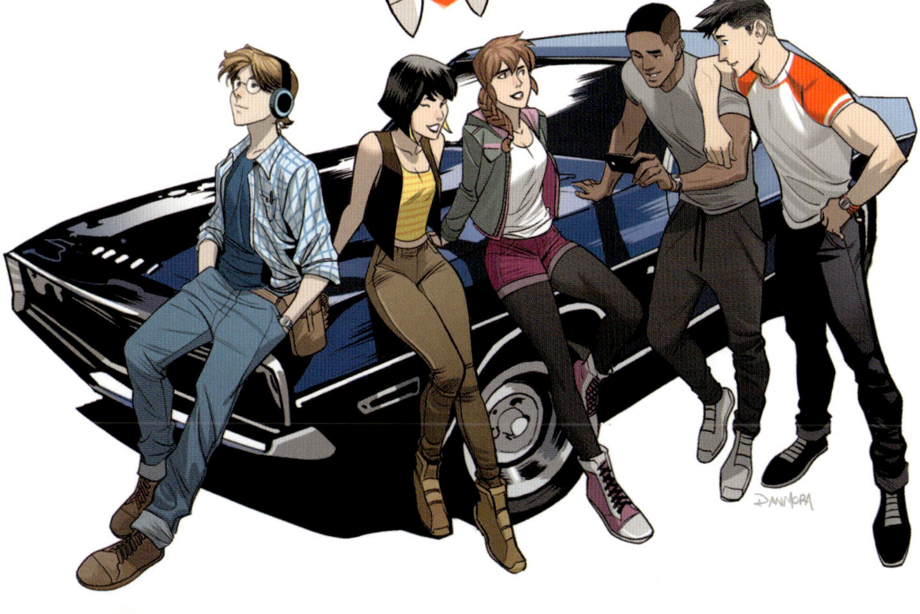

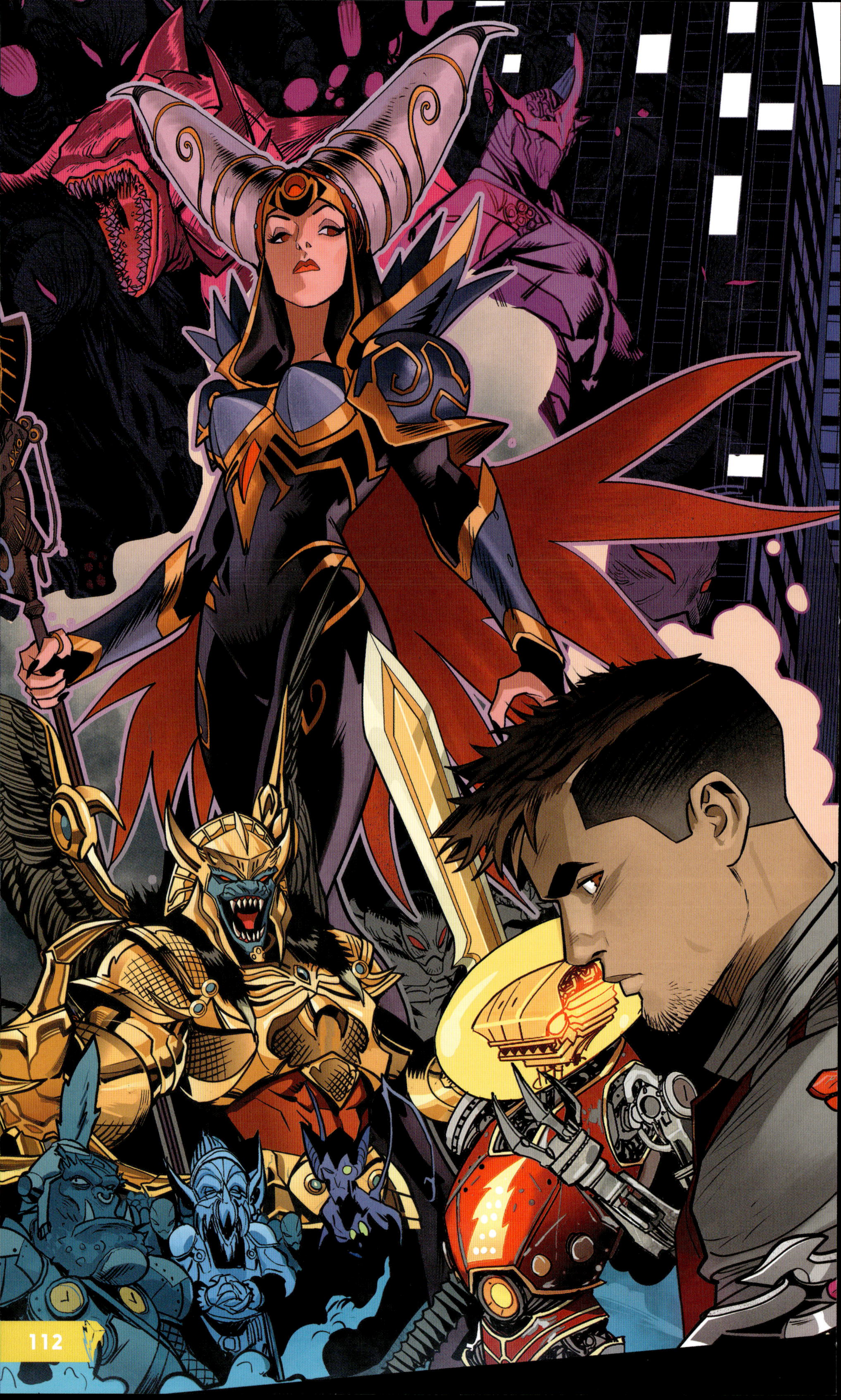

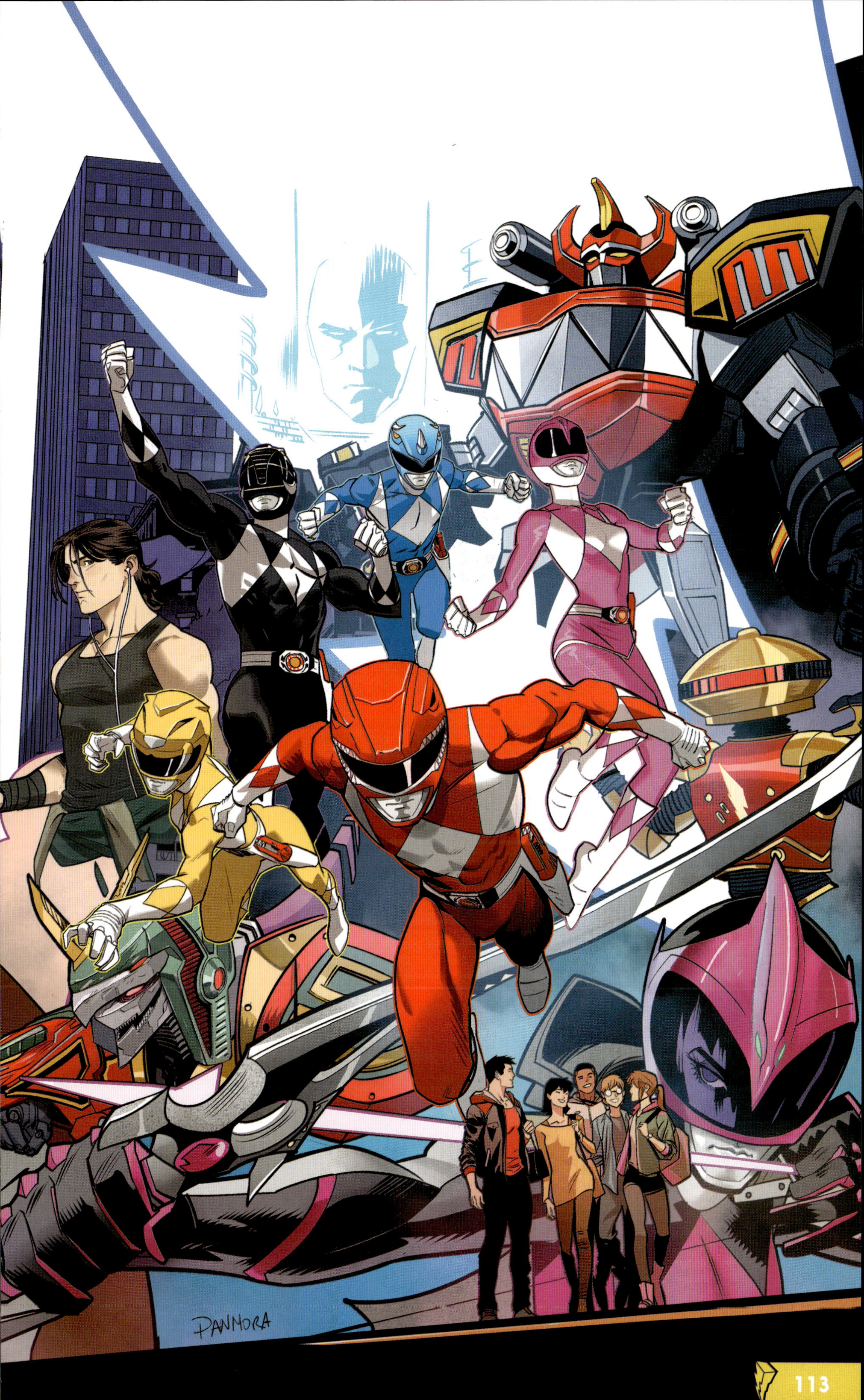
PANMORA

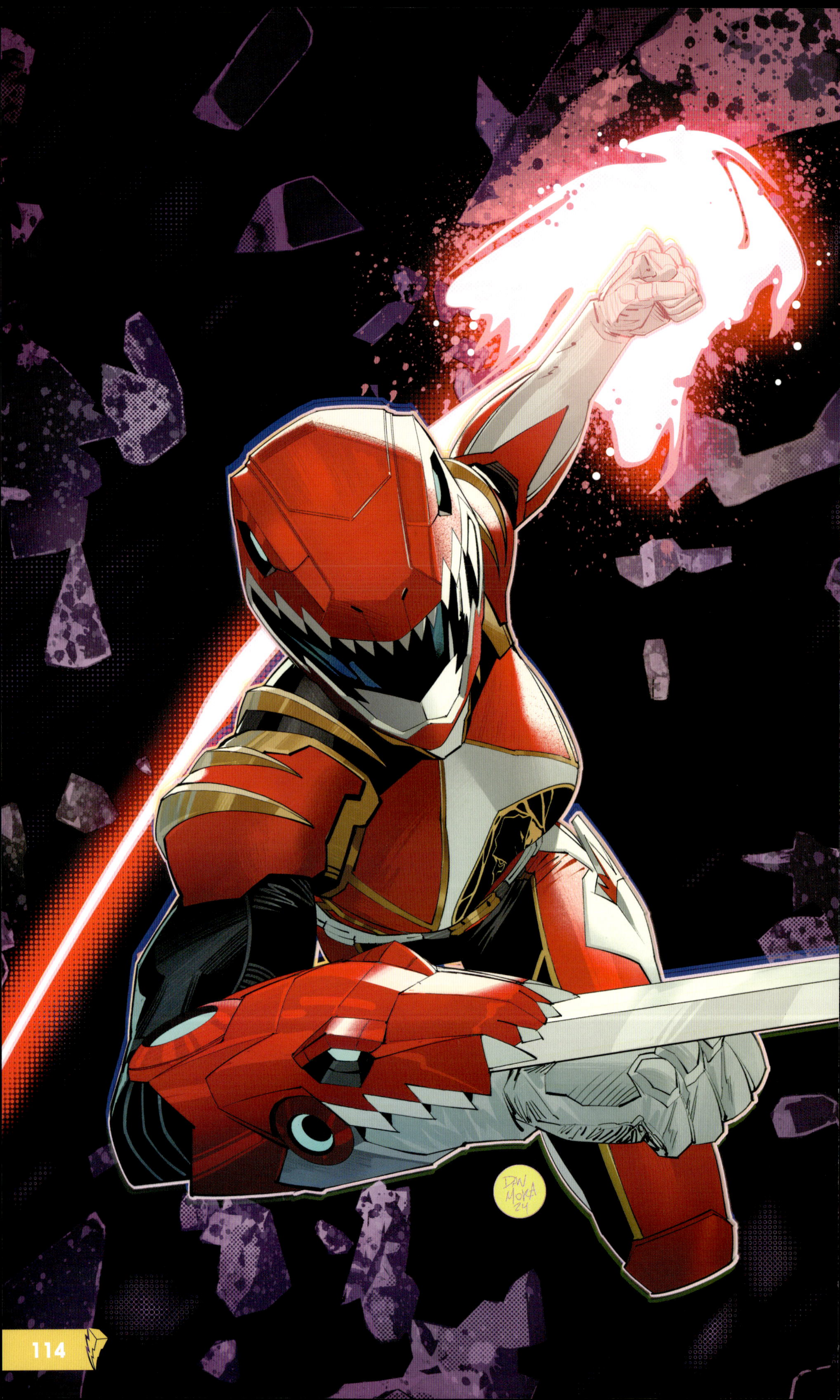
DAN
MORA
'24

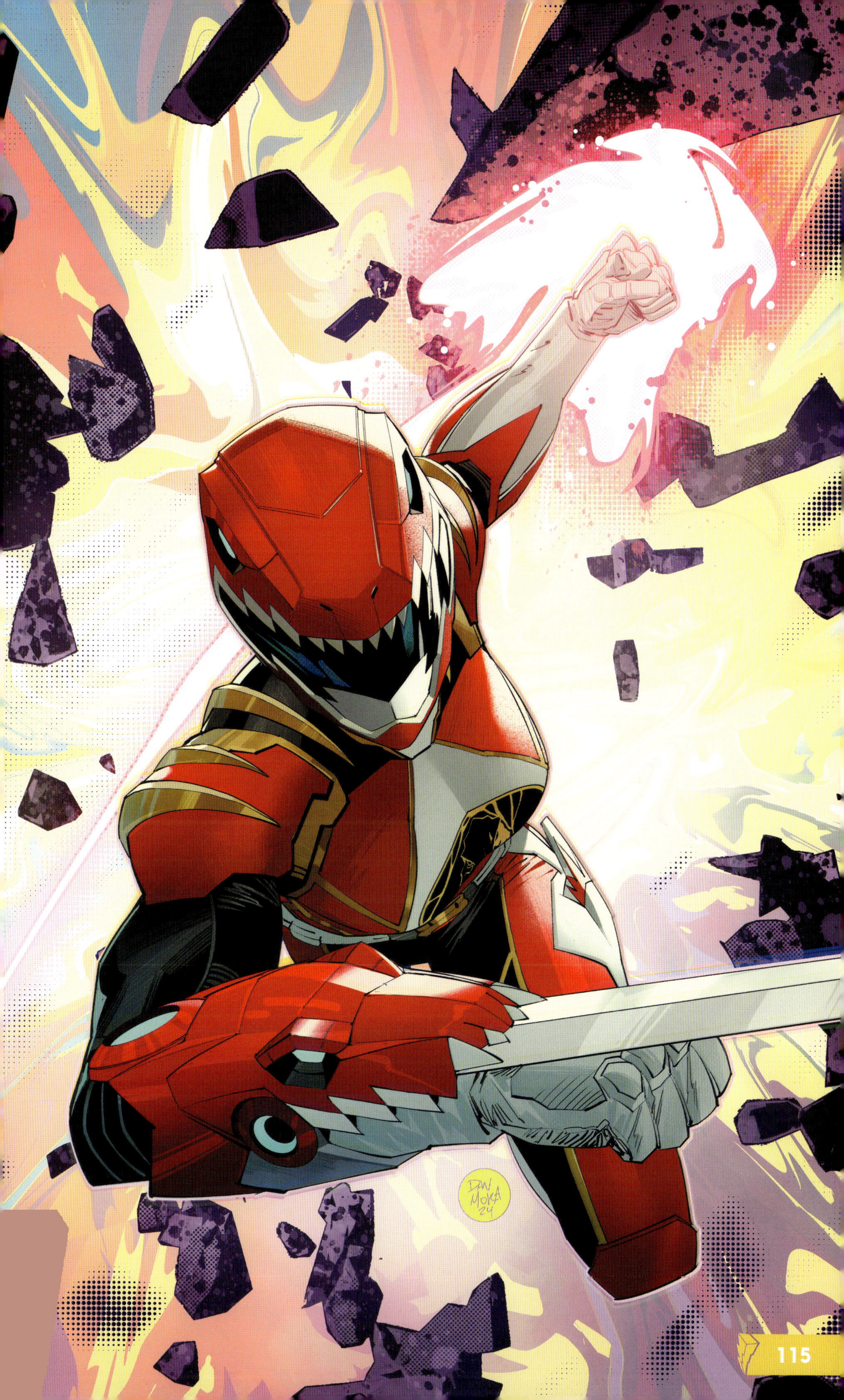

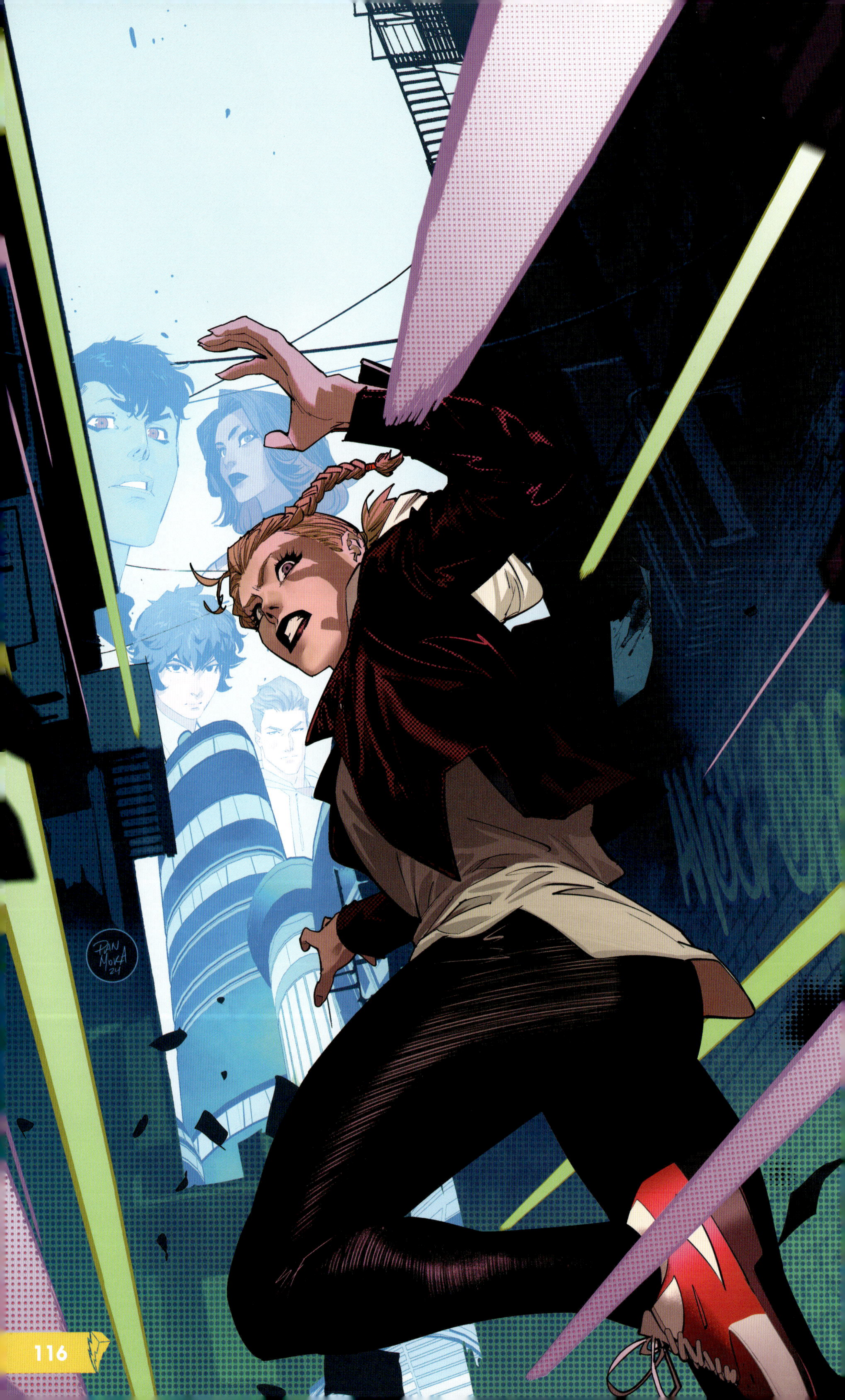

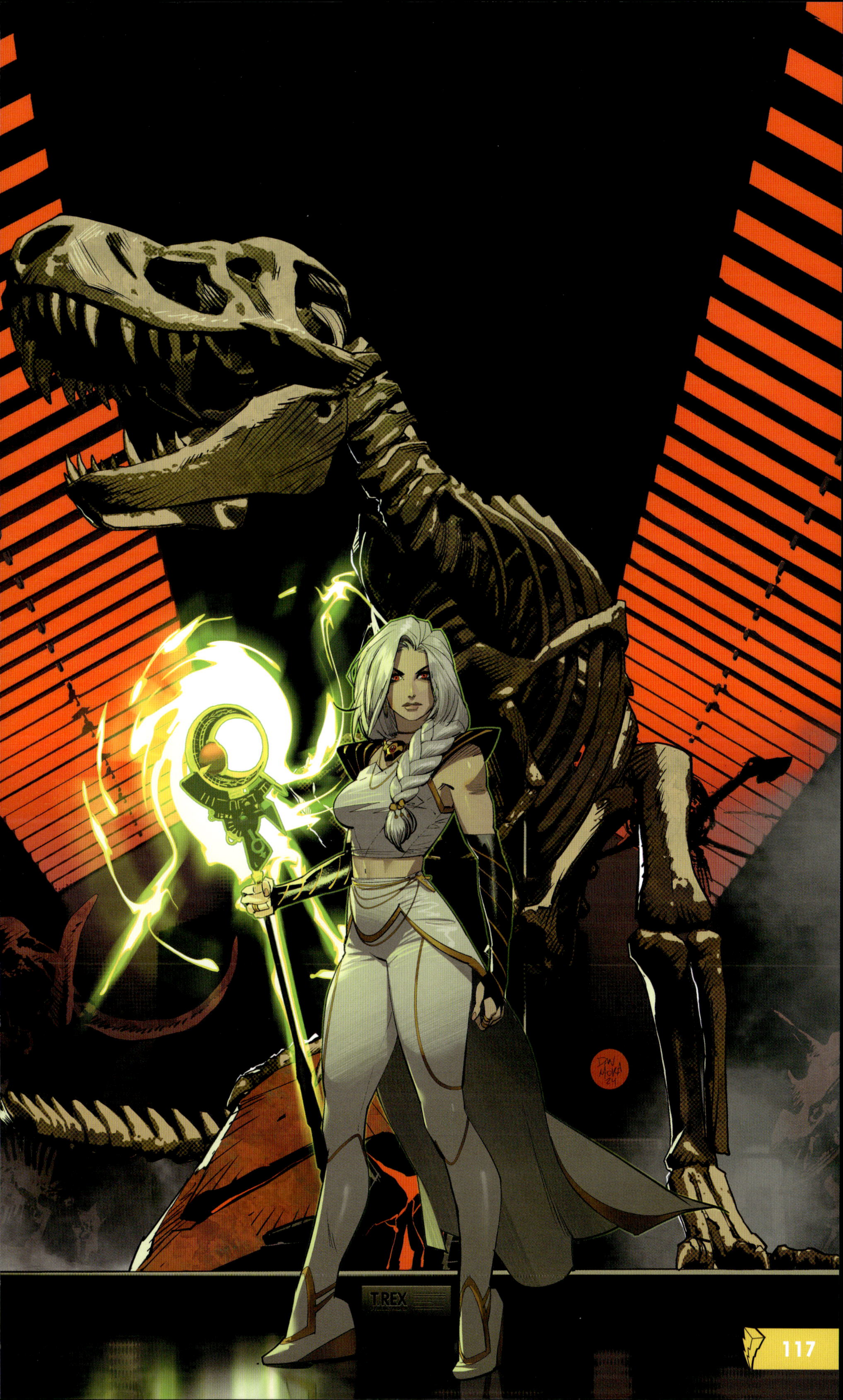
T.REX

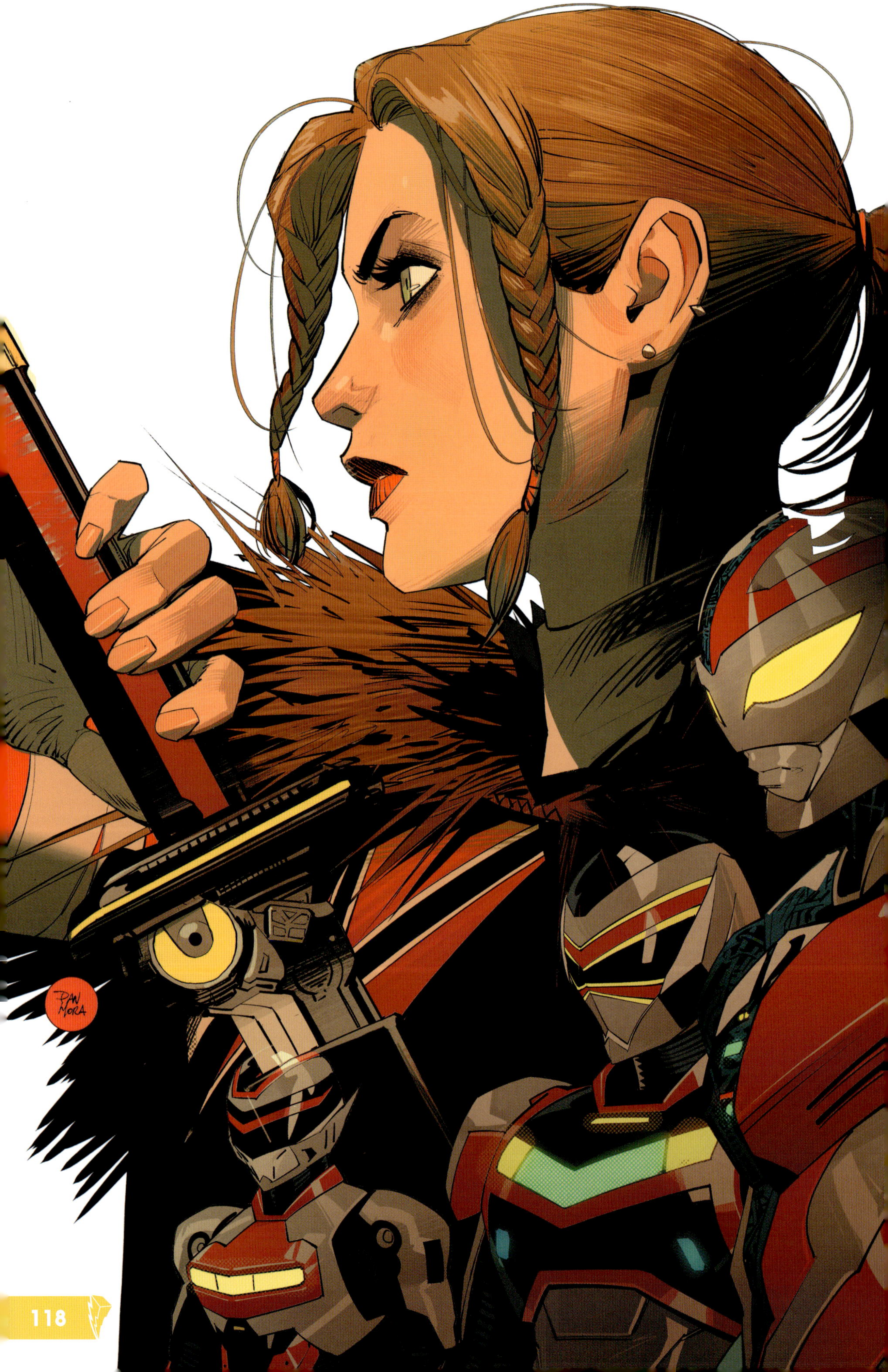
DAN
MORA

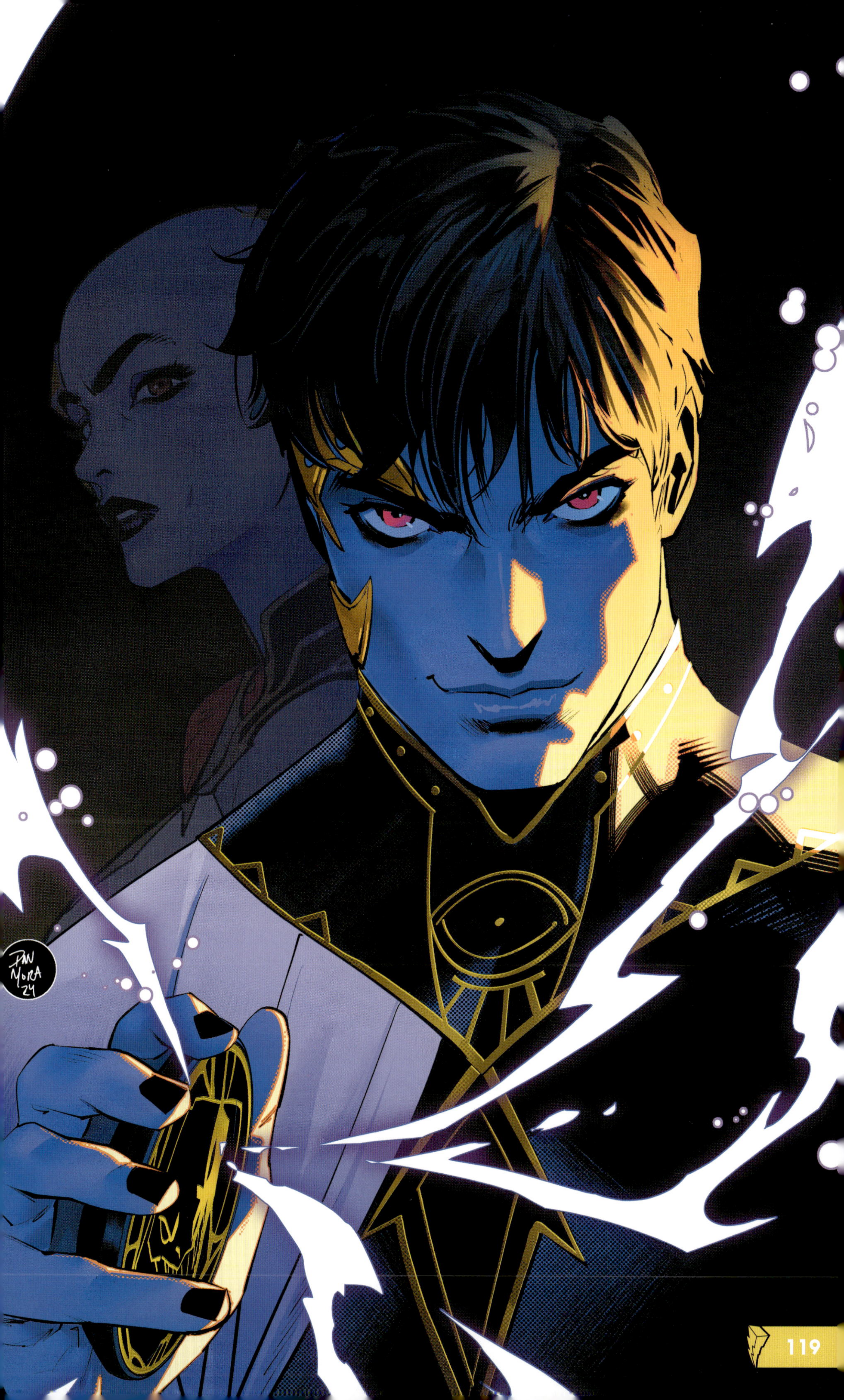
DAN MORA 24

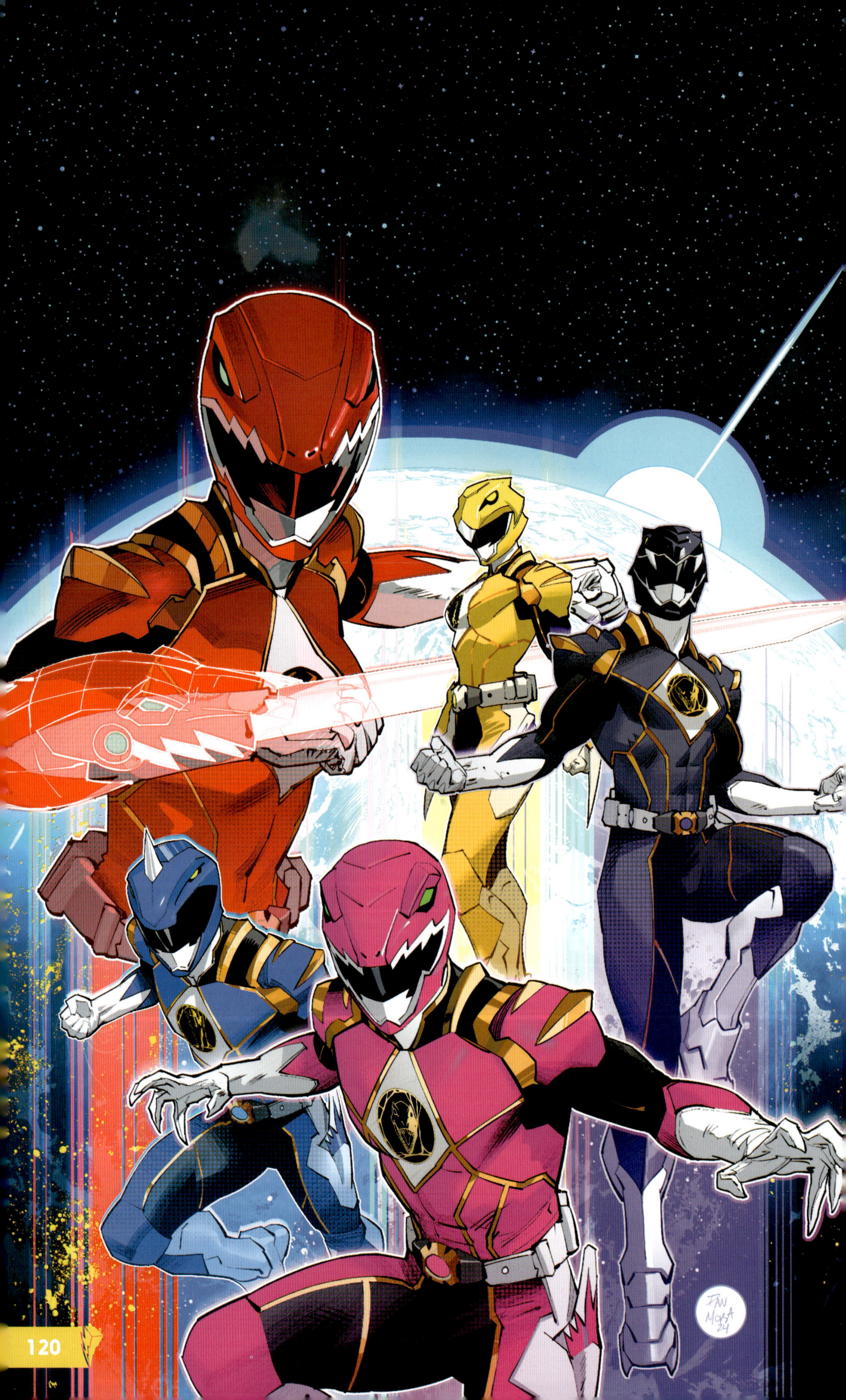

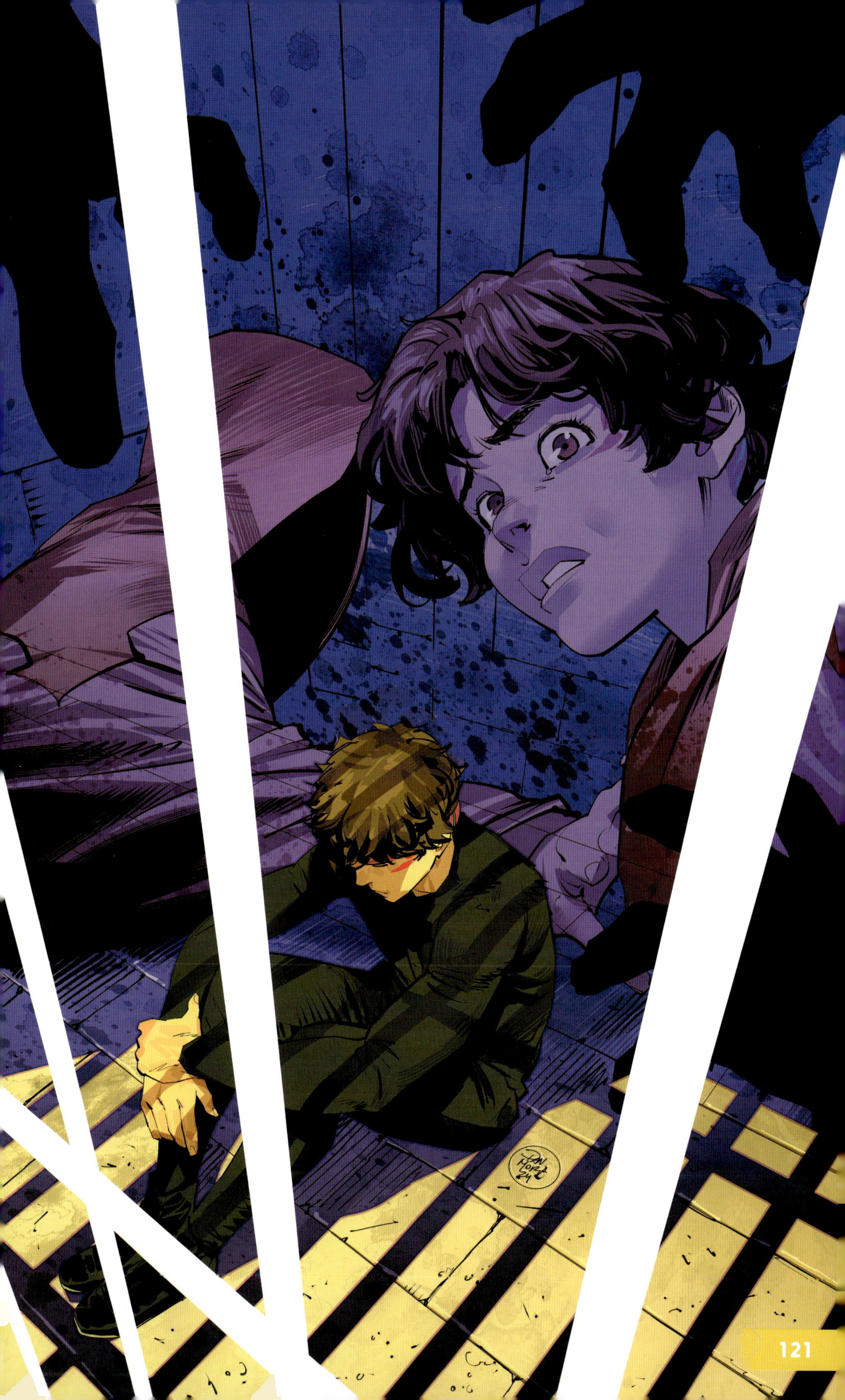

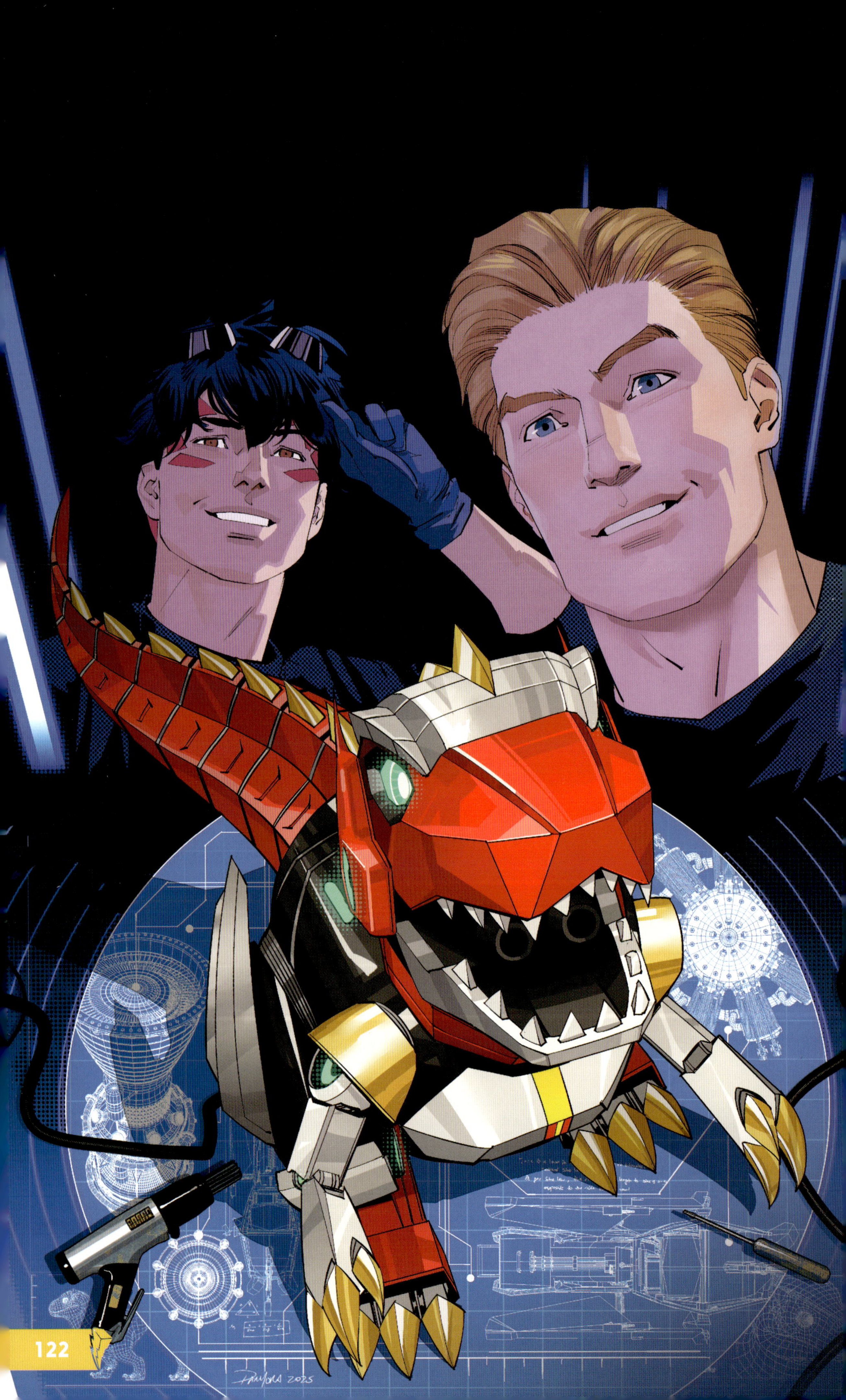

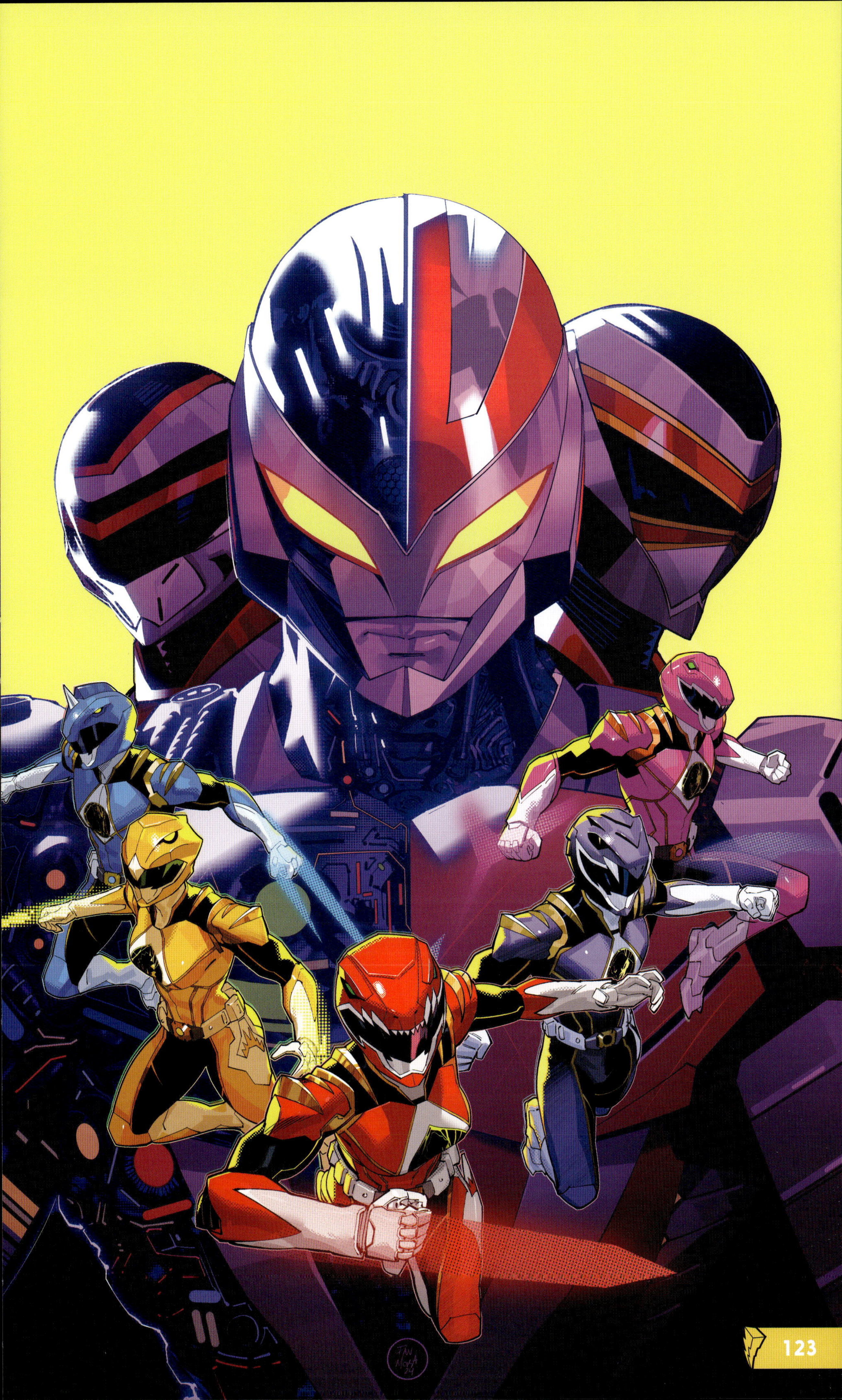

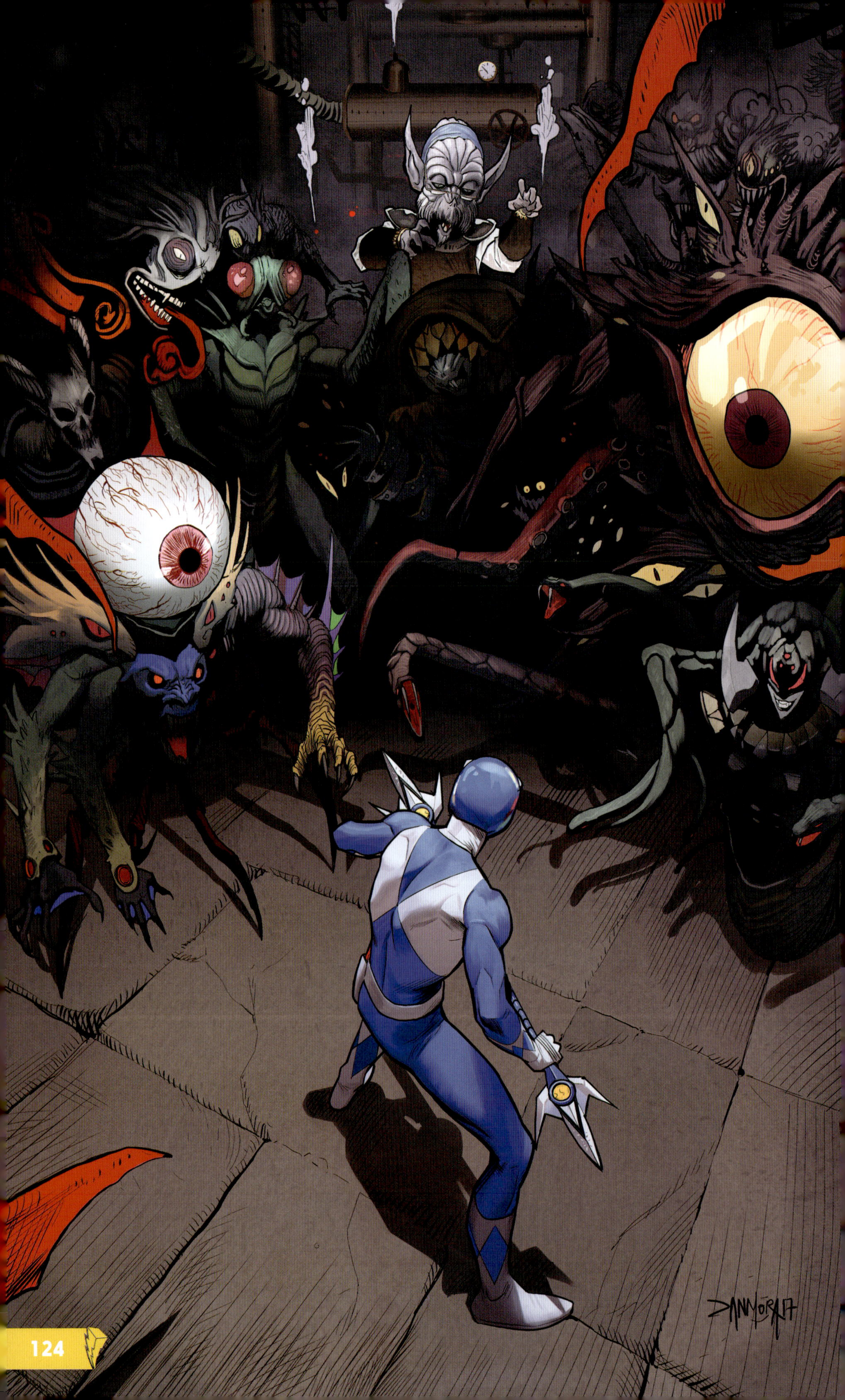

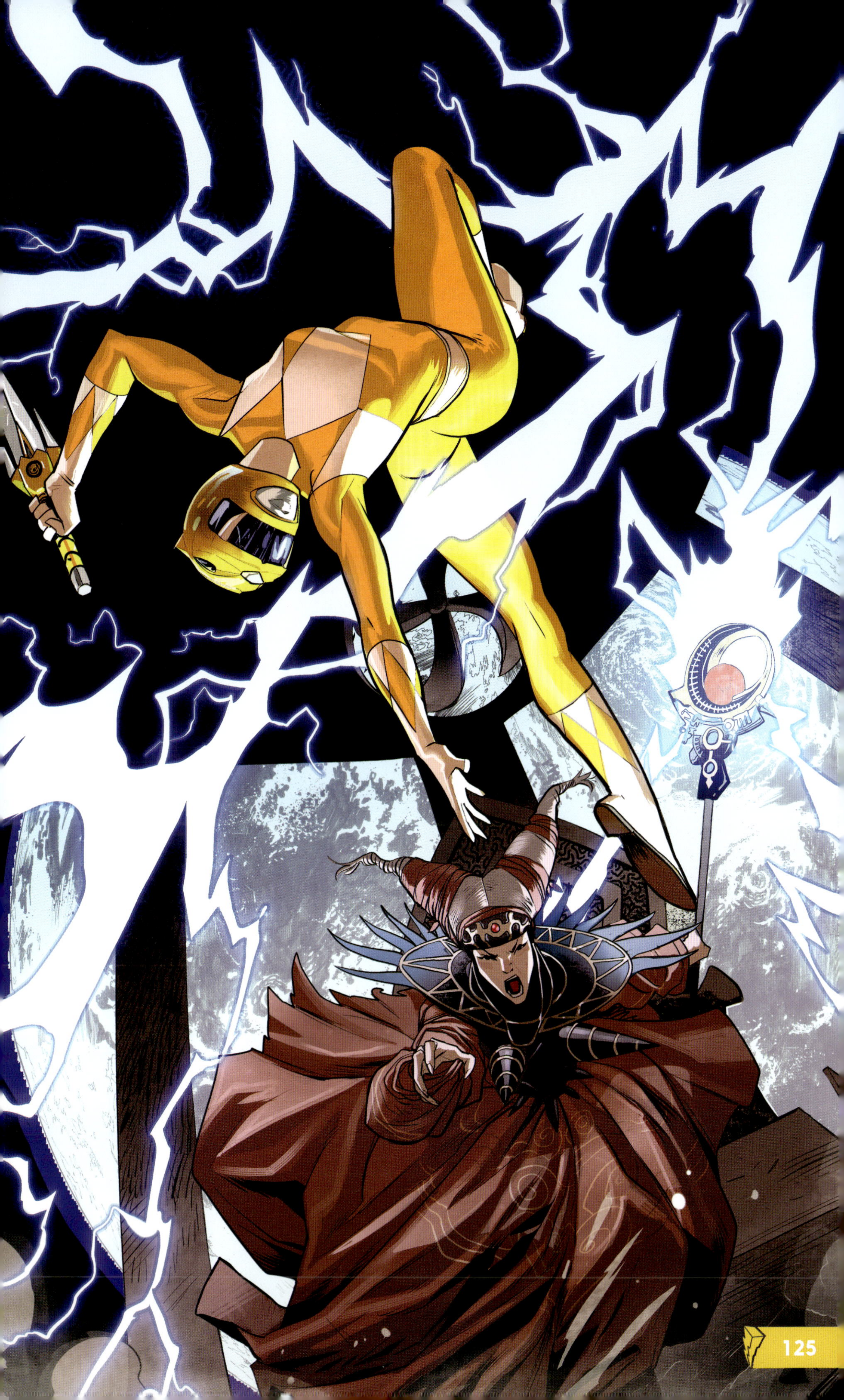

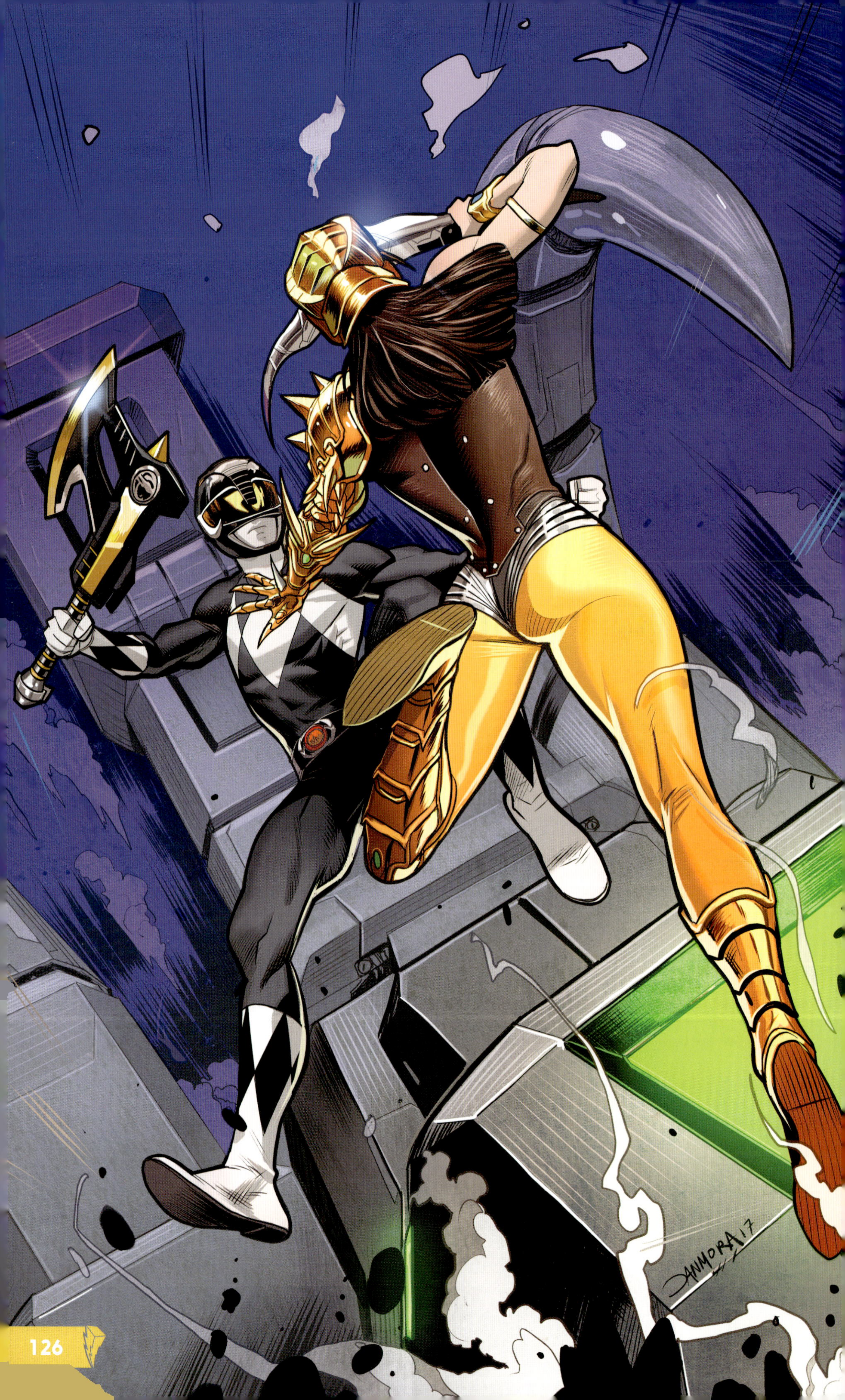

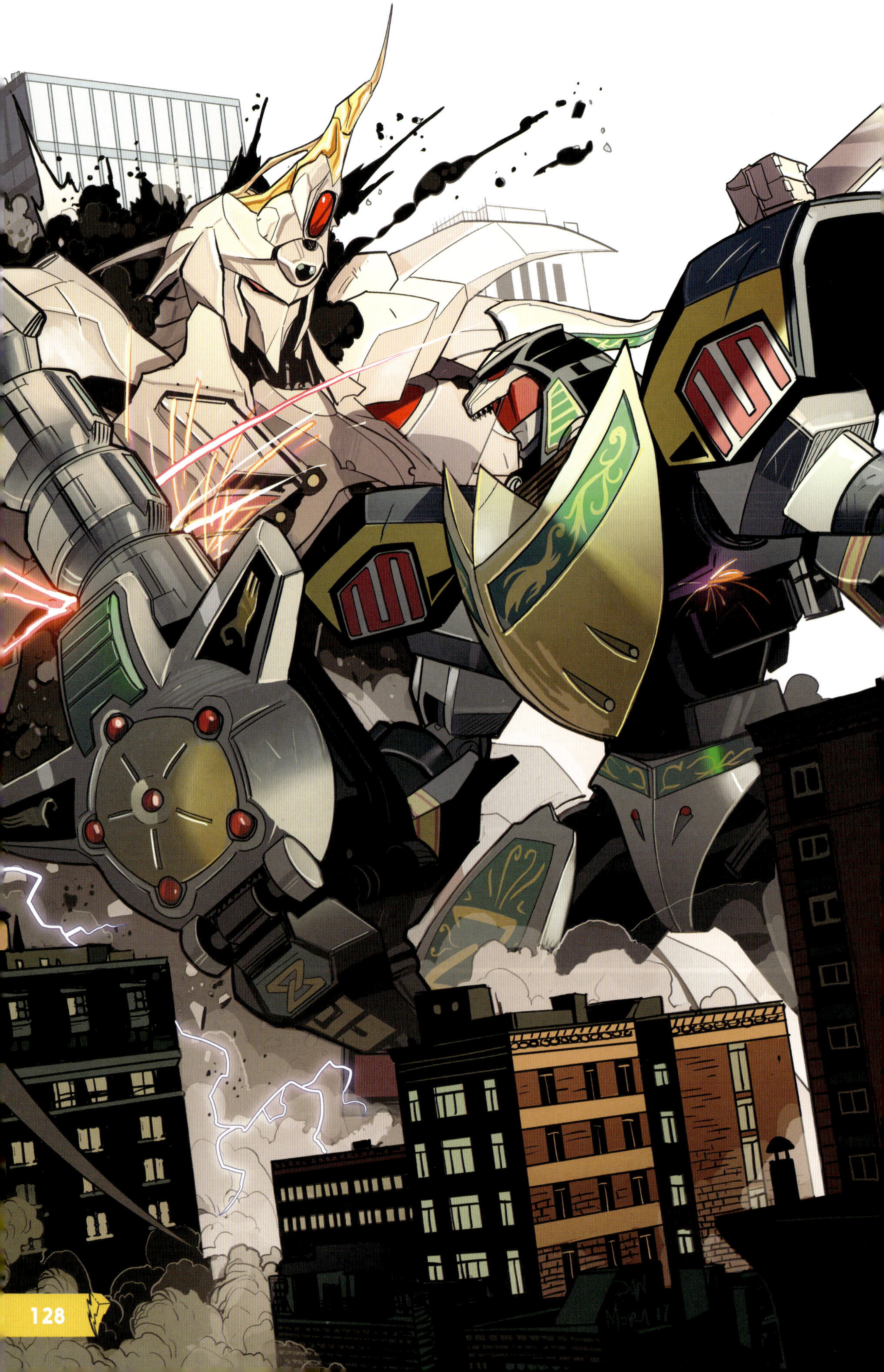

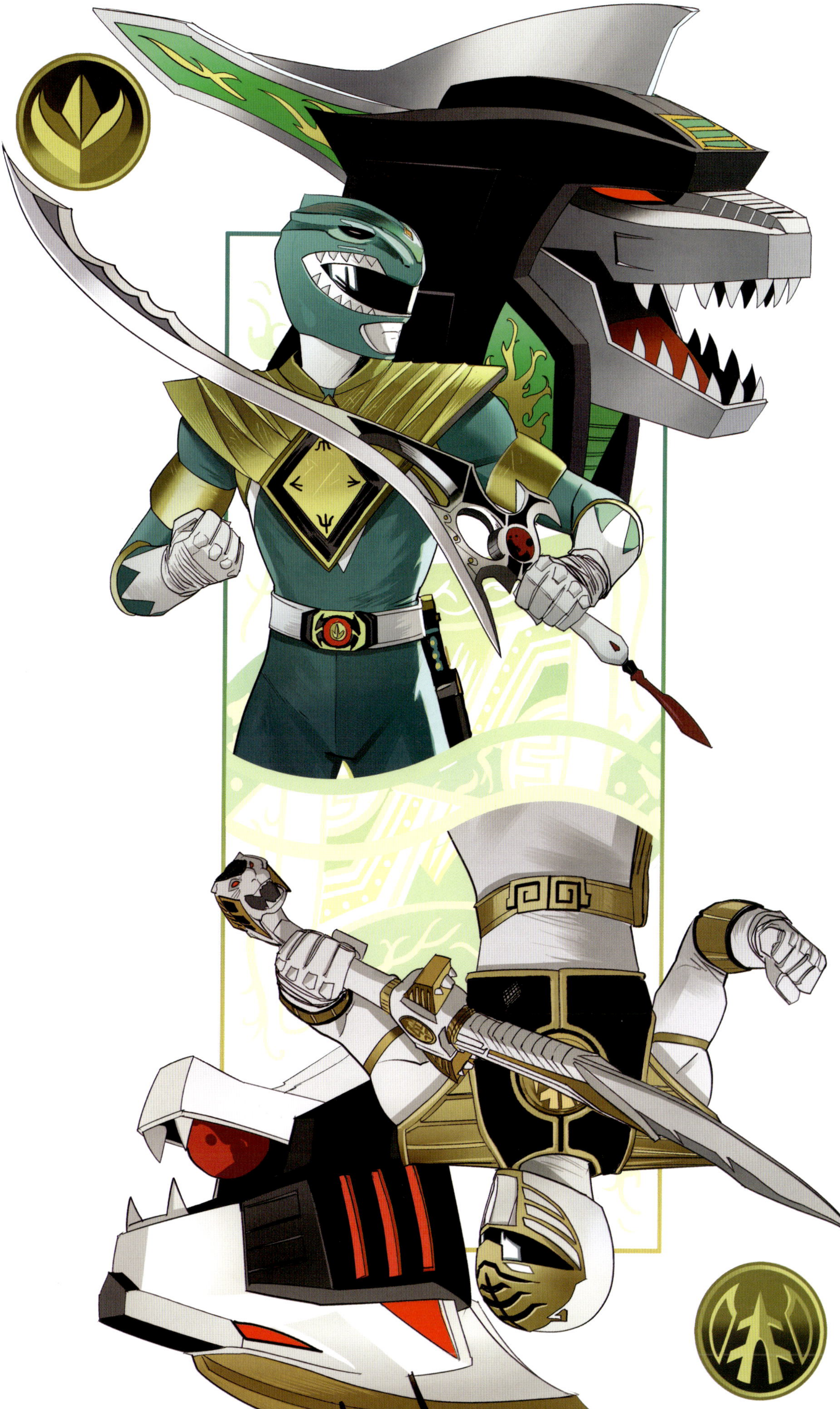

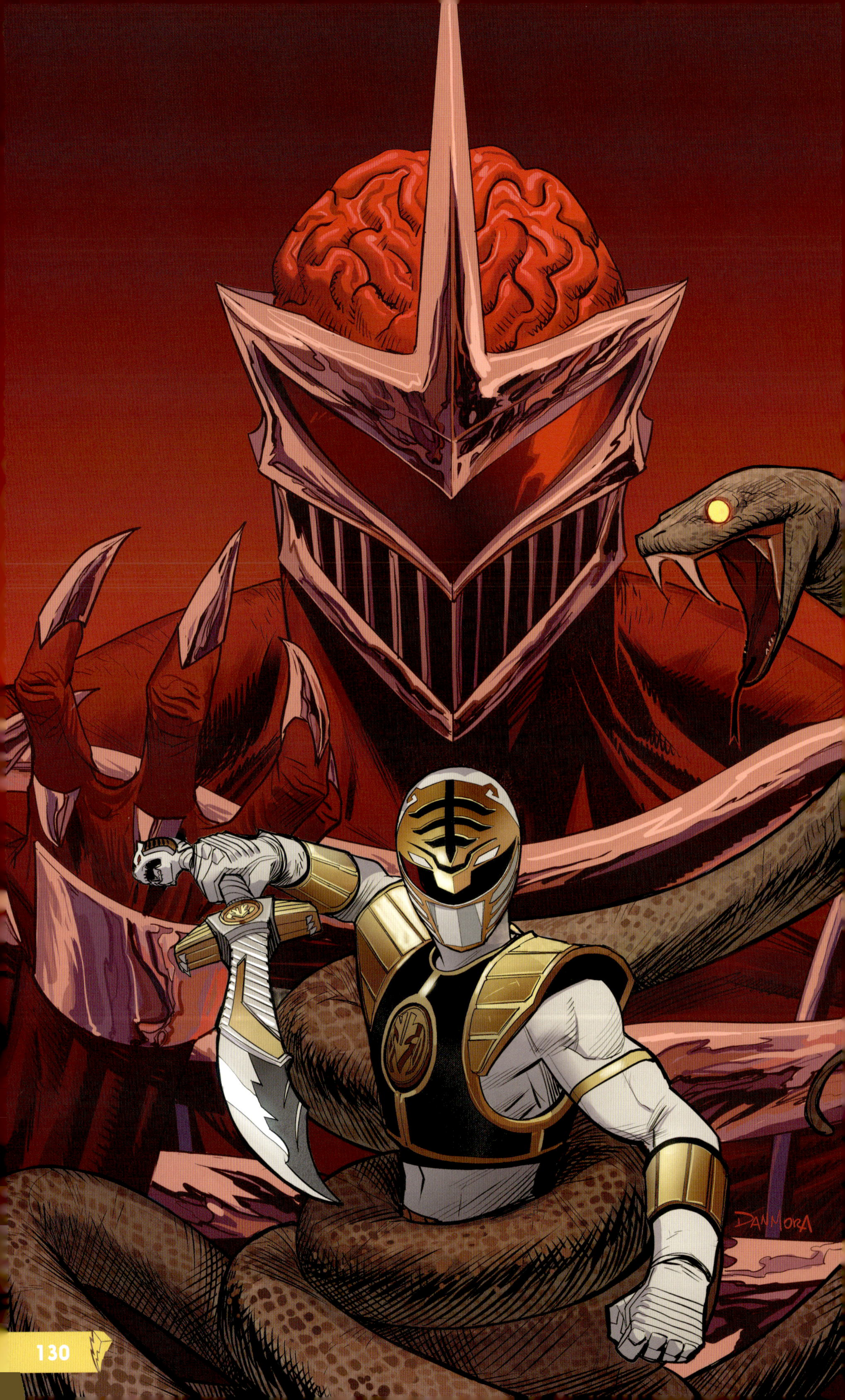
DANMORA

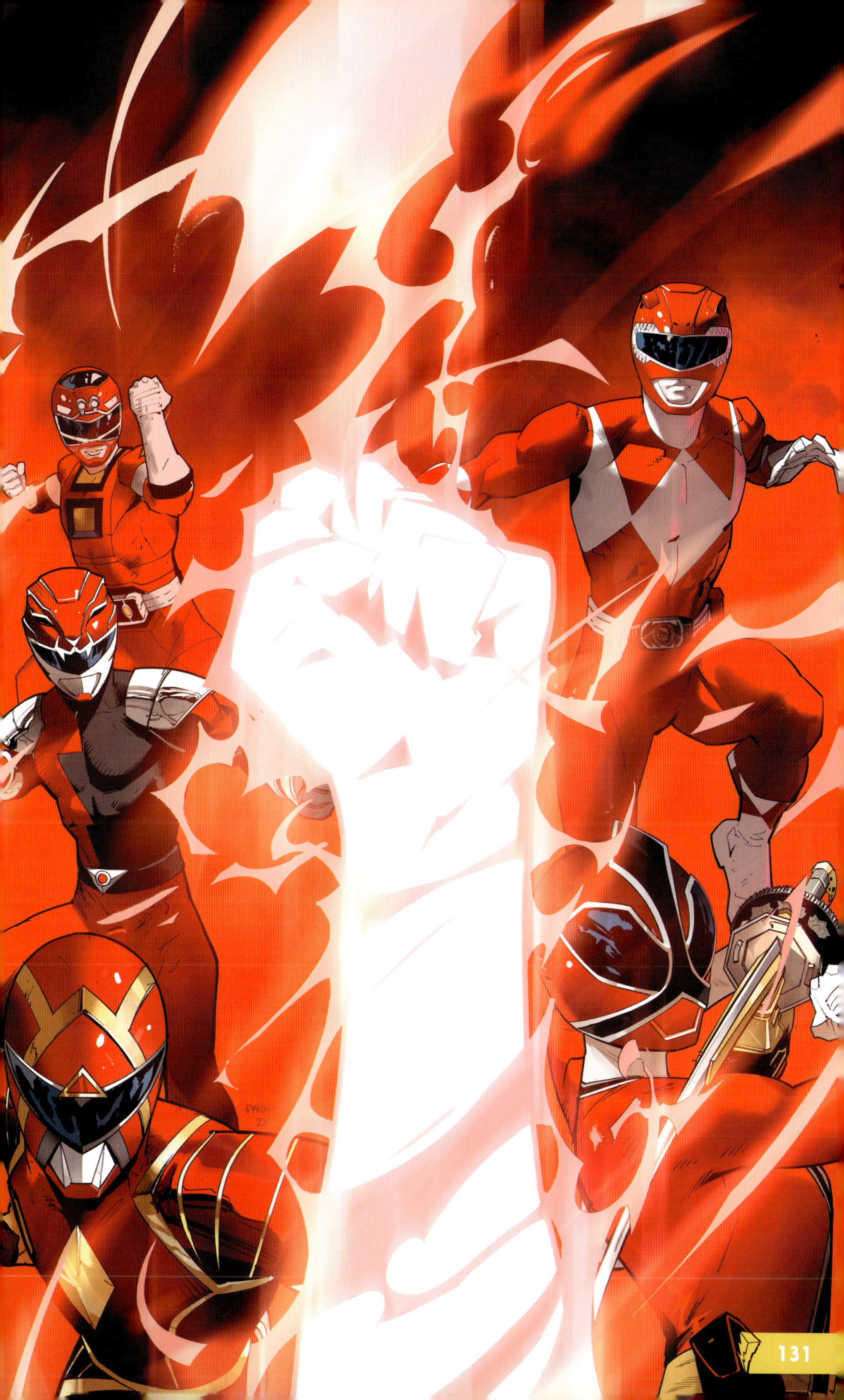

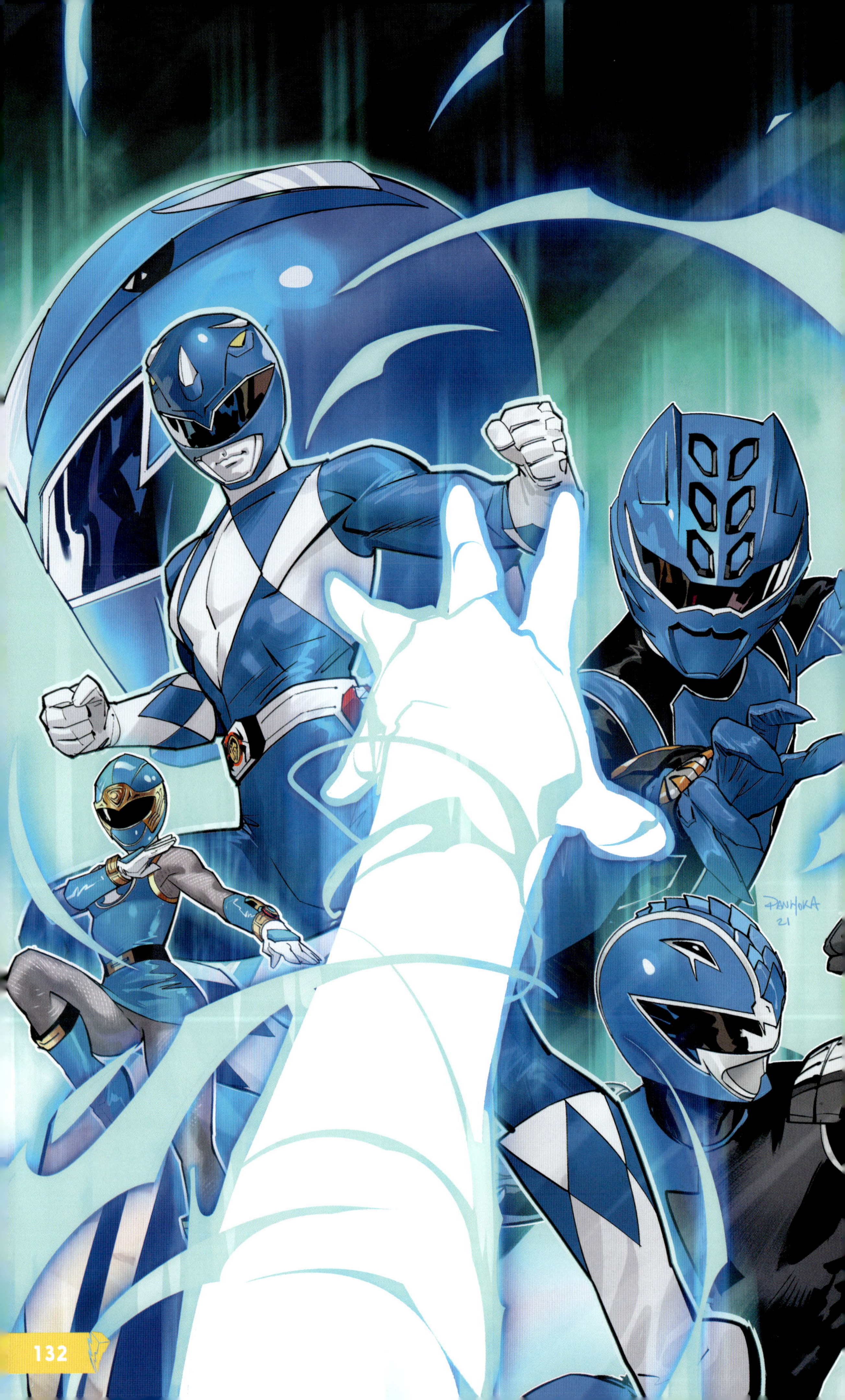

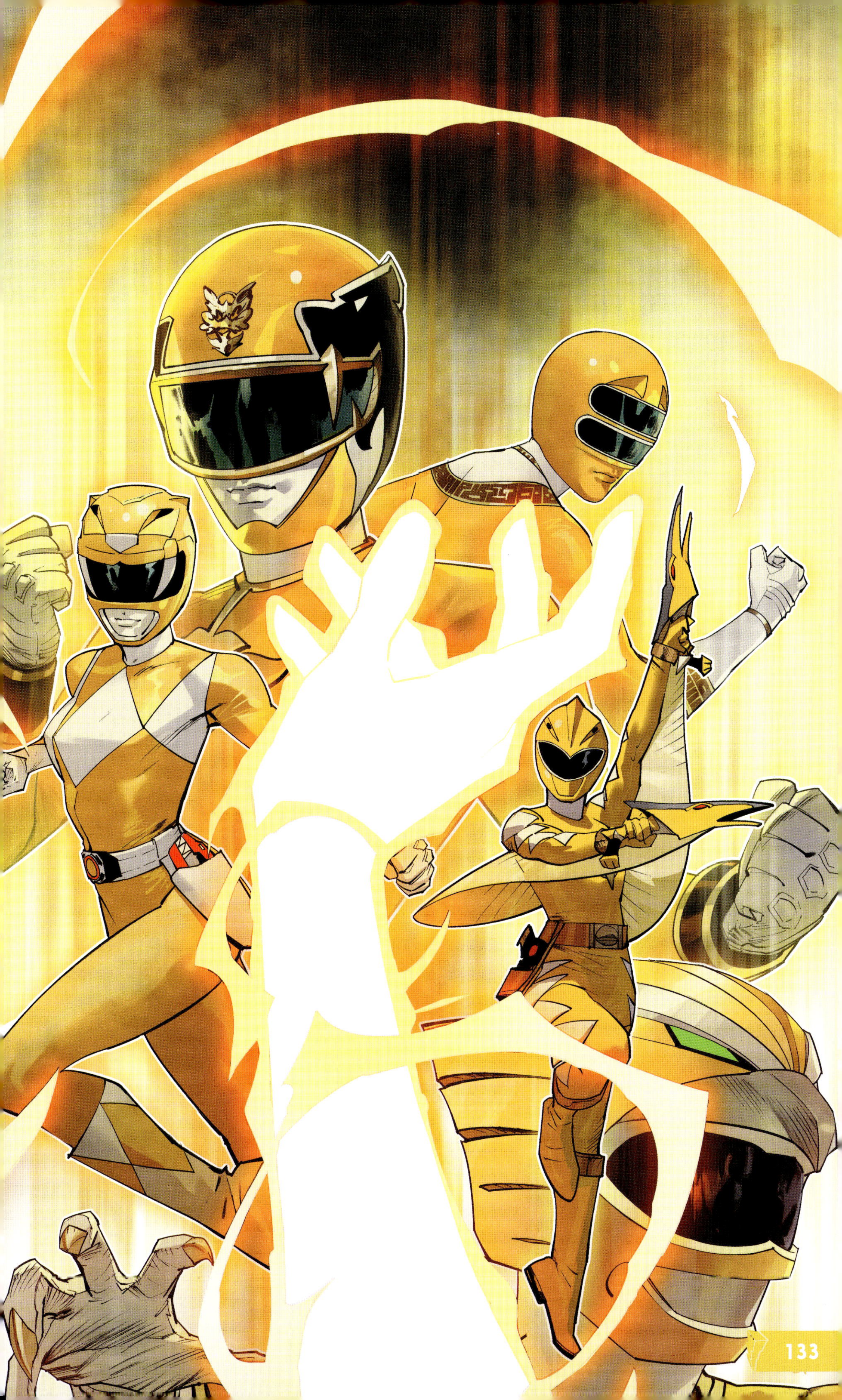

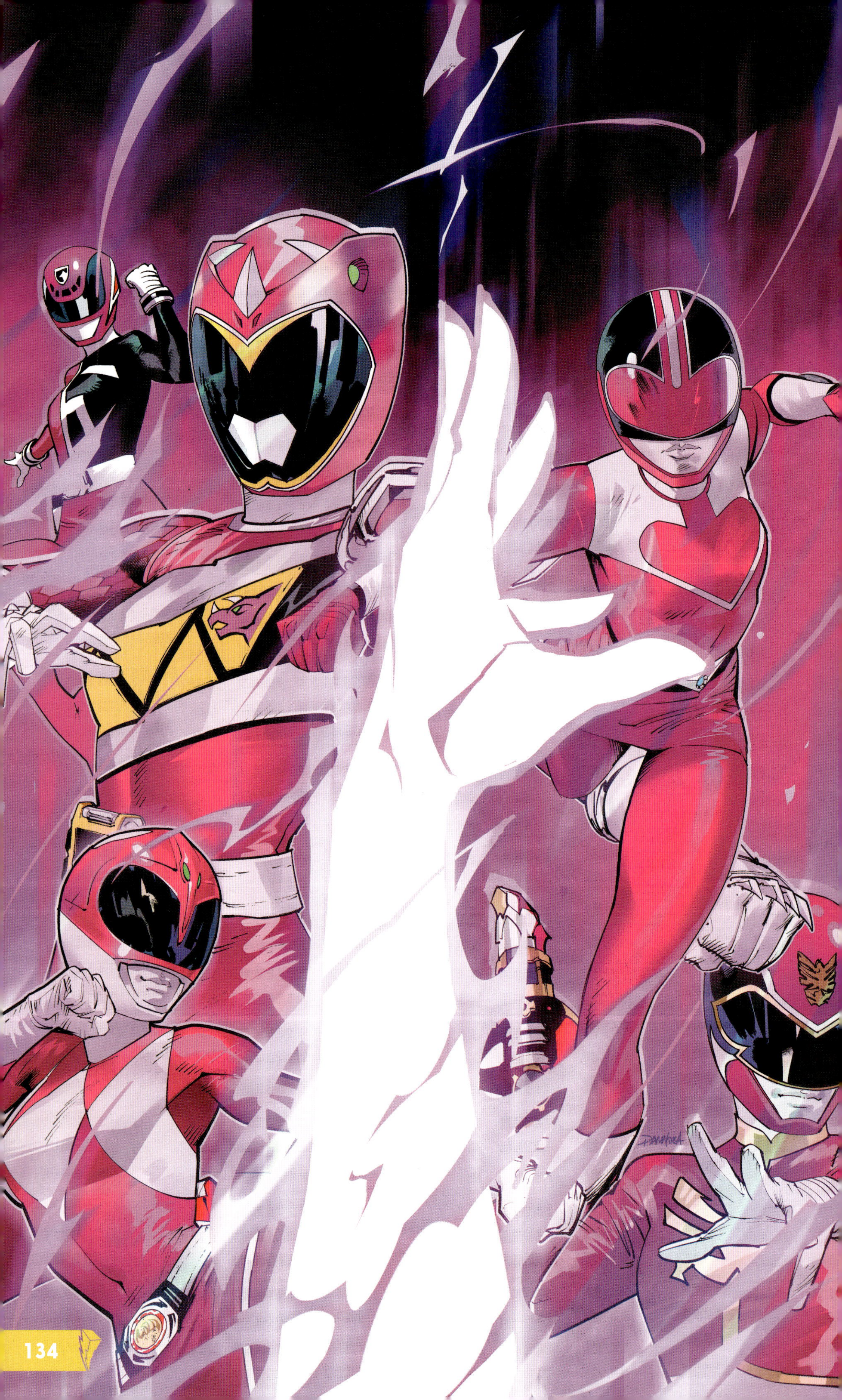

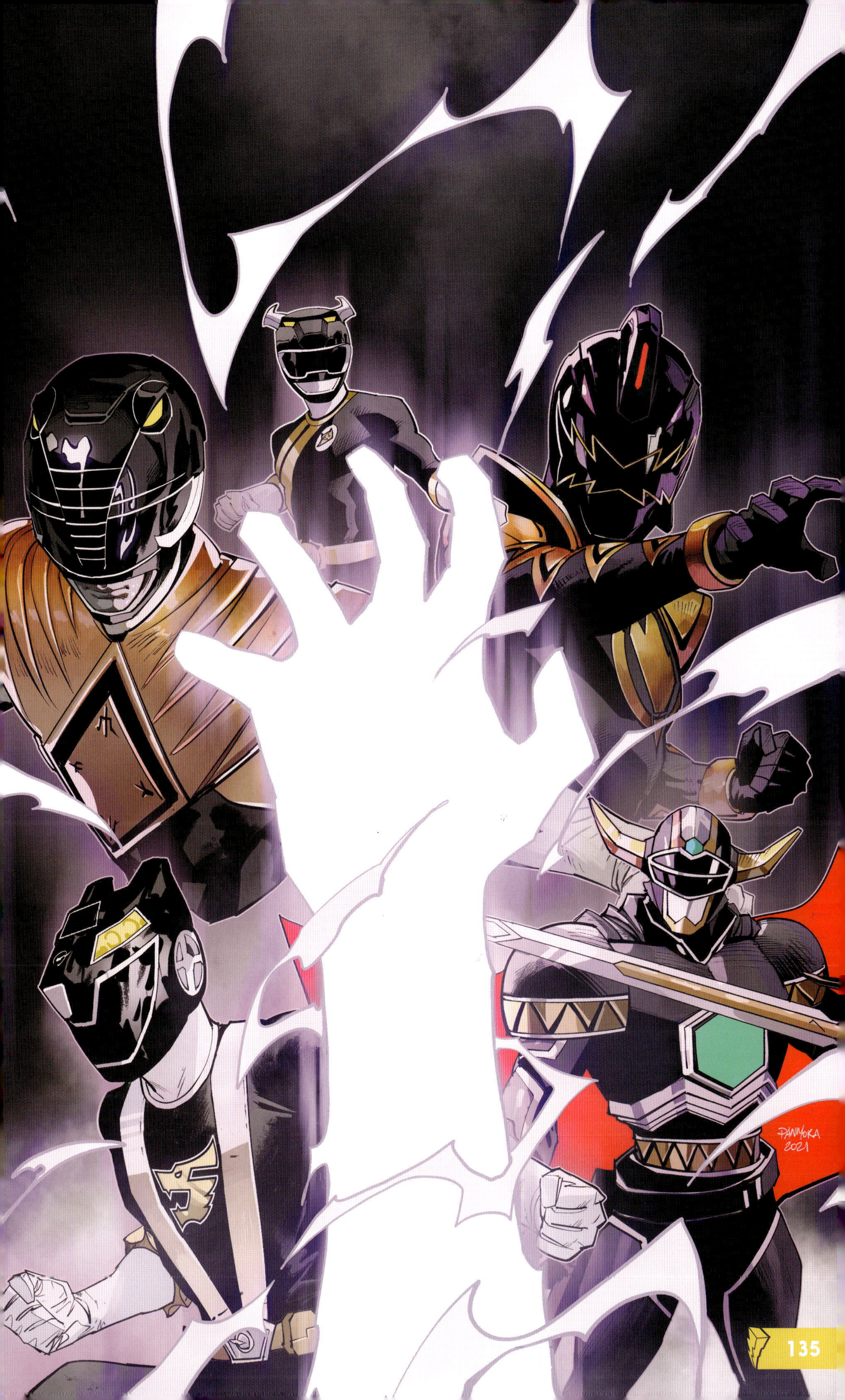
PANMOKA
2021

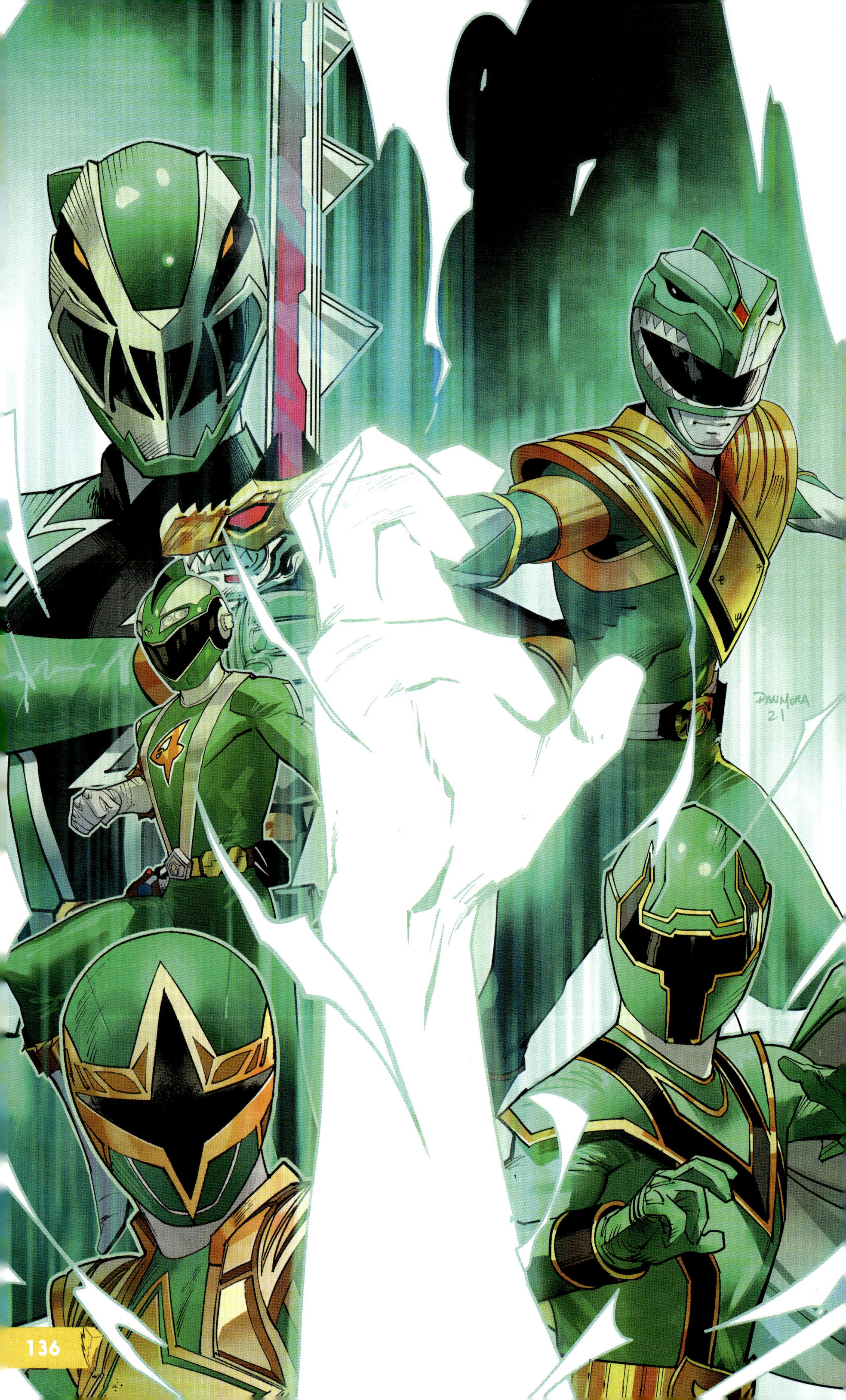
DAN MORA
21

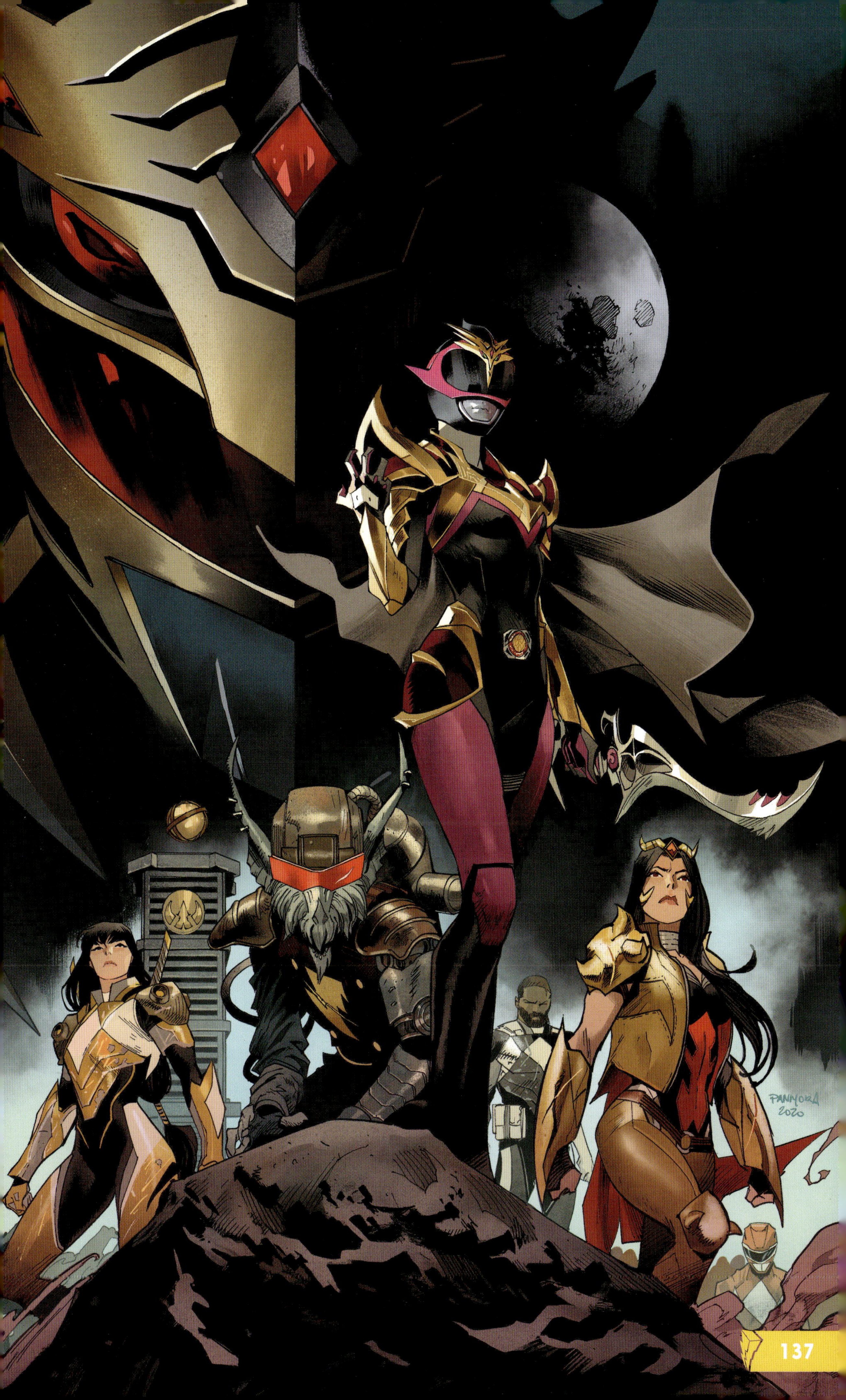
PANMOKA
2020

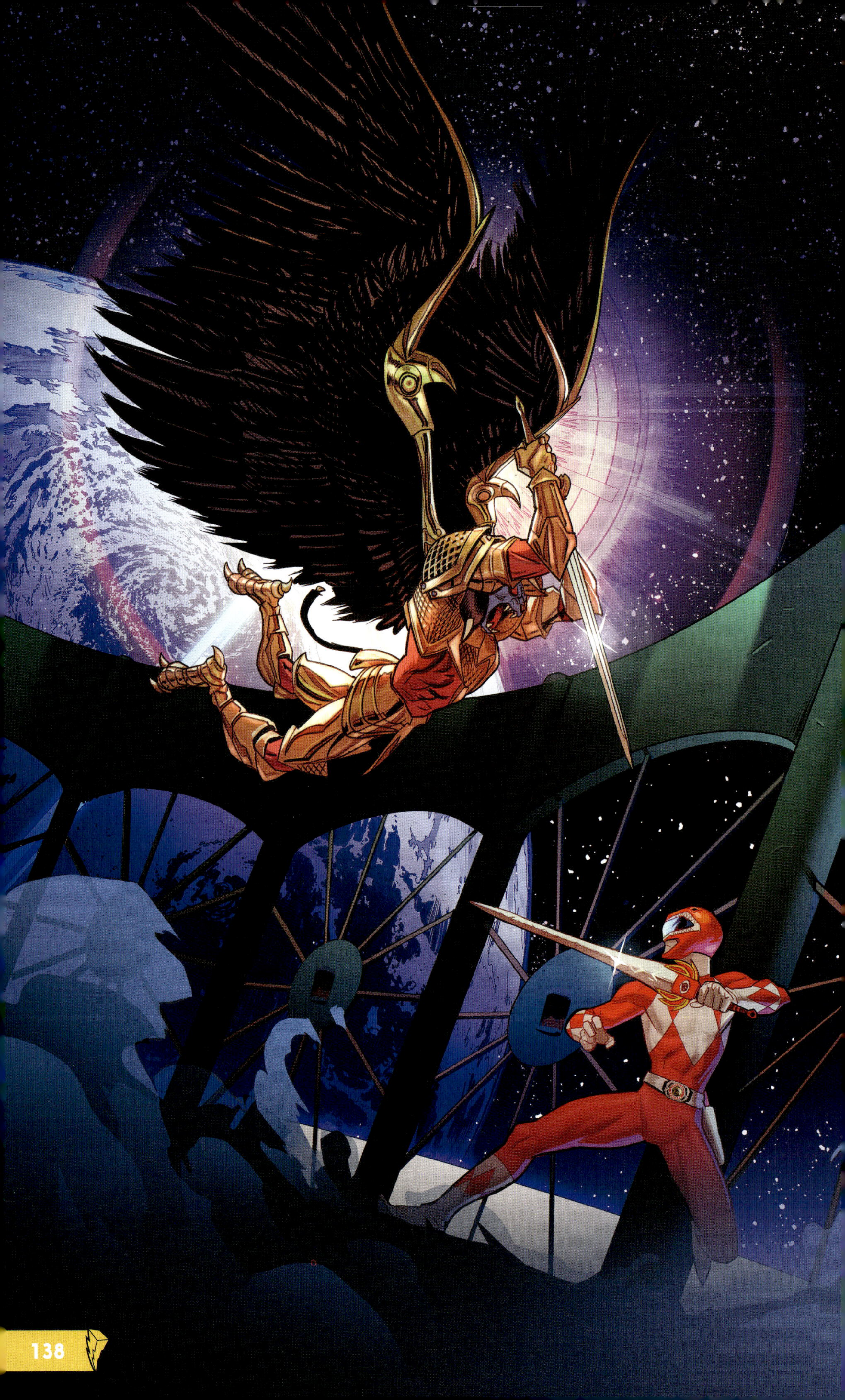

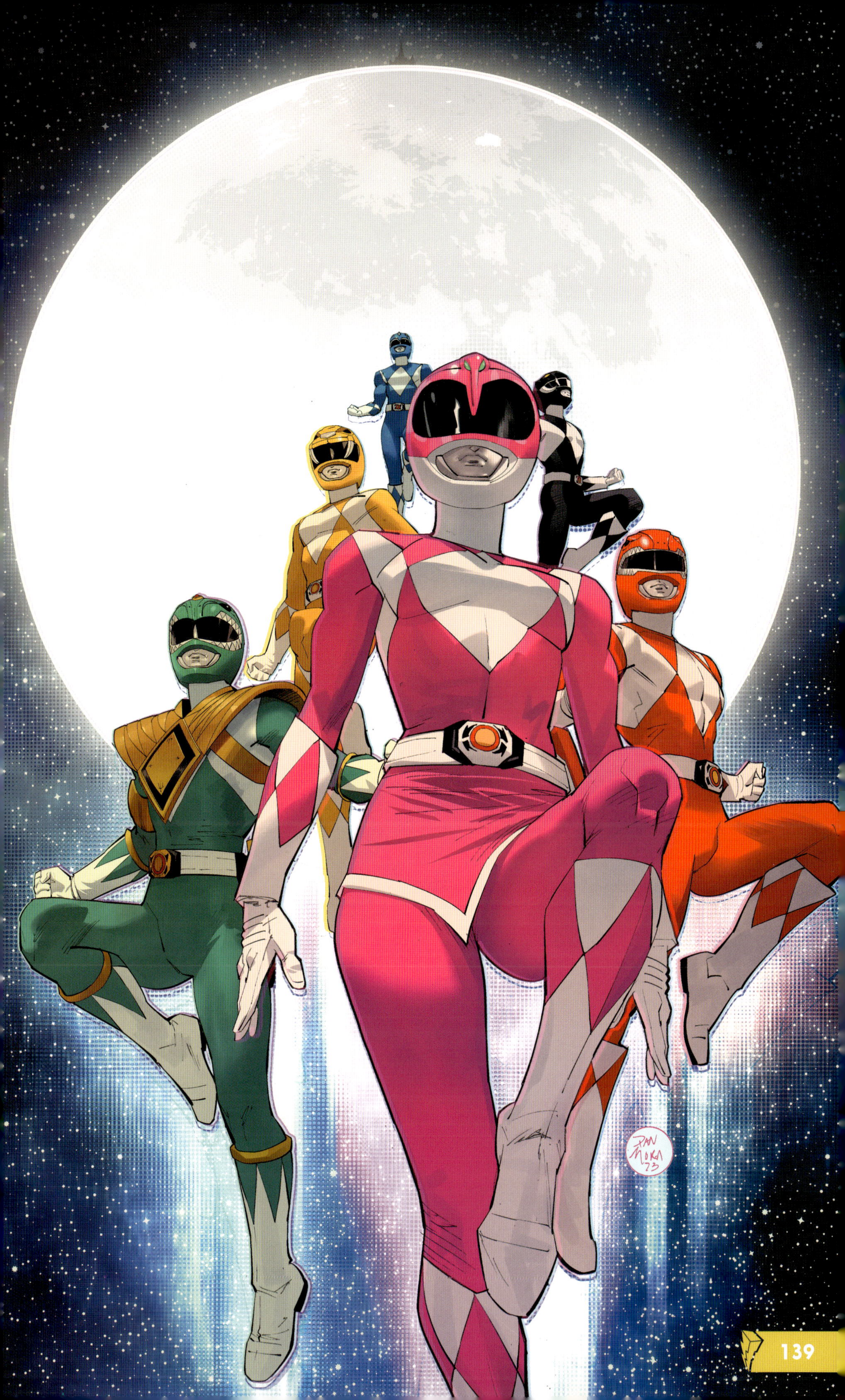

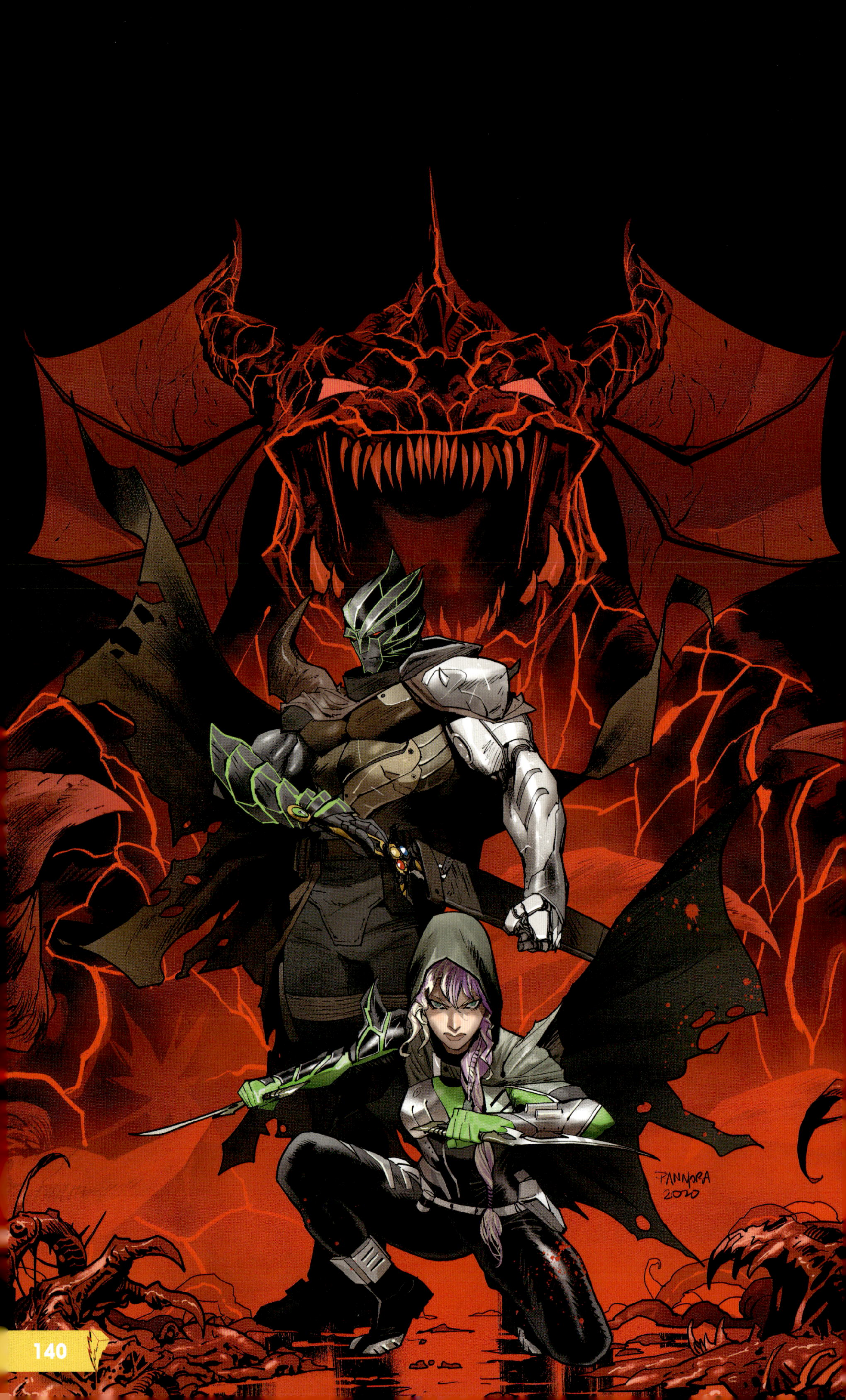
PANNORA
2020

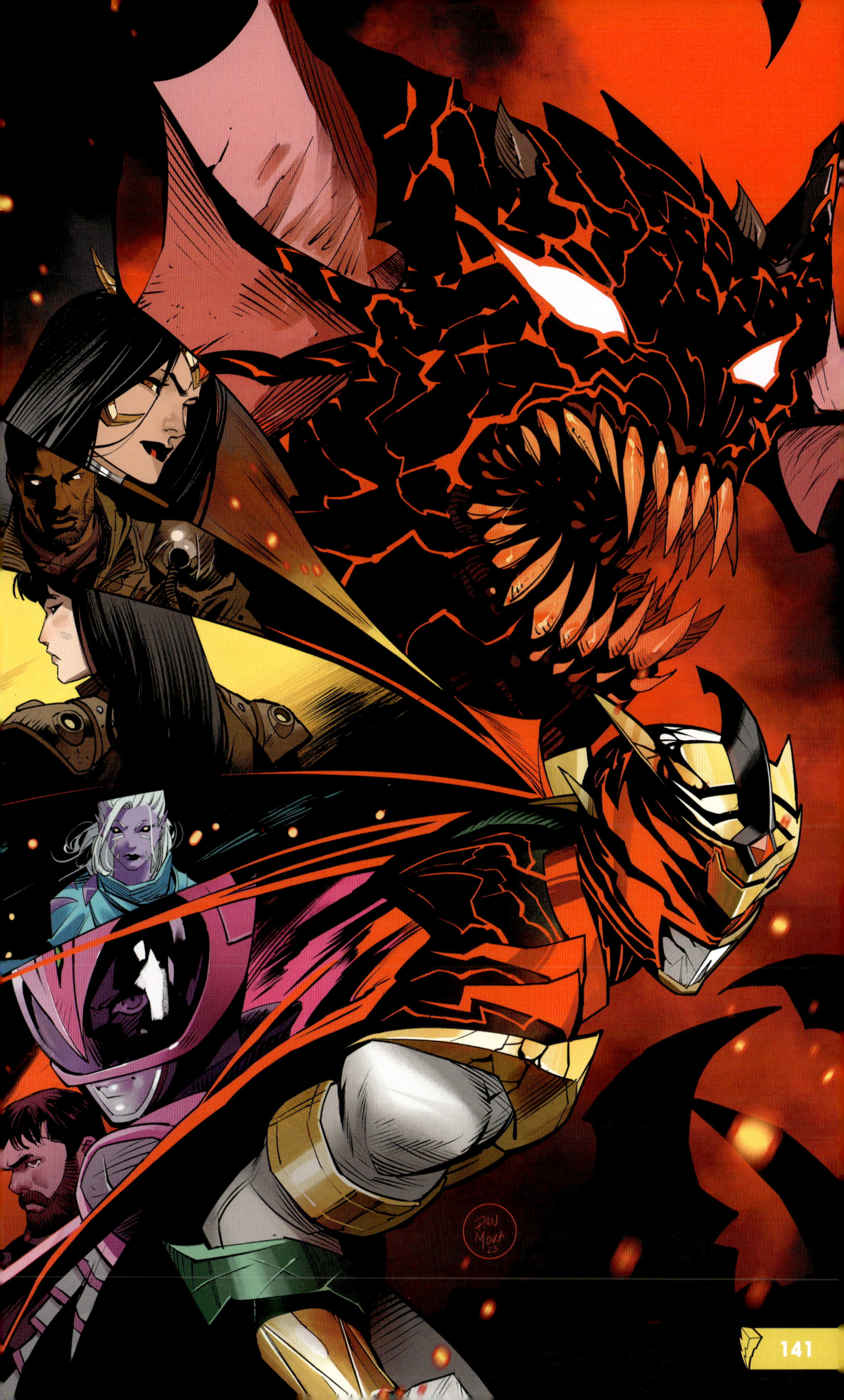

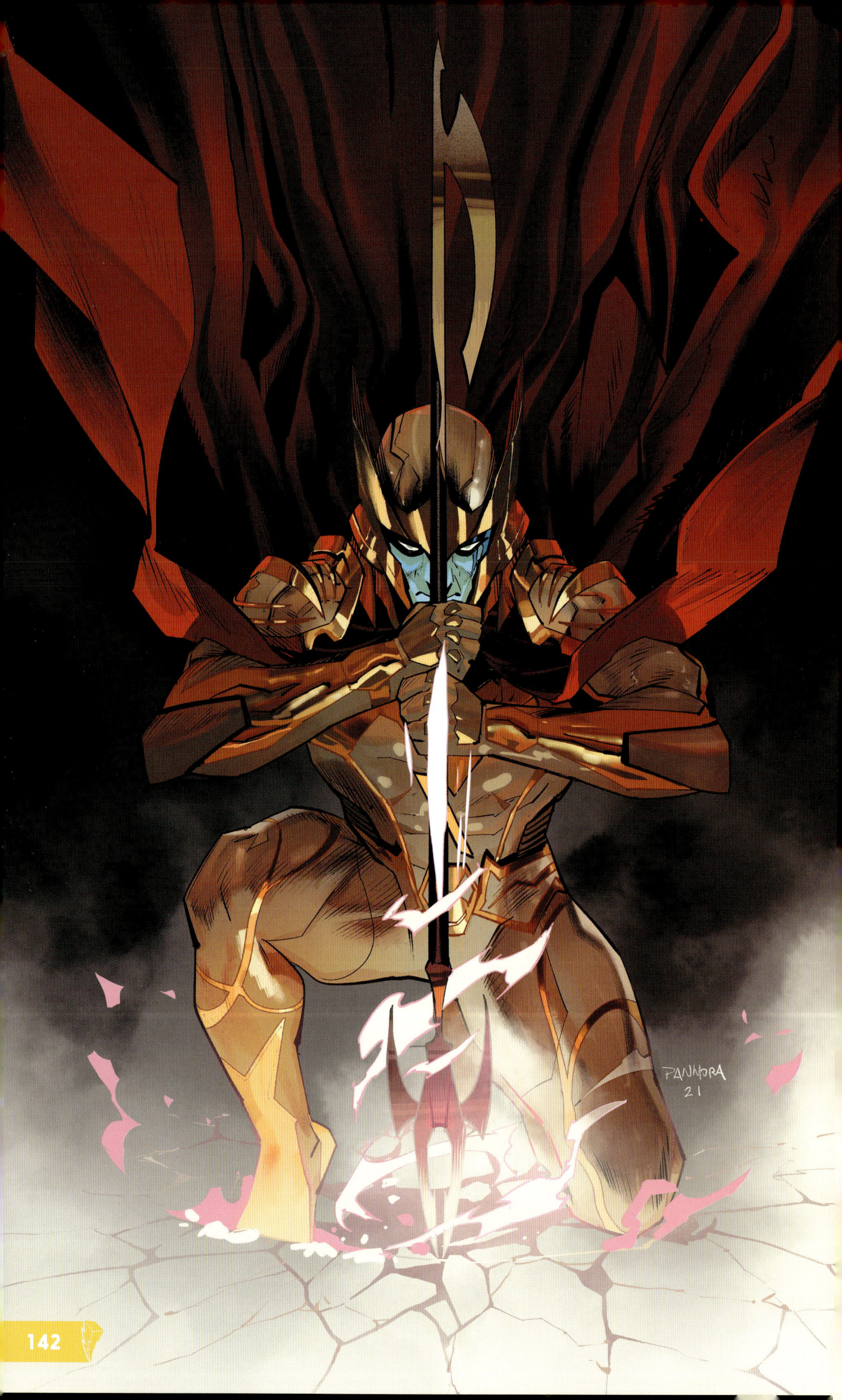

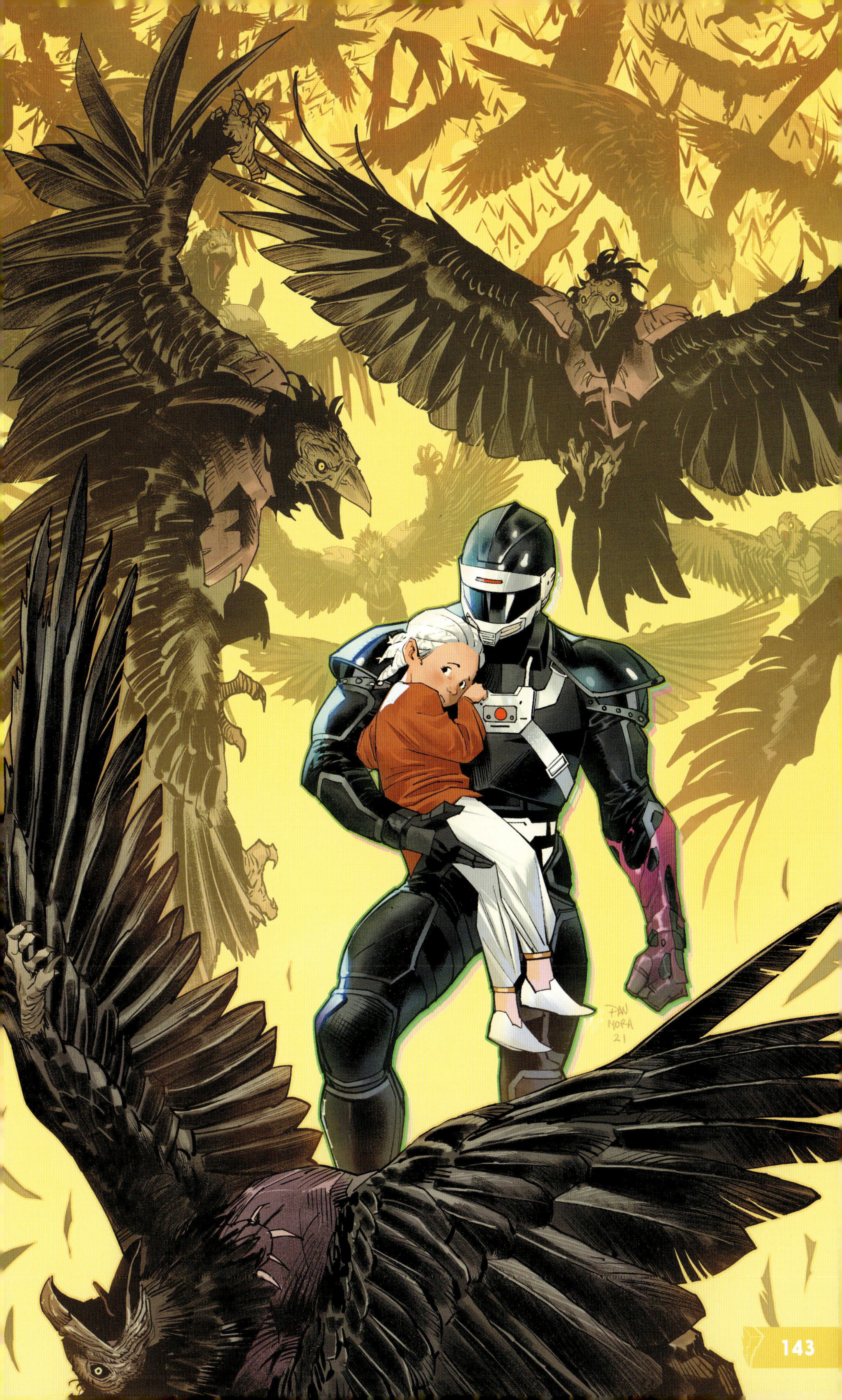
DAN
MORA
21

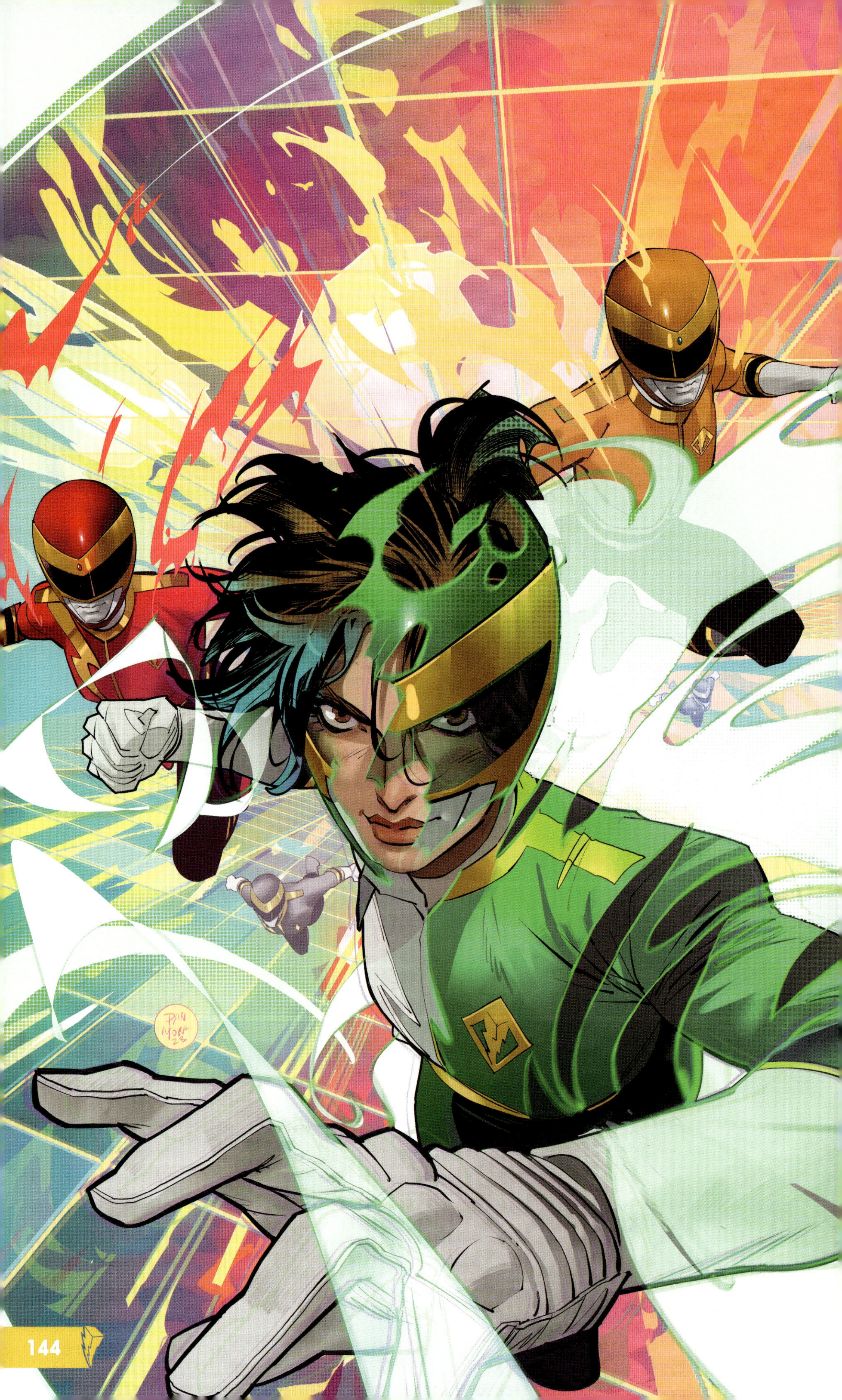

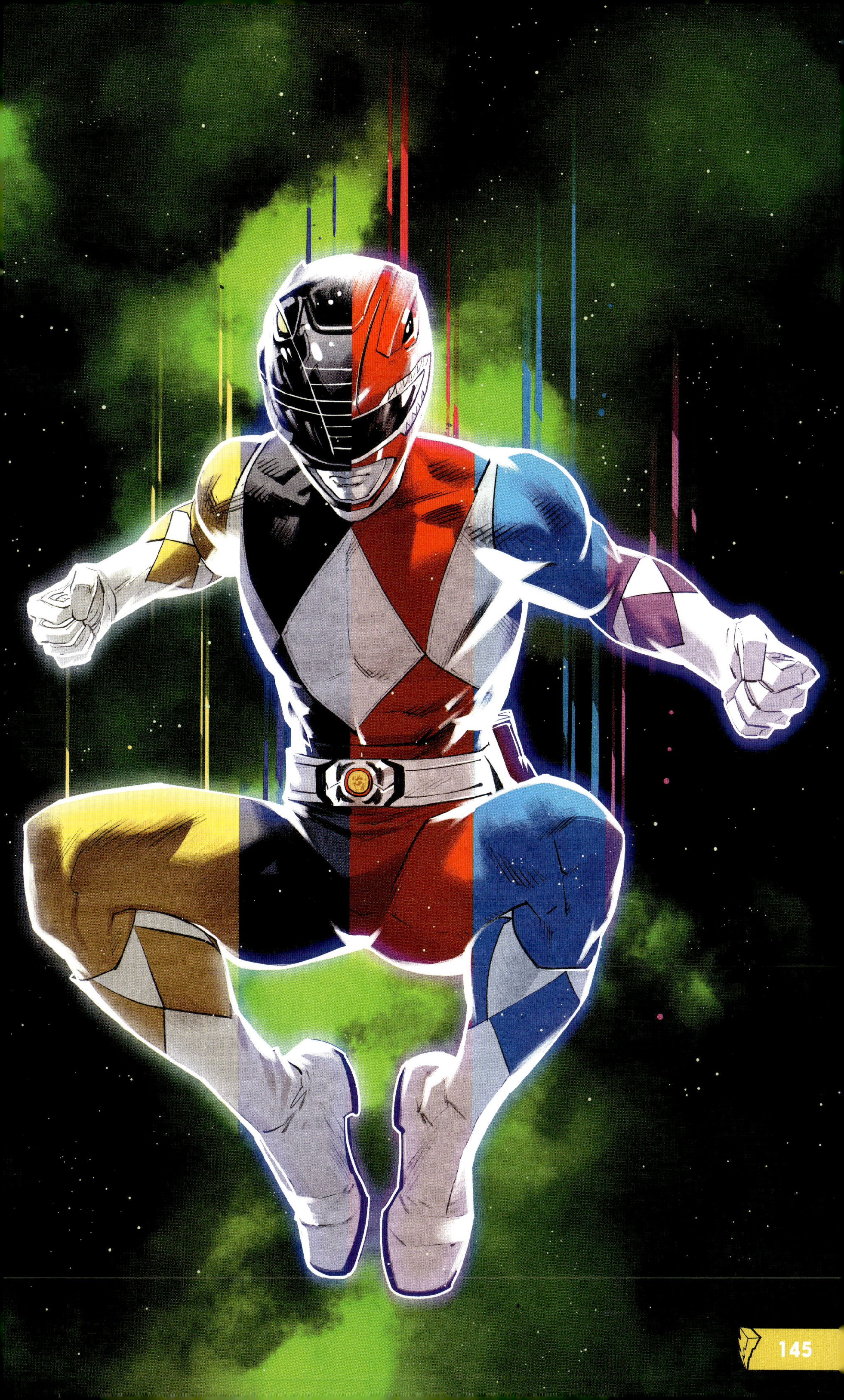

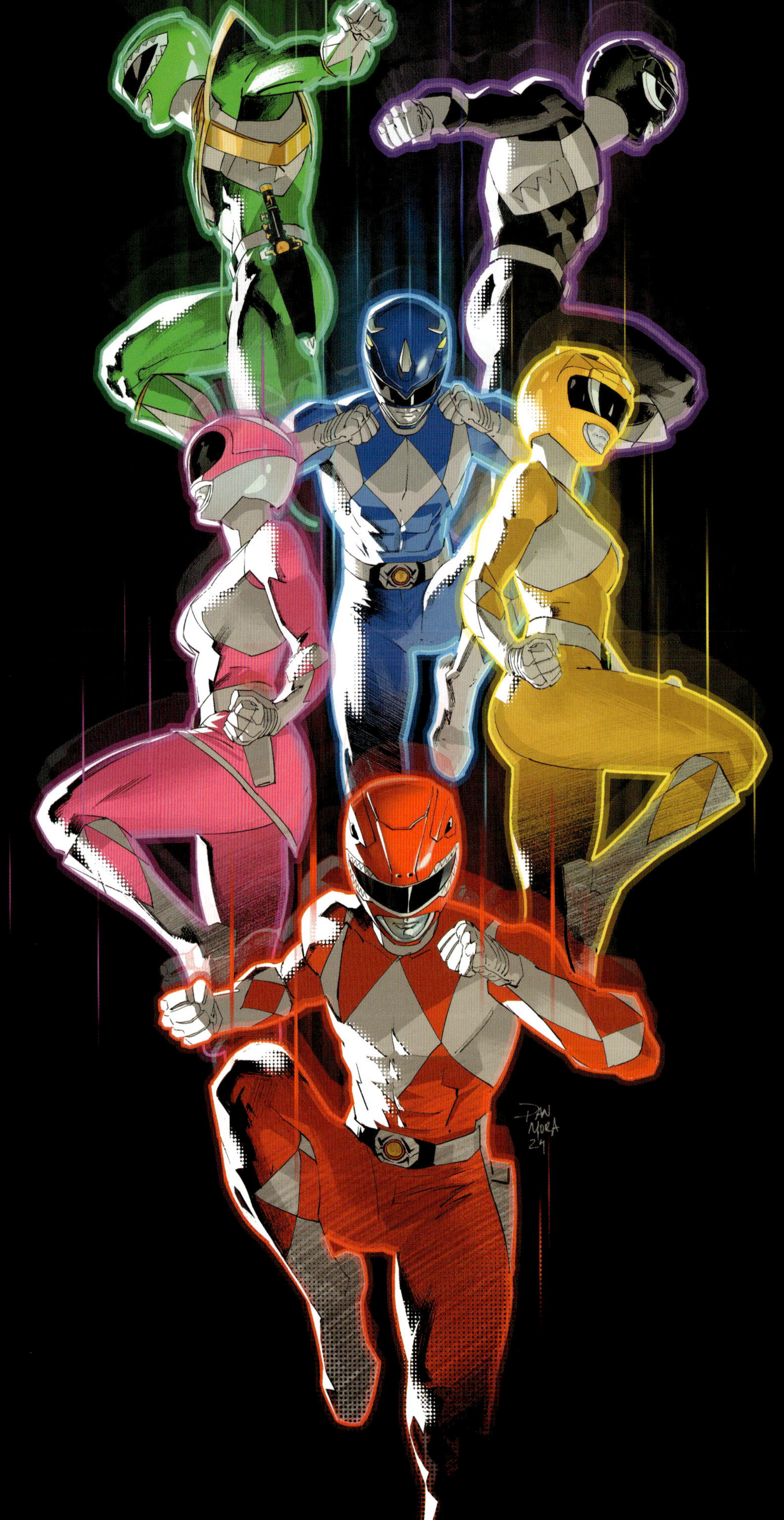
DAN
MORA
24

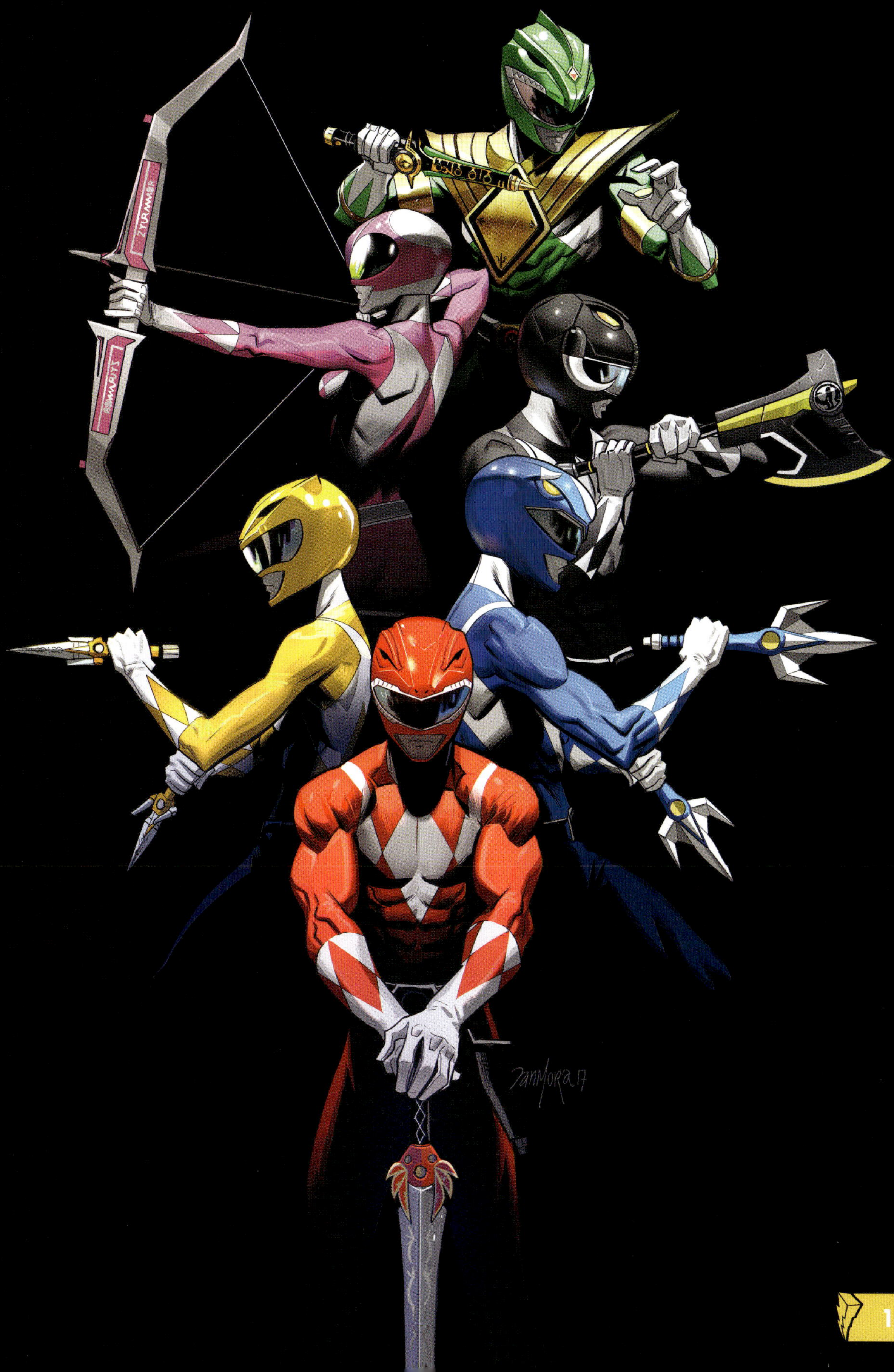

PAGES 150-151 Every Ranger Ever - Layouts to Finished

PAGES 152-155 Every Ranger Ever - Inks

PAGE 156 Ranger Slayer - Roughs to Inks

PAGE 157 Ranger Slider - Final

PAGES 158-161 Interior Art - From Roughs to Final

PAGE 162 Alternate Timeline Rangers - Inks

PAGE 163 Alternate Timeline Rangers - Colors

PAGES 164-165 Mighty Morphin Power Rangers 41 - Rough to Finished

PAGE 166 Power Rangers 100 Cover - Inks

PAGE 167 Power Rangers 100 Cover - Finished

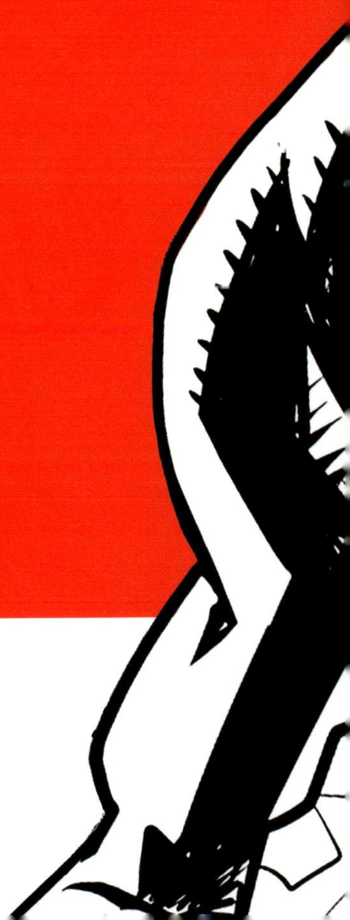

PROCESS

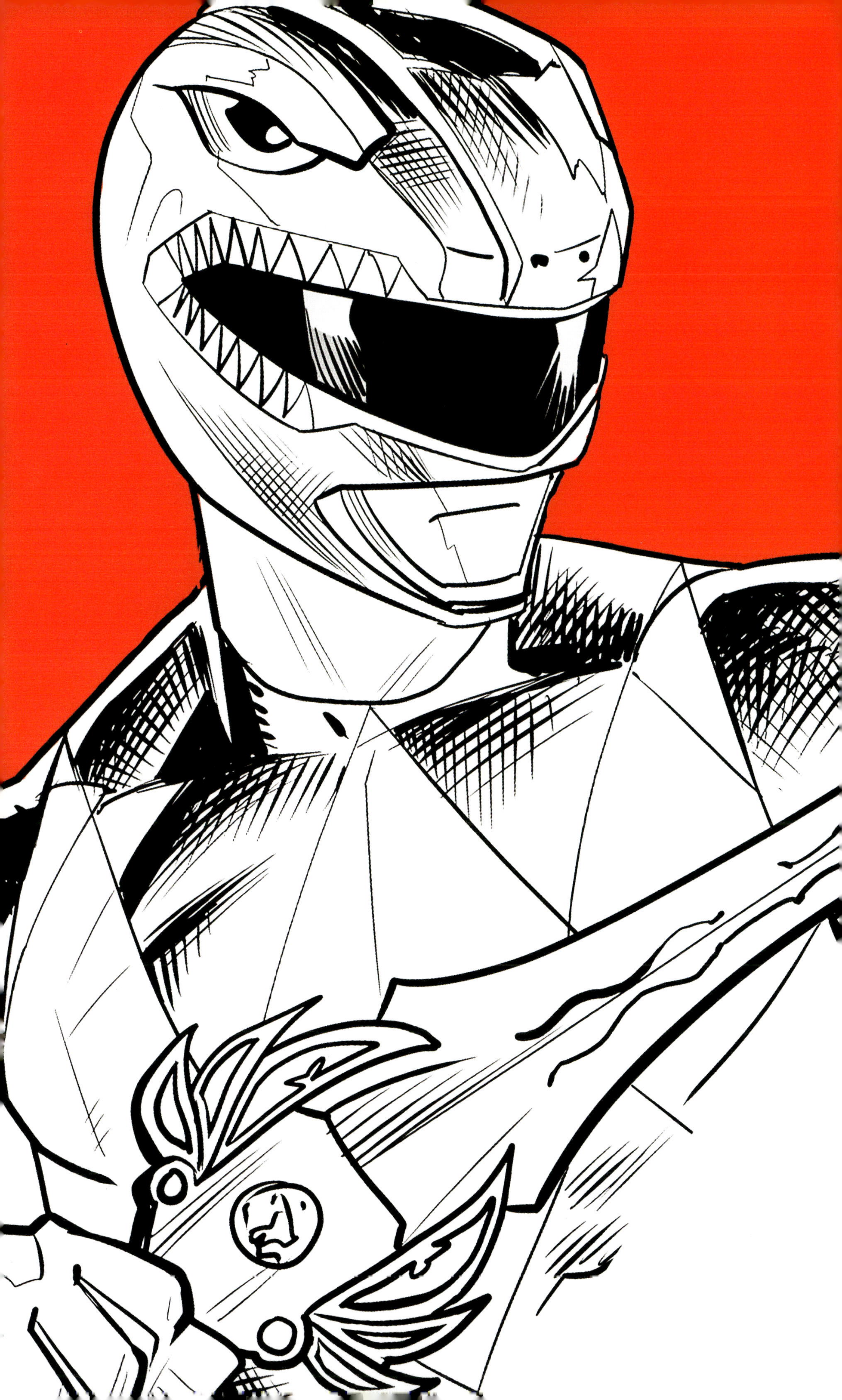

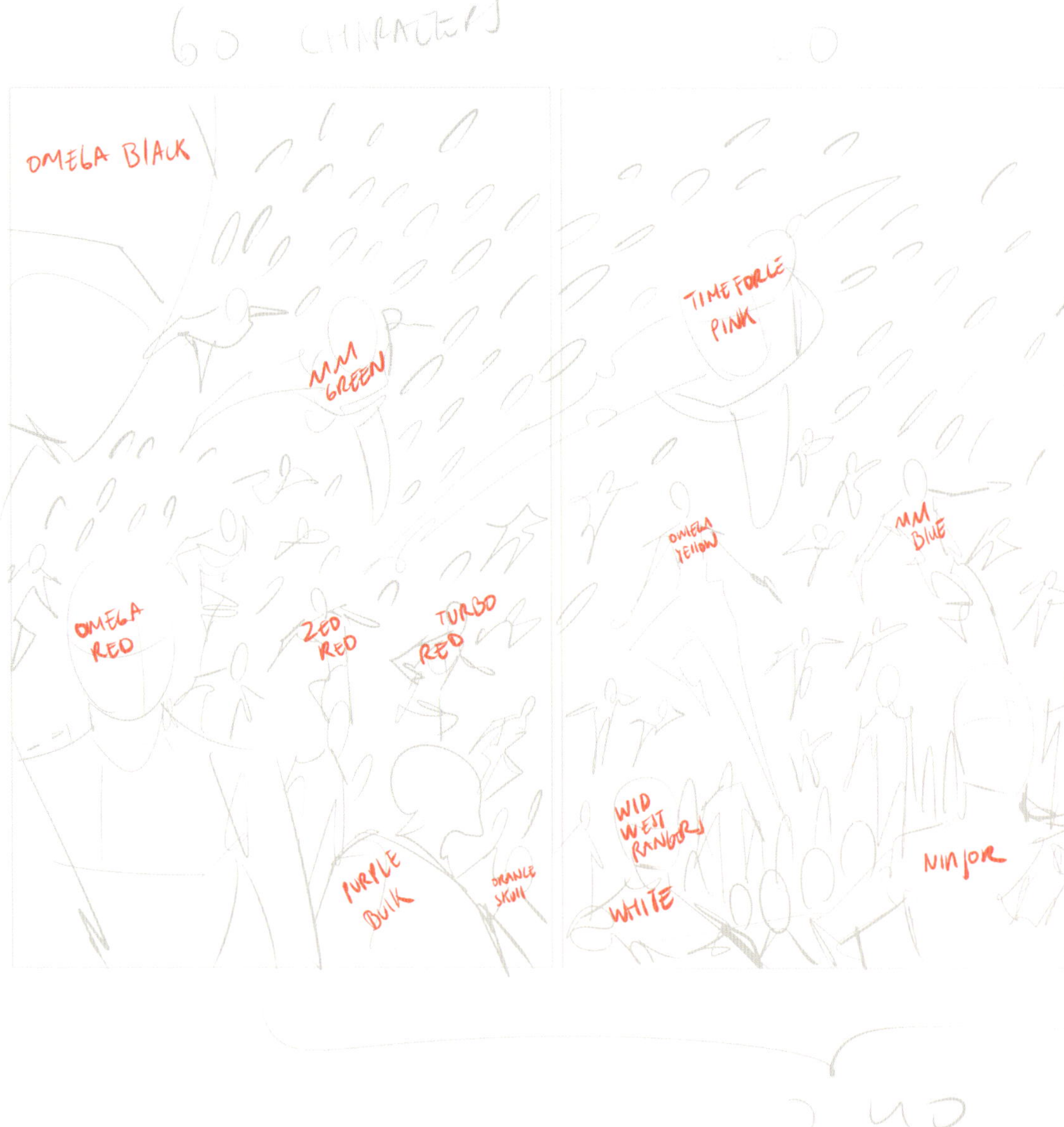
60 CHARACTERS
OMEGA BLACK
MM GREEN
TIME FORCE PINK
OMEGA YELLOW
MM BLUE
OMEGA RED
ZEO RED
TURBO RED
WILD WEST RANGERS
WHITE
NINJOR
PURPLE BULK
ORANGE SKULL
240

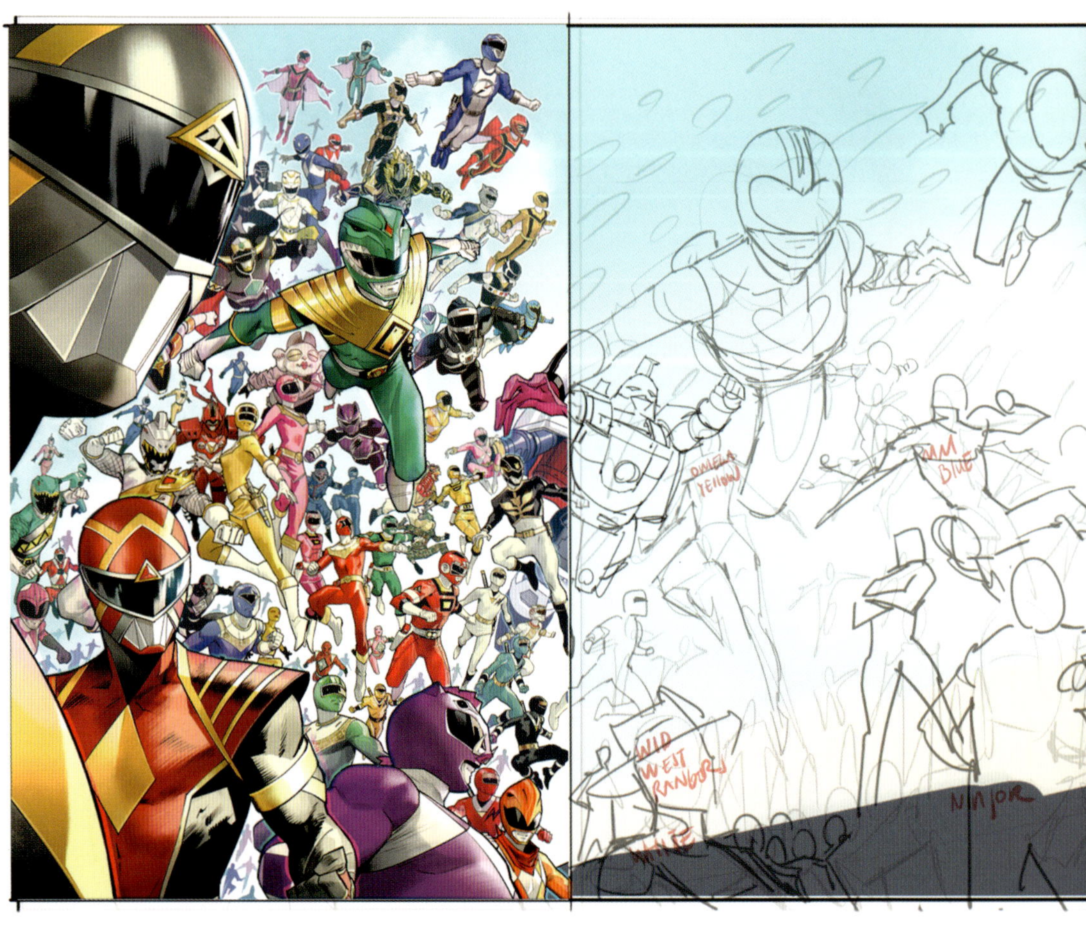

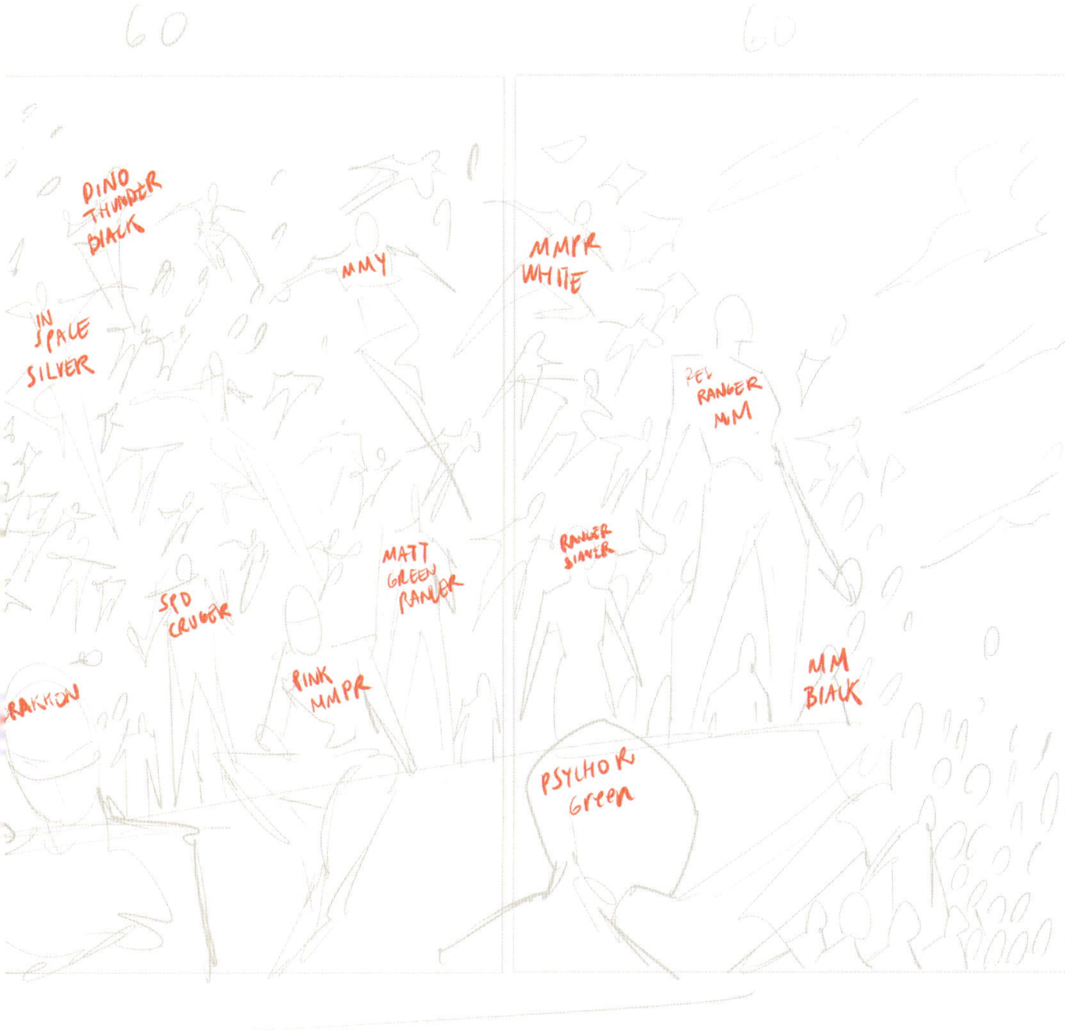
60
60
DINO THUNDER BLACK
MMY
IN SPACE SILVER
MMPR WHITE
RANGER MM
SPD CRUGER
MATT GREEN RANGER
PINK MMPR
MM BLACK
PSYCHO R Green

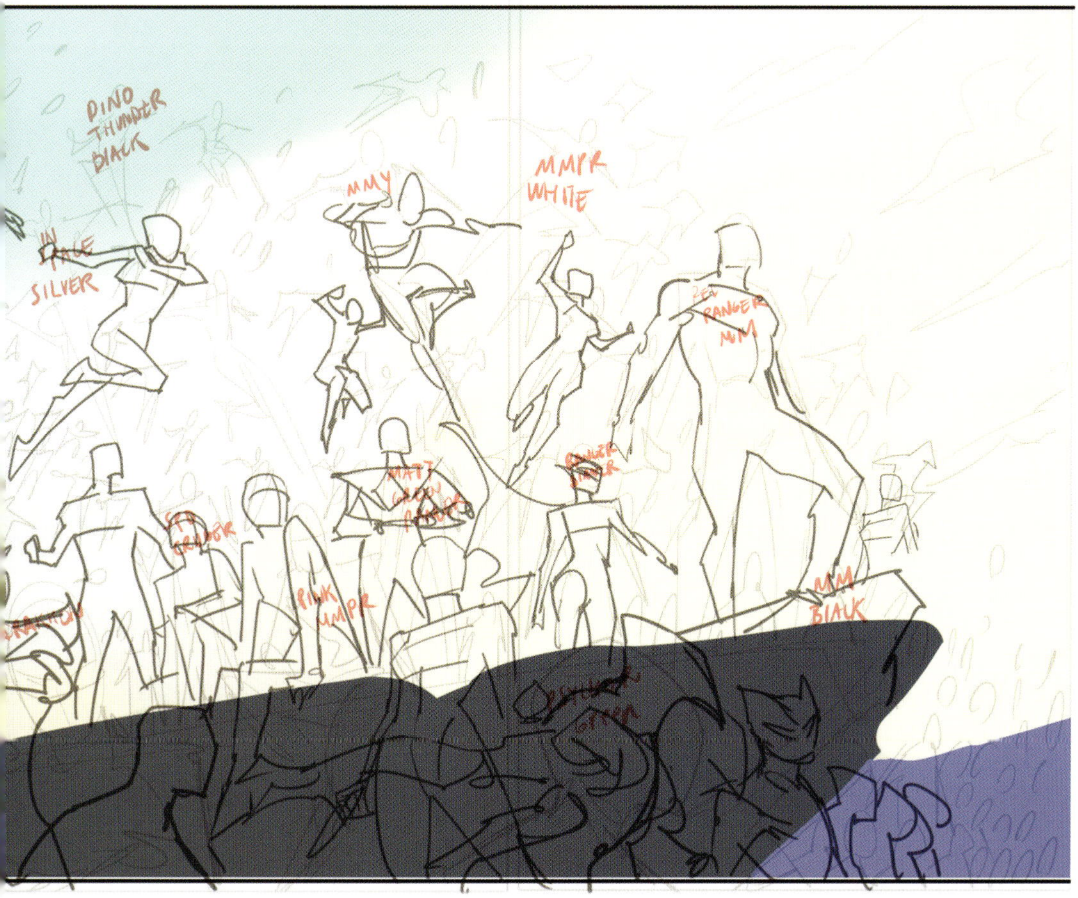
DINO THUNDER BLACK
MMY
SILVER
MMPR WHITE
MM BLACK

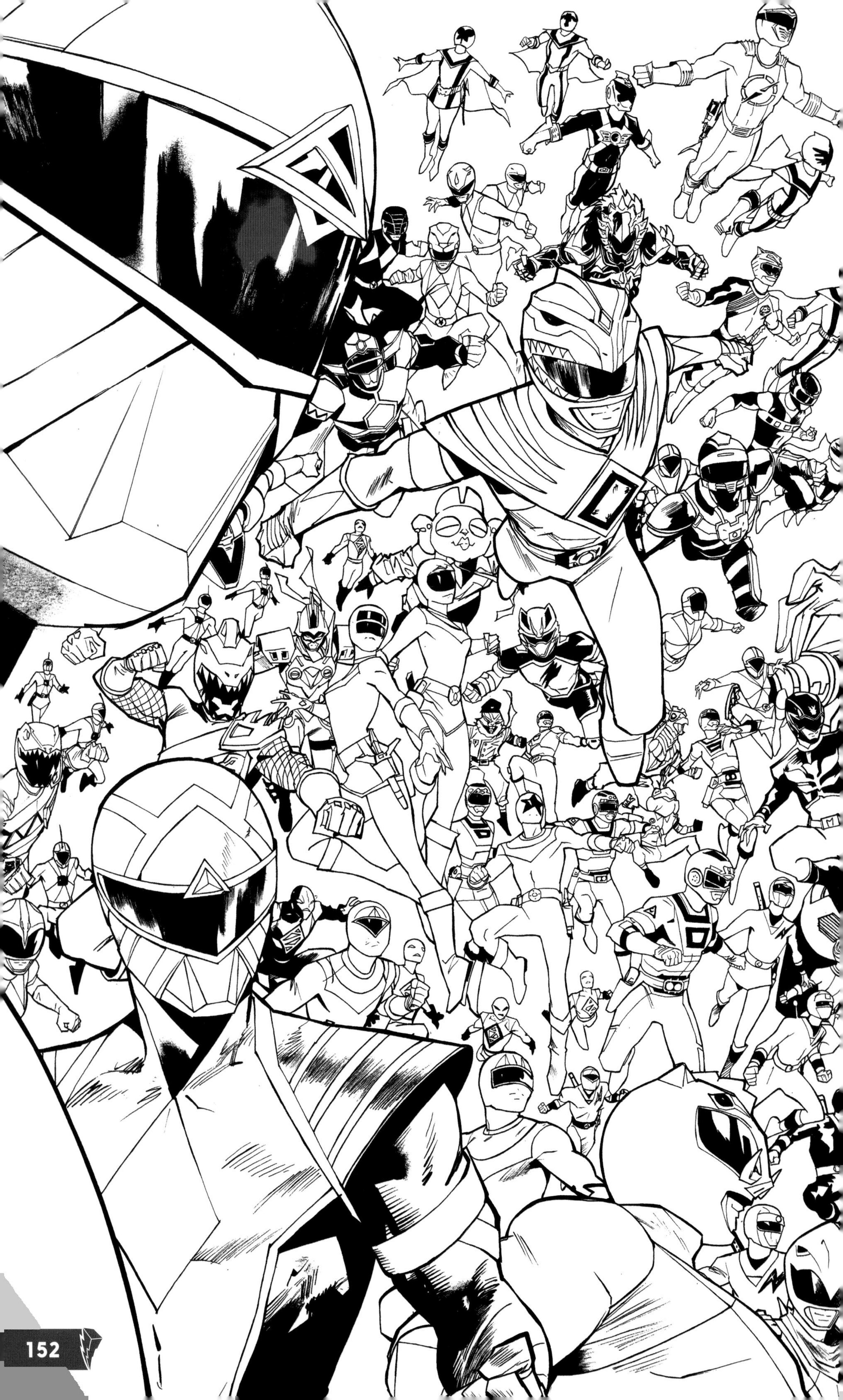

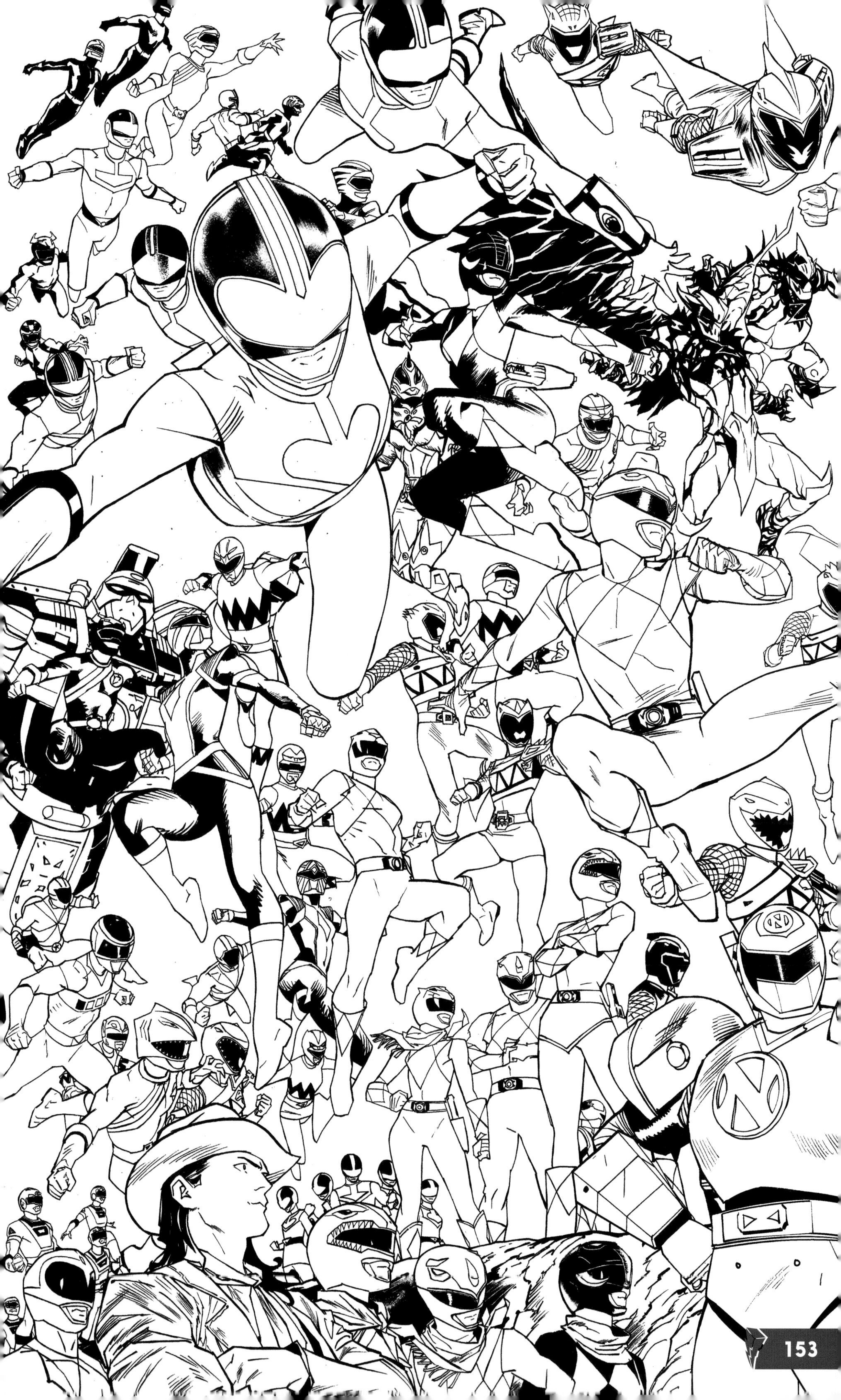

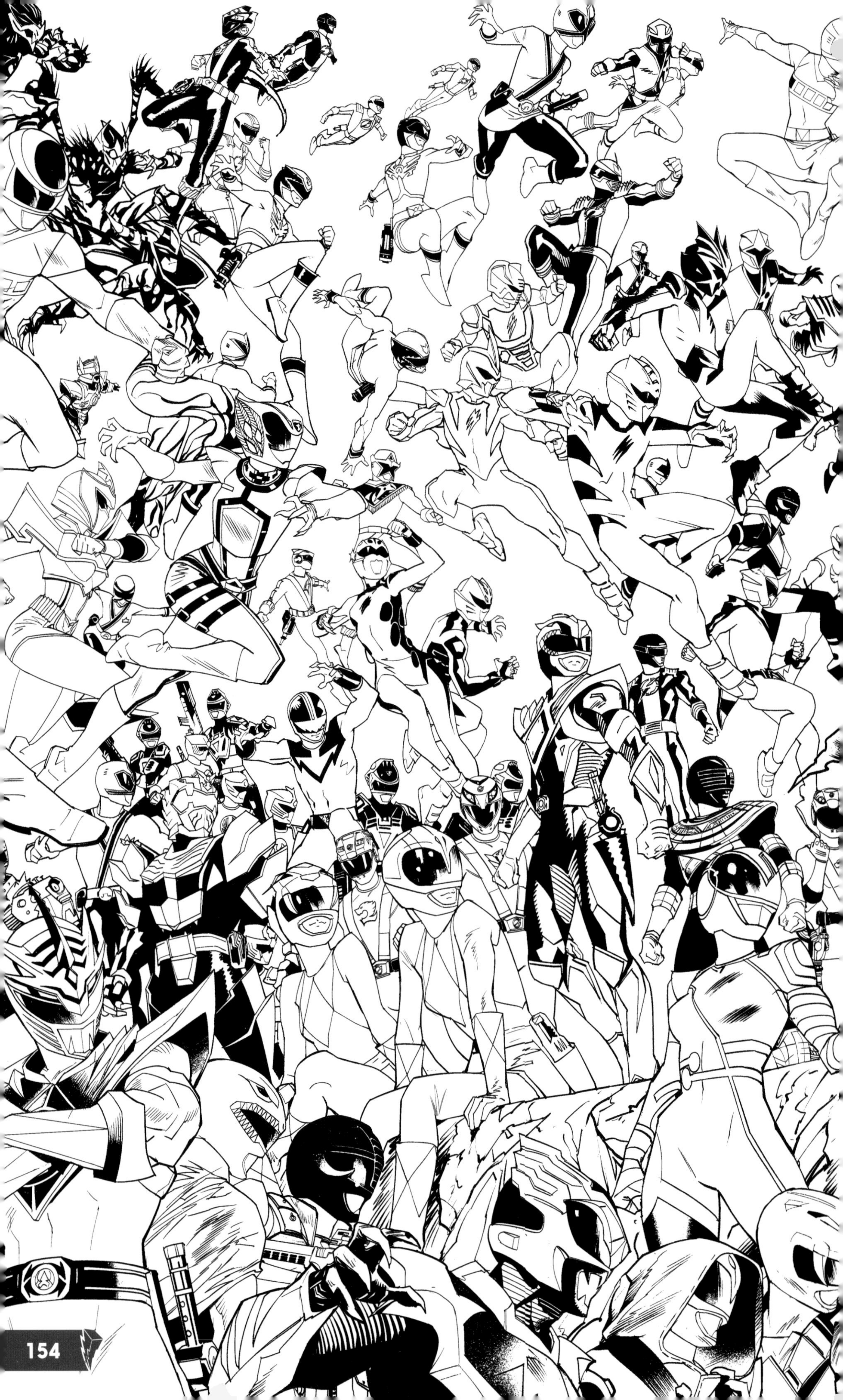

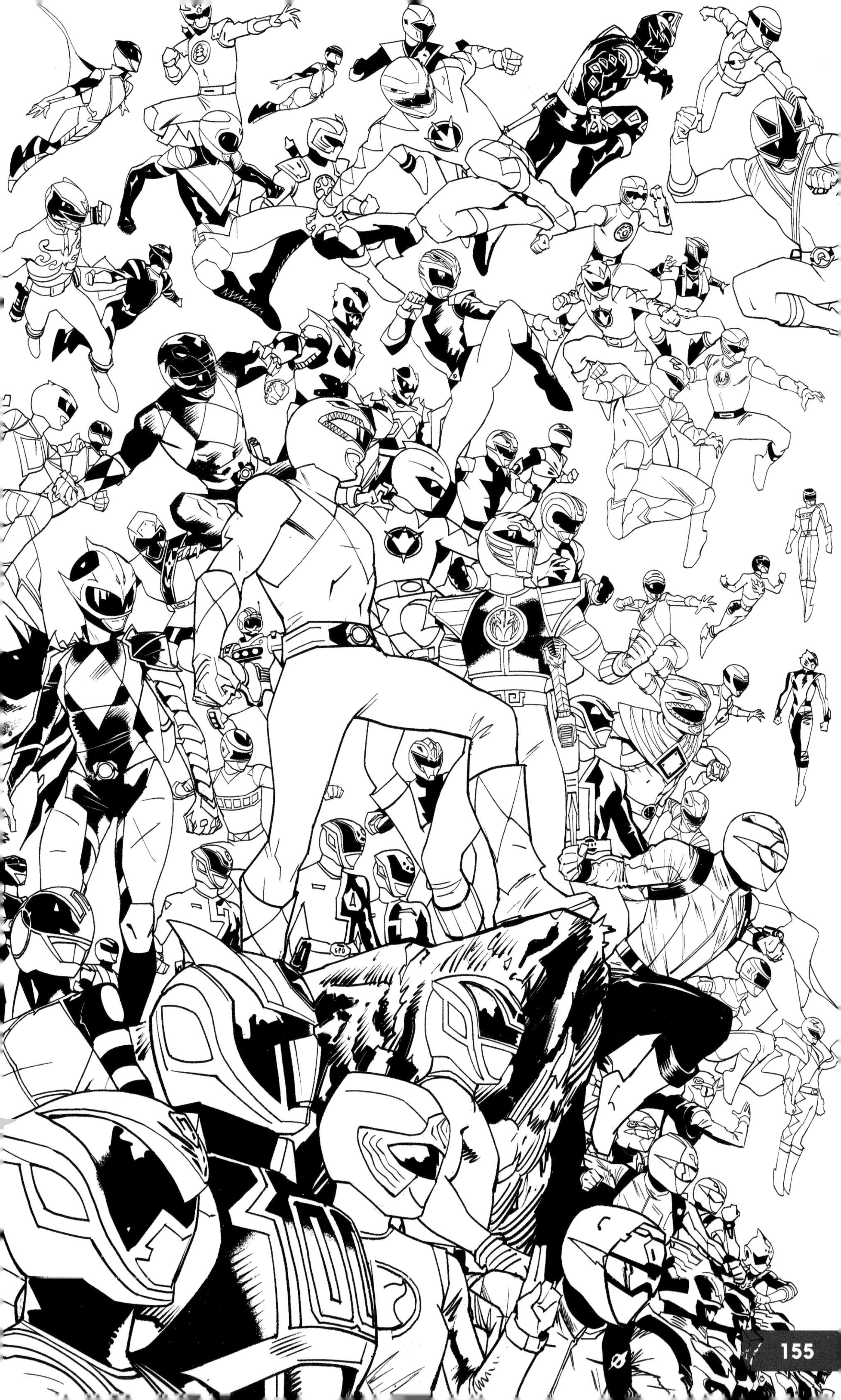

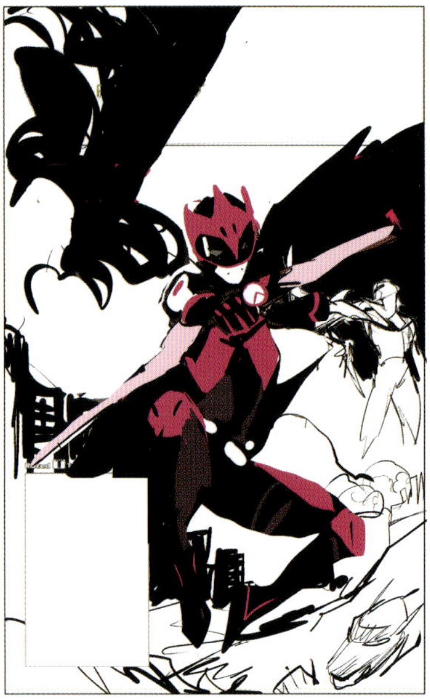

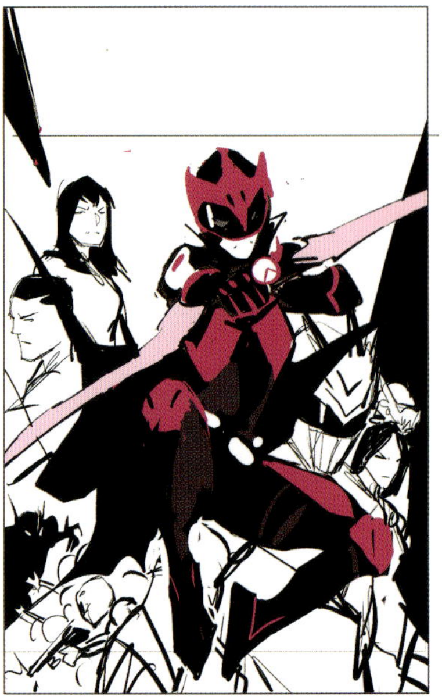

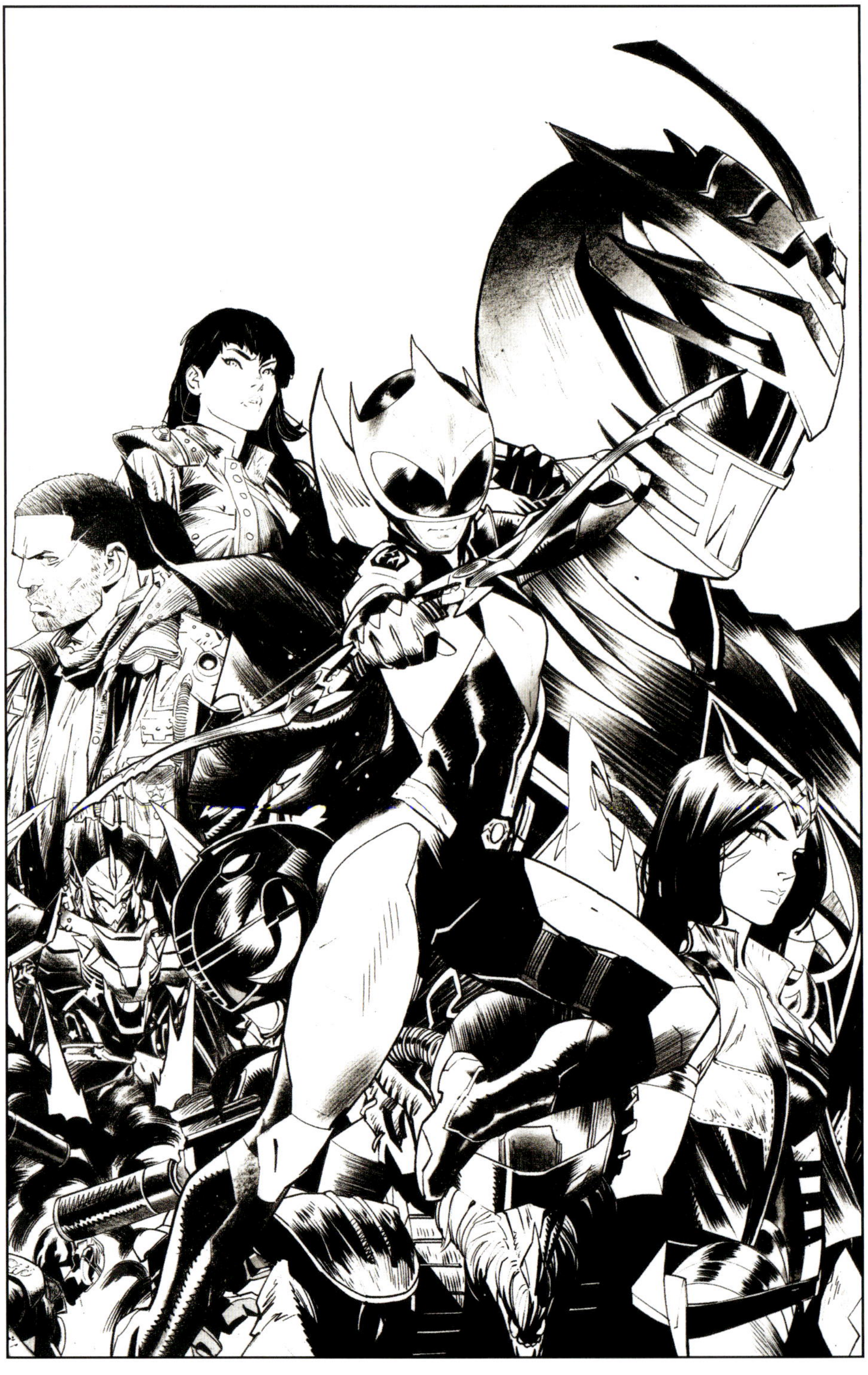

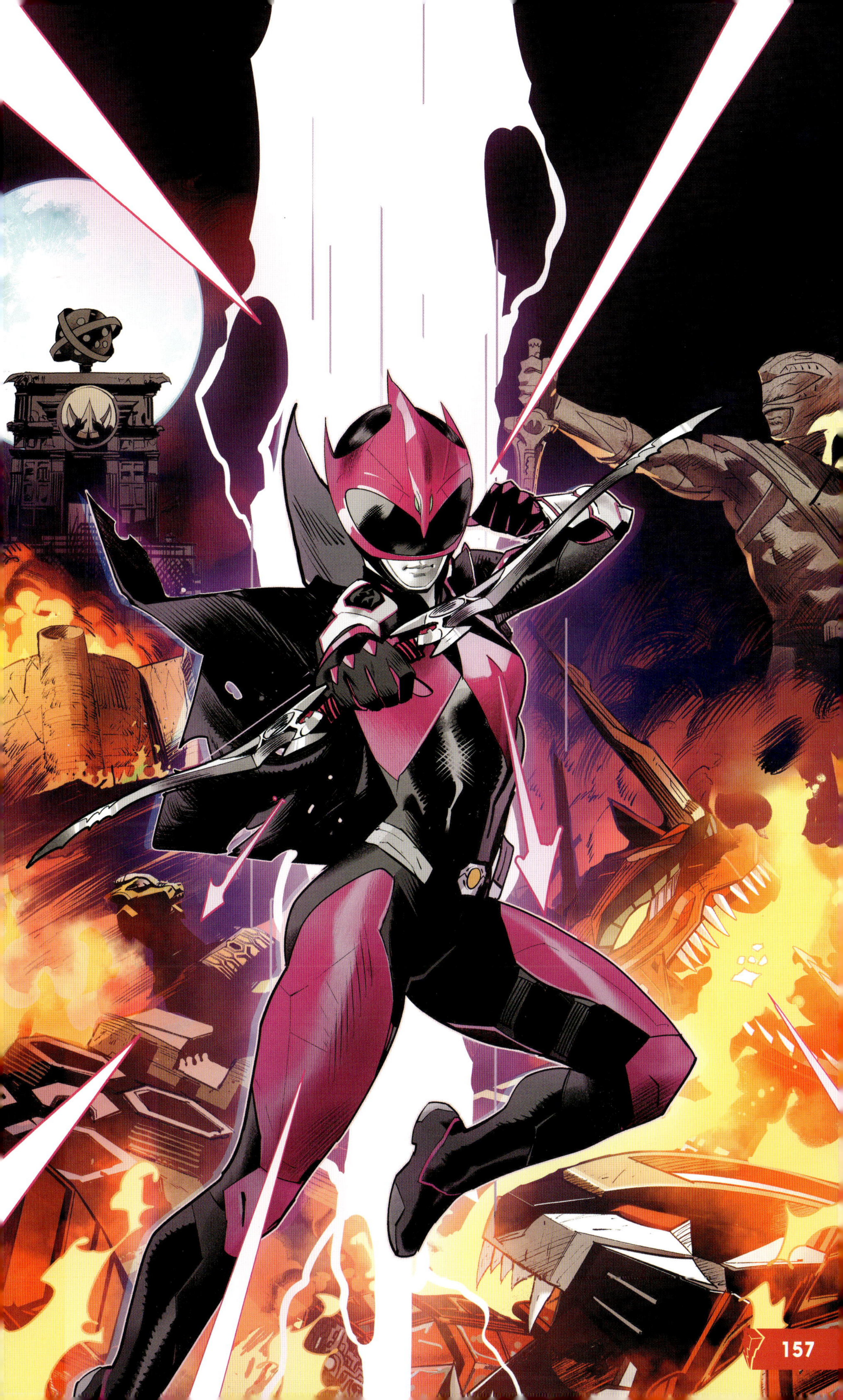

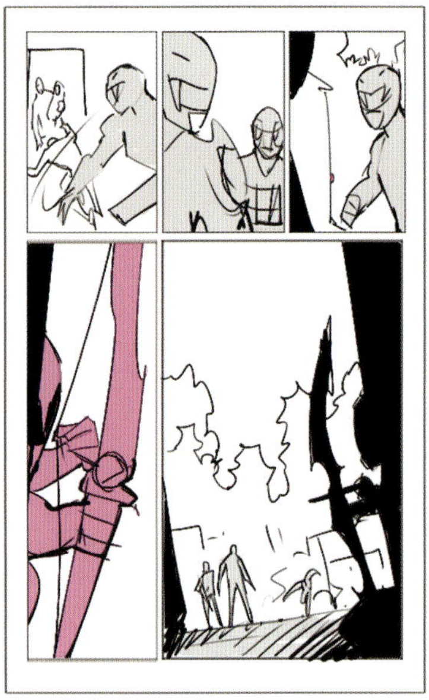
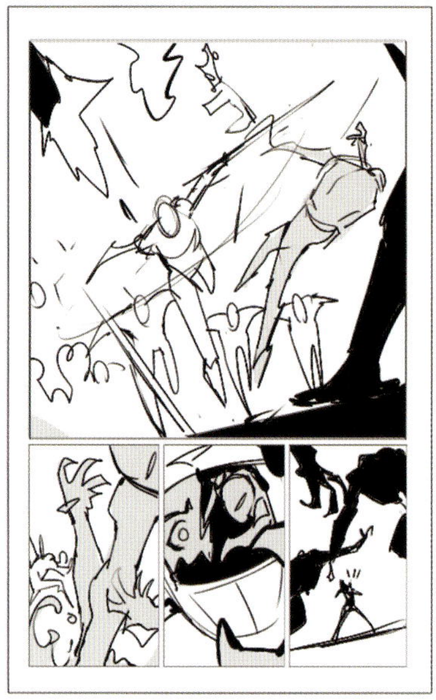
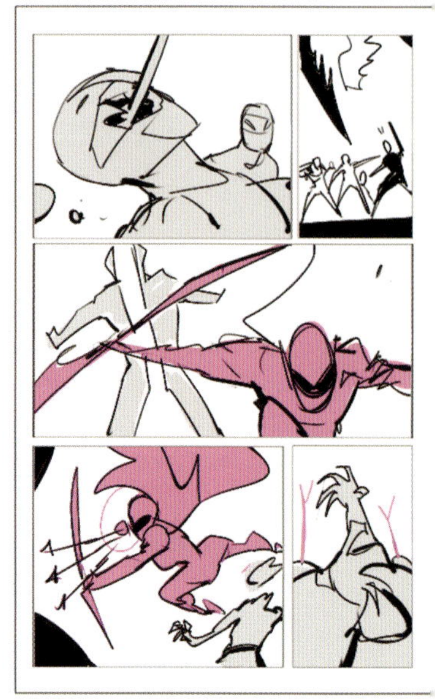
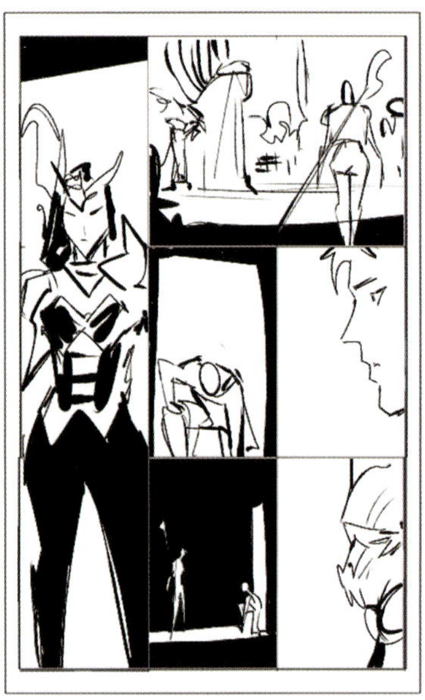
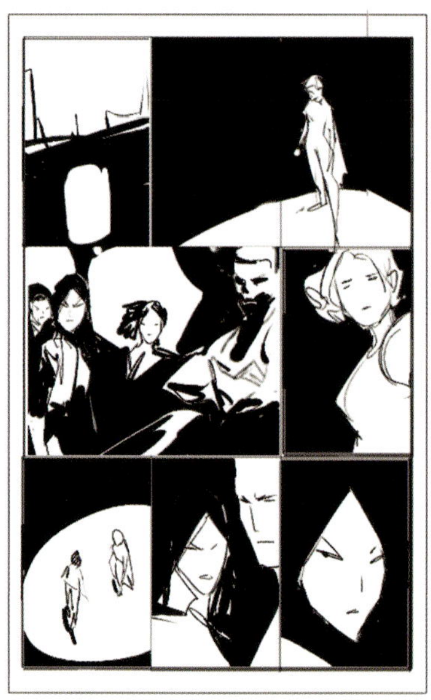
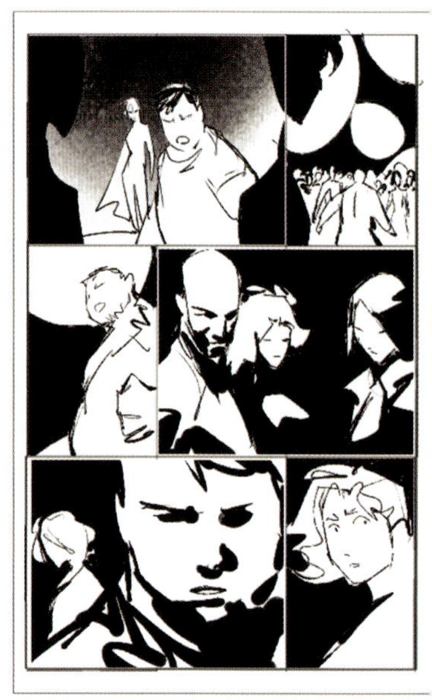
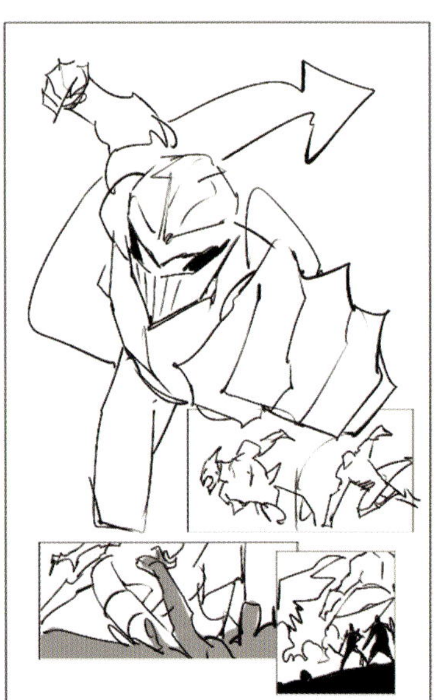
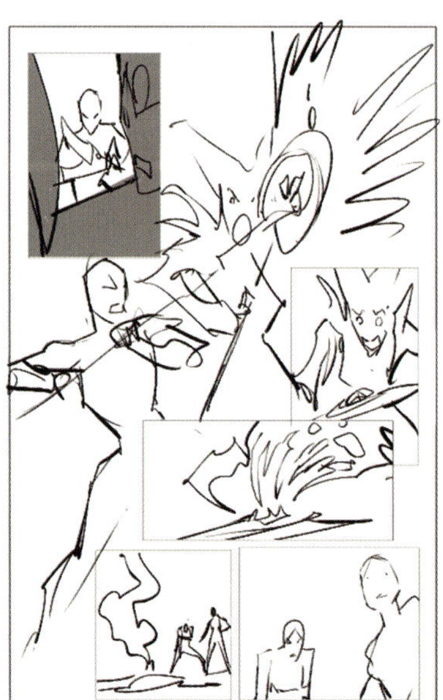
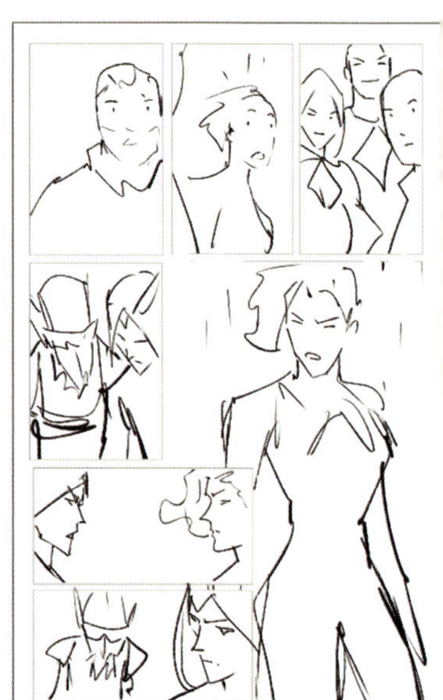

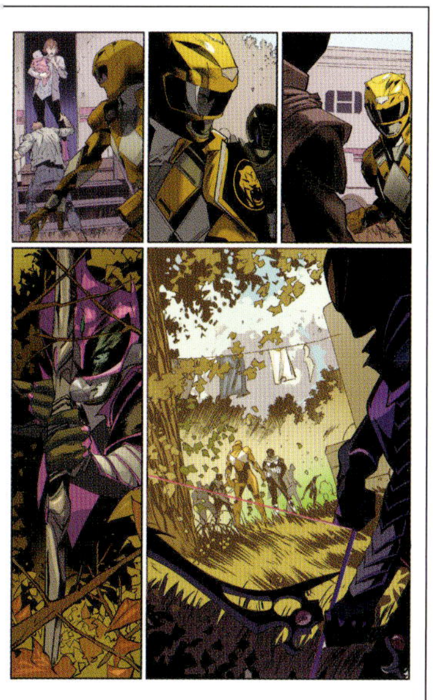
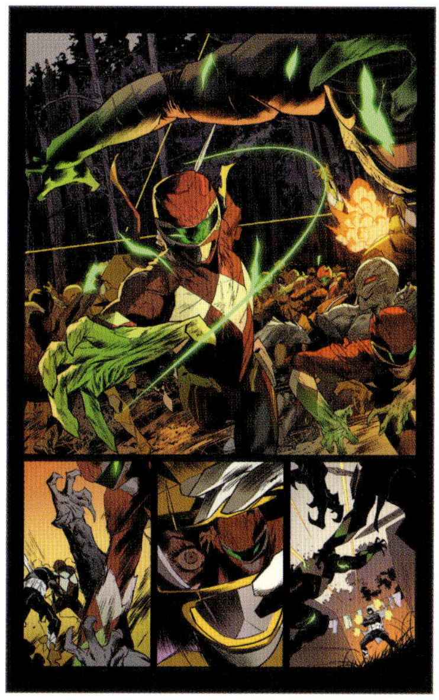
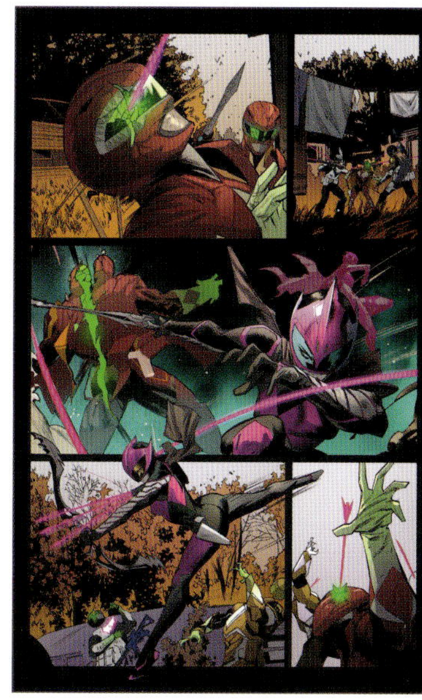
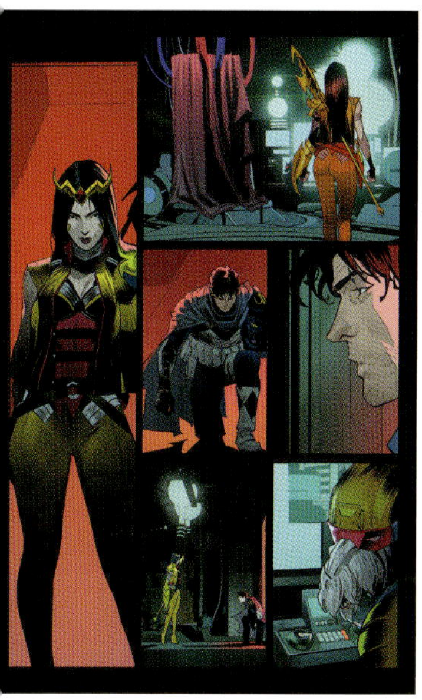
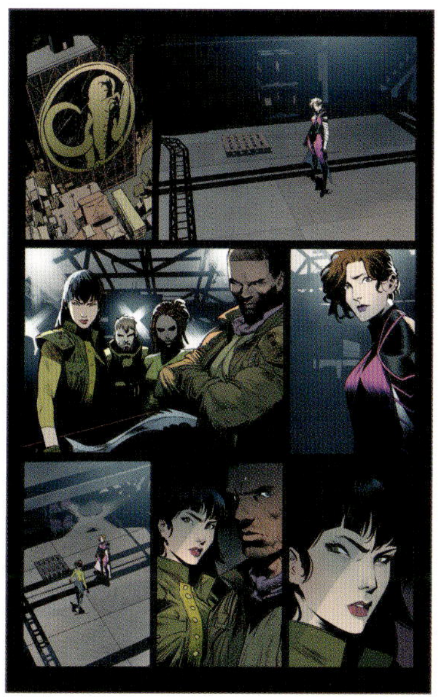
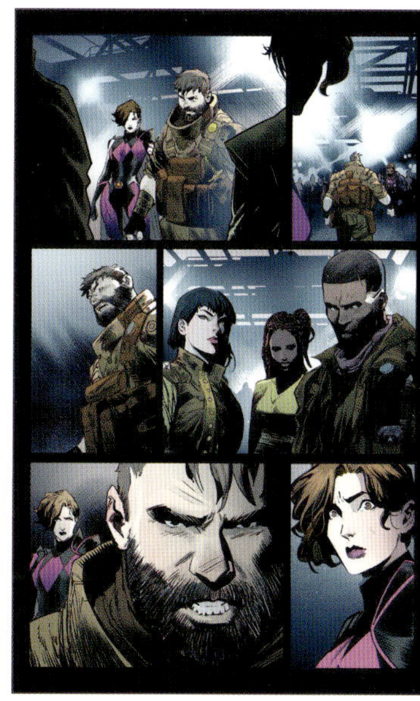
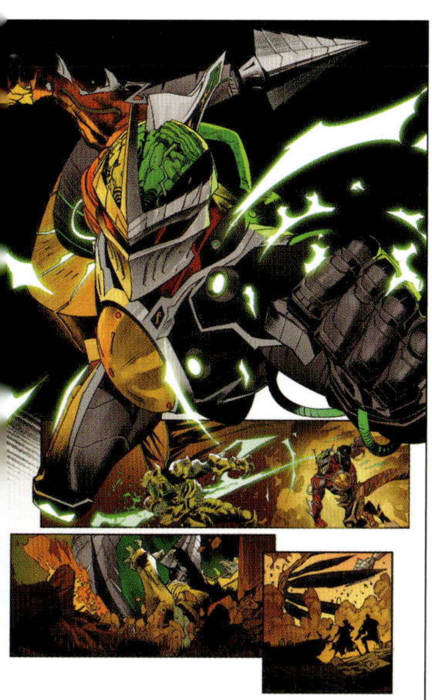
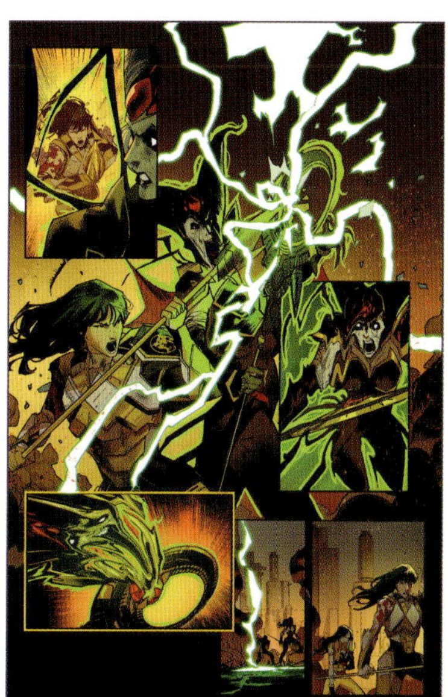
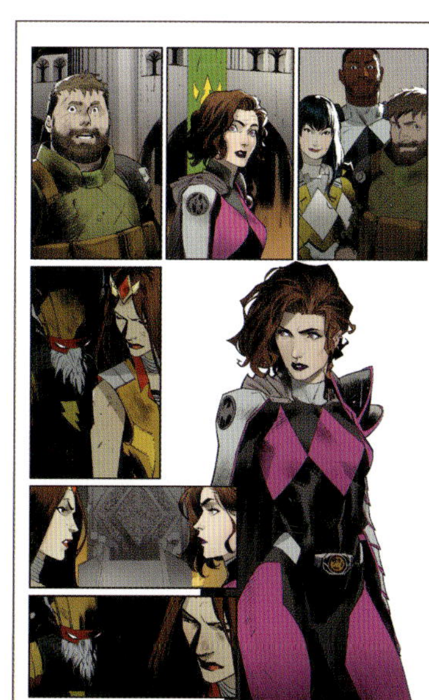

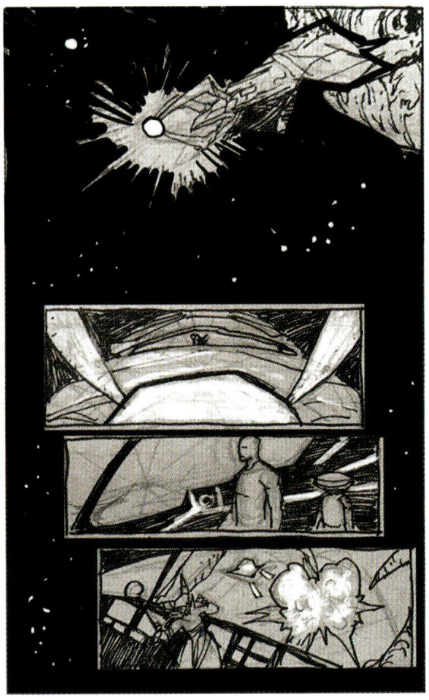
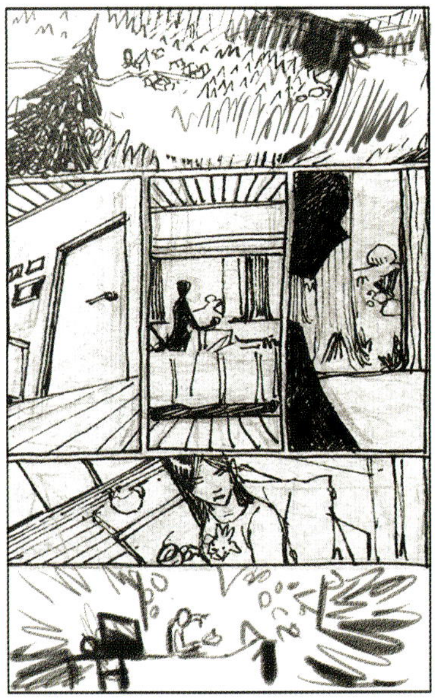
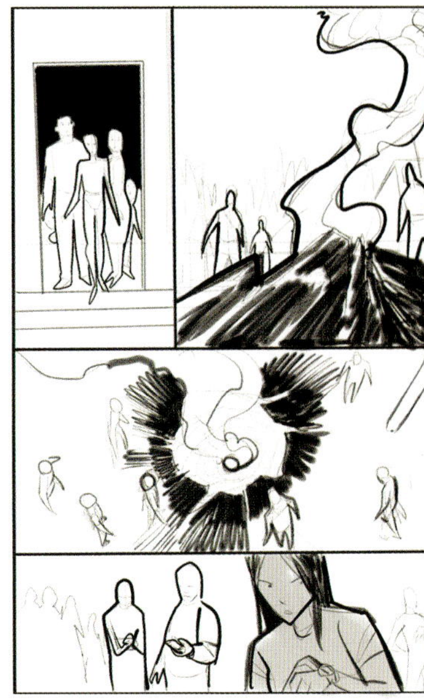
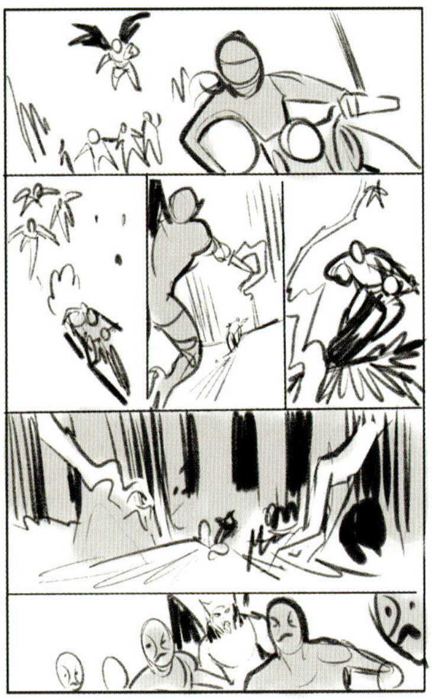
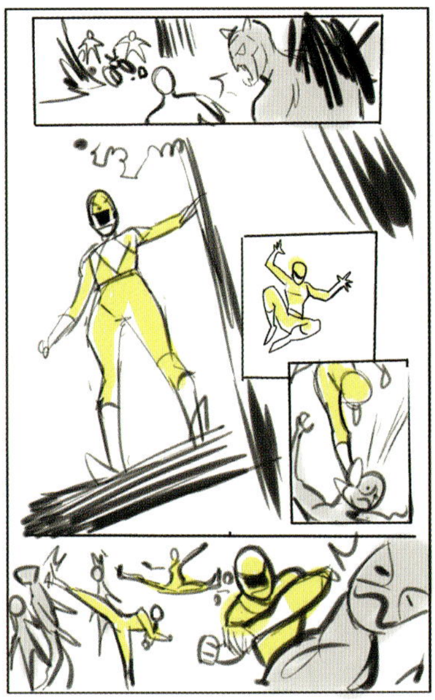
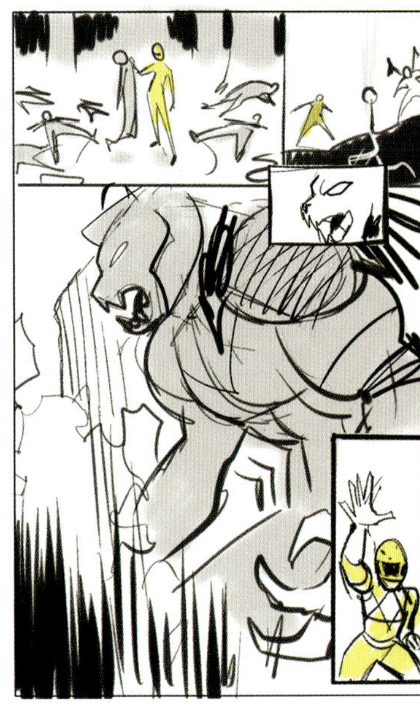
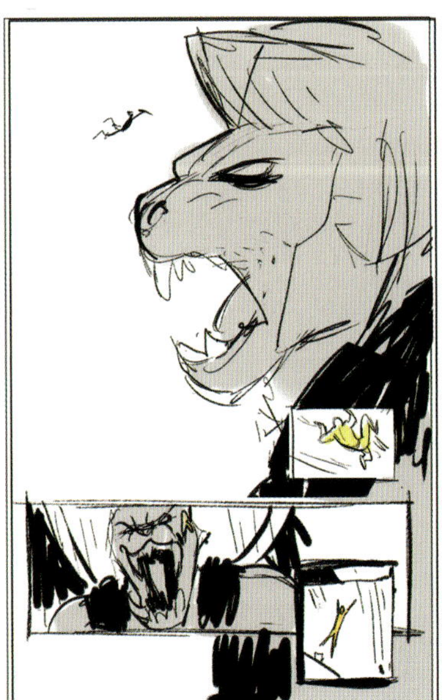
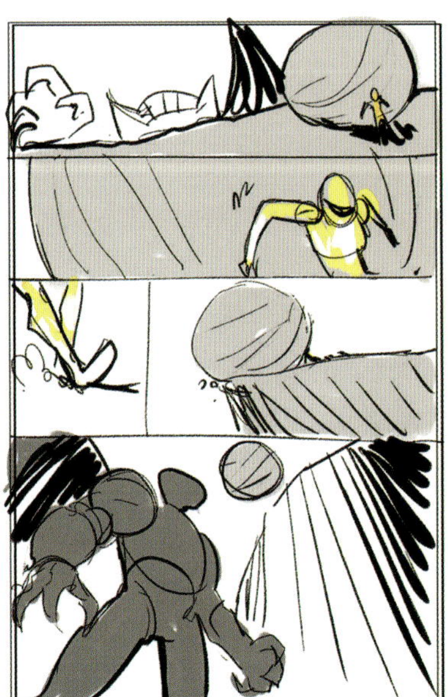
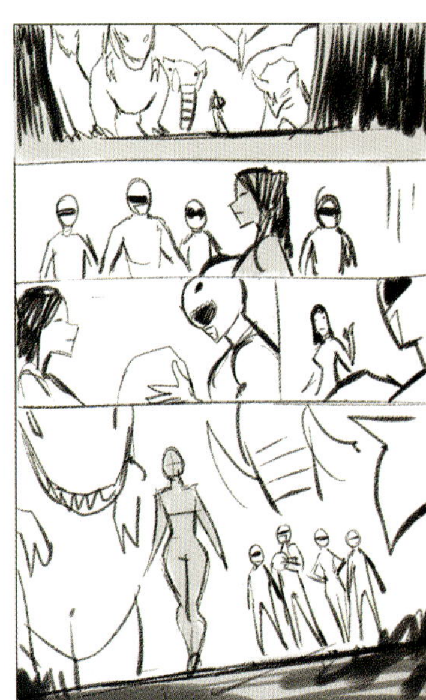

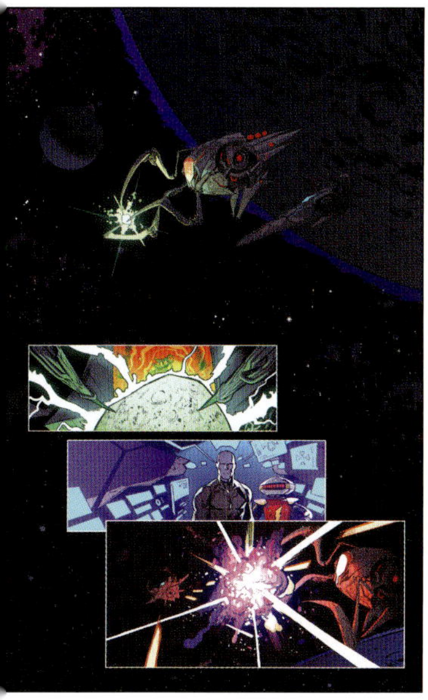
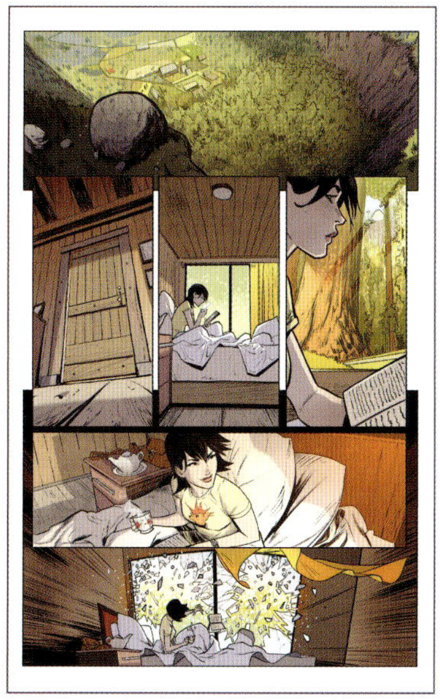
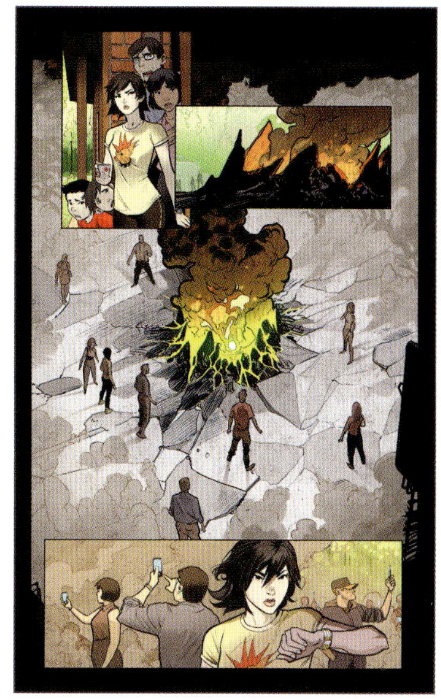
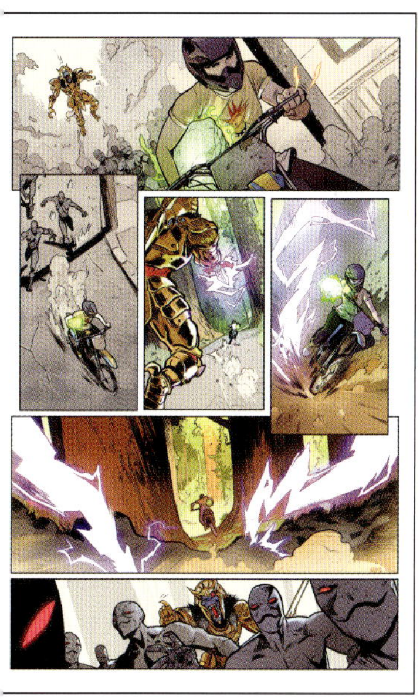
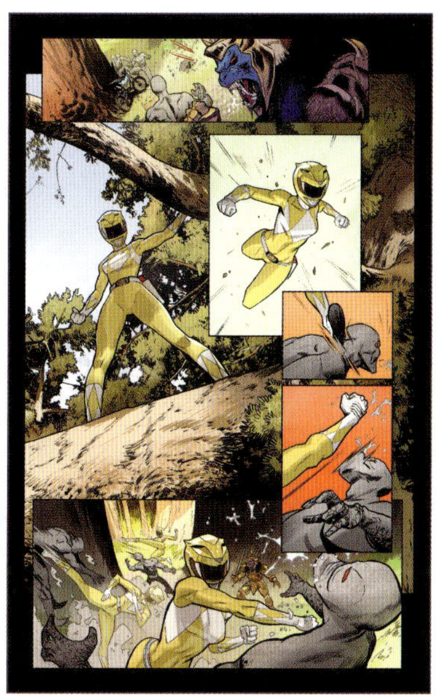
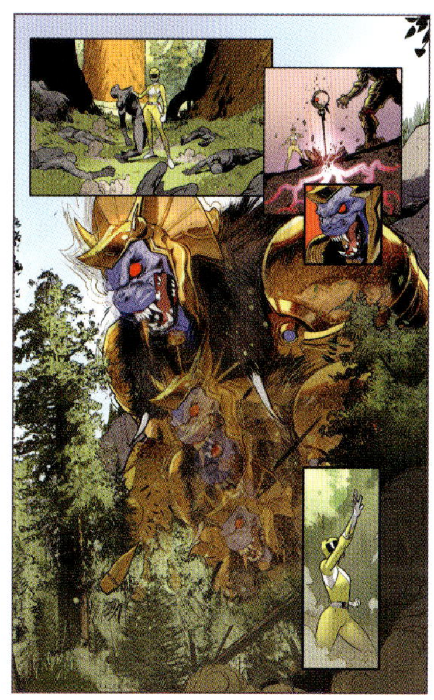
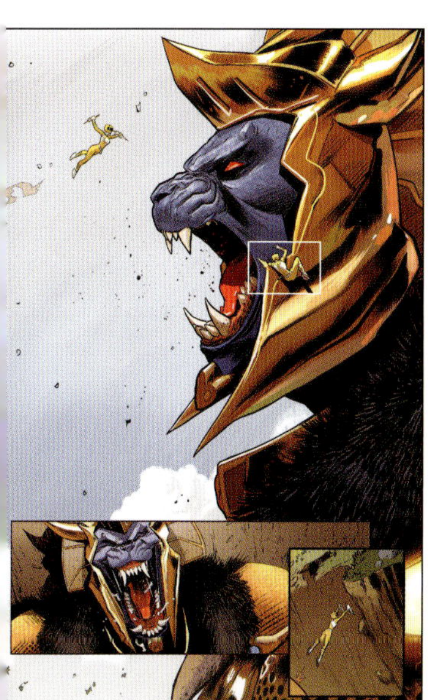
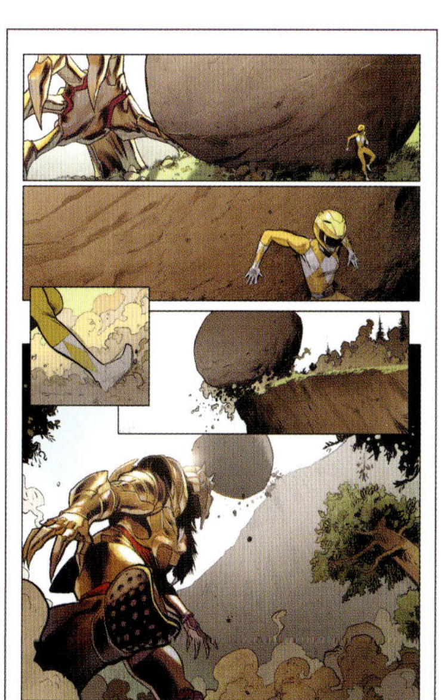
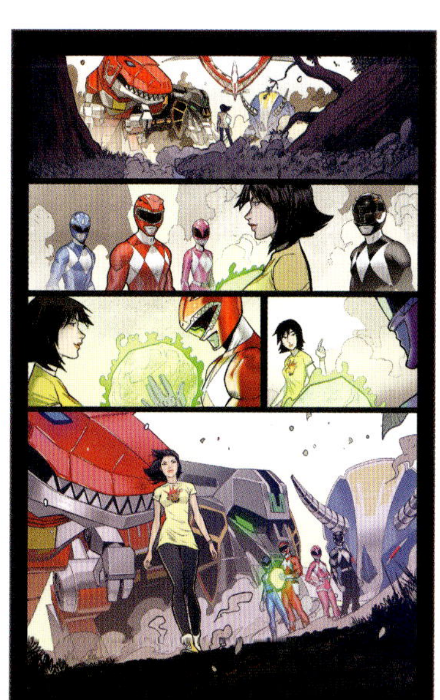

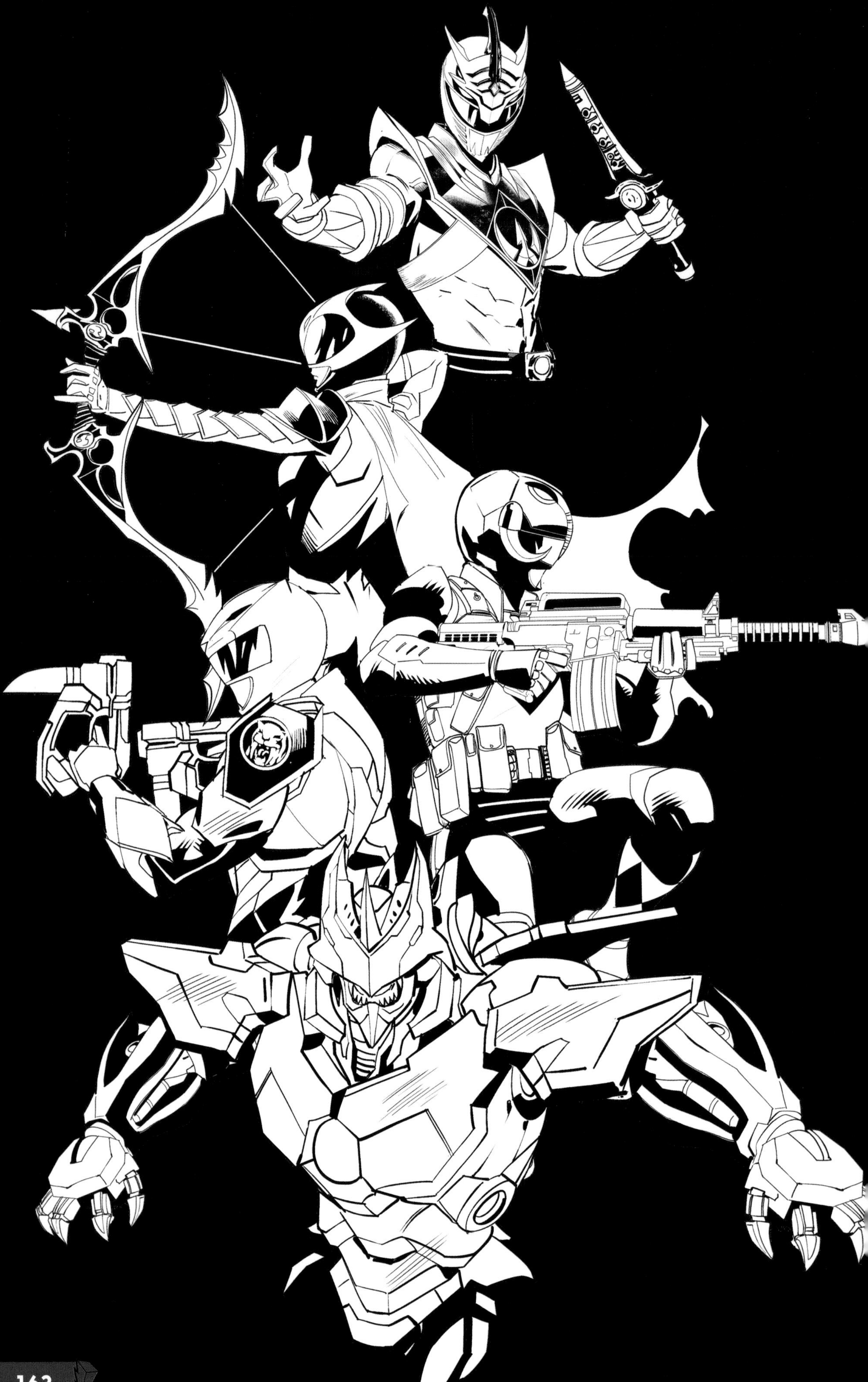

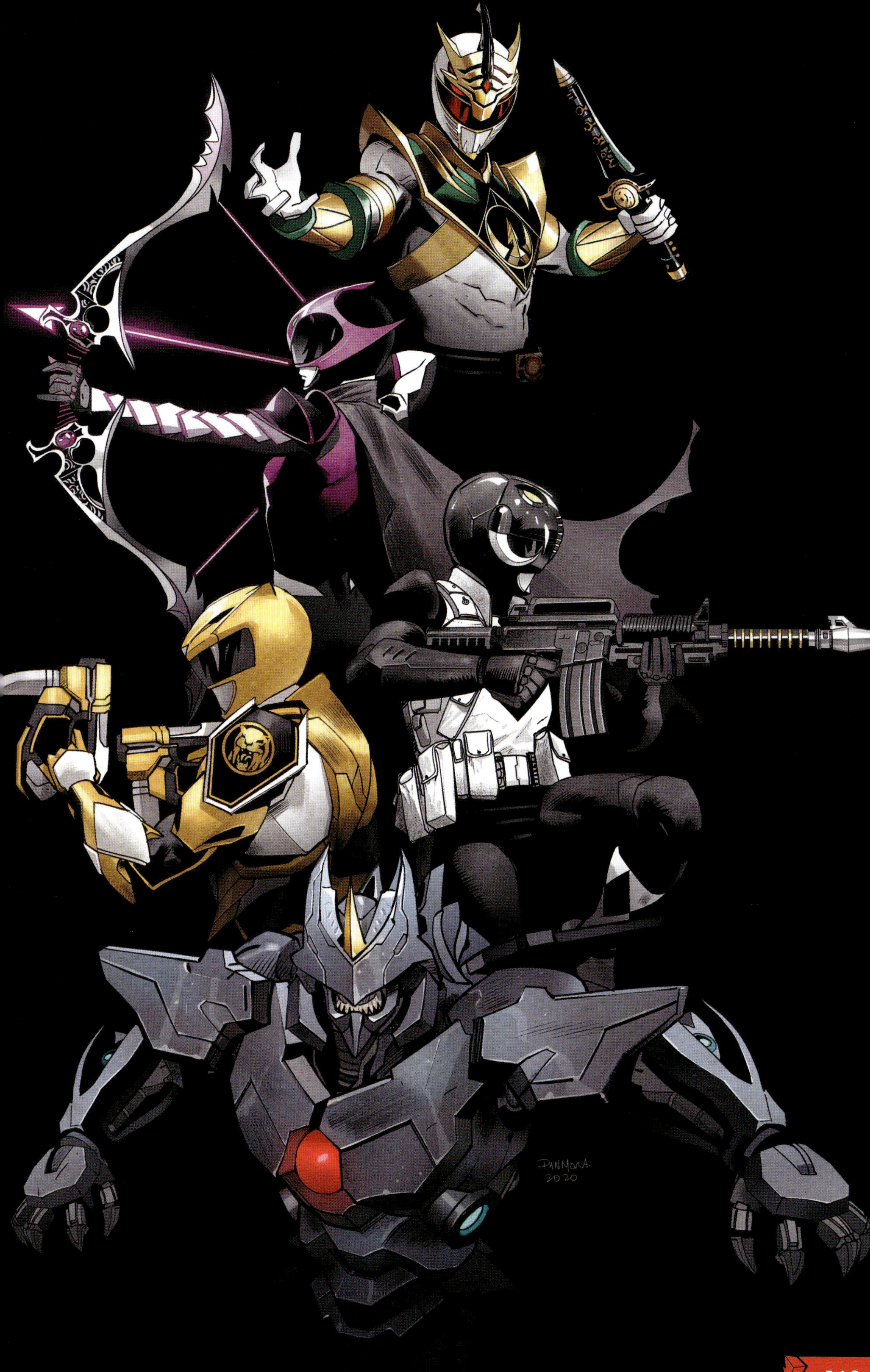
DAN MORA
2020

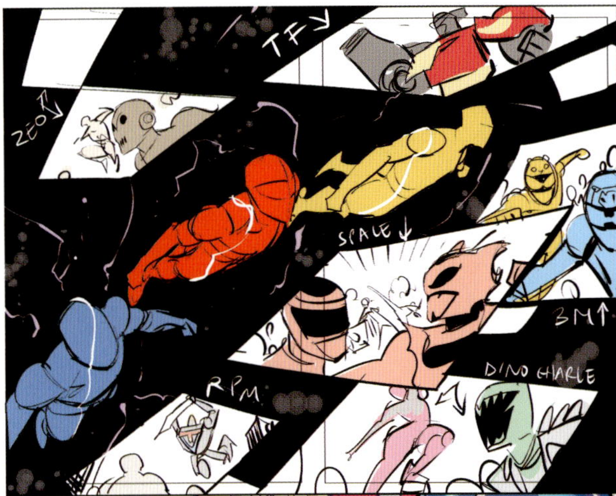
TF
ZEO
SPACE
3M
RPM
DINO CHARGE
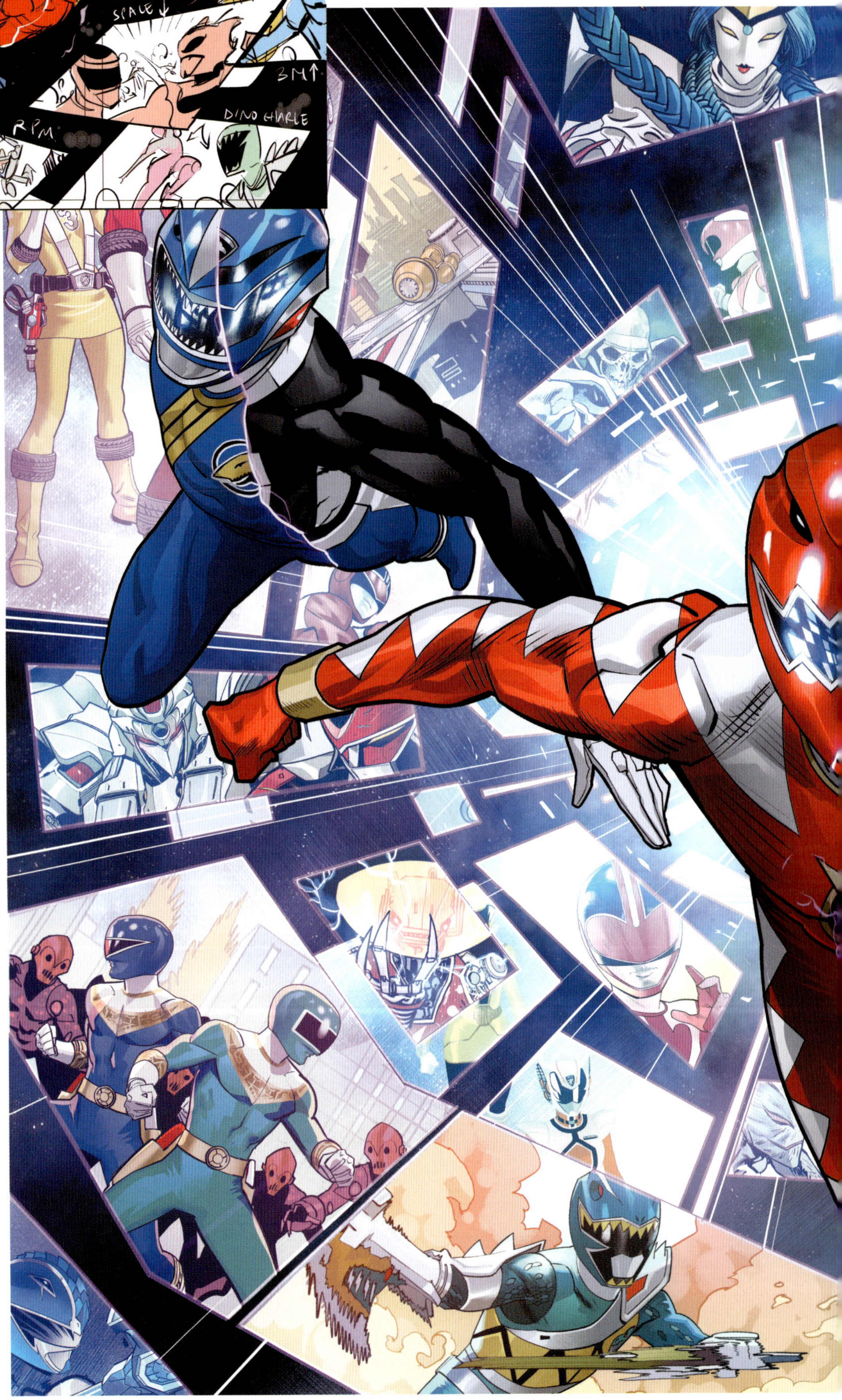

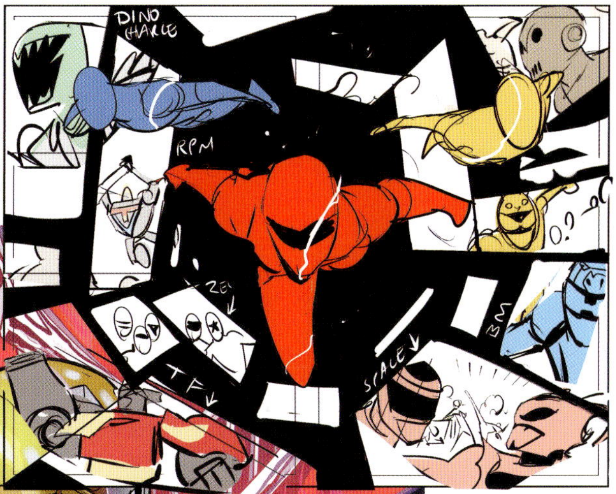
DINO CHARGE
RPM
BM
SPACE

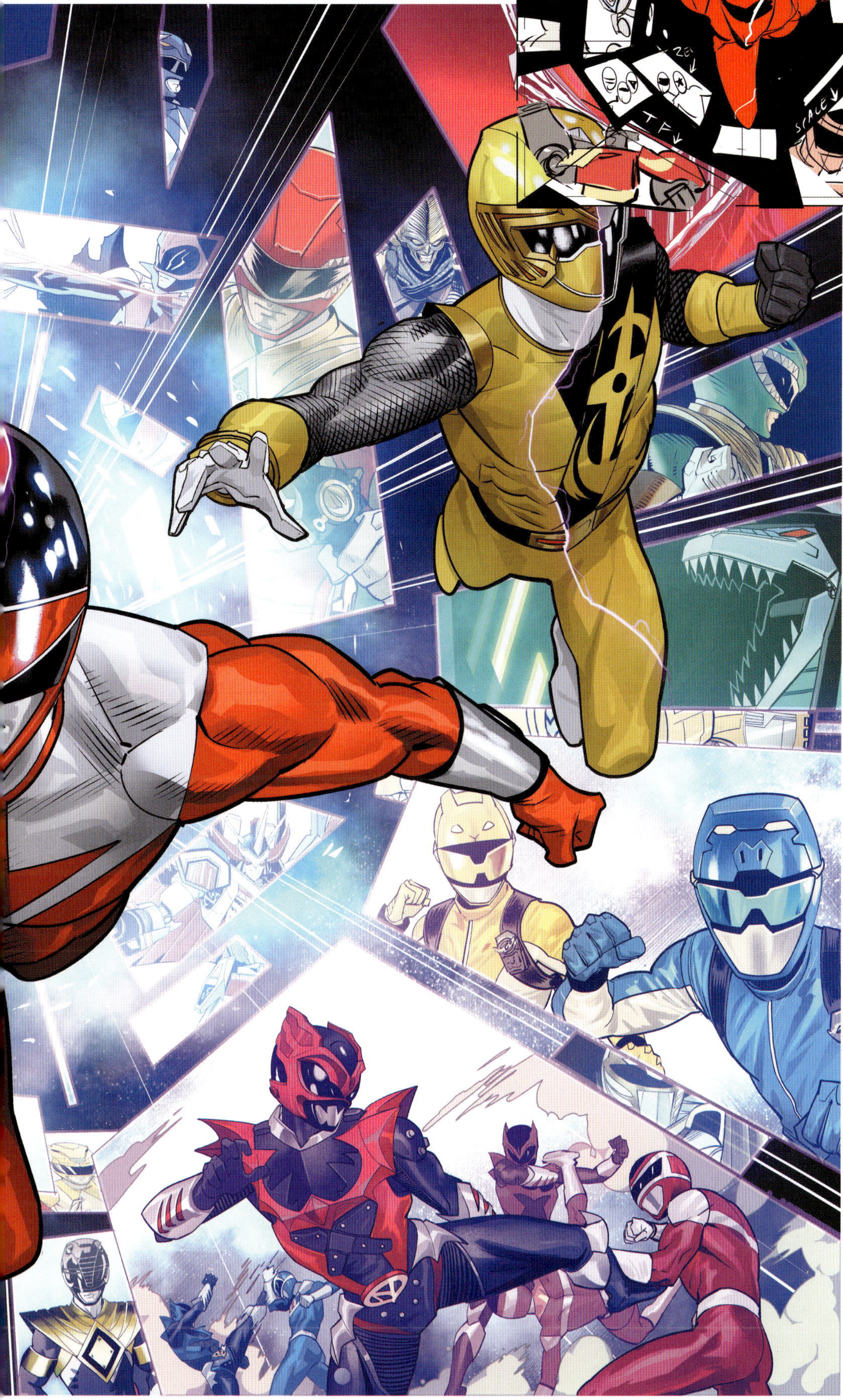

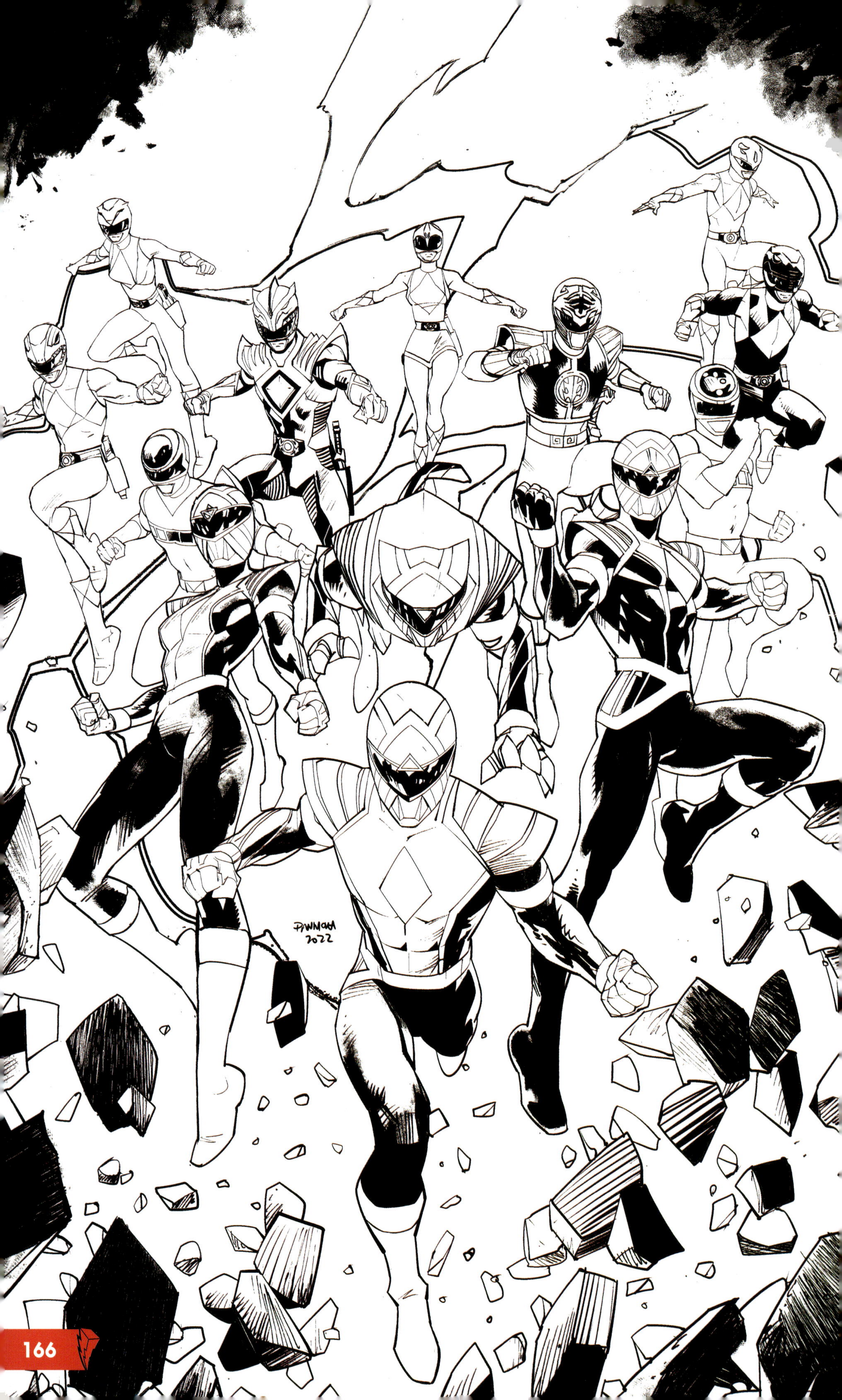
DAN MORA
2022

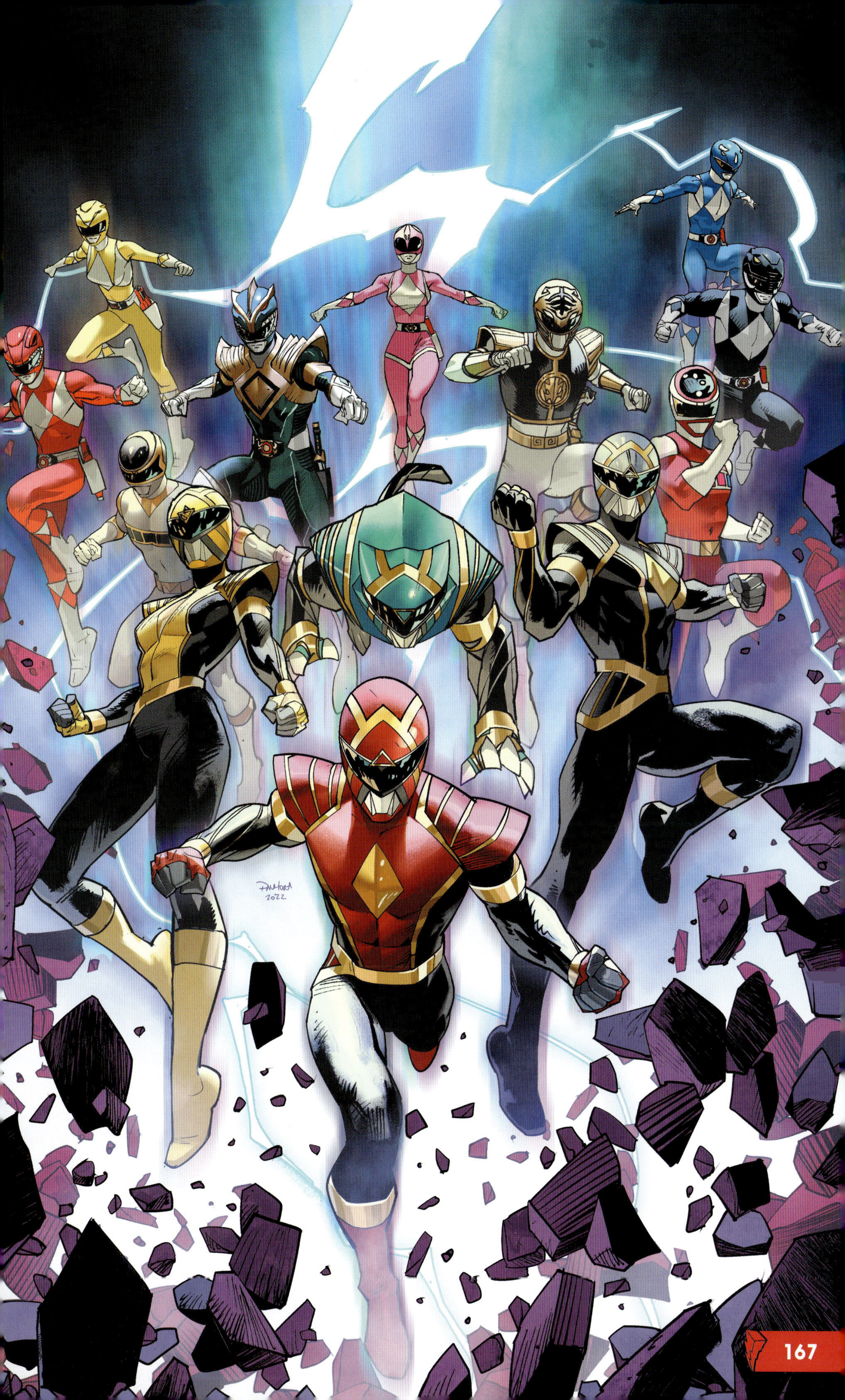

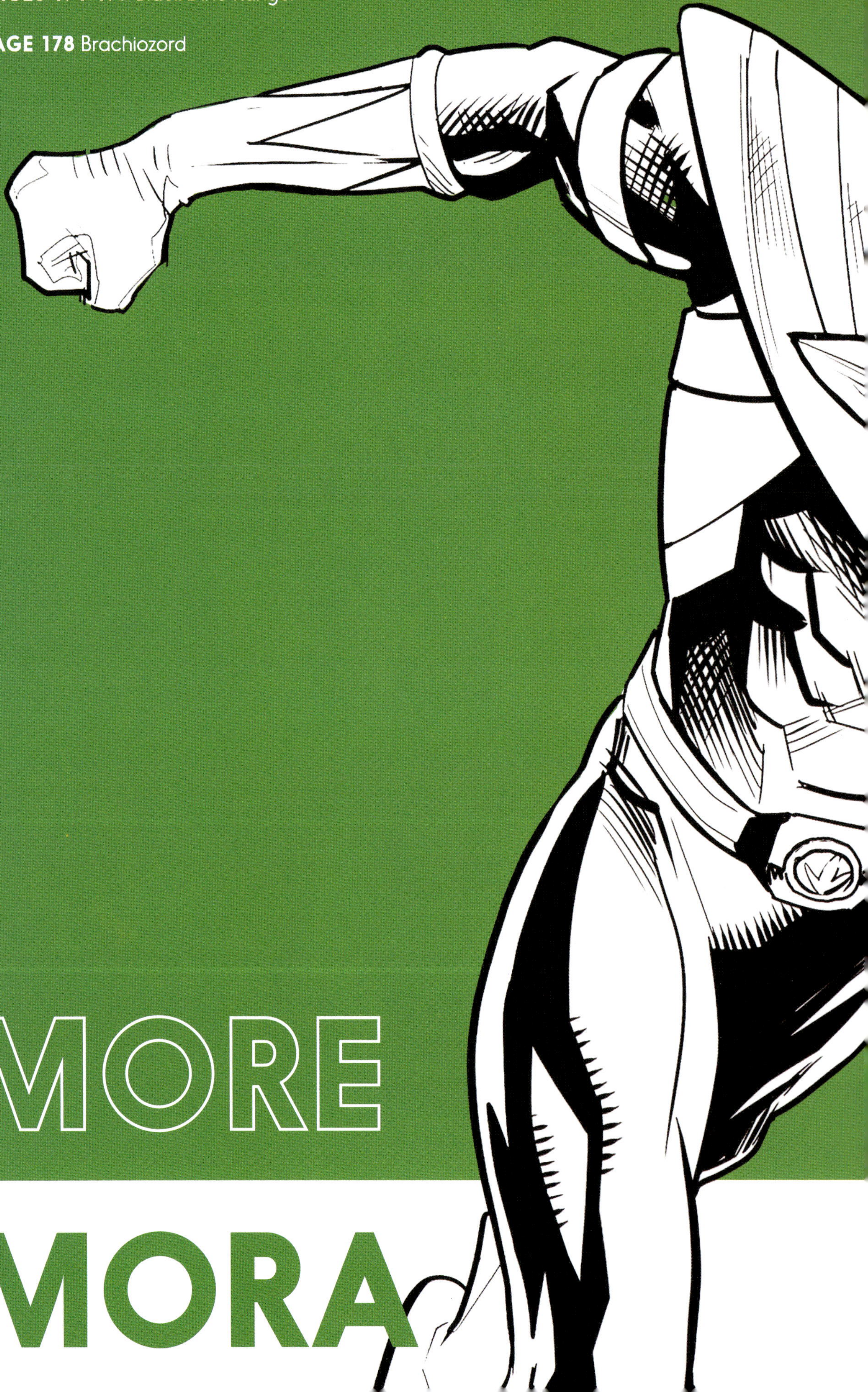

MORE

MORA

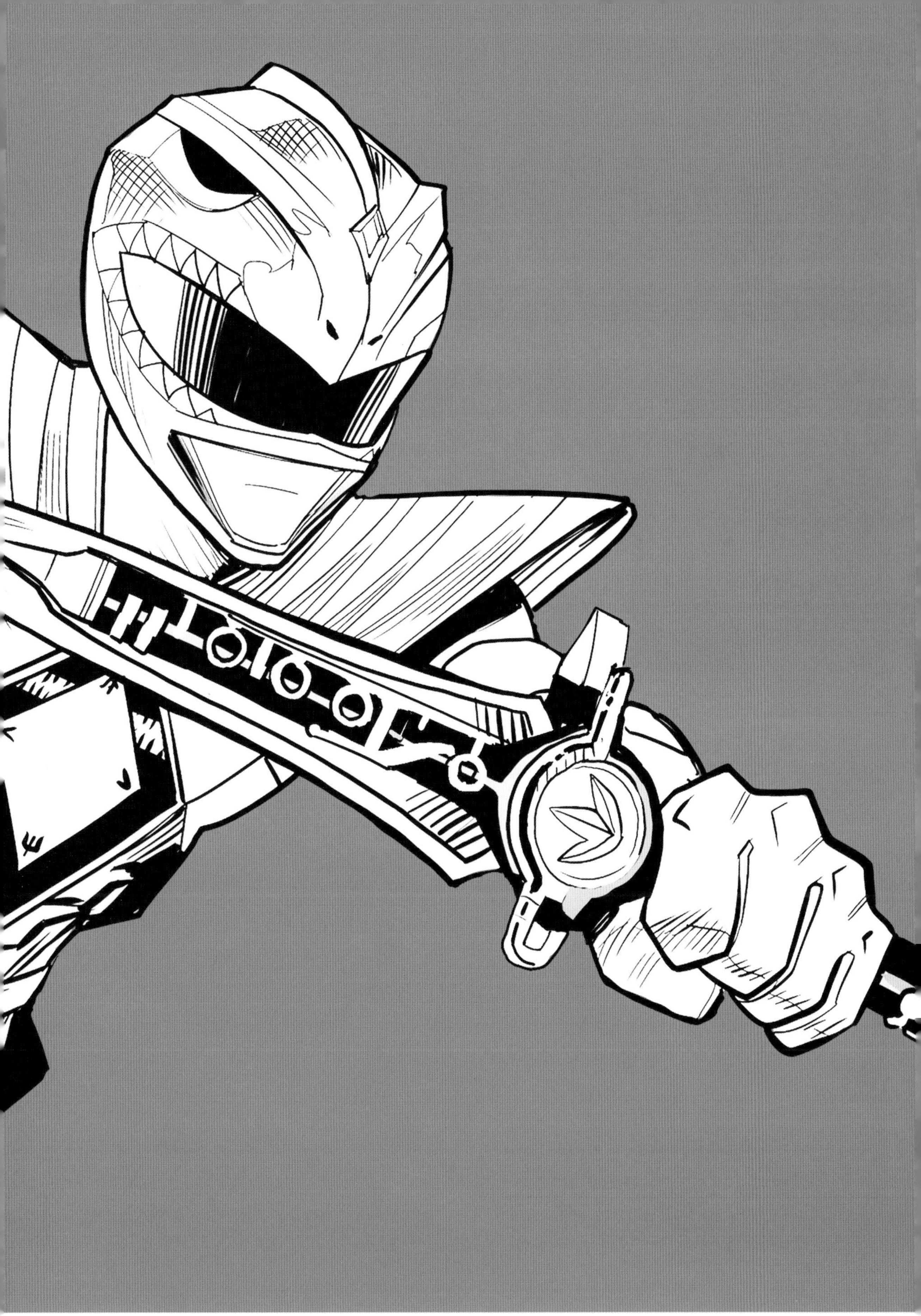

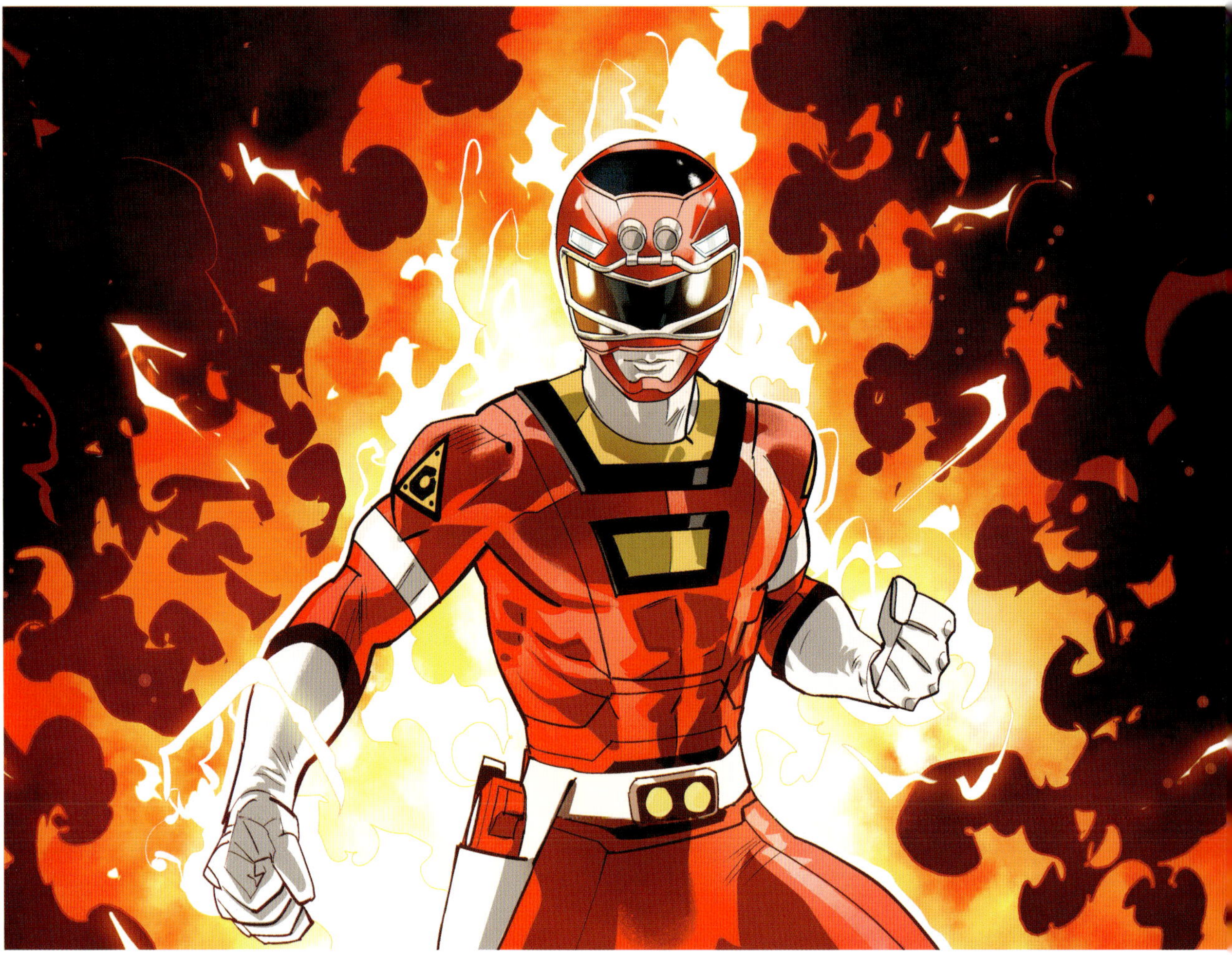

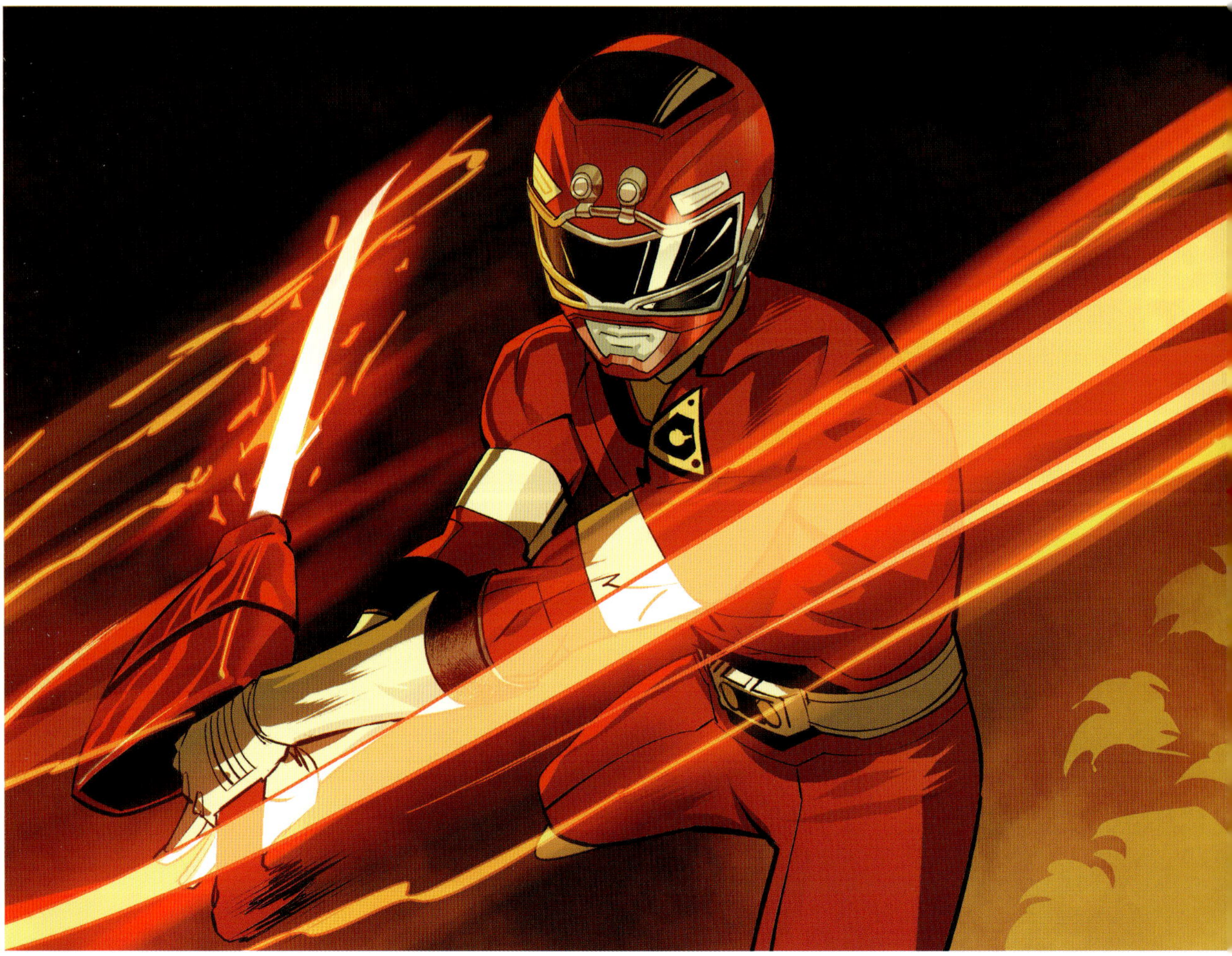

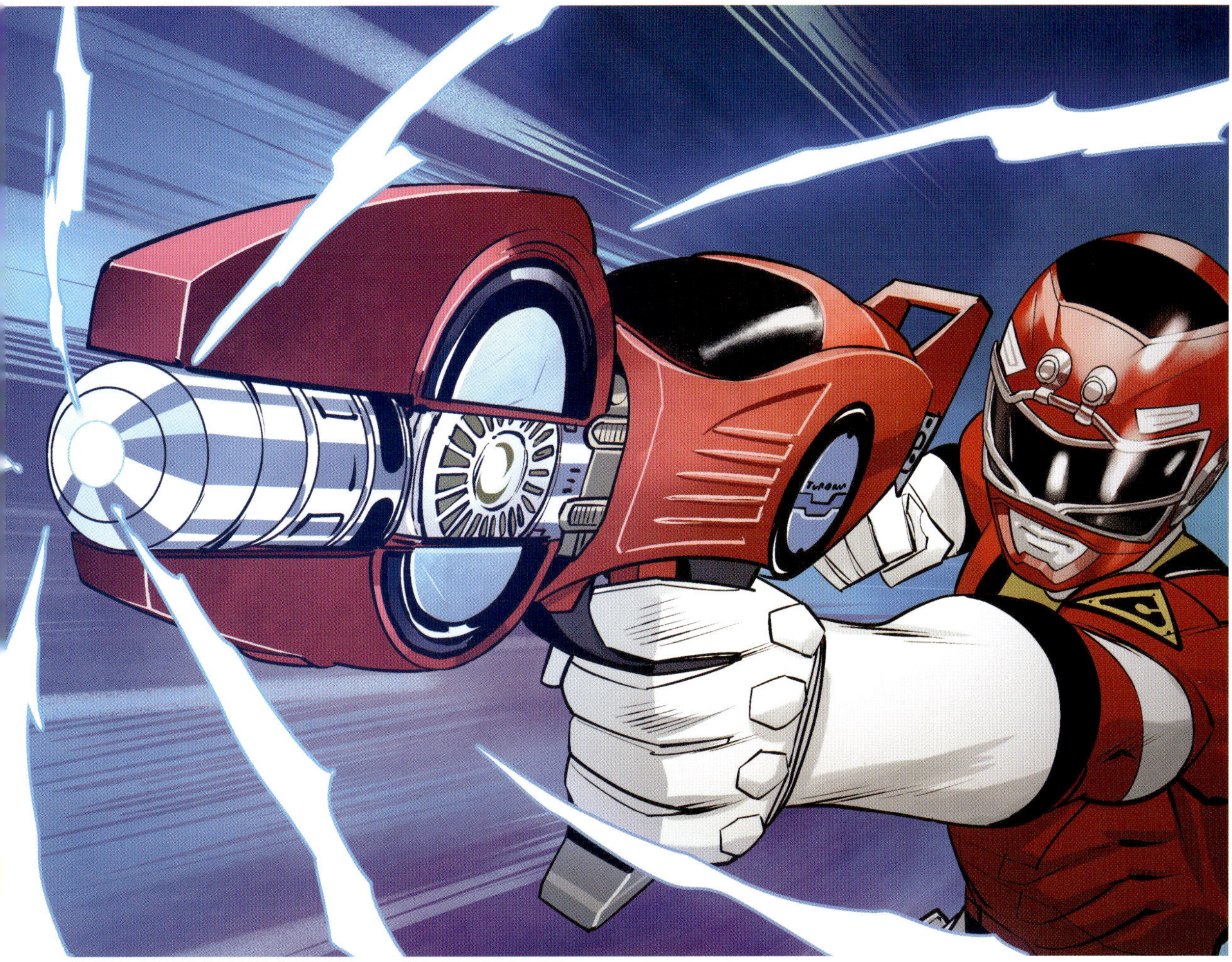

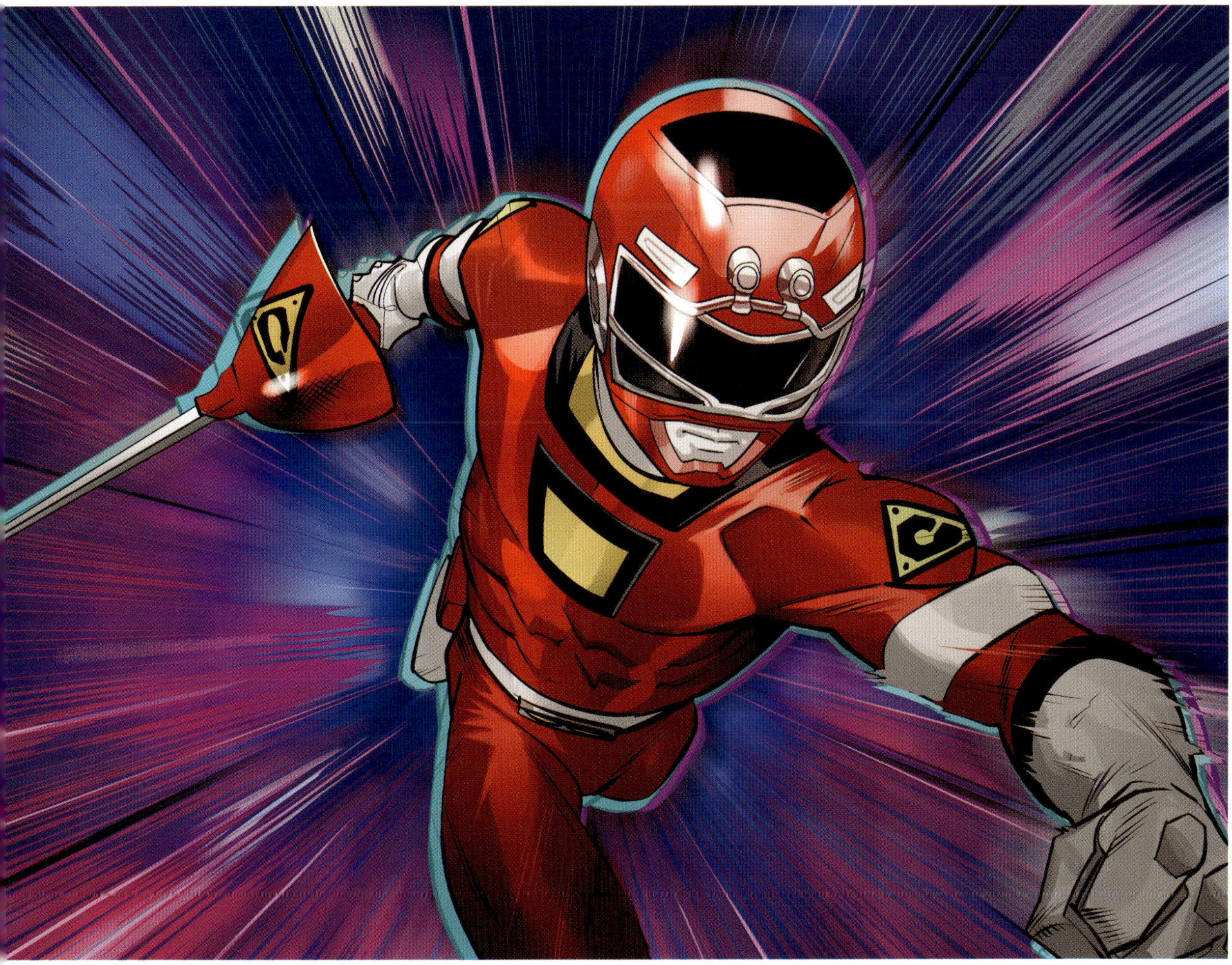

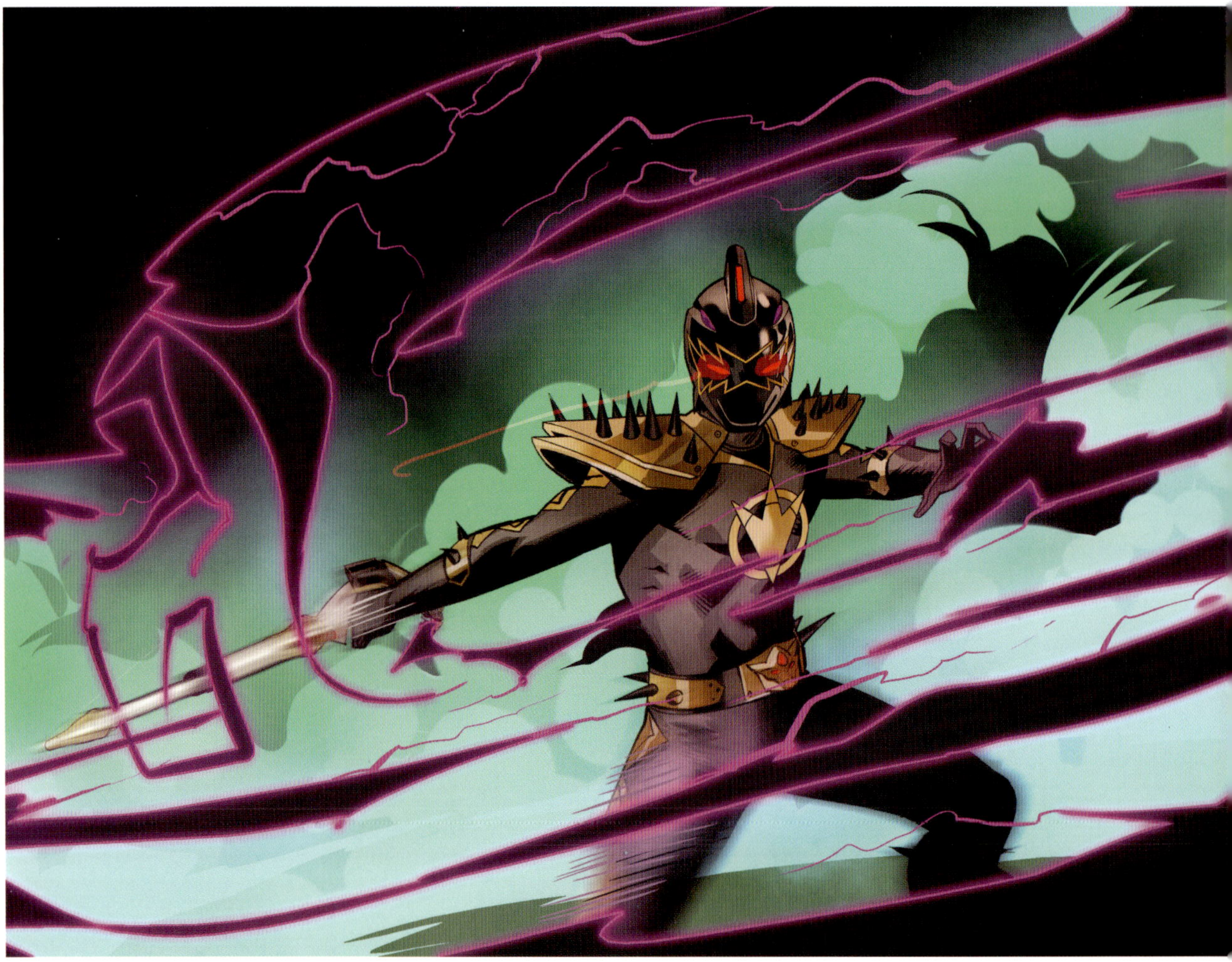

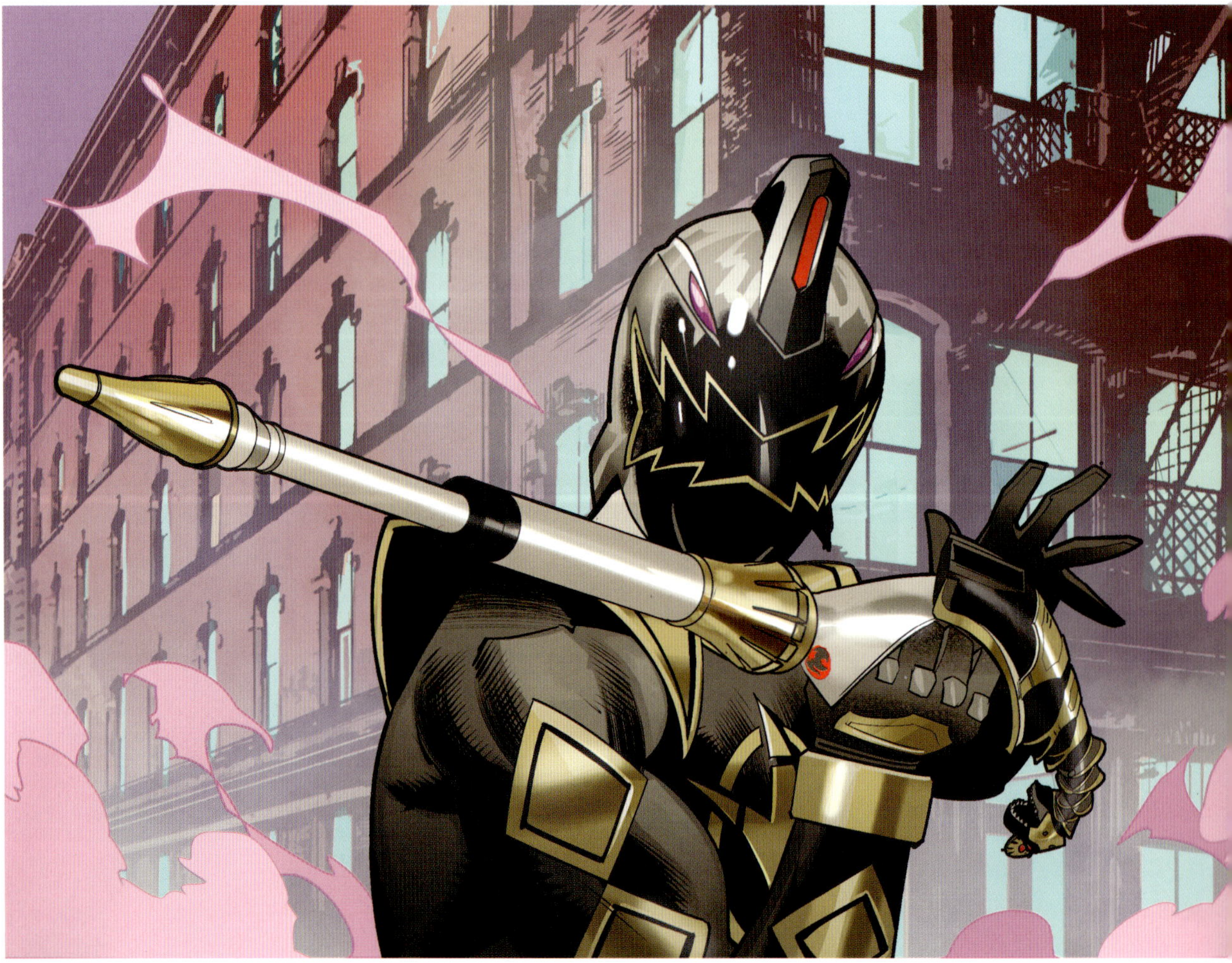

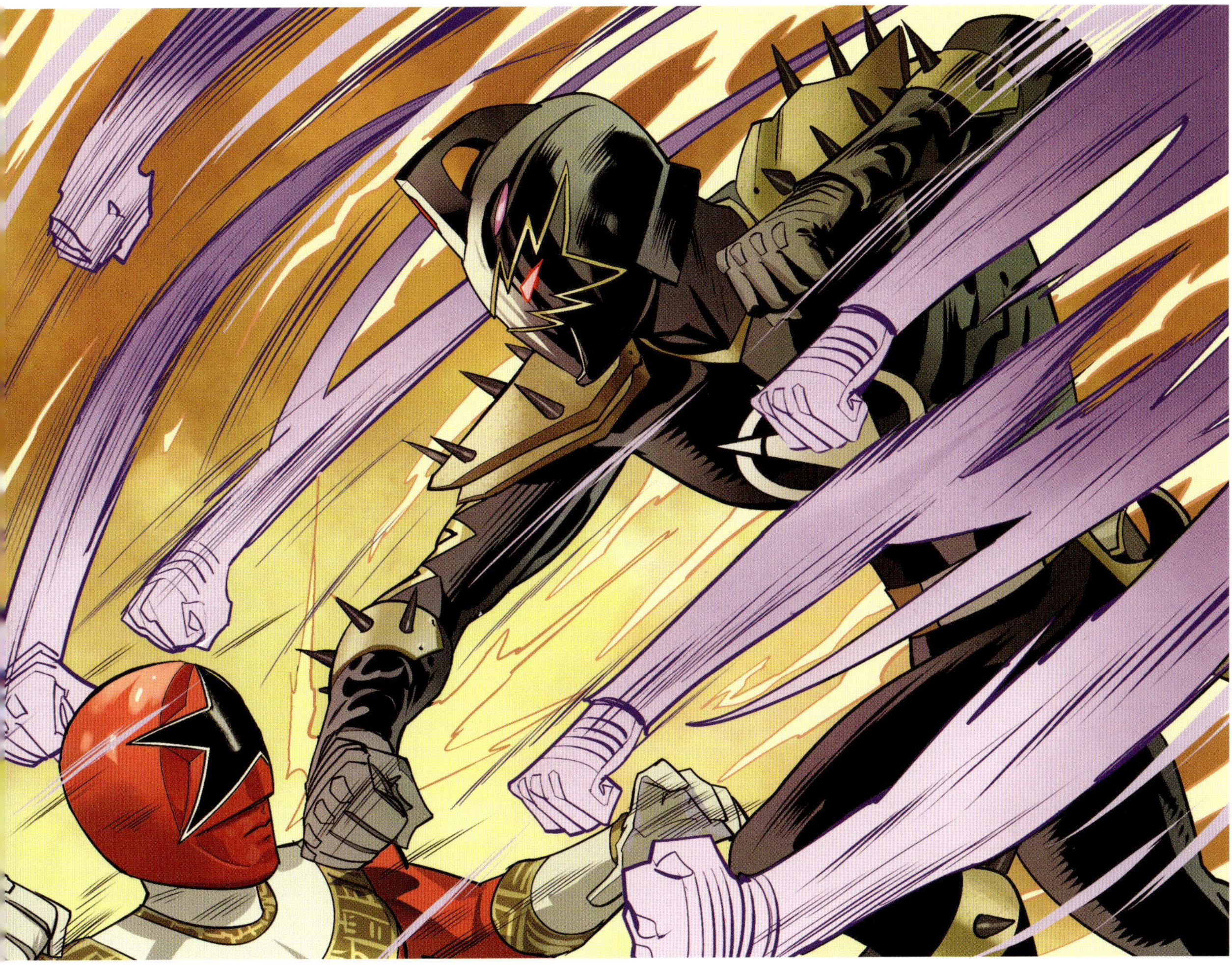

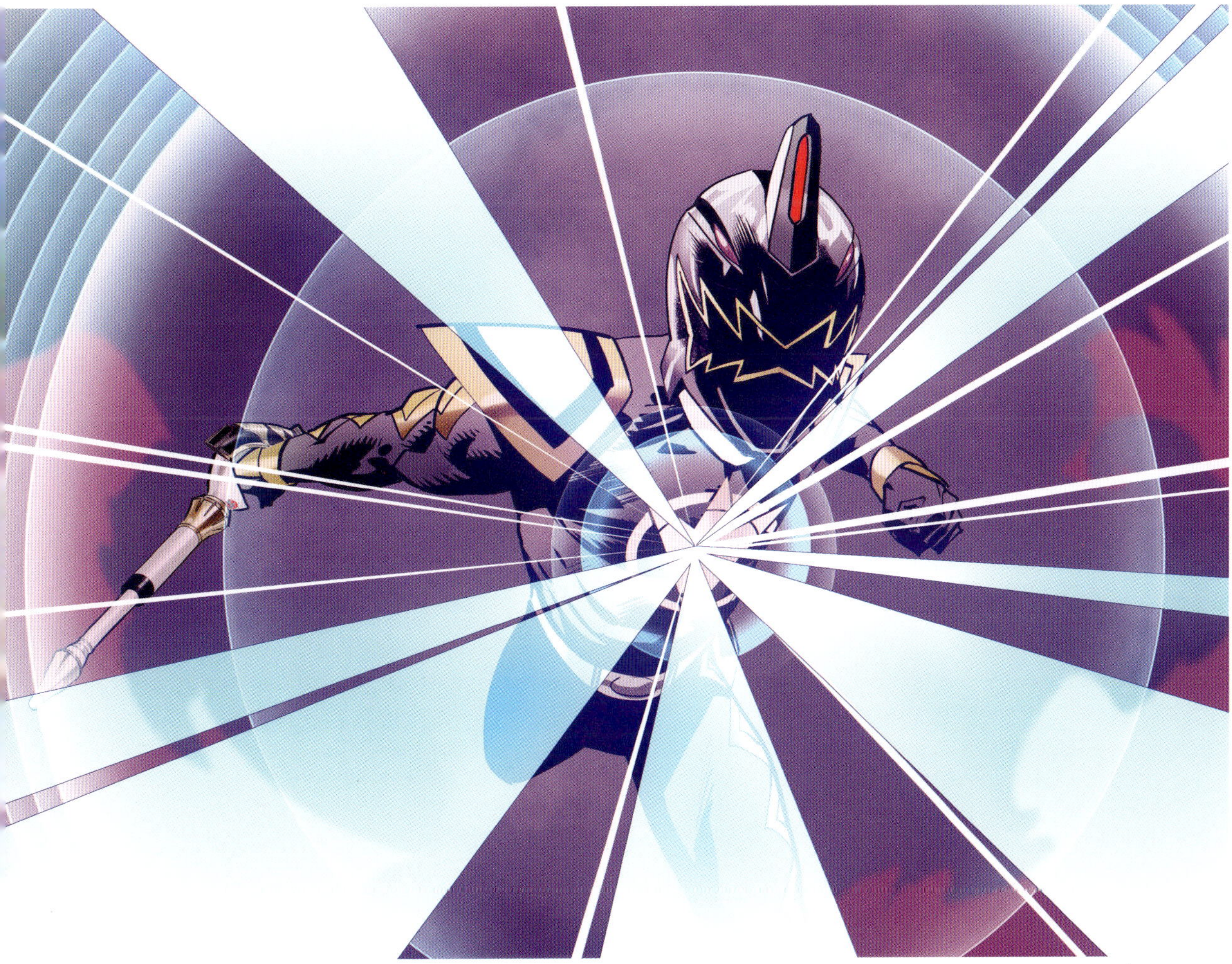

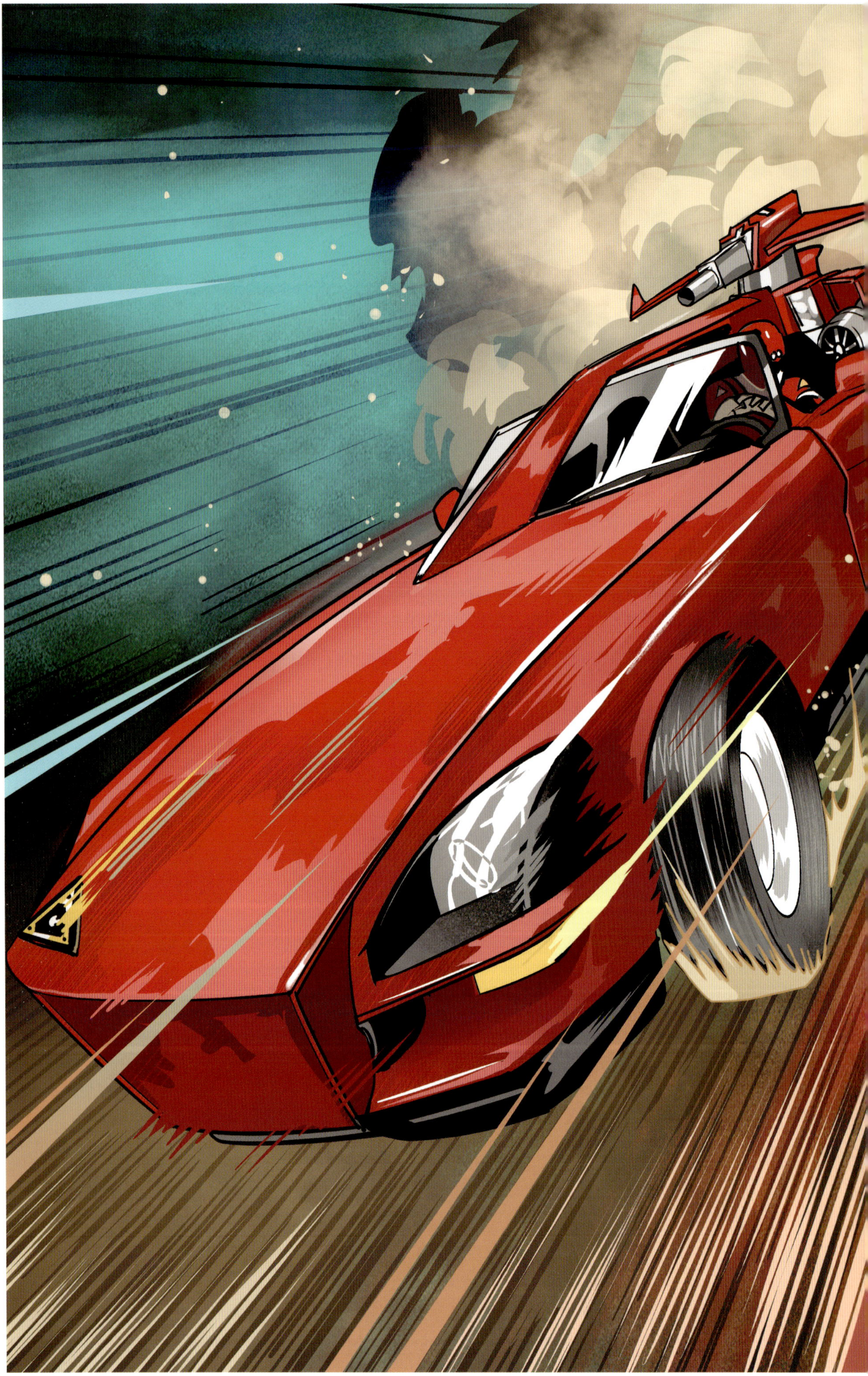

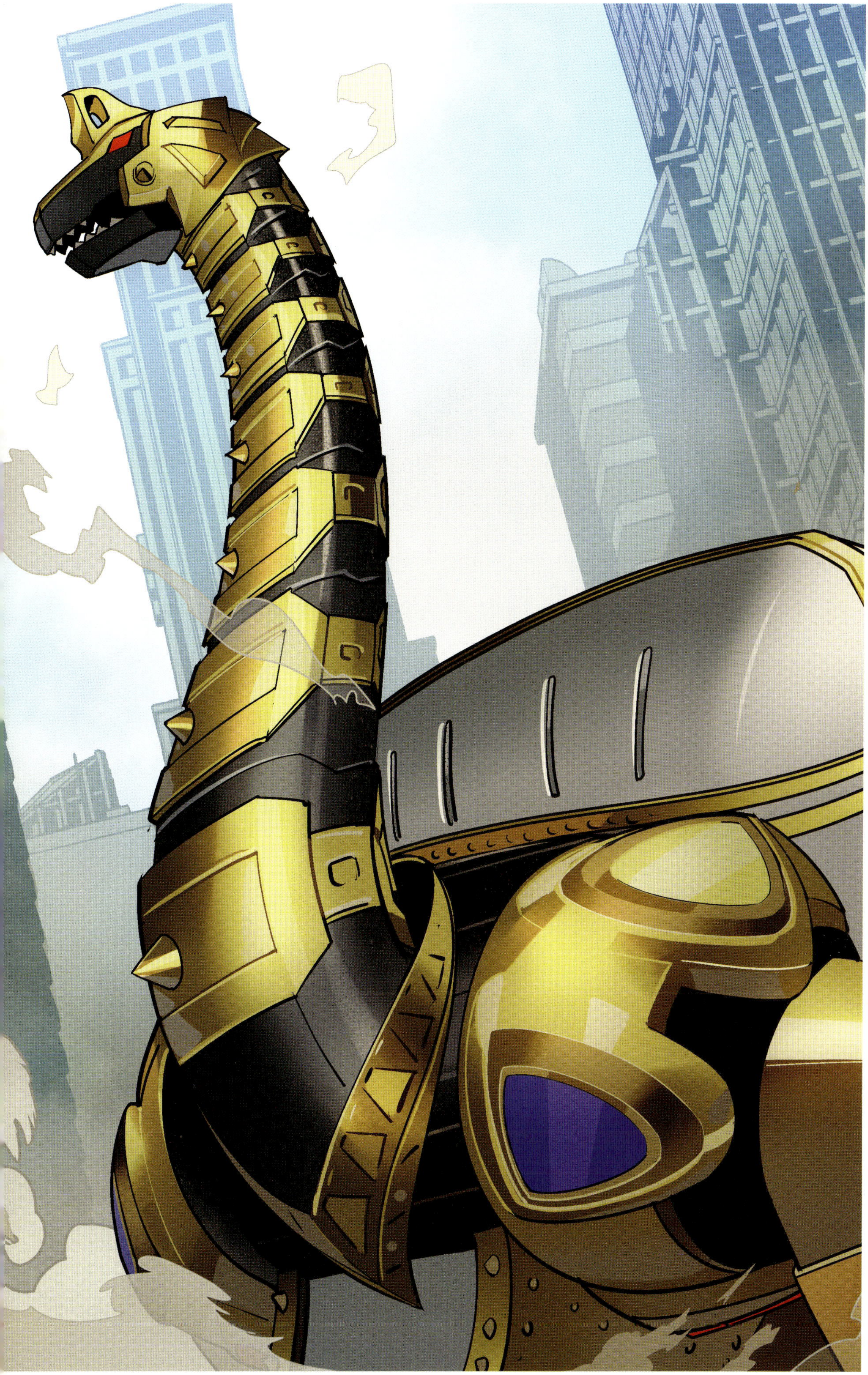

DAN MORA

is a Costa Rican comic artist whose clean linework, expressive acting, and camera-ready sense of movement have made his pages instantly recognizable and relentlessly readable. In 2016, he received the Russ Manning Promising Newcomer Award, a major early-career honor presented at San Diego Comic-Con.

Mora first broke out at BOOM! Studios with *Klaus* (with Grant Morrison), then became a defining visual force on *Saban's Go Go Power Rangers*, helping modernize the franchise's look while delivering some of its most memorable new imagery. BOOM! has also credited Mora as co-creator of the fan-favorite *Ranger Slayer* (with writer Ryan Parrott), a character and design that quickly became central to the mythology.

From there, Mora's range expanded fast: the Arthurian-horror epic *Once and Future* (with Kieron Gillen) showcased his ability to balance scale, speed, and atmosphere without losing emotional clarity. At DC, he has become a marquee storyteller on titles including *Batman/Superman: World's Finest* and *Shazam!*, where his compositions hit with the punch of an action sequence and the precision of classic superhero draftsmanship.

He is also one of the medium's most in-demand cover artists, earning multiple Eisner Award nominations, including recognition for Best Cover Artist.

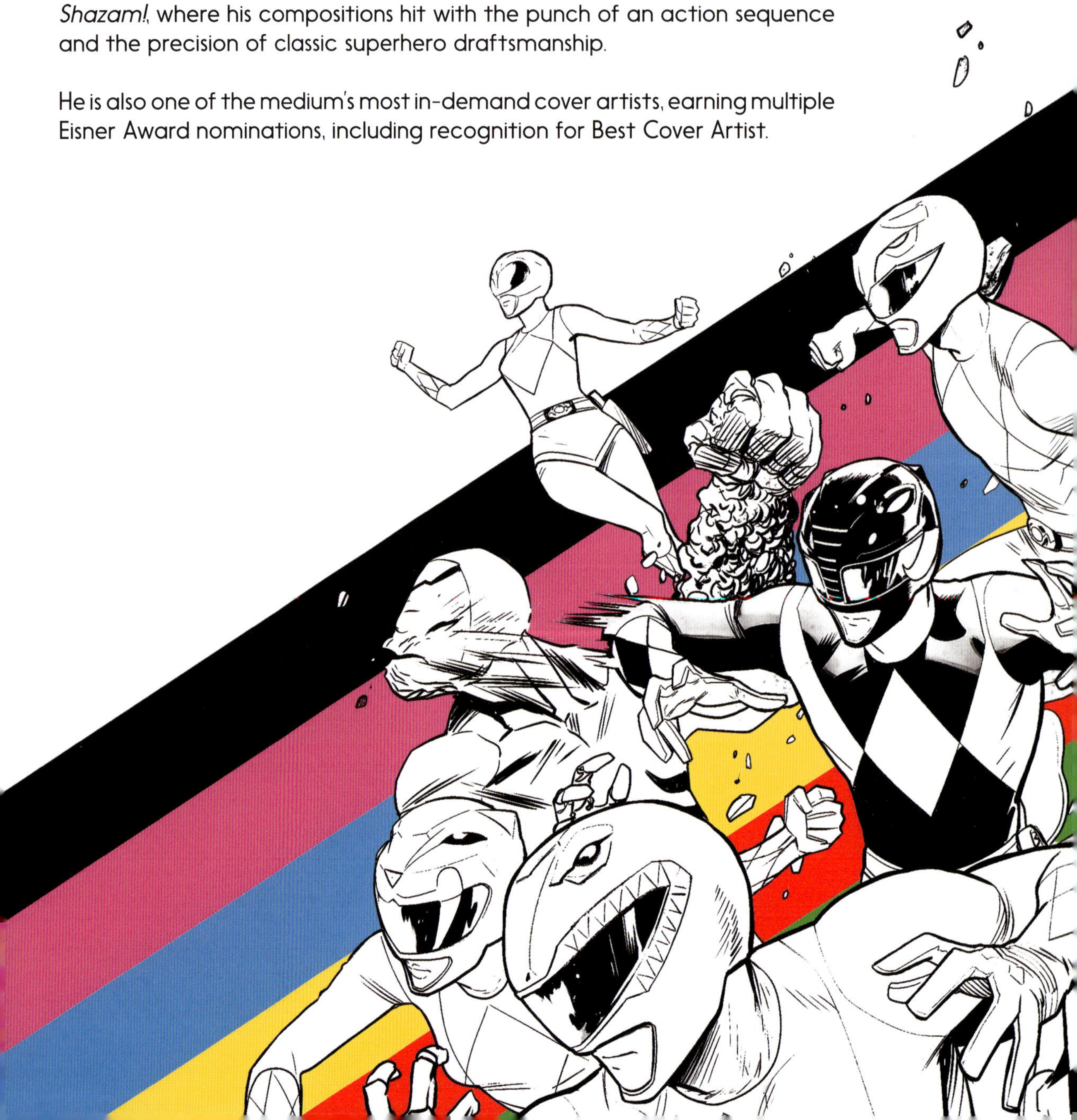